FROM HEGEL
TO
EXISTENTIALISM

FROM HEGEL
TO
EXISTENTIALISM

Robert C. Solomon

New York   Oxford
OXFORD UNIVERSITY PRESS
1987

Oxford University Press

Oxford   New York   Toronto
Delhi   Bombay   Calcutta   Madras   Karachi
Petaling Jaya   Singapore   Hong Kong   Tokyo
Nairobi   Dar es Salaam   Cape Town
Melbourne   Auckland

and associated companies in
Beirut   Berlin   Ibadan   Nicosia

Library of Congress Cataloging-in-Publication Data
Solomon, Robert C.
From Hegel to existentialism.

1. Hegel, Georg Wilhelm Friedrich, 1770–1831.   2. Philosophy, Modern—19th century.
3. Philosophy, Modern—20th century.   I. Title.
B2948.S65   1987   142′.78   86-12528
ISBN 0-19-504147-X (alk. paper)

1. "Hegel's Concept of *Geist*," *The Review of Metaphysics,* vol. 23, no. 4 (1970).

2. "Hegel's Epistemology," *American Philosophical Quarterly,* vol. 2, no. 4 (Oct. 1974).

3. "Hegel: Truth and Self-satisfaction," *The Review of Metaphysics,* vol. 28, (June 1975).

4. "The Secret of Hegel (Kierkegaard's Complaint: A Study in Hegel's Philosophy of Religion)," *Philosophical Forum,* vol. 9, no. 4 (Summer 1978).

5. "Kierkegaard and Subjective Truth," *Philosophy Today,* vol. 21, no. 3 (Fall 1977).

6. "Nietzsche, Nihilism, and Morality," by Robert C. Solomon, from *Nietzsche.* Copyright © 1973 by Robert C. Solomon. Reprinted by permission of Doubleday & Company, Inc. Reprinted by the University of Notre Dame Press, 1979.

7. "A More Severe Morality: Nietzsche's Affirmative Ethics," reprinted with the permission of the editors of the *Journal of the British Society for Phenomenology,* vol. 16, no. 3 (Oct. 1985).

8. "Sex and Perversion" first appeared in *Philosophy and Sex,* ed. F. Elliston and R. Baker (Buffalo, N.Y.: Prometheus, 1975).

9. "Freud's Neurological Theory of Mind," by Robert C. Solomon, from *Freud,* edited by Richard Wollheim. Copyright © 1974 by Richard Wollheim. Reprinted by permission of Doubleday & Company, Inc.

10. "An Introduction to Phenomenology," from *Phenomenology and Existentialism,* ed. R. Solomon, originally published by Harper and Row, 1972; reprinted by the University Press of America, 1979).

2 4 6 8 9 7 5 3 1

Printed in the United States of America
on acid-free paper

11. "Husserl's Private Language" is reprinted with the permission of the editors of *Philosophical Topics,* formerly *The Southwestern Journal of Philosophy* vol. 5 (Nov. 1974).

12. "Sense and Essence: Frege and Husserl," *The International Philosophical Quarterly,* vol. 10, no. 3 (Sept. 1970).

13. "Husserl's Concept of the Noema," from *Husserl,* ed. F. Elliston, P. McCormick (Notre Dame, Ind.: University of Notre Dame Press, 1977).

14. "An Introduction to Existentialism," from *Existentialism,* ed. R. Solomon, reprinted with the permission of the editor and publisher, Random House, Inc., first published 1974 by Modern Library College Editions.

15. "Camus's *L'Étranger* and the Truth" is reprinted with the permission of the editors of *Philosophy and Literature,* vol. 2 (Oct. 1978).

16. "Sartre on Emotions" is reprinted from *Sartre,* in the Library of Living Philosophers series, ed. P. Schilpp, with the permission of Open Court publishers (first published 1981).

17. "Jean-Paul Sartre, 1905–1980: An Interview," reprinted by permission of the Hackett Publishing Company, Inc., Indianapolis, Indiana from *Introducing the Existentialists* (1981).

For Kathleen Marie Higgins

A PERSONAL PREFACE

"I am not an existentialist."

So insisted Camus, and Jaspers. So, too, growled Heidegger with existential indignation. But if you were to ask me, I suppose that I would have to say, if awkwardly, "I am an existentialist." At a time when American philosophy is well on its way to becoming a respectable branch of cognitive science and a mandated prerequisite for law school, I find myself quaintly worrying about the significance of feelings, about who or what I really am and about the kinds of personal responsibilities that don't concern national policy and jurisprudence. In an age when philosophers have finally become professionals instead of street-corner kibitzers, I stubbornly believe that philosophy ought to speak to ordinary, intelligent people about personal worries, reflections, and experiences. It's embarrassing to be so out of style.

Existentialism, I am often told, is now out of date, a philosophical rage from the past—as, no doubt, the newest French fad will soon be as well. Hegel enjoyed a resurgence of academic popularity in the 1970s; the recent Nietzsche renaissance is just waning now. One gets the sense that current European philosophy, unlike philosophy elsewhere, is strictly a matter of fashion. It is a great virtue for a scholar to spend a lifetime studying Aristotle or Aquinas or Frege or Russell, but it is considered pure foolishness to devote one's attention to such ephemeral folk as Hegel, Nietzsche, or Sartre. "They will pass," I am told, as if these eccentric thinkers in Europe fly by like comets while the truly great philosophers are fixed navigational stars. But they provide another kind of beacon: philosophical inspiration rather than established scholarly constellations. There may be scholars and serious studies, but enthusiasm is still the proper approach to Hegel, Nietzsche, Sartre, and existentialism. They have, happily, not yet become institutions.

It is no secret that philosophy has been a battleground in recent years, and one misleading way of describing this has been the antagonism of "analytic" versus "Continental" methods and approaches. But the watershed of contemporary philosophy, I would argue, is not a matter of method—be it analytic, ontological, historical, phenomenological, or deconstructionist. (I have never understood—except as campus politics—the supposed clash between these, nor have I understood "method" as such in philosophy; it seems to exist only to satisfy that peculiar professional need to subscribe to an established routine—and to avoid saying anything that might be personally revealing, heartfelt, or just plain interesting about a subject of general concern.) Nor is the battle one of tradition. Do philosophers really disagree about more than one or two names on the standard "top ten" chart in philosophy (Socrates, Plato, Aristotle, Aquinas, Descartes, Spinoza, Leibniz, Locke, Hume, Kant)? I think that the battle is phony, and that the various dividing lines have been artifacts: matters of personal (or impersonal) style, matters of emphasis and mutual misunderstanding. If pressed, I would say that the essays in this book utilize the application of analytic techniques to phenomenological issues with inevitable—if usually undeveloped—ontological implications arising from widespread personal concerns and the urge to combat, if not "deconstruct," a transcendental pretension to objectivity that has defined much of traditional philosophy, and threatened to submerge the personal and the subjective. But, as J. L. Austin once replied to a similar question about method, "that would be quite a mouthful."

If there is a dividing line, I would suggest that it is a question of temperament: whether philosophy should be an "art"—a literary form of personal expression—or an impersonal "science" like logic or abstract law. But even this, I think, is a false antagonism. Philosophy can be as serious as science and as rigorous as the law, but it can also be playful and personal. Philosophy serves a special purpose and is something more than a janitorial service for sloppy concept-keeping in the sciences or a prep course in careful thinking—or worse, a caustic corrective for earlier concept-mongering in philosophy. Philosophy is also vision, a statement of purpose, the development of a point of view—"perspectivism," perhaps, but the articulation of particular perspectives, rather than the teasing thesis that "there are only perspectives." Philosophers have tried to understand and even change the world in so many ways; the point, however, is to stand for something.

Existentialism is a philosophy that insists on standing for something. The abstract thesis of existentialism, which insists that one must take a stand, is not yet the taking of a stand. It is a gross limitation of the existential (or Hegelian) "engagement" thesis that it is always thought to be purely political, as if "to stand for something" could only mean being a Marxist or a libertarian. One can also stand for the examined life, for the importance of the arts and humanities, for sympathy and passion, for a way of thinking and living. Existentialism encourages a sense of personal urgency that is often missing in philosophical debate today. Kierkegaard did not spend his career just harping on the importance of emotions and choice; he also expressed his emotions, and brilliantly, "seductively," articulated his own dramatic choice of a way of life, a "sphere of existence," worth living for—or dying for. Nietzsche occasionally viewed himself as a "scientist" (he, too, suffered from the old *Wille zu Wissenschaft*) but what overwhelms the reader of Nietzsche's work is not science, nor even literary brilliance, but his passion, the almost buffoonish confidence he has in himself and his mission. Sartre may have found his eternal niche in philosophy with his thesis that "man makes himself," but he demonstrated that thesis in his life through his devotion to his art and to the (sometimes dubious) political purposes it served. In the essays that follow, I do not argue (as I do elsewhere) for any particular philosophical position, but I do try, by example, to represent a certain way of doing philosophy: historical yet personal; serious yet entertaining; academic yet "relevant." It is the sort of philosophy I like to think that Hegel would do today, if he had enjoyed the debatable benefits of a late twentieth-century analytic graduate program.

It is perhaps unfortunate that we are still importing our best ideas from abroad, but intellectually, at least, America is still a "young" country. Our philosophical founding fathers bought their ideas wholesale from the Scots and the French. My philosophical generation spent an obligatory year or two in Oxford or Cambridge. A few students squandered their tough-minded training in logic and analytic philosophy in pursuit of the Gothic secrets (then referred to as "pseudo-problems") of Hegel, Husserl, and Heidegger. I was one of them. We inherited our arguments and our sense of strategy from Quine and Wittgenstein; we got our ideas and inspiration from Nietzsche, Sartre, and Camus. But existentialism, whatever its roots, is in fact a very American style of philosophy. Its emphasis on individual responsibility and freedom, its wary confusion about the importance and nature of interpersonal relationships, its manifest (if not negligent) view of history and its distrust of established institutions, its sensuous and skeptical (but not cynical) vision of the meaning of life—these ideas may have found a soft spot in the postwar European sensibility, but they found their natural soil in America. Existentialism is not an intellectual fashion. It is a way of life, and it is ours.

The temptations of existentialism must be balanced, however, by a broader historical picture, and the best proponent of that global perspective is Hegel. Against the enthusiastic individualism of the existentialist, there is always Hegel to remind us of the profound *un*importance of the individual; against the existentialist's overly anxious focus on the present and the near future there is the Hegelian perspective of history as a whole, in which the present cannot even be understood except as a historical product. Hegel and existentialism, it has always seemed to me, form the two poles of the twentieth-century philosophical dialogue, between our inescapable concern for our own worth and happiness and the grand vision that alone can give our existence some sense of profundity. I do not believe that one can study and advocate one side without bumping up against and getting drawn into the other. Hegel and existentialism form a natural dialectic, whose vicissitudes have come to define not only continental philosophy but much of life in both Europe and America. Together they form the subject matter as well as the inspiration for this book.

Rapprochement (or At Least Détente)

> There is one goddess who, amidst all the gaiety and pastimes, wears ever
> a coat of mail, the helmet on her head and the spear in her hand. She is
> the Goddess of Wisdom.
> —HEINRICH HEINE, *Reflections on German Religion and Philosophy*

The chauvinist antagonism between "hard-headed" Anglo-American and "soft-hearted" European philosophy has always seemed as absurd to me as it seemed important to its professionally hostile protagonists, among whom mutual illiteracy was typically counted as a virtue. Phenomenologists shook their heads and complained that they found "nothing but fiddling with symbols" in the works of the analysts, and some of the great minds of analytic philosophy proclaimed with pride that they wouldn't dream of wasting their time reading such "nonsense" as Hegel or Nietzsche, though they might proudly admit that they once had tried to read a page or two and "didn't understand a word of it."

There is an oft-told popular (and perhaps apocryphal) story about two philosophical giants, Gilbert Ryle and Maurice Merleau-Ponty, seated together at a conference. "Aren't we after the same thing?" asked Merleau-Ponty. Replied Ryle, "I hope not!" It is a scene that has been repeated thousands of times with lesser figures and less polite language, and, to correct a possible misimpression, the Europhiles are just as often just as narrow and nasty as the analysts. Against the one side, there are the residual logical positivist charges of "gibberish"; against the other, there are more ponderous charges such as the "denial of death" and "ignoring the meaning of man." What is at stake on both sides are entrenched professional interests which have little to do with philosophy.

From the moment I emerged from graduate school, full of respect and appreciation for the power of analytic techniques as well as enthusiasm for the visions and insights of the great and (then) neglected post-Kantian idealists, phenomenologists, and existentialists, I knew what I wanted to do in philosophy. Eventually, of course, I wanted to *be* a philosopher, to spin out, like a spider, a system to encompass my world—as Hegel had done, as Sartre had done. Or, perhaps, to pierce the world from a hundred angles (cosmic acupuncture?), as Nietzsche had done. But first, I wanted to be part of that then very small movement devoted to "rapprochement," bringing together the seemingly incompatible methods of analysis and phenomenology, the supposedly incongruent concerns of the emotivists in ethics and the existentialists, the modest and much qualified claims of the analysts and the ambitious visions of the Europeans. Without reducing or simply explaining the one to the other, it seemed obvious to me that whether or not they were "after the same thing," they were certainly much more akin than different. One had the discipline to be clear and precise; the other had the imagination and the daring. Both traced their inheritance from Plato, Descartes, and Kant. Both insisted that their interests had been generated from "real-life" problems of ordinary people, even if the language employed on both sides made that claim somewhat dubious. Why not bring them together—at least into détente, if not exactly camaraderie?

In 1986, that blunt conversation between Ryle and Merleau-Ponty would be all but unimaginable. If there are lines to be drawn of a serious philosophical nature, they will not appear down the middle of the English channel but, as other détenteniks are realizing, in a complicated nongeographical zigzag that will place Husserl, for example, on the side of the analysts (or the angels, as some would have it) and such paradigmatically analytic and American philosophers as Wittgenstein and John Dewey on the side with Heidegger and Sartre. Of course, one could carve up this continent in a hundred other ways: one can imagine a perverse chorography with Quine and Hegel together against Kant, Carnap, and Sartre. One can easily divide Heidegger and Wittgenstein against themselves (as they did so well in their own works). And it is of no small interest that neo-Hegelian Habermas is reading John Searle to prop up his attacks on neo-Heideggerian Gadamer, while Searle himself calls on Foucault to give transcultural legitimization to his own attack on post-Heideggerian Derrida.

My aim in this book is to present one picture of rapprochement; how analytic techniques and concepts can lend clarity and some rigor to the more polemical and imaginative claims of Hegel, Nietzsche, the phenomenologists, and the existentialists; and how a broad philosophical outlook can illuminate issues that extend far beyond the realm of professional philosophy. If there is one thing that these essays have in common, it is the attempt to break down artificial barriers, such as those between Anglo-American and Continental (i.e., northwestern European south of Helsinki) philosophy, and between "analytic" and "phenomenological" techniques. (The usual contrast between "analytic" and "Continental" is a confusion of these two.) The essays also attempt to break down the academically spurious boundaries between philosophy and its kindred disciplines: art, literature, history, psychology, sociology, and anthropology, as well as science and linguistics. Many of those divisions are based on a distinction that I do *not* talk about in this collection—the much maligned, and in any case suspicious, "analytic-synthetic" distinction, which I have come to believe is more of a political distinction between university departments than a question of certain sentence types. So, too, I see the battles between analysts and "Continental types" not as philosophy but as politics, not as intellectual positions but as excuses to limit one's thinking, refusals to leave the intellectual security of graduate-school dogmas.

I have also avoided—at all costs—trying to say anything at all on that hateful intramural metaquestion, "What is philosophy?" Today, many students are only too happy to find out that the history of philosophy is in fact the history of abortive epistemology. An earlier generation was taught that the history of philosophy was the history of abortive metaphysics. If there is a view of philosophy that is implied in these pages, it is that philosophy is first of all a multidimensional tradition and practice, not a unified body of techniques or doctrines—much less an abortion of anything. It is a tradition as broad and as varied as Western culture—not a footnote to Plato or Plotinus or anyone else—and it is a practice that is as diversified, and often as eccentric, as the temperaments of its practitioners. Both as a tradition and as a practice, philosophy is a realm of immigrants, some of whom came from mathematics and the sciences, others from religion and theology, still others from literature or random reading or, occasionally, from "real life." Fashionable philosophers today call this—following James—pluralism. But pluralism isn't a position—much less is it the wholesale rejection of "the tradition." It is the horizon of positions within and a looking beyond that tradition. Pluralism means seeing the limits of one's own view and understanding others', but at the same time (and of equal importance), it means standing for something oneself. Nietzsche said that a philosopher ought to be an example. At least he or she ought to be a person with cares and desires, rather than merely the transcendental critic to whom all ideas appear equally dubious or dogmatic.

The essays that follow are for the most part reprinted in their original published form, though I have made some additions to bring material up to date, and deletions and qualifications to correct some current qualms about my earlier interpretations. I have tried to provide a spectrum of readings not only in terms of subject matter but style as well. Unfortunately, to keep the chronology straight it was necessary to begin with some of the more difficult studies (on Hegel), while the more accessible essays (on Freud, Sartre, and Camus, for example) got shoved to the back of the book. Throughout, I have benefited from the kind criticisms of numerous friends, colleagues, and students. Special thanks to my editor, Cynthia Read, and to Shari Starrett, for her help with the final proofs. The mistakes and eccentricities that remain are entirely my own but might with equal validity be blamed on the Zeitgeist. Be that as it may, it is my hope that this collection can provide both a serious introduction to recent European philosophy and a number of interpretations which will bring together issues that have too long divided the philosophy profession in America.

Los Angeles, Calif.   R. C. S.
June 1986

CONTENTS

FROM HEGEL
TO
EXISTENTIALISM

1

Hegel's Concept of *Geist*

Geist[1] is a central conception of Hegel's mature philosophy, and much of the misunderstanding and hostility toward his "system" is due in part to the obscurity and quasi-mystical haze surrounding his employment of this concept. Concepts translatable as "Spirit" have been part of philosophy since ancient times; but Hegel's ambitious attempt to introduce an immanent God and World-Spirit into Christianity and philosophy has all but driven the term out of circulation. If we cannot understand *Geist,* then we cannot understand Hegel's philosophy: the "philosophy of Spirit" is only as comprehensible as the concept of "Spirit."

What clearly emerges from Hegel's writings is that *Geist* refers to some sort of *general consciousness, a single "mind" common to everyone.* The entire sweep of the *Phenomenology of Spirit* is away from the "disharmonious" conceptions of us as individuals to the "absolute" conception of humanity as one. In the *Phenomenology,* we are first concerned with the inadequacy of conceptions of oneself as an individual in opposition to others (in the "master-slave relationship") and in opposition to God (e.g., in "contrite consciousness"). The opposition is first resolved in ethics, in the conception of oneself as a member of a family, of a community, of Kant's "Kingdom of Ends," as a citizen of the state, and then in religion, in which one conceives of oneself as "part" of God and a religious community. Absolute consciousness is the explicit recognition of one's identity as universal Spirit. The concept of *Geist* is the hallmark of a theory of self identity—a theory in which *I* am something other than a *person.*

The first version of this paper was presented at the American Philosophical Association meetings, Eastern Division, in Washington, D.C., December 1968.

Of course, this theory of superpersonal identity is not all there is to the notion of *Geist* in Hegel's writings. *Geist* is fundamentally a religious concept, and Hegel's central purpose in employing *Geist* is to resolve the "disharmonies" of traditional Christianity which he had discussed in his earlier "theological" writings. Because Hegel's conception of an "immanent God" is dependent upon the peculiar theory of identity embodied in *Geist,* we shall be indirectly, but only indirectly, concerned with Hegel's philosophy of religion. *Geist* also represents an ambitious attempt to resolve certain far-reaching epistemological problems, characterized as the "disharmony between subject and object." However, this aspect of Hegel's notion of *Geist* goes far beyond the problem of superpersonal self identity with which we shall be concerned.

1

Most interpreters have accepted the notion of "universal consciousness" without serious criticism. It is often pointed out that *Geist* is one more in a long history of such concepts, particularly common in certain mystical traditions in Christianity and Eastern religions, and more recently adopted by Fichte and Schelling as the "Absolute Ego" or simply "the Absolute." But does the notion of a universal mind make sense? If two persons' minds are identical, then it would seem to follow that whatever would be experienced or known by one would be experienced or known by the other: in Sartre's terminology, consciousness is *translucent*—it has no "parts," and nothing can be "hidden" in it. Conversely, two minds would seem to be distinct if what is experienced or known by the one is not experienced or known by the other; in a very different language *privacy* is the defining trait of minds: one mind is distinguished from another by the "private access" each has to its own "contents." The fact that different persons have different memories, experiences, and knowledge has been often enough used as a criterion for personal identity (e.g., in Locke). How then can we make sense of the claim that *we* are all one consciousness-*Geist,* when the evidence so overwhelmingly proves that different persons have different ideas, thoughts, and feelings, and *ipso facto* different minds? I cannot remember what Julius Caesar was thinking as he crossed into Britain; I cannot speak Polish in spite of the fact that there are persons who can; I feel pains that you do not: therefore, I do not have the same mind as Julius Caesar, the same mind as any Pole, not the same mind as you. Now this is all so obvious that Hegel surely cannot be denying the privacy and individuality of the minds of persons. "Universal Spirit" cannot be the claim that we are all one consciousness in this sense.

A more plausible account of Hegel's *Geist* would not *deny* individual mental differences, but it could *ignore* them. Thus we might reject *Geist* as a name for a single universal mind, but maintain that *Geist* is the name of an *abstract entity,* like "the average American taxpayer." *Geist* abstracts from the peculiarities of individuals and focuses attention on their similarities: *Geist* is a convenient way of talking about the common properties of a society, of a people, or of *all* people while ignoring, but not denying, their differences. This sympathetic account of *Geist* eliminates the absurdity of talking about some actual mind common to all people. *Geist* is universal only in that it is the name of those properties had by every human consciousness: it is *not* universal in the sense that it is the name of a single entity (mind) common to every individual. Thus, "the spirit of the proletariat" or the "mind of middle-class America" does not refer to a single Spirit or a single mind shared respectively by all proletarians or all middle-class Americans. It refers to a set of concerns, goals, beliefs, and feelings which each of (or most of) the members of those groups share. Similarly, we may sympathetically interpret Hegel's *Geist* as an abstraction ranging over all human beings, an attempt to talk about humanity as a whole without being concerned with particular individuals, an attempt to talk about human consciousness without being concerned with the minds of any particular individuals.

This interpretation is reasonable, of course, and it does make perfectly good sense out of Hegel's very difficult notion of *Geist.* But what a bad joke Hegel's philosophy becomes on this interpretation! The aim of the entire *Phenomenology* is to give us a realization of *Geist,* and eight hundred tedious pages are solely directed to the demonstration of "absolute knowledge," "the goal, [of] which is Spirit knowing itself as Spirit."[2] But according to this interpretation, this grand effort is an attempt to prove only the humble and obvious thesis that we can talk abstractly about people without referring to individuals. Are we to believe that the philosopher who has been called the "Aristotle of our Renaissance world" spent his entire philosophical effort proving to us only that we can make abstractions and that in philosophical reflection we need to make abstractions? Are we to take seriously an *interpretation* which reduces a discovery which Hegel himself equated to divine revelation to the simpleminded claim that philosophers are not specifically concerned with people as individuals? However digestible the interpretation of *Geist* as an abstract entity might be, it can do no credit to Hegel's philosophy. Moreover, it is clearly contrary to Hegel's own insistence that "Spirit, of all things, must be looked at in its *concrete actuality*" (*LL,* sect. 34. Italics mine).[3] The *Phenomenology of Spirit* is a study of *something* called *Geist:* it is not the invention of abstraction.

If *Geist* refers neither to a literally general consciousness nor to an abstraction from all men, what else might it be? We might reasonably suppose that *Geist* refers to some sort of consciousness apart from the particular manifestations of consciousness so that sense can be made of "universal mind" without denying the obvious fact that different people have different experiences, knowledge, and the like. Traditional doctrines of *soul* would give us such a theory. If we distinguish "empirical psychology" from "rational psychology," as both Kant and Hegel have done, then we may say that *Geist* is a conception of rational psychology only, and that the identity thesis embodied in the concept of *Geist* is a claim about *souls,* not about *minds* with their particular experiences, beliefs, and so on. The soul is that which *underlies* particular mental states and events, and the notion of *Geist* embodies the claim that all individuals share the same *soul.* This interpretation at least offers us a specific and significant rendering of Hegel's notion of *Geist:* the concept of *Geist* is then as clear as the concept of "soul." However, Hegel sharply distinguishes between *Geist* and *soul,*[4] "soul being as it were the middle term between body and Spirit, or the bond between the two" (*LL,* sect. 34 [*Zusatz*]).[5] Furthermore, Hegel insists that the traditional doctrine of soul as a stable *thing* underlying all the more particular manifestations of mind, is wrong as an analysis of *Geist*. *Geist* cannot be separated from its manifestations, is not a thing, is not stable, and therefore is not soul:

> One word on the relation of rational to empirical psychology. The former, because it sets itself to apply thought to cognize mind and even to demonstrate the result of such thinking, is the higher; whereas empirical psychology starts from perception, and only recounts and describes what perception supplies. But if we propose to think the mind [*Geist*], we must not be so shy of its special phenomena. . . . It is wrong therefore to take the mind for a processless *ens,* as did the old metaphysic which divided the processless inward life of the mind from its outward life. (*LL,* sect. 34 [*Zusatz*])

An all too common interpretation of *Geist* relates it to the traditional doctrine of the soul but avoids the traditional metaphysical arguments concerning this soul by rejecting argument and appealing to mystical (or "intellectual") insight. Accordingly, Hegel is traced to Meister Eckhart, and *Geist* is identified with immanent God-soul discoverable through special experience: Hegel the arch-rationalist is interpreted as a mystic. However, regardless of what Hegel's *Geist* and Meister Eckhart's "God" have in common, Hegel discovers his *Geist* by strictly *rational* procedures. *Geist* is not "seen" in a single experience or set of experiences: it is a *conception* of mind which can only be defended through careful *thinking* about mind. We need only remind ourselves of Hegel's various attacks on Schelling's mystical tendencies (one of which occupies several pages of the preface to the *Phenomenology*) to see how very distant he is from this mystical tradition.

We have said that *Geist* is not the name of an abstract entity, that it cannot refer to the soul of traditional theology, and that it cannot refer to individual minds with their peculiar thoughts, feelings, and such. Yet it seems that *Geist* cannot ignore these peculiar manifestations of individual minds either, and it appears that *Geist,* although it is "concrete," can be discovered not through experience alone but only through "scientific" philosophical thought. But if *Geist* is neither soul nor abstraction from particular minds, what sort of thing can *Geist* be?

It has been remarked that Hegel's conception of *Geist* has its philosophical origins in Kant's *transcendental ego*.[6] However, the transition from Kant's talk of "consciousness in general" and the "synthetic unity of consciousness" to Hegel's conception of a *literally* general consciousness has been understandably challenged as one of the most confused and notoriously invalid moves in the history of philosophy. Against the influential picture of Hegel as misinterpreting and abusing Kant, however, I shall argue that this transition is neither confused nor invalid, and that the notion of *Geist* embodies an important attempt to resolve an important problem in Kant's philosophy.

How is Hegel's *Geist* related to Kant's *ego?* Kant's *ego* serves a function in his epistemology: Hegel's *Geist* functions primarily as an ethical-religious conception. But both authors are concerned with the possibility of "absolute" knowledge, and Hegel was deeply dissatisfied with the Kantian critique of reason. His dissatisfaction is not given full hearing until the *Science of Logic,* but the too often neglected introduction to the *Phenomenology* is clearly a complaint against Kant's theory of knowledge as well. For both Kant and Hegel, self-consciousness is the key to all knowledge, and both the *Critique of Pure Reason* and the *Phenomenology of Spirit* must be considered treatises on self-knowledge. Thus, for both Kant and Hegel, the nature of the knowing subject is the key to all philosophical understanding, and *Geist,* I shall argue, plays the same role as subject that the *transcendental ego* plays in Kant's philosophy.

2

If Hegel's *Geist* is reinterpretation of and improvement over Kant's *transcendental ego,* where in Hegel can we locate a critique of Kant's *ego,* and where are the arguments to show that *Geist* is an improvement over the *ego?* Although there are a few passages in Hegelian texts to indicate that Hegel did consider *Geist* as a reinterpretation and improvement of Kant's *ego* (e.g., *LL,* sect. 20), the comparison between *Geist* and *ego* is not to be found in Hegel's writings. What then can we use to defend our interpretation, which will argue that the two concepts are intimately related?

A nagging problem in the study of Hegel is his tendency to discuss a very specific problem without identifying it—to pluck an idea out of its specific context and display it as a problem for every philosopher. In the *Phenomenology,* for example, we are accustomed to seeing obvious references to Kant, Locke, Schelling, which conscientiously avoid any mention of Kant, Locke, or Schelling. Similarly, theses are often advanced in answer to a long-standing philosophical problem with no mention of the problem itself: in fact the "system" as a whole is an attempt to answer philsophical problems which are never stated in Hegel's mature works. This troubelsome philosophical style cannot help but create despair for the student of Hegel. We can piece together what references we can find and attempt to formulate a commentary to Hegel, adding what insights we have to the difficult text. And, we can do meticulous biographical research, attempting to use Hegel's more personal remarks in letters and influences which he obviously felt as clues for the construction of a hypothetical structure which might explain what is going on. But all of this produces shoddy philosophy, for we cannot possibly understand a philosopher if we do not understand what he is trying to do. The first step in understanding Hegel, therefore, is to reject his classic opening line of the *Phenomenology:*

> In the case of a philsophical work it seems not only superfluous, but, in view of the nature of philosophy, even inappropriate and misleading to begin, as writers usually do in a preface, by explaining the end the author had in mind, the circumstances which gave rise to the work, and the relation in which the writer takes it to stand to other treatises on the same subject, written by his predecessors or his contemporaries.

Can we understand Hegel when we violate the two central Hegelian methodological dictates? Does it make sense to try to understand Hegel by seeking out just those historical influences and unstated intentions which Hegel claims are irrelevant, and, worse, by plucking a single concept out of the context of his philosophy as a whole and attempting to analyse it? Hegel repeatedly warns us against considering philosophical concepts in isolation from the systems in which they are given significance. But what if instead of focusing on these statements of method which have had such disastrous effects on Hegel scholarship, we look at Hegel's own treatment of the history of philosophy? Hegel did not restrict himself to textual analysis, and when considering the writings of others he surely did not consider it inappropriate to question an author's intentions or to relate a work to its predecessors and contemporaries. Hegel's historical technique, perhaps his most valuable contribution to philosophy, is his attempt to see historical trends and developments in a philosophy which even its author did not see, to find advances in philosophy which had not been seen as advances, to see influences on thought of which even the thinker was unaware. What we must do for Hegel, therefore, is read his work not as he insists that we read it, but as he read the work of his predecessors. Whether or not Hegel saw the important relationships between *Geist* and Kant's *ego,* we shall find ourselves able to better appreciate Hegel's philosophy when we see what perhaps even Hegel did not fully appreciate in his own work.

If *Geist* is an answer to a problem which is never stated, then what reason do we have to accept it as an answer to that problem *for Hegel?* Hegel nowhere argues for the interpretation which we are about to present, and nowhere indicates that *Geist* is introduced to solve a problem derived from Kant. What Hegel does is simply present us with a "system" of philosophy in which *Geist* is the featured concept. But this sort of philosophy has been often attacked—for example, by Kierkegaard and Nietzsche, by Husserl and J. L. Austin—as a sort of philosophical dishonesty, a mode of presentation of philosophical prejudices which are thereby protected from all criticism. Hegel's lack of argument for his system is taken as grounds for dismissing his system as indefensible. But all of this is a profound misunderstanding of Hegel and his attempts to do philosophy. It is true that a philosophical system is well insulated from attack from the outside, but this does not mean it cannot be attacked, even if it is internally consistent. A system is not an arbitrary body of propositions: it is not even a coherent and consistent arbitrary body of propositions. A philosophical system is a super-theory, which attempts to resolve certain perplexities that brought us into philosophy in the first place. A system is successful insofar as it is adequate to eliminate those perplexities; it fails insofar as it leaves those perplexities intact or substitutes for them new problems of equal difficulty. Therefore, when we read Hegel, we must ask questions like: "What problem(s) is he attempting to solve?" and "How well does this system attempt to solve those problems?" When we are investigating a single concept in Hegel's philosophy, we must ask why Hegel included X in his system rather than Y and what perplexities X is supposed to help resolve. Specifically, we must ask why the special concept of (universal) Spirit is introduced instead of the traditional concept of "soul" or "consciousness" or "transcendental ego." In thus examining an individual concept, we must notice that we are not really taking it out of the system itself in examining it even though we are examining it without thereby examining the system as a whole. In other words, it is possible to examine individual Hegelian concepts without at the same time examining the system as a whole. Hegel commentators often neglect examination of crucial concepts, particularly *Geist,* because they confuse Hegel's insistence that concepts be investigated within a particular system of thought with the reasonable demand that we should examine particular concepts within a system by asking how this particular concept aids our resolution of extrasystematic perplexities.

We may thus restate the argument of this essay: *Geist* replaces Kant's *ego* in Hegel's philosophy because it removes certain philosophical perplexities which Kant's *ego* is incapable of resolving. Enough said about the uncommon historical method which we shall employ in this paper. We are not arguing so much *from* Hegel's philosophy as *for* his philosophy.

3

The concept of *Geist* is a successor both to Kant's *transcendental ego* or *"I think"* and Descartes' celebrated *cogito.* For both Descartes and Kant, the *cogito* or *"I think"* holds a precious place in philosophy: it is not merely one self-evident truth among others, but the "highest principle in the whole sphere of human knowledge" (B134).[7] The *cogito* or *"I think"* is the first principle of a philosophical methodology and a criterion for philosophical truth, as well as a philosophical truth itself. Were it not for the very specific significance now given to the notion of "phenomenology," we might call this philosophical method the "phenomenological method." Instead, we shall utilize a less popularized but more descriptive name in current employment, and call it *methodological solipsism.*

Methodological solipsism requires that every philosophical proposition must be justified from a first-person standpoint. If I wish to know what an X is, I must ask: "How can I and must I come to regard any X?"; if I wish to know whether there could be any X's, I must ask: "Could I come to know any such?" The methodological solipsist view is forcefully expressed by one of its most important advocates, Edmund Husserl:

> Anyone who seriously intends to become a philosopher must "once in his life" withdraw into himself and attempt, within himself, to overthrow and build anew all the sciences that, up to then, he has been accepting. Philosophy— wisdom—is the philosopher's quite personal affair. It must arise as *his* wisdom, as his self-acquired knowledge tending toward universality, a knowledge for which he can answer from the beginning, and at each step, by virtue of his own absolute insights. . . . All the various inferences proceed, as they must, according to guiding principles that are immanent, or "innate," in the pure Ego.[8]

According to the methodological solipsist starting-point, every philosophical problem must be construed as *my* problem: I must determine whether it is justifiable for me to believe in any theory which attempts to answer that problem, and I can justify my acceptance of this theory only by appealing to evidence that I have, and treating this evidence according to methods which I am also able to justify. To this solipsist demand is often coupled the insistence that only propositions of which we are certain may be allowed into our philosophical inquiry.

Together, the demands for self-evidence and certainty require that philosophical inquiry will restrict itself to an examination of the necessary features of the "first-person situation." For Descartes, the resultant method limits its appeals to the clarity and distinctness of ideas and the natural light of reason. One could not appeal to natural science or the teachings of religion or "common sense," for these were not self-evident. Similarly, one could not appeal to his own beliefs unless these were self-evident, so that my believing that X is not sufficient to ascertain X. In Kant, the dual restrictions of certainty and appeal only to the first-person case yeild a "transcendental method," whose aim to provide us with those features of (self-)consciousness which are necessary.

According to the methodological solipsist, my mind is not one mind among others, and I am not one person among others. Every philosophical proposition (and therefore every proposition) depends upon *my* mind for their justification, but every other mind can only be a philosophical problem. I know the existence of my own mind without doubt: if I can know of the existence of other minds at all, it must be the result of a calculation derivative of certain facts about my own consciousness. This is not to say that the methodological solipsist openly accepts solipsism as a philosophical truth, of course: it is only his starting-point. Solipsism is an initially given problem to be resolved, and one of the central efforts of all who have adopted this method has been to show that solipsism is false in spite of the method. This is obvious for Descartes and Kant (in the "Refutation of Idealism"): it is not always understood in discussions of Hegel (and Husserl).

The supreme test of methodological solipsism turns out to be the analysis of the basic concepts of the method itself (as Husserl never tires of telling us). Thus we should not be surprised to find Descartes, Kant, and Hegel very much concerned to analyze the concepts of "first person" and "self-consciousness" which lie at its foundation. Before philosophy can insist upon "appeal to the first-person case," we must understand what this first person case is. Thus, the epistemology of Descartes is dominated by the *cogito;* and the "Transcendental Analytic" of Kant's *Critique of Pure Reason* rests upon the necessity of the "possibility for the 'I Think' to accompany all my representations" (B131). For Descartes and Kant, methodological solipsism is a position which must be explained and defended; for Hegel, it is simply there to be used. As a result, we do not get from Hegel an elegant expression of his starting-point: he simply starts. Yet it is clear that his "phenomenology" does accept this beginning:

> A self having knowledge purely of itself in the absolute antithesis of itself. . . .
> The beginning of philosophy presupposes or demands from consciousness that
> it should feel at home in this element.[9]

4

How can an analysis of "self-consciousness" be carried out from a methodological solipsist position? We cannot appeal to a scientific study of consciousness or even other philosophical analyses of "self-consciousness"; we cannot appeal to other persons, to be sure, or to other persons' experiences of themselves, or to the language *we* use to communicate about ourselves. I cannot even appeal to myself as a *person,* for persons have *bodies,* and the existence of my body or of any connection between that body and my mind is still being held in philosophical suspension. According to methodological solipsism, I must ask: "How can I and must I come to be conscious of myself?"

For Descartes, the "I" of the *cogito* is clearly not dependent upon other persons and not itself a person. But its exact nature is a matter of great concern for him; in the second of his *Meditations on First Philosophy,* he thinks:

> I do not yet understand what is this "I" that necessarily exists. I must take care, then, that I do not rashly take something else for the "I" and thus go wrong even in the knowledge that I am maintaining to be most certain and evident of all.

Descartes concludes (in the sixth *Meditation*) that the "I" is neither person nor human body but the thinking mind:

> I recognized I was a substance whose whole essence or nature is to think and whose being requires no place and depends on no material thing.

In Kant, the "I think" is a *formal* necessity, a unifying principle which constitutes a necessary precondition for any consciousness:

> Only insofar as I can unite a manifold of given representations in *one consciousness* is it possible for me to represent to myself the identity of the consciousness in these representations. (B133)

The formal principle of this unity, "all my representations are mine," is analytic, but, according to Kant, the unifying principle of consciousness is itself not analytic:

> The *analytic* unity of apperception is possible only under the presupposition of a certain *synthetic* unity. (B133)

The introduction of the "I think" as the "vehicle of all concepts" (B399) must be carefully distinguished from two other concepts of "self" with which it is naturally confused. First, this "I" that thinks is not equivalent to a *person* but only to that nonmaterial conception of the "I" that thinks which is transcendentally necessary for there to be consciousness at all. Secondly, and more dangerously, this transcendental "I," which "can have no special designation because it serves only to introduce all our thought as belonging to consciousness" (B399–B400), is naturally but mistakenly spoken of as a "thing," as a *substance,* as a *soul.*

The inference from the necessity of the "I think" to the existence of the "I" as a thing, Kant argues, is the result of a paralogism—an invalid syllogism—which mistakenly argues from the formal conditions for consciousness to a conclusion about supersensible objects—in this case, the soul or the "self-in-itself." But no such doctrine about the "I" as object can be established by appeal to the necessity of the "I think," the "bare consciousness which accompanies all con-cepts," because

> consciousness in itself is not a representation distinguishing a particular object
> (the soul) but a form of representation in general. (B404)

The analysis of the "I think" will admit only inferences which state necessary conditions for employment of the understanding. The argument against the par-alogisms,[10] therefore, proceeds by demonstrating that all talk of the "I" as sub-stance does not state such necessary conditions. The "I" that thinks and is nec-essary to consciousness is only the subject of experience, not an object of experience. Because the "I" by its very nature cannot be an object of experience, the categories of the understanding cannot be applied to it, which means that this subject cannot be considered as unit or plurality of substance(s), cannot be exhib-ited in causal relationships with anything else and, in summary, cannot be *known:*

> The unity of consciousness . . . is only unity in thought by which alone no
> object is given. . . . Consequently, this subject cannot be known. (B421–422)

Thus, on Kant's account, the substantial "I think" postulated by Descartes is nec-essarily unknowable, for it corresponds to no intuition and thought alone can proceed to it only fallaciously.

5

With this analysis of the "I think," Hegel is in general agreement, and the concept of *Geist* reflects much of the Kantian transcendental "I." *Geist,* like the "I," is the subject of all possible experiences, and is not itself a "thing" to which the cate-gories can be applied. *Geist,* like the "I think," is an activity, and not a "soul-thing" lying "behind" our thoughts. *Geist* is the "universal in action," as the "I think" is the unifying activity of employing universal concepts (of reason and of the understanding). The only sense in which the "I think" exists is the sense in which it knows of itself or is "reference-to-self." *Geist* is "being-for-itself," and its existence and its knowledge of its existence are the same.[11] Finally, Hegel speaks mysteriously of *Geist* as "infinite and negative" (*LL,* sect. 94–97) and as "infinite negativity."[12] But these obscure phrases can be unpacked as an equivalent of what Kant says of "negative" or "limiting" concepts, "the function of which is to curb the pretensions of sensibility" (B311). The concept of the thinking "I," considered as an object, is just such a concept, for it represents a thought for which there can be no corresponding intuitions. *Geist,* like the "I think" is indicated in every experience but it is not itself experienced in any of these.

Most importantly, considering the frequent charges that Hegel ignored Kant's critique of metaphysics, Hegel accepted Kant's rejection of the paralogism for their "confounding of one kind of truth for another" and the "replacing of empirical attributes by categories" (*LL,* sect. 47). He commends Kant for

> emancipating mental philosophy from the "soul-thing," from the categories
> and consequently from questions about the simplicity, complexity, material-
> ity, etc., of the soul. (*LL,* sect. 47)

> By his polemic against the metaphysics of the past Kant discarded those pred-
> icates from the soul or mind. He did well, but when he came to his reasons,
> his failure was apparent. (*LL,* sect. 47 [*Zusatz*])

Hegel does qualify his commendation, however, with a criticism of some of Kant's arguments, most notably, his argument that to get rid of the soul as a supersensible thing was to get rid of it as an object of knowledge altogether. For Hegel

> this style of abstract terms [the categories of the understanding] is not *good
> enough* for the soul which is very much *more* than a mere unchangeable sort
> of thing. (*LL,* sect. 47 [*Zusatz*]. Italics mine.)

But Hegel's refusal to return to the metaphysics against which Kant argued is clear, and the concept of *Geist* does not refer to the supersensible or the unknow-able. Hegel is neither a metaphysician, in the old sense, nor a mystic, and *Geist* is neither metaphysical nor mystical.

The disagreement between Kant and Hegel was not, however, a simple dis-pute over the correct reasons for accepting a mutually agreeable thesis. They did concur on the nonsubstantiality of the "I think," but Hegel charged that Kant ignored his own prohibitions and inadvertantly reintroduces to philosophy just those notions which his most brilliant doctrines sought to eliminate. Kant rec-ognizes the importance of the differences between the transcendental "I think" and the empirical self or person and the metaphysical notion of the soul, but, complains Hegel, he "never went into the details of this."

6

The *Critique of Pure Reason* is notably obscure on the relationship between the "I think" and personal identity. As two recent commentators, Bennett and Straw-son, have pointed out, Kant pays so little attention to the problematic connec-tions between the thinking subject and his body, and the "I" that thinks and the person, that questions concerning the attribution of mental predicates to other persons, or even questions concerning ourselves as persons remain unanswerable. Yet Kant's free use of the pronouns "my" and "mine" throughout the *Critique* make it quite clear that the "I think" is a *personal* "I think": there is one such subject *per person.* In the *Critique of Practical Reason,* however, it becomes evi-dent that the noumenal acting ego there discussed is the same ego presupposed by the "I think" in the first *Critique:*

> We should become aware that in the consciousness of our existence there is
> contained a something *a priori,* which can serve to determine our existence . . .
> as being related, in respect of a certain inner faculty, to a non-sensible intelli-
> gible world. (B430–431)

And this ego, whether applying concepts in the employment of the understanding or reason or whether willing in the employment of practical reason, is a *personal* ego. For every *person,* there is an "I" that both thinks and wills.

Now this almost tautological thesis raises immense problems for Kant's doc-

trine of the *transcendental ego* within the demands of his methodological solipsism. First there is the question of how I can know whether there are any other
subjects or "I think's"—or, if you like—whether there are any other *persons,* by
arguing from my own case. From Kant's own characterization of the "I think," it
is clear that the existence of other subjects can never be established as an a priori
truth. If it is to be established at all, it must be some form of inductive argument—by analogy, or as an inference to the best explanation or theory about the
"behavior" of certain objects. Within Kant's first *Critique* we are forced to adopt
a provisional behaviorism with respect to other persons. But this is not a moot
point here—first, because it is not a problem unique to methodological solipsists
of Kantian persuasion, but mainly because it is not a problem that seriously
seemed to confront Hegel. It is only in the second *Critique* that recognition of
other persons becomes a matter for *practical* concern (it cannot, therefore,
become an object of *knowledge*). For Hegel, first recognition of others arises in
the conflict of the master-slave confrontation. (But for Hegel, who does not distinguish between theory and practice, this recognition does constitute knowledge,
but knowledge of a relatively unsophisticated sort.) However, the problem with
which we must be concerned here is not this problem of *other* minds so much as
the problem of identifying *our own mind.*

According to Kant, the nature of the "I think" is such that it abstracts from
all empirical content, or, in his terms, there are no true empirical propositions
applicable to it. This means, foremost, that any statement about human bodies
cannot be statements about the "I think," for Kant clearly states the independence of all talk about bodies as part of the empirical ego which has no place in
transcendental deduction of necessary states of consciousness. We have already
seen that Kant, like Descartes, considers the relationship between "me" and my
body a strictly empirical relationship, albeit a very special empirical relationship.
But neither can any statements about what Kant calls the *content* of consciousness, for example, particular thoughts, be statements about the "I think," for the
fact that a consciousness "contains" any particular thought or sets of thoughts is
again strictly empirical, but also again, as exemplified by, for example, memories
of childhood, these facts might be very special facts indeed.

But what this means is that any criterion which we would normally use to
identify *persons* does not suffice to help us identify the "I think," Thus the "I"
that thinks is not a person, and, moreover, considerations about the "I think" are
quite independent—logically and causally independent—of considerations about
myself as a person. This independence results in a most embarassing consequence
for Kant's thesis of *transcendental ego.* Because "I think's" cannot be individuated by individuating persons, it is possible, on Kant's analysis, that I share a
transcendental ego with others, or that there are several subjects occupying "my"
body, or that there are several of us, though not knowing of each other, who are
sharing the same thoughts, memories, feelings, and the like. The almost trivial
thesis that human "I think's" are commensurate with persons turns out to be no
more defensible on Kant's theory than the bizarre thesis that my body is "inhab-
ited" by two "I think's," one of which my body shares with an automobile. If we
have no way to identify and individuate "I think's," then any thesis about the
number or distribution of (transcendental) subjects is as defensible as any other.

This argument may be further reinforced when we consider the privileged status of the "I think" in Kant's philosophy which leads him to reject the paralogisms. The categories cannot be applied to this "I," says Kant, because the categories presuppose the "I." The errors of rational psychology result from the attempt to categorize the "I think" as soul. But what Kant evidently fails to notice, as Hegel's system brings out, the individuation of the "I think" as a personal "I think" presupposes the categories just as surely as do the paralogisms. Individuation requires the discussion of the quantitative categories of the unity and plurality just as surely as do Kant's rejected theses that the "I" is noncomposite, simple, and so on. Furthermore, any talk of the "I think" as being *in* space and time embodies the same confusion, for it is the "I think" which imposes these forms on any possible experience. (This, of course, is how Kant himself manages to introduce his own doctrine of immortality of the soul in the second *Critique.*) But this means, again, that we have no way of individuating "I's"; in fact, we are not even justified in talking as if subjects (transcendental subjects) can be individuated at all. We must, as Kant argues, attribute all thoughts and experiences to a subject; but we cannot, by Kant's own insistence, identify or individuate subjects as we individuate persons.

7

Why does Hegel use the concept of *Geist* instead of the concept of the *transcendental ego?* The traditional use of *ego* carries with it the more or less explicit stipulation that there is one such ego for each *person.* Similarly, *"I"* and *"I think"* are used to refer to individual persons. But any attempt to use these concepts in transcendental philosophy constitutes a serious confusion. The subject of transcendental philosophy does not individuate individual persons, and it is therefore nothing like the ego or "I" of traditional philosophical and everyday discourse.

We might interestingly compare Hegel's rejection of the traditional concepts of self-reference to Peter Geach's rejection of Descartes' *cogito.* In *Mental Acts,*[13] he argues that Descartes uses "I" to refer to a self not seen by others, whereas "I," insofar as it has any intelligible use in our language, is

> used to draw attention to the speaker. . . . "I" can refer only to a human being;
> "I" in this special [transcendental] context is idle and superfluous.

In other words, the "I" of the *cogito* is no more than a confused parasitic use of our ordinary grammar of self-reference. But in philosophical discussions of the transcendental "I," there can be no reference to persons and therefore no intelligible use of "I" to denote at all. If we wish to talk, as the methodological solipsist supposes we must, of the transcendental subject in philosophy, it cannot be through this traditionally misleading use of the *personal* pronoun "I." The subject of philosophy is not a person, is not an individual, but must be referred to *simpliciter* as *subject,* without any pretense toward identification or individuation with persons. But this notion of *subject* is precisely Hegel's notion of *Geist.* For Hegel, the *transcendental ego,* as *Geist,* is a literally general or universal consciousness, as it *ought* to have been for Kant. Hegel's *Geist* is Kant's ego without the unwarranted claim that there is one ego per person. *Geist* is simply the underlying unifying principle of consciousness and, at the same time, the underlying rational will "behind" all practical reason and action. Hegel does sometimes speak as if there is only *one Geist,* particularly in the preface to the *Phenomenology* where he attempts to personify *Geist* as the divine subject. But these mostly grammatical attempts at individuation are not frequent, and the movement of the *Phenomenology* as a whole seems to indicate clearly that the transition from Kant's *ego* to Hegel's *Geist* is a transition from a personal subject to a universal subject. Kant's "consciousness in general" with its necessary "I think" is forced to become universal *Geist,* no longer stating the laws necessary for any consciousness but also stating that every consciousness is *transcendentally* indistinguishable from every other.

8

One cannot help but mention here a fascinating modern analytic analog to this contest between Kant and Hegel. In Wittgenstein's notes after the *Tractatus Logico-Philosophicus,* we also find a brilliant philosopher who, through his commitment to a methodological solipsist approach to philosophical truth, is forced into a position of admitting that he cannot explain our accepted correlation between persons and subjects. This leads him into hesitantly admitting what Strawson, in *persons,* characterizes as a "no-ownership theory of consciousness," not very far from Hegel's universal ownership of consciousness theory. One striking difference, of course, is that Strawson and later Wittgenstein took this conclusion as a *reductio ad absurdum* argument against any such first-person oriented theory of persons, while Hegel took the argument to establish an interesting and true ("absolutely" true) proposition. Of course, in philosophy we are not unused to seeing what is established as uncontrovertible theory in one conceptual age to later constitute a manifest absurdity. Nonetheless, if the result of Hegel's introduction of *Geist* is outrageous, it is not peculiarly Hegel's outrage. A rejection of the bizarre consequences of Hegel's *Geist* should not call for the "return to Kant" so often urged by his detractors, but rather for a renewed attack on Kant's most treasured methodological presuppositions.

NOTES

1. *Geist* is usually translated as either "spirit" or "mind." I shall use both English terms interchangeably with *Geist.*

2. *Phänomenologie des Geistes,* ed. by J. Hoffmeister (Hamburg, 1952), p. 564; *Phenomenology of Mind,* trans. by J. B. Baillie (London, MacMillan, 1931), p. 808.

3. All references to Hegel's *Logic* are references to his *"Lesser" Logic* from the *Encyclopedia.* This work will be abbreviated to *LL,* and followed by section numbers. Translations are those of William Wallace, *The Logic of Hegel* (Oxford, 1892).

4. Cf. *LL,* sect. 34.

5. The *Zusätze* are additions to the *Encyclopedia* made by Hegel's editors from his lecture notes. Quotations from the *Zusätze* instead of from the original text will be so noted.

6. One recent source of a remark is J. N. Findlay's *Hegel: A Re-examination* (London, Colliers 1958), ch. 2.

7. Immanuel Kant, *Critique of Pure Reason,* trans. by N. Kemp Smith (London, MacMillan 1929). All references to Kant are to the second edition.

8. Edmund Husserl, *Cartesian Meditations,* trans. by D. Cairns (The Hague: Nijhoff, 1960), pp. 2–3.

9. *The Phenomenology of Mind,* p. 86.

10. In this brief discussion, I have avoided discussing the various doctrines of rational psychology individually as Kant does in the first edition. It is the first three theses, that the soul is substance, is simple, and remains identical in time, which would be relevant to a more detailed discussion of the relation of the paralogisms to Hegel's *Geist.*

11. Hegel's general thesis, so often attacked, that essence and existence, thought and being, are one and the same, clearly makes perfectly good sense in this particular context.

12. *Phenomenology,* p.96.

13. P. T. Geach, *Mental Acts* (London: Routledge and Kegan Paul, 1956), p. 117.

2

Hegel's Epistemology

Until very recently, the philosophy of Hegel was sufficiently disreputable in this country, despite the rebirth of interest in Kant, Marx, and Kierkegaard, that an essay on Hegel typically turned into a defense of his philosophy, and then of its intelligibility rather than its truth. Accordingly, I do not want to begin by claiming that Hegel is doing something ingenious and revolutionary—that is still commensurate with being disreputable—but by showing how he was doing something respectable and defensible. I here want to examine one aspect of Hegel's thought—his epistemology (or perhaps we should say, his "ontology of knowledge," for reasons which will soon become clear.) My aim is to establish this epistemology within the tradition usually traced from Descartes to Kant, where it is eclipsed by Hegel's shadow for a century before being brought back to the light by Moore and Russell. But Hegel took Kant's philosophy to be "the basis and point of departure of modern German philosophy."[1] Accordingly I want to argue that Hegel's epistemology is an attempt to rework and make consistent the key arguments in Kant's "Transcendental Analytic" of the *Critique of Pure Reason*. The focus of my attention will be the introduction, the first three chapters, the first few pages of "Self-Consciousness" and section AA(V), "Certainty and the Truth of Reason," in Hegel's *Phänomenologie des Geistes*.[2] But, in addition to the more substantial agreements that I shall illustrate between the two works, there is the further similarity in style—both hastily written transcriptions of ideas and arguments not yet fully digested and formulated, and so what I present here is a defensible reconstruction of their thinking rather than a line-by-line commentary on the texts.[3]

The basis of the interpretation I wish to defend is this: Kant's great anti-sceptical move in the "Transcendental Analytic" is the mutual rejection of the Cartesian claim to the epistemological priority of the mental and the empiricist model of knowledge as passive-receptive "representation." In place of both, Kant supplies the revolutionary notion of *a priori synthesis,* the idea that objects are not simply *given* in experience but rather constituted or synthesized as a necessary condition for experience by the pure concepts of the understanding. Similarly, Kant argues that the idea of necessary connection between events (e.g., causal connection) is not given in experience (thus agreeing with Hume) but is supplied by the Understanding as a necessary condition of every experience. But Kant, like most great revolutionaries, is not quite bold enough to step surefootedly onto the new intellectual ground he had liberated. Even as he attacks the Cartesian epistemological priority of the mental, he still finds problematic the idea that we could know things-in-themselves. And even as he attacks the "myth of the given" of empiricism and the "blindness" of nonconceptualized experience, he hangs onto the empiricist notion of "impressions" *(Empfindungen)* which are given in atomistic bits and then synthesized to give us objects. And as he argues for the active role of the Understanding and the Imagination in perception, Kant retains the conservative belief that there is but one set of categories and consequently but one possible conception of the world. The move from the idea that *we* supply the categories by which objects are synthesized to the idea that we might supply *other* categories doesn't entice him. But the idea that necessary truths are not in turn necessary (a denial of Becker's reiteration of modalities theorem in the material mode) did not bypass Fichte, who saw there the germinal idea of Kant's philosophy. Unfortunately, Fichte was not equal to the task of redoing and "systematizing" Kant's philosophy, and so the challenge passed to Hegel. Working a quarter century after the publication of the revolutionary *Critique,* whose ideas were now as cool and established as the banal slogans of the great political revolutions of the same period, Hegel, without Kant's timidity and with newfound transcendental *Arroganz,* pursued to the limits Kant's ideas of a priori synthesis and his rejection of the idea that objects are simply *given* in experience.[4]

The interpretation falls into three parts: First, I provide a cursory and barely adequate summary of the three chapters on "Consciousness" in part A of the *Phenomenology.* Second, I offer a semiformal account of the arguments which I find contained, presupposed, and suggested in these chapters together with the preceding introduction and succeeding transition to later sections of the *Phenomenology* on "Self-Consciousness" and "Reason." Third, I attempt to support this account by establishing Hegel in a methodological tradition within which I think his epistemological claims can best be understood.

1

Each of the first three chapters of the *Phenomenology* presents us with what Hegel calls a "form of consciousness;" together, these three are entitled "Consciousness." It is important to stress from the beginning that "consciousness" here does not refer to the specifically "mental," but is rather more like "knowing something." "Knowing something," after Hegel has rejected the idea of the "knowledge by acquaintance" in the first chapter, means *"knowing that* something is the case." Each "form of consciousness" is a different philosophical analysis of knowing. In these chapters, Hegel does not simply "take up" a form of consciousness, as is often suggested, but examines and criticizes each of them as *theories.* In the text, we often find reference to "we who are watching the process" or "we who perceive the contradiction." In other words, Hegel's text often says something of a form of consciousness which it could not say of itself. "Consciousness" is an examination of theories of knowledge which themselves are reflections on knowing, but not self-reflective. "Sense-Certainty," "Perception," and "Understanding" are each a philosophical theory of knowledge. The knowledge they theorize about—even if it should be "theory-laden"—is not self-reflective, and neither are these theories themselves self-reflective. It is only with Hegel that philosophy is forced to be fully self-reflective.[5]

The common link of all forms of "Consciousness" is the fact that the object is taken as "more essential" than our knowledge in the sense that "the object exists, indifferent to whether it is known or not, . . . but the knowledge is not if the object is not" (75/B151). Accordingly, the most primitive of these "forms of consciousness" is "Sense-Certainty," which Hegel describes as

> That knowledge, which is in the first place or immediately our object of concern, can be no other than that which is itself immediate knowledge, knowledge of the immediate or what *is.* (73/B149.)

It is "mere apprehension [*Auffassen*] free from conceptual comprehension [*Begreifen*]" (149). In "Sense-Certainty," it is suggested, as in naïve realism but also as in many empiricisms, romanticisms, intuitionisms, mysticisms, etc., that knowledge of objects begins with *acquaintance.* An object *has* properties, but it is first of all a mere "this," that of which the properties are predicated. Included here is what recent epistemologists have called "the myth of the given," Kant's "blind" intuitions without concepts, and what recent metaphysicians have called a "bare particular." But, Hegel argues, there can be no knowledge that is not knowledge by description as well. "Sense-Certainty" is the barest form of "the myth of the given," and Hegel's argument against it is intended as a general argument against all philosophical claims—whether of naïve realism or sophisticated phenomenalism—which argue that it is possible to identify the objects (or sensations) of one's immediate acquaintance without presupposing categories and descriptions. In a familiar Wittgensteinian argument, Hegel shows that a "this" presupposes an understanding of "what," that identifying a particular presupposes being able to describe it in universal terms. Since the idea of "the given" in philosophical theories depends upon the claim that what is given can be identified independently of and prior to any particular description of it, Hegel, in denying this, undermines its role in epistemology. It must be stressed that Hegel does not deny that knowledge has its sensuous component. He insists, as much as Kant, that it is sensibility that allows us to distinguish between the objects of experience and objects which are only "thought" and merely possible. But, Hegel argues, there is nothing to be said about sensibility insofar as it is "given" and preceedes conceptualization. Accordingly, it drops out of the dialectic from the very beginning. To understand knowing, Hegel continues, is to understand how we *describe* the objects of our knowledge. Knowing surely depends upon the sensible but not upon "given" nonconceptual sensible particulars. Our analysis of knowing must turn to universals, the subject matter of the remainder of Hegel's philosophy.

The second chapter is called "Perception." Perception

> takes what is given to it as universal. As universality is its overall principle, so too are its moments distinguished in their immediacy [that is, as universals], *I* is a universal, and the object is a universal. (84/B162)

"Perception" is an attempt to replace the ineffability of the "bare particular" of "Sense-Certainty" with a conception of knowledge which suggests that *all* that we are acquainted with are properties ("sensuous universals") and that an object is nothing but a unit of properties. Within this quasi-Leibnizian view (but some empiricist sense-datum theories would also fit here) Hegel also finds it necessary to defend the principle of the identity of indiscernibles, the only way to avoid the fatal conclusion that there might be two objects with all their properties in common and which therefore could not be individuated on this account of knowledge. But, even with this principle, "Perception" will not do. How is it, Hegel asks, that we take properties to be properties *of* anything particular? To answer this problem, Hegel introduces the form of consciousness called "Understanding," which "takes the unconditioned universal as the *object* of consciousness" (100/B180). The unconditioned universal (the category of substance) is to be contrasted with "conditioned universals" or properties. The Understanding introduces the notion of "Force," (Leibniz' dynamic version of "substance") as the "supersensible medium" which *has* properties (its "manifestations") and which explains our ability to individuate objects and reidentify them over time and through change. With the conception of supersensible forces and substances, Hegel traces the classical retreat from the "given in experience" of both empiricists (Locke) and the rationalists. But the same problem of individuation repeats itself: How do we individuate substances and forces? And, if we are *given* appearances but intellectually *know* this "super-sensible world," how are these two related? (Kant's rationalistic problem in the *Dissertation* of 1770 and the *Poltergeist* of the *Critique*.) With the former question, Hegel is still in league with Kant, but with the latter question, he begins to turn against him. Not only the idea of "substance," but any idea of the supersensible raises the same problems. In a perplexing but delightful counterexample of sorts, Hegel creates an "inverted" *(verkehrte)* supersensible world, in which it is suggested that every proposition true of the apparent world corresponds to its *opposite* in the "real" world (black is white, good is evil). And so Hegel rejects, by making fun of, Kant's "things-in-themselves" as distinct from phenomena.

Leaving "Understanding," we also leave "Consciousness" for the famous section, "Self-Consciousness." This is now called "the native land of truth" and "a new form and type of knowledge" (131/B219). With this move, Hegel rejoins Kant and insists that any adequate theory of knowledge takes the contribution of the knower as fundamental. In other words, *reflecting* on (our knowledge of) objects philosophically ultimately must become self-knowledge.[6] At this point (for reasons we cannot discuss here) the dialectic takes a turn into what appears to be primitive social philosophy and the concept of "freedom." Hegel's theory of knowledge as such reemerges in the next section with "Reason," where "the individual consciousness is inherent absolute reality" (174/B272) and "is the conscious certainty of being all reality" (175/B273). Here Hegel leaves Kant for Fichte. His concern is "Idealism" and Hegel is concerned to protect the gains of "Transcendental Idealism" (Kant and Fichte) from the confusion (which virtually destroyed Fichte) between Transcendental Idealism (in Fichte, "Ethical Idealism") and Subjective (or what Hegel calls "Empty" or "Unintelligible") Idealism (175f./B273).

No doubt the language of this argument is unfamiliar today and its structure perplexing; in fact, it is not obviously an *argument* at all. But everyone who knows nothing else of Hegel knows that the above progression is a form of "dialectic" and that the stages are arranged in ascending order approaching what Hegel pretentiously calls "Absolute Truth." But how is this an argument? Where is the "epistemology?" Why the opaque references to Locke, Leibniz, Kant, and Fichte? Why these particular forms? And why this particular progression?

Notice that Hegel is cutting the philosophical pie in an unusual way. Unlike Kant, he does not take the competing epistemological claims of the empiricists and the rationalists as the antitheses for him to *aufheben*.[7] Rather he sees a series of competing ontological claims which are, as often as not, shared by the two epistemological traditions. (Locke, Leibniz, and Russell, for example, would have to be included at every stage.) This is why we began with the parenthetical remark that epistemology for Hegel is "the ontology of knowledge." One must distinguish two very different epistemological problems, one of which Hegel took Kant to have already solved beyond question. This is the empiricist "constitution" problem: How do our sensations or "impressions" become organized into objects? Hegel accepted Kant's answer without qualification: We so organize our experience into objects, and so it does not even make sense, Kant proved, to talk about experience except in terms of our experience of objects. Accordingly, Hegel does not talk about it in any other terms, and the familiar empiricist epistemological problems concerning the relationship between experience and objects are not even mentioned by him. However, there is a second problem—also part of Kant's "reply to Hume"—which arises independently of the "constitution problem." Assuming that we are conscious of objects, how can we know that the objects of which we are conscious are "objective"? How can we know that they exist independently of our awareness of them, that the space they occupy is "real" space, that they are not just productions of *my* consciousness? To this problem, Kant gave a promising but incomplete answer. The categories by which I constitute my experience are such that to be conscious of objects is *ipso facto* to be conscious of objects as independent, as "real" in "real space," and not just *mine*. This answer, too, Hegel accepts without question, so far as Kant had presented it. But there is still a question, left unanswered by Kant, concerning the *ontological status* of the objects of knowledge. Kant had reduced all ontological questions to epistemological problems and so used his answer to the "constitution problem" as an answer to the ontological questions as well. The mutant and subtle scepticism of Kant's notion of "things-in-themselves" is but a symptom of this ontological neglect. And so Hegel, accepting Kant's epistemological arguments so completely that he does not even consider it necessary to repeat them, goes on to provide the ontological counterparts of those arguments. What is it to know something? We need not even consider the narrow problems raised by the empiricists in their peculiar reply to this question. Hegel does not feel it necessary to give another "reply to Hume." He does not feel it necessary to restate Kant's theory of "constitution" or "a priori synthesis." But he does find it necessary to return to the epistemologies that Kant rejected to further purge them of shared ontological claims which Hegel wants to reject by similar "transcendental arguments."

The first three "forms of consciousness" are each one of these shared ontological claims: first, there is the naïve idea of a "bare particular," knowable by "pure acquaintance"—whether such objects of acquaintance are formless sense-data or impressions, a bare particular or substance, "Being-in-general" or "Absolute Ego" as known by "intellectual intuition" (Jacobi, Fichte, and Schelling; also compare pt. 1 of the *Logic*). Second, there is the idea that objects are merely "clusters" of properties (or sense-data, which are here conceptualized and describable, not "this" but "red and square"), again a thesis which can be found both in the empiricists (e.g., Berkeley) and rationalists (e.g., Leibniz). Third, there is the idea of supersensible substance or force, a thing-in-itself that in some sense lies "behind" properties and particulars and accounts for them. Substance is recruited to fill in for the rejected bare particulars, but without the naïve claim of knowledge by acquaintance: substances can only be known by "the Intellect" (for the rationalists), or inferred (e.g., by Locke). Against those commentators who loudly complain about the arbitrariness of Hegel's "Dialectic" (e.g., Findlay, pp. 55, 69–73, 93, 107, 113, 118, 143, 147), I would want to argue that the logical progression here, which focuses on the single but central ontological problem of individuation of particulars, is as rigorous as one would expect even from contemporary philosophers. There is the natural but naïve idea that "objects are simply *there,* and we know things because they are there," against which Hegel argues that one cannot know particulars (by description as well as acquaintance). Accordingly, it is suggested that what we are acquainted with is not particulars but universals, that is, properties. But Hegel argues, one cannot individuate particulars without already knowing *of what* a "cluster" of properties is predicated. And so, the idea of knowledge by acquaintance yields to the suggestion that *we* predicate properties (which are still known through acquaintance) of particulars by reference to a supersensible substance which *has* those properties. But then, stuck again, for how does one individuate supersensible substances without already presupposing individuation of (sensible) objects? Accordingly, the next move is Kant's move (from his *Dissertation of 1770* to the *Critique*); he changes the philosophical notion of "Understanding" (or "Intellect") such that its pure concepts apply, not to the supersensible things themselves but to appearances. Objects are not *given* by acquaintance with particulars or clusters of properties, but neither are properties simply given as properties *of* something (either a bare particular or a supersensible substance). *We* (in some sense) are responsible for *producing* the objects which we are apparently given. And with this, Hegel's dialectic moves from mere consciousness of objects to self-consciousness to the notion of *Reason,* that our activities are as essential to the object of knowledge as the object is to our knowledge. (Compare "Consciousness.") Hegel has arrived at Kant's conclusions through similar reasoning, but along the route of an epistemo-ontological argument in the place of Kant's epistemological "Deductions." We might here add, also against many commentators (again e.g., Findlay, pp. 67–68, 78–79, 93) that it is clear on the above interpretation that there are a number of possible routes through the dialectic to any given point, including (especially) its endpoint ("Absolute Truth").

2

The section on "Consciousness" is preceded by a brief introduction to the entire work which can function for us here as a guide to just these chapters. The focus is on Kant and the empiricists, although, as usual with Hegel, no one is mentioned by name. Kant had complained that philosophers were trying to settle metaphysical disputes concerning "things-in-themselves" before they examined the possibility of gaining any such knowledge. Accordingly, with the empiricists, he reduced all ontology to epistemology—what there is depends upon what we can—and must—know. Consequently, there can be no knowledge of "things-in-themselves" (no "metaphysics"). Hegel agrees that ontology must be limited by epistemology, but he adds that Kant is mistaken if he believes that epistemology can avoid metaphysical as well as ontological commitments. (We see precisely the same dispute repeated a century later in Heidegger's rebellion against Husserl.) In this introduction, Hegel argues this point by accusing Kant (and the empiricists) of employing an unexamined metaphor, of knowledge as an "instrument," as a "medium" through which we come to know objects:

> It is a natural idea that, before philosophy would get to the subject matter itself—namely to the actual knowledge of what is in truth—it is necessary first to understand that knowledge itself, which is considered to be the instrument through which one takes possession of the absolute itself, or as the means through which one discovers it. (59/B131)

But instruments "mould and alter" objects and media refract and distort the "light of truth" that passes through. (Compare the "spectacles" and "meat grinder" metaphors that have been suggested by two of Kant's leading British commentators, Kemp-Smith and Weldon.) Consequently, Kant finds himself with two different senses of "object" and "truth"—as known by us (as "phenomena") and as they are "in-themselves" (as "noumena").

Hegel does not attack Kant's phenomenon-noumenon distinction; he undermines it, finally reducing it to an absurd joke at the end of "Understanding." And again, he does so by using Kant's best arguments against him. Just as Kant had argued that traditional scepticism and idealism resulted from an indefensible distinction between experience and the objects of knowledge, Hegel now argues that Kant committed a similar error in his distinction between the objects of knowledge and the objects-themselves. Against traditional scepticism, Kant had leveled his "Refutation of Idealism." But Hegel does not see scepticism as a problem: rather he sees seeing scepticism as a problem as a problem.

> We should beware that this fear of erring is already the error itself. Actually, this presupposes something and indeed many things as truth; it presupposes the same images of knowledge as an instrument and a medium, and a distinction between ourselves and this knowledge. (61/B132-3)

Kant had paid too little attention, according to Hegel, to the role of philosophical *critique* in the determination—as well as the analysis—of the Understanding. It is this neglect that leads him to his "phenomenon-noumenon" thesis and his "new" scepticism. Against all forms of "idealism," Kant had argued that the Understanding not only understands but contributes to experience. Objects are not inferred from but are the very structure of experience. And now, against Kant, Hegel argues that it is similarly a mistake to suppose that philosophical criticism only criticizes rather than contributes to our understanding. Philosophy is not only reflection upon but the structuring of our knowledge. Kant's mistake, according to Hegel, is his idea that the understanding and empirical knowledge are independent of philosophical criticism, whose only function is to justify their concepts and not to determine them. Accordingly, the *Critique* succeeds in this justification only by allowing philosophy (which is, for both Kant and Hegel, a matter of *reason* rather than *understanding*) to entertain the impossible notion of things as they are apart from our understanding.

Kant's "reply to Hume" was that knowing is a self-confirming activity. Hegel's reply to Kant is that philosophizing about knowing is also. As he states this,

> Consciousness is for itself its own concept . . . Consciousness furnishes its own criterion of itself, and the inquiry [of philosophy] will thereby be a comparison of itself with its own self.

This central Hegelian claim, that knowing and philosophizing about knowing are self-confirming activities, does not entail the absurdity (with which both Hegel and Fichte were often charged) that all our knowledge is our own creation. There is nothing here that denies the possibility of error or ignorance regarding empirical propositions (let us call any such proposition *"P"*). But any proposition P is *presupposed* by a number of other propositions (*"C"*), which are not only required in order for P to be true but in order for P (or not-P) to be intelligible.[8] In any dispute over P, C is taken as unquestionably true. But there is, according to Kant, a class of propositions such that they are presupposed (in the above sense) in every empirical dispute. Let us call such propositions *"C**"*. One such proposition would be what Kant calls *the causal maxim*—the a priori principle that every event succeeds another in accordance with a rule. The claim that knowledge is self-confirming maintains that it is impossible to be mistaken concerning propositions C*, the a priori maxims which are presuppositions of *all* particular empirical beliefs. But the reason one cannot be mistaken in believing C* is not to be attributed to any peculiar indubitability of C* or the inconceivability of not-C*. Rather, belief in C* cannot be wrong because it is *taken* as unquestionably true in every empirical dispute. In other words, one *makes it true* by believing it and not questioning it.[9] It serves functionally as a rule; a rule of inference in argument, a rule of understanding in experience. A rule, however, can always be stated as an axiom—in which case it will appear as a necessary truth. For example, Kant's causal maxim might appear either as a rule, "Take every event to be . . .," or as an axiomatic principle of experience, "every event has a cause." Such principles do not have the status of necessary truths because of any conceptual necessity (although principles such as C* are, according to both Kant and Hegel, *concepts*. But, for them, concepts are *rules,* even if Kant, like

Hume but unlike Hegel, sometimes slips into a more psychological characterization.) C^*, as a rule, is the product of a decision, not a fact about the world or a description of the subject's activity. It is a basic presupposition, a self-confirming stipulation that provides a framework for empirical knowledge.

It is in this sense that both Kant and Hegel insist that knowledge is self-confirming. The key notions of "a priori synthesis" in Kant and the "universal in action" in Hegel converge in their mutual insistence that certain basic concepts of the understanding of experience are contributed by the subject. Their mutual antagonist is Locke and the empiricists who took knowledge and understanding to be a matter of correspondence of a given representation to the object represented. Against this, Kant and Hegel are arguing a material mode equivalent of a principle of great importance in contemporary philosophy; that there are no concept-free representations. What we can know is determined by the concepts—and that means by the language—we provide to describe what we know. In Quinean terms, "experience under-determines theory;" "the central fundamental theoretical commitments in the organization of experience are one's own contribution."[10]

If C^* is a necessary truth because it acts as a rule and therefore remains unquestioned in empirical disputes, it does not follow that it cannot be questioned elsewhere—for example, in philosophical criticism, Kant, of course, recognizes this, and states clearly mid-*Critique*

> . . . while the understanding, occupied merely with its empirical employment, and not reflecting upon the sources of its own knowledge, may indeed get along quite satsifactorily, there is yet one task to which it is not equal, that, namely of determining the limits of its employment . . . (B 297)

Now Hegel agrees with Kant—he was taught by Kant—that it was a mistake for Locke, *et al.,* to assume that the Understanding only understood—rather than determined—the knowledge it was apparently "given" through the senses. But now Hegel goes on to make a similar point against Kant, who makes the same mistake with regard to philosophical criticism. Philosophy does not merely recognize but determines the structures it apparently "finds" in the activities of knowledge. In other words, Kant had argued that C^* counts as a necessary truth because it functions as a rule defining empirical considerations which cannot be challenged in the course of such considerations. (In seeking a causal account of *P,* one cannot even consider the possibility that there might be no such account.) But in a philosophical discussion, C^* does not function as such a rule, and consequently does not appear as a necessary truth, and can subsequently be challenged to see whether it is a "truth" at all. Within philosophy, it can be shown that C^* has a presupposition Z, which it shares with not-C^*. Z would be a "transcendental judgment," that is, a judgement *about* another judgment which is taken to be a necessary truth (e.g., B80). For example, the causal maxim (C^*) has as its presupposition the proposition that our experiences are necessarily ordered in time. Kant so argues in the "Transcendental Analytic." But the denial of the causal maxim (not-C^*) would also take this proposition as a presupposition. Leibniz, for example, rejects the causal maxim but would insist, as a presupposition of that rejection, that our experiences are necessarily ordered in time. Kant, who holds C^*, necessarily holds Z. But Leibniz, who holds not-C^*, finds it equally necessary that he hold Z. Parodying Quine and paraphrasing Hegel, we may say that necessary truths underdetermine our philosophical theories. Empirical considerations are not capable of deciding between C^* and not-C^*, since these principles in turn are responsible for defining empirical considerations in general. Hegel's argument, then, is that whether or not one accepts a given C^* is a matter of some dispute, but not an empirical dispute, and that the philosophical model one accepts in part determines the rules for empirical knowledge one can accept and thereby determines the objects one knows. If our experiences depend upon the way we understand them, our understanding in turn depends upon the way we reason.

Kant was instrumental in rejecting the empiricist notion of the *given* in experience. But he replaced it, according to Hegel, by introducing a *given* in the Understanding.[11] Many commentators have balked at the *source* of Kant's collection of categories, the overripe fruits of the pretentious and antiquated logic of the day. But Hegel argues further, not against the source or even the particular list of categories Kant provides, but against the very kind of a fixed and determinate list of a priori concepts without regard to the kinds of reasoning that is going on about them. Differing conceptions of the understanding will in turn produce different conceptions of the concepts of the Understanding; in other words, different philosophers will produce either different categories or different views of the categories, and a philosophical critic who reflects on these differences will be forced to give up the concept of "understanding" as it had been employed by Kant and others as a faculty with a determinate set of concepts. For example, Locke, Spinoza, and Leibniz, or Plato, Aristotle, and the early Chinese philosophers are not just giving different *accounts* of similar experiences and the same activities, some of which are more nearly "correct" than others. When Hegel says, in the preface to the *Phenomenology* and elsewhere, that we should see the "difference of philosophical systems as the progressive development of the truth" (4/B68), he means more than the obvious and patronizing consolation that each philosophy has *something* right about it. In addition, he means, in the sense that we have outlined above, that each philosophy is self-confirming, and that their apparent contradiction can only lead *us* ("perceiving the contradiction") to conclude that it is the self-confirmation itself, not the *contents* of the various systems (i.e., their categories), that is the *truth* Hegel is talking about. The ("absolute") truth is that there are alternative and equally valid if not equally adequate "one-sided" ways of looking at the world of human experience: the basic concepts of our understanding are determined in these various theoretical stances. In the *Phenomenology* these are called "forms of consciousness."

Accordingly, Hegel rejects Kant's concept of the Understanding and concentrates his attention on Reason. The difference between the two is not, as in Kant, that the former applies concepts to experience while the latter does not; for Hegel, both Understanding and Reason apply their concepts *only* to experience, but the former in an unreflective, rigid, and mechanical way, the latter in a self-reflecting, freewheeling manner that takes into consideration every possible coherent alternative system of conceptualization of experience. Understanding is essential for shopkeepers, but, in philosophy, Understanding ("which, itself finite, can understand only the finite" [*Encyclopedia* 28]) is a reactionary idea, the equivalent of bourgeois morality in a revolutionary society, or Newtonian mechanics in a problem in quantum physics. It is a piece of efficient yet gross machinery, adequate to gross tasks, but not equal to the critical tasks of philosophy. As philosophies change, reason "develops," and the basic concepts of experience change also. And experience changes with the concepts of experience. It is Hegel, before Marx, who insists that the point of philosophy is to change the world, although he would add that to understand it *is* to change it.

3

> The Cartesian dictum might better be expressed, "Hey, there goes Edna with a saxophone!"
>
> —WOODY ALLEN, *Getting Even.*

It may be that there are presuppositions Z^* of all philosophical discussion which occupy a logical role similar to C^* in empirical discussions. For reasons which will become apparent shortly, I do not believe that there are any such, but Hegel—with most philosophers of his tradition—did believe in one such Z^*: the peculiarly necessary "fact" of (my) consciousness. This is famously the starting point of Descartes' Meditations, demonstrably the premise of Kant's transcendental deduction, and arguably the beginning of Hegel's entire system of philosophy. But Z^* is not *simply* an ultimate presupposition, nor a premise of these philosophical arguments. If it were, we could not possibly make sense of the fact that three of Europe's most brilliant thinkers took Z^* to be the starting point of their philosophy. If Z^* were simply a principle which was presupposed by every proposition, Z, C^*, C, and P (Kant's "regressive" argument of the *Prolegomena*) then the attempt to argue from Z^* to C^* (Kant's "progressive" argument of the *Critique*) would amount to the elementary logical fallacy of affirming the consequent. There is something most peculiar about Z^*.

Kant's brilliant if obscure "Transcendental Analytic" is a turning point *within* an epistemological tradition that includes Hegel, which began with Descartes and Locke, came to Kant through Leibniz and Hume, reached Hegel from Kant and Fichte. Basic to this tradition is a philosophical method or discipline which I shall call "methodological solipsism." (I borrow the term from Jonathan Bennett, who also helped me clarify some of the issues raised here.) Methodological solipsism (MS) is what I consider to be the defining characteristic of "Cartesianism" broadly conceived, and it was adopted by not only traditional Cartesians but also most empiricists, Kant, Fichte, Hegel, and, prominently, all those contemporary philosophers who claim to follow "the phenomenological method," which I would argue to be a tedious version of MS. One might first characterize MS by saying that it is a first-person philosophical orientation and consequently restricts the kinds of questions one can ask and the types of appeals one can make. In MS, every philosophical problem must be construed as *my* peculiar problem. The question, "What is knowledge?" must be recast as "What is it for me to know something?" I must determine what is justifiable for *me* to believe according to evidence which *I* have. Similarly, the problem of other minds becomes, "How can *I* know that other persons exist?" Needless to say, there can be no appeal to other persons, to "common" sense, to theories or models which I cannot justify for myself. MS is the mother of the egocentric predicament. But these are not identical, for it is the presumption of the philosophers who endorse this program to demonstrate that *our* common knowledge of the physical or natural world can be understood and defended only *in terms of* MS. MS, we can now say, is what lies behind the problematic Z^* of our argument.

I know this is a markedly unfashionable program in this country these days, since Wittgenstein in particular, but I believe that without it we cannot understand Hegel—or Kant or Descartes, Leibniz or Fichte, or, perhaps much of empiricism, which is a perversion of the MS program. It may be that the entire methodological solipsist program is a dead end, but I would argue that without it the awful pinch of the classical problems of knowledge isn't imaginable. Once we give up MS and "naturalize" epistemology (in Quine's and Nietzsche's phrase), these problems do not arise in any compelling way, as all the propositions which troubled the MSist are *assumed* to be true in the very statement of the problem. ("How do *we* know that there are other minds?")

I take MS to be the greatest contribution of Cartesianism—its demand for epistemological autonomy and intellectual rigor. But in substance, Cartesianism went off the track virtually at once. Even aside from Descartes' notorious retreats and circles, the method itself took a wrong turn as soon as he stated it. From the first-person stance of MS, Descartes asserted that the mind is better known than the body. Accordingly, MS became the attempt to move from immediately known mental experiences to objective reality. In fact, I shall argue, not only does MS not entail any such "phenomenalism," but it provides overwhelming grounds against any such theory. But MS was turned into a phenomenalist program by most Cartesians, by the British empiricists, and by many philosophers today. Nelson Goodman, to choose but one illustrious example from many, gives the distinction between phenomenalist and physicalist models a prime place in his *Structure of Appearance* (although, while he opts for the former, he rejects the claim of epistemological priority to either). Similarly, the sharpest critics of phenomenalism, for example, W. V. O. Quine (in *Word and Object*) begin by making the same distinction, but then reject one of its terms.

Cartesianism as I want to pursue it, as MS, does not need and ought to abandon phenomenalism and the phemomenalism-physicalism distinction. Undermining both was one of Kant's greatest contributions to the Cartesian tradition (which was by then so entrenched that it was not even thought of as a tradition). Kant himself remained a Cartesian dualist of sorts, but he was not a phenomenalist.[12] It is false, he argued in the "Transcendental Analytic" (and even more explicitly in the "Refutation of Idealism" in the second edition of the *Critique*), that the mental is better known than the physical. The very existence of a unified self-consciousness presupposes the existence of physical, that is, spacial objects. What we know are physical objects, not our own sensations.

But where Kant, betraying his empiricist influences, seems to believe that there were raw sensory materials which, by their very nature, could not be examined as such, Hegel more consistently argues that this very notion is incomprehensible. One of the consequences of the first two chapters of the *Phenomenology* is that any notion we might have of sensations or sense-data (particulars or properties) must be parasitic on our prior knowledge of physical objects.

Phenomenalism is to be distinguished from MS: There is nothing in the first-person method of MS that requires introduction of peculiarly mental entities or events. The objects of scrutiny in MS are physical objects, or perhaps we should say putative physical objects, not experiences. And if MS typically (but not always, see Hegel) considers doubts concerning the existence of physical objects, it does not follow that *experience* is better known than objects. Within MS, as in everyday discussion, our talk is physical object-talk. The notion of "experience" can be brought in, if at all, only in those special cases (toothaches, migranes, visual flashes, perhaps hallucinations) where physical object-talk breaks down. Even here, introduction of the notion of "experience" raises difficult problems, particularly within the MS standpoint. (I take this to be the thrust of the "private-language arguments" that have been squeezed out of the later Wittgenstein.) But to introduce the notion of "experience" as a general conception of the objects of consciousness is as controversial and counterintuitive within the MS position as in everyday conversation.

In fact, MS excludes phenomenalism. Consider Macbeth at the banquet table watching the procession of Banquo and his relatives. For Macbeth, any conception of "his experience of seeing Banquo" is just an unnecessarily complex way of referring to his "seeing Banquo." It is only the guests who surround him, who do not see what he sees, who could talk significantly about "Macbeth's experience." But they refer to it as "an experience" in such a case just because its objects are not shared by them. For Macbeth, were he a good Cartesian, there could be no appeal to his guests' opinions; so he could have no notion of "his experience" as opposed to simply his "having seen Banquo." In other words, the notion of "experience" comes, not from the first-person stand-point of MS where it is typically identified, but from the third-person attempt to explain the behavior of others. Quine is right, I believe, but for all the wrong reasons, in his suggestion that experiences and the like are theoretical entities which we supply to explain *other* people's behavior. However, the phenomenalists are correct—but from the *third-person standpoint*—in their insistence that such accounts are indispensable. But the Wittgensteinians are also correct that such explanations are not conclusions of analogical arguments from any notions of "experience" drawn from my own case. The notion of "experience" is peculiar to the third-person case; it has no primitive role in the first-person case and therefore has no role in any account of MS.

Properly understood, Z^* is a cryptic if not misleading statement of MS, not a "first principle" or premise, not a peculiarly necessary *fact*. Surely it is not a necessary truth that I exist, or that we exist, or that any conscious creature exists (neglecting certain traditional theological doctrines). The "necessity" of this "fact" of consciousness can *only* appear within the first person case. But even then, it is not as if there is some *principle,* "I am conscious" or "I exist," which becomes a necessary truth; in this peculiar case, the conditions for assertion of a *particular* utterance and the truth conditions for that utterance are identical. This is the point made forcefully but restrictedly by Hintikka, who argues that Descartes' *cogito* is a "performance." But it must be added that the necessity of Z^* lies not only in the peculiar status of some particular utterances. Z^* defines the context within which any utterance is permitted. Z^* is not our starting point because it is a necessary proposition: Z^* appears as a necessary truth because it is our starting point. Z^* is nothing other than MS, the insistence that all our philosophical deliberations be carried out in the first-person case.

There are well-known and outstanding problems in formulating Z^*. Descartes' *cogito* formulation is crisp, and raises fascinating problems in itself, but it is clearly not correct as a statement of MS. The status of the "I" is famously suspect, and more than one philosopher of his own time suggested that it did not belong in the formulation at all. For Hegel, notably, the first-person case of MS can only be defended as the first-person *plural*.[13] As the "I" drops out of the formulation of Z^*, the possibility of individuating "consciousness" drops out also. But even Hume, in denying the unity of consciousness, is forced to say "*I* am not aware . . . " Similarly, Kant, who reintroduces the "I" as a "principle of transcendental unity," wrongly rests his concept of the "I think" on an unwarranted and unquestioned supposition that "I think's" can be individuated by individuating persons. But neither can one simply say, as several of Descartes' contemporaries and later Hume and Nietzsche suggested, that Z^* is "there is consciousness" (or "there are thoughts"). "Consciousness" here cannot refer, for reasons now familiar, to the phenomenologist notion of "experience" (Hume's conception). "There is consciousness of objects," while compensating for the above faults, carries with it no possible way of identifying "consciousness of objects" as opposed to simply, "objects." Thus James is pushed to the absurd conclusion that "there is no consciousness." To answer this two-hundred-year-old puzzle, Hegel points out that there is no correct formulation of what we are calling "Z^*" as a first principle with the properties of self-certainty etc., demanded by Descartes. Z^* is not merely an axiom or premise but a rule for philosophical discussion. In the *Phenomenology*, it is understood from the outset (as it is also in Kant's *Critique*) that the entire investigation proceeds from the first-person case (thus the title, *Phenomenology*, as well as the titling of the first section, "Consciousness"). But Z^* does not appear, as in Fichte—whom Hegel attacks on this point—as a "first principle." It is the guiding rule for the entire work, emerging explicitly in the course of the *Phenomenology* as its importance becomes more evident. Thus the notion of "Self-consciousness," the usual formulation of Z^* (in Descartes, Kant, and Fichte) does not appear until section B, and Kant's "consciousness in general" taken literally, does not appear explicitly until the final section of the book, "Reason." And Z^* does not emerge in full glory until the still less-than-adequate formulation as "Absolute Truth." This way of interpreting Z^* can, I believe, open up a way of interpreting many of the better known opacities of the *Phenomenology*, notably the confusing discussion of the identity of results and method and subject and substance introduced in the preface and summarized in "Absolute Truth", but without much explicit help in between. Z^* is not a first principle but the rules of philosophical inquiry—preventing us at any point from stepping out of MS (the source of the most serious errors of empiricism and, Hegel would argue, of Kant's ultimate mistake: his distinction between noumena and phenomena.) Z^*, as a rule, might be made into an axiom at any point, but such a "mere result," without "the process of arriving at it" would be but a "lifeless universal,"

> The naked result is the corpse of the system which has left its intention behind.
> (5/B69)

Z^* will appear as a principle as well as maintain its function as a rule only when it is *necessary* for it to do so. In other words, Hegel begins, as his Cartesian predecessors began, by minimizing the effects of their philosophical method and

accordingly dealing with purely ontological questions. It is only when he has demonstrated that these ontological puzzles are unsolvable without a little help from
Z^* that Z^* is allowed to make its first assertive appearance in "Self-Consciousness." And it is only when the minimal and traditional interpretation of Z^* as a
personal (self-) consciousness fails that Z^* becomes increasingly prominent as the
"result" as well as the method of *Phenomenology*.

Philosophy does not start from scratch. Of course, everyone knows that
Hegel believed his own philosophy to be the extension and incorporation of all
the philosophies before him. But in particular, the method he uses, MS, is parasitic not only on two centuries of philosophers before him, but also on everyday
language and knowledge. The first-person standpoint itself is parasitic on "common sense," since there is no way one could "get into" the first-person standpoint
of MS without a prior philosophically inadequate but ordinarily adequate conception of himself—himself opposed to others, himself opposed to objects. Here
again, Wittgenstein is correct in suggesting that first-person ascriptions are parasitic on third-person ascriptions. But, to borrow a metaphor from an earlier Wittgenstein, one can always "throw the ladder away." Z^* accordingly, must first be
crudely formulated as a rule of method in everyday terms, and this means with
some essential reference to oneself as a conscious individual. But this is only a
starting point, and further refinements might well end in the elimination of the
"I"—whether implicit or explicit in the initial formulation of Z^*. Such an elimination occurs crudely in Hume, and again, far more spectacularly, in Hegel. One
might well say that Hegel's *Phenomenology* is basically an attempt to formulate
Z^* in an adequate way.

Descartes' *cogito,* Kant's "I think," and Hegel's *Geist* all function as philosophical rules, ultimate *within,* but *only* within, the first-person case. And, of
course, a rule can always be employed as an axiom, as a premise, as Descartes
used Z^* in his Meditations, and as Kant has been argued to use the "I think"
("the synthetic unity of apperception") in his Transcendental Deduction (e.g., by
R. P. Wolff).

And, taking Z^* as a premise or as a first "synthetic" principle, Descartes and
Kant (at least according to several commentators, including Kemp-Smith, Paton,
and, more recently, Wolff) attempt to argue from Z^* to C^*. But the form of this
"transcendental argument" is, as we pointed out, seriously misleading. If Z^* is
characterized as the ultimate presupposition of C^*, then surely Z^* cannot entail
C^* (assuming that the two propositions are not logically equivalent, which I take
to be obvious). The mistake here is thinking that these presupposition and entail-
ment relationships hold (semantically) between two (sets of) propositions, rather
than (pragmatically) between a set of utterances C^* and the philosophical context
in which they are placed (as defined by Z^*). Z^* is a presupposition of C^* only
within the MS standpoint; it is MS that dictates the status of Z^*; not C^* alone,
and so it might be validly argued, *within the context of MS,* that Z^* entails C^*.
(This is the hidden trick to Wolff's insightful reconstruction of Kant's arguments
of the Analytic; MS provides the contextual emphymemes for all his recon-
structed arguments.) Z^* is the "ultimate presupposition" of C^* only in the sense
that it is the ultimate rule for a certain type of philosophical accounting of C^*.
Within the MS standpoint, C^* (and also other transcendental principles Z) appear
as "necessary" insofar as they are accepted as rules and not called into question.
And Kant, Hegel critically points out, never challenged the principles C^*:

The Kantian philosophy allows the categories and methods of ordinary knowledge to remain completely unchallenged. (*Encyclopedia* 60)

Thus the dispute between Kant, Fichte, and Hegel becomes the following: Is there any set of principles with the status of C^* or Z that is necessary and indispensible for human experience? According to Kant, there is such a set of categorical principles of the Understanding; according to Hegel, there is no such set, and so for him, strictly speaking, there can be no "transcendental deduction" of a particular set of categories, but only attempts to show what turns on the acceptance of any one set of categories rather than any other. But what is not in dispute between them, or even debatable, is whether some set of C^* principles or other is necessary for human experience. This is, of course, Kant's proof in his Transcendental Deduction, which Hegel reaffirms in the first part of the *Phenomenology* and again in the first part of his *Logic*.

The ultimate problem, for Hegel, is Z^*, which, although it is a rule, is an ultimate rule. One can, we might argue, step out of MS at any time, and see that Z^* is only a methodological principle, and a dispensible one. But Z^* was truly the limit of Hegel's investigations, and so Z^*, for him, remained unquestioned and unquestionable, and so, it became "absolute truth." But it is important to notice what happens if one does step outside of MS: if Z^*, Z, and C^* are self-imposed rules, looking at them as if they were someone *else's* rules means that one is not following those rules but only scrutinizing them, which, as we have seen, removes their necessary status. With regard to C^*, that means that C^* cannot, in the third-person standpoint, be regarded as necessary, but will always appear as a contingency, "the rule that *they* follow," a "habit," a physiological structure or "human nature." A rule that I am following is a necessity within the limits of my enterprise, but it is simply a contingency of my behavior to someone else. Accordingly, the Kantian notion of "necessity," from the third-person standpoint, cannot even arise. Again, Quine and other "naturalized epistemologists" are correct, but only because they neglect the MS position altogether. One might add that Kant and Hegel, of course, would not accept this characterization of their position at all: they would agree with my analysis of Z^*, Z, C^* as rules, but then would object that, because the "enterprise" for which these function as rules is the whole of human experience, there can be no "outside" or third-person point of view available to us. Accordingly, they would argue, one must treat these principles as one's own, and treating them as others' principles always presupposes their use in one's own case.

Kant argues that C^* principles function as rules, but he was not clear about the status of Z, describing C^* and Z alternatively as rules and as "structures," and so he was not willing to entertain the idea that C^* might be a matter of choice. Fichte then suggests that Z principles and consequently C^* principles are a matter of choice, that "the philosophy one chooses is the kind of man one is." Hegel takes up Fichte's suggestion, and the "forms of consciousness" of the *Phenomenoloy* are systems of self-imposed rules Z. Only Z^* is not a matter of choice.

The ultimate challenge to MS is scepticism, the threat that Z^* might degenerate into solipsism. Traditional scepticism was a direct consequence of phenomenalism. Once one separates experience and physical object, even the love of God won't validly bring them together again. And so Kant rejects phenomenalism by insisting that our experience is necessarily experience of physical objects; and that must be so because of the rules by which *we* constitute our experience. And so, as Kant argues most explicitly in his "Refutation of Idealism," there is no place for the sceptic to get his wedge in between experience and object.

But the sceptic gets a second chance with Kant. There is no longer the vulnerable gap between experience and object, but there is a new gap, between the physical object as phenomenon and the object in itself. Now where did this gap come from? From an inconsistency in Kant's MSist analysis! Having completed his argument against phenomenalism and scepticism by pursuing more thoroughly that his predecessors the MS position, he now slips back into a naturalistic or third-person standpoint and questions the MS position itself. Accordingly, he asks, in effect, "Even if it is necessary because of my a priori synthesis that I see objects in accordance with conditions which I impose (and by the a priori forms of intuition) is it not possible that the objects themselves do not obey these conditions?" But, the question is, from the MS position, illegitimate. Of course, one can question the MS position, as many recent philosophers have done, and reject it. But in that case, you reject it in the beginning, not when entering the climax of your epistemological deliberations. If Kant were consistent, he would have avoided this final slip out of the MS position. From the MS position, the philosopher tries to prove the objectivity of what he knows; he cannot, and it does not even make sense for him to ask what things are like apart from one's possible knowledge of them. Here Kant falters, and Fichte picks up the Cartesian banner—against the fading Kant's will—and carries it to Hegel. Hegel, a thoroughgoing MSist, never leaves the MS standpoint. Within it, he establishes, as Kant almost established, that from the MS standpoint, consistently carried through, there is no intelligible way to talk about, point to, grunt toward, or otherwise acknowledge the possibility of a world beyond our possible knowledge.

Now, stepping out of MS, its Hegelian conclusions might seem intolerable, much as waking up after a fabulous party the morning after: not only the particular festivities but the very idea of such merriment appears absurd. Stepping back into our everyday non-MS standpoint, it might appear that MS does end in the absurdity of the egocentric predicament after all. But this cannot be shown within the MS standpoint. Perhaps there are only two ways to follow consistently and honestly through the MS program in philosophy. There is Hume's schizoid way out, to leave his scepticism in his study and pick up his cue stick and his belief in the C^* belief in universal causation on the way to the billiards table; and there is Hegel's Kafkaesque pertinaciousness, maintaining the MS position by expanding its scope to the extent that, because there is no place else to go, there can be no question of a "predicament." There is ultimately "absolute truth," that MS, once taken up in earnest, can be consistently pursued beyond the point of possible refutation.

NOTES

1. *The Science of Logic* trans. by Johnston and Struthers (London, 1929), I: 44. "Modern German philosophy" in Hegel means "Hegel."

2. All quotations from Hegel's *Phänomenologie des Geistes* are from Johann

Schulze, Ed. (Berlin, 1832). The translations are my own, with reference to Baillie's translation (*The Phenomenology of Mind* [New York: Harper and Row, 1967].) All references to the *Phänomenologie* are given in the text, first to the Schulze edition, then to Baillie's rendition (e.g., "(59 B131)"). All references to Kant's *Critique of Pure Reason* are to the Kemp-Smith translation (New York, 1966), 2d ed., in parentheses in the text prefaced by "B."

3. I have provided such a commentary, upon which my argument here ulitmately depends, in my *In the Spirit of Hegel* (Oxford and New York: Oxford University Press, 1983).

4. The Copernican revolutionary had died two years before, but one can imagine his ire had he had the opportunity to read Hegel. We recall his "Open Letter" on Fichte (Aug. 7, 1799): " . . . I am so opposed to metaphysics, as defined according to Fichtean principles, that I have advised him in a letter to turn his fine literary gifts to the problem of applying the *Critique of Pure Reason* rather than squander them in cultivating fruitless sophistries. . . . "

5. In contemporary terms, Hegel does not presuppose the truth of any "knowing entails knowing that one knows" thesis. Nor would he hold even the weaker thesis that "knowing entails believing that one knows." All such theses, Hegel would rightly argue, presuppose a confusion between the Kantian thesis that reflection on knowledge shows that, if we know something (prereflectively), that we can know (reflectively) that we know, and the very different thesis that knowledge itself is necessarily reflective.

6. This claim must be distinguished from a superficially similar trivial claim and two false claims. The trivial claim is that knowledge is always predicable of somebody (there cannot simply be knowledge, there must be somebody's knowing). The first false claim is that to know something is to know something about yourself (e.g., that you know something or believe something). But, as I argued above, Hegel need not and does not hold that knowledge itself is reflective: his claim is that *reflection* on knowing shows that the conditions for knowledge are provided by the knower (see above). The second false claim is that one can ultimately only know himself. But the very point of Kant and Hegel's joint polemic is to prove the contrary, that what we know are objects "outside" of ourselves. (This and the earlier similar point were stimulated by Paul Ziff.)

7. The best definition I know of *aufheben* has been proferred by the hardly Heglian philosopher Frank Ramsey in his *Foundations of Mathematics* (pp. 115–16); "the truth lies not in one of the two disputed views but in some third possibility which has not yet been thought of, which we can discover by rejecting something assumed as obvious by both the discussants."

8. It must be insisted that the same propositions might be either *P* or *C* depending upon the theoretical role they played in a particular context. *C* is a proposition which must be taken to be true if *P* is to be considered either true or false. In the terms of the current controversy in linguistics, the conception of "presupposition" I am employing here is "pragmatic" rather than "semantic." I do not believe that my argument here turns on these issues. Cf. Stalnaker, "Pragmatic Presupposition," unpubl.

9. The obvious analog here is J. L. Austin's notion of a "performative," but the more apt comparison is Carnap's discussion in Appendix *A* of *Meaning and Necessity: A Study in Semantics and Modal Logic* (Chicago: University of Chicago Press, 1956).

10. "Two Dogmas of Empiricism," in *From a Logical Point of View* (Cambridge: Harvard University Press, 1953), pp. 42–43. Of course, the theoretical commitments here would include, for Hegel, philosophical commitments as well as the ontological commitments of scientific (empirical) theories. We might also add that Quine, still an empiricist at heart, takes the "observational edge" to be the key to conceptual change. For Hegel, always a rationalist, it is rather the "form of consciousness" that takes priority, not the evidence.

11. Cf. Nietzsche (*Beyond Good and Evil,* §11), "Why should we believe such judgments to be necessary?"

12. This claim would appear to contradict the findings of several important commentators, notably, J. Bennett in his *Kant's Analytic.* (Cambridge: Cambridge University Press, 1966). The contradiction is only nominal, I would argue, but will not here, due to small but significant differences in the use of the term "phenomenalism." "Phenomenalism," as I am using that term here, is the thesis that there exist discrete atoms of experience identifiable independently of identifications of physical objects (leaving open questions of how these are identifiable and what the relationship is between experience and physical objects).

13. See my "Hegel's Concept of *Geist," The Review of Metaphysics,* vol. 23 (1970), pp. 642–61 [chapter 1 in this collection].

3

Hegel:
Truth and Self-satisfaction

Jesus declared, "I am the truth." Does that make sense? Even Pilate jested, not "who" but "*What* is truth?" And most philosophers today are arguing among themselves that *what* is true must be what is *said,* a sentence or a statement, perhaps an abstract proposition, but hardly a person, even a divinity. But what then are we to make of Keats' celebrated equation of truth and beauty? A category mistake, perhaps? What of Kierkegaard's much discussed notion of truth as "subjectivity," as passion and commitment? And what of the "true man," the "true friend," and "true-life adventures"? Is the marksman with "true" aim one who systematically makes true certain propositions concerning the trajectory of his bullets? What is truth? Or at least, what is true? Philosophers today seem a long way from an adequate answer.

It is by way of clue but not argument that we remind ourselves that the etymology of "truth" and "true" takes us back to an old Anglo-Saxon word, *treowth,* and the Old English *treowe* and *trywe,* which mean "faithful" as well as "true," applying to friends and servants as well as to statements. Similarly, the Latin *veritas* and its modern Romance-language derivatives and the German root *Wahr* carry the meaning of "fidelity" as well as epistemic "correctness."

"True" in English often means "genuine" or "ideal." Applied to religious sects and patriotic orders it may mean "orthodox." Applied to foods and drugs it may mean "unadulterated." And, in addition to saying what is true, a good man will be true *to* his word. "True" has a great many literal contexts beyond the bounds of epistemology, and most of them have to do with the agreement with an ideal, whether in "true friend," "true aim," "true American" "true antique" or "true margarine." "The truth," in this broad context, is an ideal manifestation, a paradigm case or a "thing itself." Thus Jesus was at least intelligible when he declared, "I am the truth"; Keats was not confusing epistemic and aesthetic categories in his "Ode"; and Kierkegaard was not philosphically confused when he argued that the truth of human existence lay in individual passion rather than in anonymous knowledge of the truth.

What is the relationship between the narrowly epistemic notions of "truth" and "true" and the broader notions concerning ideal? Most philosophers would insist, at least implicitly by their own focus of interest, that the primary senses of "true" and "truth" are epistemological and that these can be analyzed without reference to or even passing mention of the nonepistemic senses.[1] The latter, it seems, are secondary or extended senses of "truth" and "true," cousins by marriage, perhaps, but not part of the immediate family. This, however, seems to me to be a serious mistake, for an adequate analysis of the narrowly epistemic notion of "truth" is identical to an adequate account of the broader notions of "truth." In what follows, I should like to argue that an adequate analysis of "truth" and "true" extends far beyond the narrowly linguistic and epistemic, that the bearers of truth may be beliefs, desires, people, abilities, faith, fruits, and vegetables as well as sentences, statements, and propositions. But the "problem of truth" usually begins, as it did with Aristotle and has continued to since, by attending to what is *said,* and so that is where our analysis will begin.

Our analysis will draw heavily from Hegel studies over the past several years. It is commonly recognized, at least by writers on the subject, that Hegel's *Phenomenology of Spirit*[2] is, and he says that it is, a theory of truth. Yet that theory has rarely been spelled out in analytic terms or been applied to the standard puzzles regarding truth in epistemology, and, where it has received some mention, for example, from Russell, Moore, and the early logical analysts, it is not Hegel's theory but some bastardized British versions of it, usually by Bradley, that have been examined. Similarly in this country, it is more often Royce, Joachim, and Blandshard, with their "coherence" theories of truth, that have passed for Hegelian. But in fact, Hegel had done with the coherence theory, as well as the other standard theories of truth, before he was half finished with the *Phenomenology.* And so, a second purpose of this essay is to give Hegel a fair hearing on truth, and to defend the sometimes puzzling pronouncements of his first and, in my mind, his greatest work.

1

The notion of "truth" has always had its obvious analysis: so obvious that Aristotle, who could go on at length on minor problems, felt that he had done with the matter in a single platitudinous sentence, (into which more recent commentators have struggled to read an encapsulated "theory"): "To say of what is that it is, or of what is not that it is not, is true . . ." (*Metaphysics* 1011^{b}26). And there he left the problem for two thousand years. In fact, this primitive "correspondence" conception would never have been suspected of being a *theory* at all, were it not for a radically opposed conception of truth that emerged during the nineteenth century. Kant is usually credited with its discovery, although Leibniz and Spinoza, at least, held it before him, and Kant himself did not clearly hold it at all. But their suggestion that truth was not "correspondence with the facts" but rather a matter of "internal and systemic *coherence*" elevated the former notion, barely philosophical and hitherto considered too obvious to be worthy of elaborate philosophical defense, into a theory of its own, one which now required careful formulation and defense. The motivation, lacking before, was inspired by the bold and sometimes wild arguments put forward, supposedly in Hegel's name, by the British idealists, notably Bradley, Royce, Joachim, and more recently Blandshard, which apparently did much violence to our everyday and primitive philosophical conception of truth as "correspondence with the facts." Truth, the idealists argued, was a matter of systematic coherence of our beliefs, perhaps in accord with a transcendental skeleton such as Kant devised, but without need of support or anchorage from any "facts" with which at least some of our beliefs need to agree. "There are no facts," they argued, but only the sum of "internal relations." A true belief is one that is actually true only "to a degree" ("the Truth being the Whole") by virtue of its harmonious membership in the system. Against this, Bertrand Russell—quick to the defense—reacted, indeed overreacted, in his defense of "the facts."[3] Truth, he reasserted, was correspondence of our propositions with the *many* (not the One) facts of life. But even in the hands of the most skilled theoretician in English philosophy, the correspondence theory fared badly. Every attempt to tie down the nature of propositions and facts and every attempt to spell out the sense in which they do and can be known to "correspond" resulted in conceptual disaster. The key elements of the common-sense theory—propositions, facts, and the correspondence between them—defied analysis. Furthermore, the correspondence theory always seemed to slide into skepticism and thus fall dangerously close to the antagonist's idealistic camp. But as the inadequacies became more apparent, Russell, at least, dug his heels in further, becoming even more of an atomist and more of an empiricist. Even when he became convinced that it was necessary to give up the key notion of "propositions," he resisted the consequence, as A. N. Prior argues,[4] that "if propositions must go, facts must go too." There had to be *something* discrete and mind-independent for our beliefs to correspond to, otherwise we would fall disastrously into the solipsistic, mutually supportive and consequently unverifiable circle of beliefs, without a world to hold on to, which Bradley and the dragons of idealism were using to threaten the fact-filled world of empirical science.

In the twentieth century, the requirements of science and the apparent inadequacies of the "correspondence theory" culminated in a third theory of truth, the so-called "pragmatic theory." An essentially crude theory, it has always been best stated in its crude form: "It's true if it works." It was basically an American theory, originating in the work of Pierce, James, and Dewey, and accordingly it shifted the emphasis from truth to utility, from science to technology, and from correspondence to convenience. In a Kantian sense, the pragmatic theory appears to be an apt synthesis of the earlier antitheses, for the pragmatic theory saves what is essential to each, "the facts" of the correspondence theory (James, for example, continued to hold the correspondence theory, but insisted that it was, by itself, "unilluminating") and the interrelationship of beliefs of the coherence theory, adding to the latter the idea that the system of coherence includes not only other beliefs but also projects, predictions, plans, problems, plumbing, and whatever other uses we find for our beliefs. (With this stretching of the notion of truth to include the pragmatic, Hegel is ultimately in agreement, and it would not be far-fetched historically to suggest that Hegel's theory may have been a strong influence on the early pragmatists.)

Of course, Hegel did not refer to these conceptions of truth by their present names, nor did he see them as the textbook polarities that they have become. Yet he did deal with them explicitly, and he anticipated most of the dominant observations and objections current today. He saw (with J. L. Austin), that the undeniable, but possibly "misleading," kernel of truth in the correspondence theory was its insistence that a belief is true if and only if it corresponds to "the facts."[5] But Hegel distinguishes this everyday conception of truth as "correctness" *(Richtigkeit)* from philosophical truth *(Wahrheit)*, and, like P. F. Strawson, argues that it is incorrect to suppose, in a philosophical argument, that "the facts" are discrete and independent existences or that truth is best understood as "correspondence with the facts." Rather, in Hegel's terms (following Kant), we might say that consciousness "determines" or "constitutes" or "synthesizes" the facts as we find them. Even if "the facts" are necessarily "found" "outside of us, in the world," we are in some sense responsible for their being there. "The facts" are independent as a son away to college is independent; in other words, only apparently. Hegel's argument against the correspondence theory, borrowed from Kant and dominating the first three chapters of the *Phenomenology,* is an argument against the idea of "the facts" as discrete and independent of us.[6] But yet the kernel of the correspondence theory is always retained, that truth is a relation of belief to something other than belief. Similarly, true knowledge is knowledge of "the world outside us," but it does not follow that we are not instrumental in "determining" or "constituting" that world, nor does it follow that, if we are responsible for "determining" or "constituting" the world, then we *ipso facto* make our beliefs true. It is the world that makes our beliefs true, but it is our beliefs, in general, together with our desires, practices, etc., that give us the world, that is, *our* world. "True aim" requires hitting a target at some distance; yet *we* choose the target beforehand, and that does not seem to presuppose that we thereby guarantee ourselves success in hitting it.

Thus we can see that Hegel both did and did not endorse the correspondence theory of truth. It is one of those "one-sided truths" which are "*aufgehoben*" in the course of the *Phenomenology,* "cancelled but preserved." And we can also see that the coherence theory will have a similar fate. On the one hand, Hegel sees that isolated beliefs can never be true nor false, for it is by virtue of the *system* of beliefs (desires, practices, etc.) that a particular belief has a world to correspond to. Yet *within* that conception, which Hegel clearly endorses ("The Truth is the Whole" [*Phenomenology,* p. 81]), it yet remains true that truth is correspondence. A belief is never true *simply* by virtue of its coherence within our system of beliefs, but by virtue of its coherence *and* correspondence with the facts. Thus Bradley's coherence theory, which is often identified with Hegel, is another half-truth, and the notorious doctrine of "internal relations," which suggests that every true belief entails every other true belief, is clearly unsound. This may hold true for purely systematic beliefs, for example, those of elementary arithmetic or the putatively a priori truths of philosophy, but it cannot plausibly be said to hold of straightforward empirical claims. This is true even if, as Kant and Hegel argued, the fundamental beliefs upon which our empirical beliefs are grounded (i.e., Kant's categories and principles of the understanding), are arguably true only by virtue of their logical relations with each other and with "the transcendental unity of consciousness," not by appeal to "the facts." Similarly, the truth of what Hegel calls a "form of consciousness" or of a "category" may depend only upon its consistency, coherence, and completeness, and it may in turn determine the *form* of any particular belief within it. But it does not follow that it determines the content of those particular beliefs, which are not true only by virtue of consistency, coherence, and completeness, but by virtue of "the way the world is."

A frequent objection to the coherence theory is the following: Any system of coherent beliefs can be turned into an equally coherent system by the systematic application of some logical operator, for example, by turning each belief into its contradictory. That is, there might be equally coherent but mutually incompatible systems of belief, and it would not seem to make sense to say that they are both equally "true." This argument has its clear instantiation in the *Phenomenology.* Hegel offers us the absurd counterexample of a "*verkehrte*" or "inverted" world, in which black is white, light is heavy, good is evil, and so on. His ultimate target is Kant's distinction between noumenon and phenomenon, but the example holds as well against coherence theory. It is a material equivalence of the replacement of each true proposition with its contradictory, and the result is absurd. Truth cannot be mere coherence. But neither, Hegel argues, can truth be divorced from our beliefs, from the categories or our "forms of consciousness." If mere coherence is *not enough* for truth, the Kantian insistence that our beliefs correspond to the world as it is independently of us is *too much* for an adequate notion of truth.

In the preface to the *Phenomenology,* Hegel offers us two examples of alternative conceptions of truth which he juxtaposes against what he insists will be an adequate theory of truth ("philosophical truth"). The first is "historical truth" (p. 100); the second is "mathematical truth" (pp. 100–104). The first of these is the usual paradigm for the correspondence theory; against it, Hegel argues that we know a "naked fact" only insofar as we know "the reasons behind it." In other words, we need criteria of coherence as well as correspondence. The second "kind" of truth is typically the basis of the coherence theory; yet there are theorems which we can "see" to be true which we cannot prove, and one can prove, in an "uninterpreted" calculus, theorems that would be nonsense "in fact." What Hegel has in mind here is the Kantian thesis that mathematical truths have an applicability to the world which is essential to them. Therefore, mere coherence is not sufficient for their truth.

2

"Truth" is a peculiar notion. Unlike most concepts, it cannot be used, traditional metaphysics aside, to talk "about the world." It is what logicians are now accustomed to calling a "metalevel" concept, which means that it can be used only to talk *about* the world. To say that a given statement *p* is true is not only to state *p,* although in an important sense it does entail the statement that-*p*; it is to talk *about p.* Logicians distinguish an "object language" and a "metalanguage," which is used to talk *about* the object language. The concept of "truth" appears only in the metalanguage.

If "truth" is a metalevel concept, it would follow that discussions *about* "truth" are metametalevel discussions. Thus "'p is x' is true" is a statement of the metalanguage; the question "What is it to say that 'p is x' is true?" or "What is the relation between the truth of 'p is x' and the fact that p is x?" are questions in the metametalanguage. One of the early upsets in the barely formulated correspondence conception of truth mentioned in passing by Aristotle was a series of ancient paradoxes, of which the best known are the "liar" paradoxes (e.g., the Spartan who claims that all Spartans are liars, or the inscription of a sentence which asserts "This sentence is false."). The need for the distinction of object and metalanguages might be traced to these paradoxes, which disappear once one has distinguished between a statement about something and a statement about a statement, with suitable restrictions on self-reference. Russell's theory of types was one such attempt to distinguish propositions about objects from propositions about propositions from propositions about propositions about propositions, and so on. More recently, the logician Alfred Tarski has argued a "semantic conception of truth," which we shall consider shortly, which employs the same strategy, restricting "truth" to the metalanguage and discussions of truth to the metametalanguage.

Using this simple but elegant apparatus drawn from logical theory, the distinction between object language, metalanguage, and metametalanguage can be simply formulated by use of quotation marks, that is, p vs. "p"vs. "'p'", and so on. But if the elements involved are not assertions or propositions, (the logician's favored but metaphysically suspect element), but beliefs, there is no suitable apparatus for making these distinctions. Yet the disctinctions are necessary whether or not it is a peculiarly "semantic" conception of truth that is at stake.

The problem facing Hegel is that he must make the object, meta, metameta, distinctions regarding belief without the convenient modern apparatus for doing so. So he makes the distinction in another way. Periodically, in the early chapters, on "Consciousness," for example, he includes a phrase like "for we who are watching the process" and frequently uses this "we" and "for us" to distinguish the level of philosophical discourse from the matter under discussion (See, e.g., *Phenomenology,* p. 162.) This effort on Hegel's part to distinguish what is being described from the metalevel of discription finds a respectable philosophical name: *reflection.* Hegel's key notion of "reflection," which he states in the preface is the "medium of the truth," is just what we might say in semantics by saying that "truth" is a metalevel concept. But where the semantic apparatus is suitable primarily for statements or propositions, the notion of reflection is appropriate for beliefs (and, more generally, for nonepistemic mental "acts" and states as well.) Reflection is belief about our beliefs. The key concept of Hegel's philosophy, "The Concept," is also necessarily a reflective or metalevel notion. We *use* concepts in talking about objects, but we have the concept of a concept only in reflection.

Similarly, Hegel must distinguish between reflection and the employment of the concepts of "truth" and "Concept" (in "Understanding") and reflection *about* reflection and *about* concepts and truth (in "Reason"). [See also Kant *CPR* B, 359] Without the semantic apparatus, this is no easy task. (Russell, using propositions and quotation marks in his theory of types, could simply generate an infinite series of semantic levels p, "p" "'p'", "'"p"'", and so on.) What Hegel does is talk about the "truth about truth" (e.g., *Phenomenology,* p. 71, *Logic* 19[7]);

about the "highest truth" and "absolute truth," and about "philosophical truth" *(Wahrheit)* as opposed to everyday truth as "correctness" *(Richtigkeit)* (*Logic* 24, 172, 213). He adds that such distinctions are not usually made in everyday life, nor need they be. But philosophical truth (*Logic* 24, *Phenomenology,* preface, p. 100) is not concerned with facts as such or with what is true. It is only concerned with truth itself, that is, with the nature of truth, what it is for a belief to be true. Thus the oft-repeated mockery, which Hegel suffered in his own time from a critic who thought that Hegel's philosophy claimed the ability to "deduce the pen with which he was writing," is based upon a profound misunderstanding of Hegel's thought. Similarly, the doctrine of "internal relations" argued by Bradley to infuriate his colleagues, the idea that any empirical truth is in some sense entailed by a philosophical truth, for example, the idea that one can deduce the number of rabbits in Australia from a knowledge of the "absolute truth" in Hegel's philosophy, is nonsense. "Absolute truth" refers to a philosophical conception of truth, to a truth *about* truth, not to an absurd and pretentious (despite "absolute") claim to omniscience of truths. "Absolute Truth" is a philosophical account of truth which avoids skepticism and shows how it is that what we believe to be true can be known to be true.

<h1 style="text-align:center">3</h1>

There was a time when philosophers allowed themselves to speak freely of "the Truth," which meant, roughly and unhelpfully, "the way the world is." After centuries of abuse by metaphysicans, however, "the Truth" acquired a foul taste. Kant rarely mentions "the Truth" in his *Critique*; he restricts his attention to "knowledge." In the same spirit, contemporary philosophers have turned away from "the Truth," with its suspicious metaphysical ring, and turned to the less substantial and therefore less committal predicate, "is true."[8]

The modern problem of truth has been well-circumscribed in the 1950 debate between J. L. Austin and P. F. Strawson on "Truth,"[9] The agreed-upon and sole candidate for the role of truth bearer was "What is *said,*" and the problem of truth became the dual problem of identifying *what* it is that is said and *how* it is that this *what* is true or false. Sentences were excluded from this role on the grounds that the same sentence (e.g., "It is raining") might be sometimes true, sometimes false, and sometimes neither. A sentence, in order to be true or false, must be further specified according to its context, its speaker, its time of utterance. Thus Quine has insisted upon "external sentences" as the bearers of truth ("It is raining in Austin, Texas at 5:31 P.M. (Central Time) August 24, 1973"), and Davidson has added semantic markers identifying speaker and time ("'It is raining' uttered by *p* at *t*"). Austin insists that what is true or false is not a sentence of any kind, but a "sentence used by a person on a certain occasion" (p. 20). For him, what are true are sentences-uttered, or *statements:*

> A statement is made and its making is an historical event, the utterance by a certain speaker or writer of certain words (a sentence) to an audience with reference to a historical situation, event, or what not. (P. 20) (See also Quine, *Philosophy of Logic* [Englewood Cliffs, N.J.: Prentice-Hall, 1970], *PL,* p. 13)

But then, in a significant footnote, he adds,

> Historical does not, of course, mean that we cannot speak of future or possible
> statements. A "certain" speaker need not be any definite speaker. "Utterance"
> need not be a public utterance—the audience may be the speaker himself."

Agreeing with the view that the bearer of truth could not be a sentence, Strawson
argues that neither could it be a sentence-uttered. What is true is *what* is uttered,
not the uttering of it:

> It is of prime importance to distinguish the fact that the use of a "true" always
> glances backwards or forwards to the actual or envisaged making of a state-
> ment by someone, from the theory that it is used to characterize such (actual
> or possible) episodes. . . . (Ibid.)

A statement for Strawson is neither a speech-episode nor a sentence, but an
abstract creature similar in function but not name or ontology to the "propositions" what Moore and Russell had invoked in their early theories. Because several sentences or several people can "say the same thing," what is true or false
must be this "same thing." Strawson's "statements" can be uttered by any number of people, in any number of sentences, or need not be uttered at all.[10] What
is essential to these accounts is that what is true (or false) is not, in Austin's terms,
a "historical event," does not require a speaker (even an "indefinite speaker") or
an "audience."

As the Austin-Strawson debate continues, the central issue comes to be one
of ultimately little traditional interest. Austin maintains that "What is said is
true" means that someone who says, "That is true" or "What he said was true,"
is himself *saying something about a statement;* roughly, that "It corresponds with
the facts." Strawson, in rejecting this notion of "statement" as the event of a person's saying something, also rejects the idea that in ascribing truth to a statement
we are saying something *about* it. To say that a statement is true, according to
Strawson, as Ramsey had suggested some years earlier,[11] is to say nothing more
than that statement itself. This is sometimes called a "redundancy theory of
truth;" but even if it were plausible as an account of what it is to say of a statement that it's true, it is not remotely plausible as an aswer to the classical inquiry,
"What is it that *makes* a statement true?"

Retreating back to the standpoint of German philosophy at the turn of the
last century, the hotly debated differences between Austin and Strawson appear
to be a family quarrel. Why the agreed-upon emphasis, a philosopher from Jena
might have puzzled, on the truth of what is *said?* The problem, he would have
said, is whether what we believe in general, is true. Once we have rejected the
idea that the bearers of truth are distinctly linguistic items (e.g., sentences or
speech-episodes), it would seem that we are considerably less justified in insisting
on the formal mode of speech, focusing on the truth of what is said, as if *what* is
said is peculiar to what is *said.* Rather it would seem, as in the older proposition-
view, that what is said is also what is thought, what is doubted, what is questioned, what is denied, and what is believed. It is to the notion of "true belief"
that we should, following G. E. Moore (in his later writings), now turn.[12]

It is necessary to distinguish two sense of belief much as Strawson has done for two senses of statement. On the one hand, belief is a psychological predicate that can be predicated of one and only one person. Thus I have my belief that x is p and you have your belief that x is p. My belief may be insecure and ill-formulated while yours is a matter of dogmatic insistence and catechismically formulated. Let us call this psychological conception of belief "belief-ψ." It is what Frege had in mind by the "idea" *(Vorstellung)*, a mental image which one and only one person can have, and what Husserl discussed as the individual "*act* of believing" (doxic act). To be distinguished from "beliefψ" is that notion of belief such that one and the same belief can be shared by any number of people. And it is thus that one can speak of a belief which is believed by no one ("No one believes *that* any more"). We shall call this epistemic and nonpsychological sense belief-ϕ". Beliefs-ϕ are not psychological, but, because they are beliefs, they can and must be predicated of persons. Like Strawson's "statements," they are not, like propositions, ontological entities which can be cut free of persons. "Holding a belief-ϕ" is more like the concept of "having the same build as Churchill." There may be many people with the same build as Churchill, but each of them, in a trivial sense, can have his and only his own build.[13] But yet it may be the case that, at a given moment in history, no one has the same build as Churchill. This does not relegate Churchill's build off to a Platonic heaven, awaiting the participation of some newly born squat Englishman. Rather we can say, "having Churchill's build," like belief-ϕ must be predicated only of people, has no existence apart from the people of whom it could be predicated, but yet it is possible to talk sensibly of it without knowing that or whether it can at the moment be truly predicated at all. (Historically, of course, this anti-Platonic view is similar to that argued extensively by Aristotle.)

The bearers of truth, we may now say, are beliefs-ϕ. Beliefs-ψ might be said to be true or false on the basis of the beliefs-ϕ which they instantiate. Statements are true or false on the basis of whether or not they express, in a particular context of utterance, a true or a false belief-ϕ (which is not to say that a person must believe-ψ what he says).

4

The coherence conception of truth is highly unfashionable today, virtually a matter of bad taste among philosophers, and so the standard objections to it are generally considered to be fatally conclusive. The pragmatic theory was always suspected of a certain polemical flimflam and disregarded for the subtleties of philosophy, and, while graced with inclusion as one of the three traditional theories of truth, it has rarely been treated as more than "the third suggestion." The correspondence theory, however, stripped of its problematic formulations and reduced to the idea that what makes a belief true must be something other than the belief or any set or system of beliefs, is undeniable. And so modern discussions of truth, for example the Austin–Strawson debate, are generally discussions of the correspondence theory. And this discussion concerns, not the correspondence theory *vs.* alternative traditional theories, but rather, fine points aside, whether we need any *theory* of truth, that is, correspondence theory, at all. As

Strawson says, "the correspondence theory requires, not purification, but elimination" (p. 32).

The central problem of the correspondence theory is, as might be expected, "What corresponds to what and how?" It is undeniable that what makes our beliefs (or statements) true must be something other than those beliefs (or statements), something "in the world," for example, "the facts." Where Russell and other theorists have erred is in pushing this necessary independence and discreteness of "the facts" too far. Of course what makes our beliefs and statements true are the facts: but it does not follow that the facts exist independently and discretely apart from our true beliefs concerning them. And this is Hegel's argument, again following Kant, which states essentially *both* that the facts are independent of us and that the "mediation or determination" or "constitution" of the facts is our doing ("subject . . . is the process of splitting up what is simple and undifferentiated, a process of duplicating and setting factors in opposition") (*Phenomenology,* p. 80).

The early empiricist versions of the correspondence theory took "correspondence" rather literally as "congruity." It was supposed that our ideas were representations or *Vorstellungen* of reality, and so the correspondence was literally one of "picturing" or "agreement." But the representational theory lost its literal interpretation, a loss that appeared irreversible when Wittgenstein turned on his own picture-theory in the 1930s, and the correspondence theory suffered as well. The idea of a picture corresponding to what it is a picture of has a certain undeniable appeal. But once one rejects this picture view of ideas, propositions or beliefs, as, for example, Austin does explicitly in his argument, correspondence becomes "correlation," and the problem then becomes to explain this correlation between such very different elements as statements or beliefs and "the facts." Austin argues that the correlation is by way of the conventions surrounding the speech-episodes: Strawson replies that, although "Austin is correct . . . in his description of these conditions which must obtain if we are correctly to declare a statement true," he is mistaken in supposing "that in using the word 'true' we are asserting such conditions to obtain" (pp. 52–53). Strawson joins a long line of critics in arguing that the notion of "the facts" is specious and does not bear critical examination. But this argument comes to us from Kant and Hegel. It is the claim, simply stated, that there are no facts except as we "determine" or "constitute" them. In their terms, there is no truth apart from concepts and "mediation," and there are no facts without our conceptualization or "synthesis" of them. Kant tells us that "intuitions without concepts are blind" (875). Hegel adds that they are inarticulate and shallow, "untrue and irrational," as well (*Phenomenology,* p. 160). And what they both have in mind, Kant as the central conclusion of his first *Critique,* Hegel as the starting point of his *Phenomenology,* is that there are no independent and discrete facts. Yet there can be no adequate notion of truth that does not begin with the recognition that it is the facts that make our beliefs true, even if we ultimately "determine" them.

Borrowing a standard example (from White, *Truth,* op. cit., ch. 4 pp. 104f.) my belief (or statement) that the battle of Waterloo occurred in 1815 is made true, not by the battle or by the occurrence of the battle, but by *the fact that* the battle of Waterloo occurred in 1815. The fact, unlike the battle, neither is nor was a "thing in the world." Strawson makes this point when he claims, "If you prize the statements off the world you prize the facts off too; but the world would be none the poorer" (p. 39), and when he counters Wittgenstein, "the world is the totality of things, not facts" (p. 40). On the one hand, the fact is not identical with the belief; on the other, it is not altogether separate and discrete either. The fact makes the belief true, but it is our system of beliefs and what Hegel and Kant would call our "consciousness in general" that determines or constitutes the fact. Here is the often neglected kernel of truth of the coherence theory: We cannot manufacture a particular fact to satisfy a particular belief (this much in agreement with the correspondence theory), but we do *make true* the framework (the fashionable word today is "paradigm") within which particular beliefs are made true (or false) by "the facts." This is what Hegel means when he argues that "categories" are themselves true, in the sense of "agreement with itself," by virtue of which an application of a category to an object (or a fact) might be true (*Logic* 24). The same point follows Hegel's declaration, "the Truth is the Whole" repeated by Bradley and capturead in somewhat different form by D. Davidson's argument that, if there are any facts at all, there can be at most one of them.[14] Accordingly, it cannot be a discrete fact that makes a belief true, but rather, as the coherence theorists have argued, a system of beliefs *within* which a fact makes a particular belief true (or false).

How is it that there are "facts"? Or, in nineteenth-century terminology, what is "determination" or "constitution" of the facts? The Kantian-Hegelian reply charges our imaginations, but is ultimately equivocal. The metaphor is typically one of "giving form to," and the tool of the metaphor is "the concept" or "rules of the understanding," But it is never clear, in Kant, Fichte, or Hegel, to what extent this means *creation* and to what extent it means only *interpretation.* It is not as if our experience in general follows the model of our "constituting" the shape of a buxom woman in a grey mass of threatening cumulus clouds, or Camus' prisoner trying to "constitute" the head of Christ in the shadows of his stucco cell wall. This dramatic model of epistemic creativity appears to leave out what many philosophers (e.g., Locke) have seen as a "natural" and uncreative association between our ideas and our words and the matters which they "represent." One is reminded of the childhood joke, in which Eve calls out to Adam, "Let's call that one a hippopotamus." "Why?" "Well, because it certainly looks more like a hippotomas than anything else we've seen so far."

One suggestion, very much in the spirit of Kant (although it is more usually insisted to be an updating of Aristotle), has been elegantly argued by the logician Alfred Tarski. His "semantic theory of truth" has been dismissed by many "informal" (not "less than logical") philosophers as a technical trivialization of the problem of truth. At the same time, he has been celebrated by many recent semanticists, notably Davidson, as having solved the traditional problem. Both interpretations are excessive, and I shall try to show in what sense Tarski's theory can be used informally to fill out the details of the Kantian and Hegelian theory of truth.

Tarski's theory responds in a formal way to Locke[15] and begins with the insistence that what is true, namely a *sentence,* is true only *within* a given language. Quine states a similar thesis when he insists (in *Word and Object*) that the smallest unit of truth is ultimately a *theory,* not isolated by hypotheses or sentences. Similarly, Bensen Mates (*Elementary Logic,* Oxford, 1965, p. 45) takes truth to be determined by the "semantic properties of a logical framework," a matter which Quine (PL 35) takes as "logic chases Truth up the tree of grammar." The Kantian flavor of this move is evident when we switch to the material mode, and say rather that a belief is true (or false) only within a system of beliefs. Of course, it must also be said that belief, and therefore the truth of belief, presupposes a particular language, within which the belief is formulated. (This is just what Hegel has in mind when he takes "the medium of truth to be the concept.") But it does not follow that items of language, not beliefs, are the primary bearers of truth (and falsity). We might say that, by virtue of a system of beliefs made possible by language, beliefs are true or false.

In Tarski's theory, truth is defined, not in terms of "correspondence," although there is a superficial resemblance to correspondence theory, but in terms of "*satisfaction*." A sentence is said to be "satisfied" by a class or classes (Quine: "sequences") of individuals. *For each sentence* (Quine: "case by case"), satisfaction is determined by the "interpretation" or "assignment" of a class or classes of individuals to sentences, according to what Tarski calls "convention T," for example,

"Snow is white" is true if and only if snow is white.

This formula, which is often all one sees of the Tarski theory, might appear trivial, nothing more than a restatement of the correspondence theory. But the significance of the formula lies behind it. There is nothing "natural," despite orthographic appearances, about the satisfaction of "Snow is white" by the fact that snow is white. Consider the German translation "*Der Schnee ist Weiss*": There is nothing trivial in "'*Der Schnee ist Weiss*' is true if and only if snow is white."[16] Truth is a matter of convention, "convention T." This is not to say that the logician *makes* his sentences true: the universe of individuals does that. But the logician sets up the language in such a way that it is designated that certain individuals satisfy certain sentences and not others. Thus if the basic sentences of L are "Fa," "Ga," "Fb," and "Gb," and the individuals of this tiny universe are a and b, with properties F and G, then "Fa" is satisfied by a and not by b, and so on. But this satisfaction-relation must be set up for each basic sentence of the language, and so there can only be a finite and manageable number of such sentences. (Though the number of complex sentences built upon these basic sentences can be indefinitely large.) This is to say that there is no single formula for convention T, such as

"p" is true if and only if p.

For there is nothing in the convention which accounts *in general* for the connection between any particular item of language and a class of individuals in the world. The above formula can only be interpreted, therefore, as "the sixteenth letter of the alphabet is true if and only if some unspecified state of affairs is the case."

The function of convention T and Tarski's theory is to allow the logician to introduce the notion of truth into formal contexts without running into traditional and more recent logical paradoxes surrounding "is true." Thus, for familiar reasons (see sect. 3), the predicate "is true" appears in Tarski's theory only in the *meta*language (M), while the formulation of the theory appears only in the *meta*-

*meta*language (*MM*). Accordingly, the notion of satisfaction, the key to truth, is defined in *M* by *MM* for each case in *L*. But it is the philosophical moral of Tarski's formal theory that truth is not simply "in the world" (i.e., "is true" is not a possible predicate of *L*), that the relationship between a sentence in *L* and its satisfaction cannot be further explained except to say that it is conventional, and that there cannot be, in the sense traditionally demanded by correspondence theorists, a *theory* of truth at all. Accordingly, Tarski has often been accused of not providing a theory of *truth* at all, but rather only a theory of translation (e.g., A. N. Prior, op. cit.). Of course, it is true, and Tarski has formally proved this, that "satisfaction" cannot be given any such accounting, and convention *T* cannot apply to a "language of infinite order" (e.g., everyday English). Satisfaction can be defined only recursively, a well-established procedure in mathematics, but in philosophy, a complex way of "begging the question." That is, on the basis of convention *T,* one can determine the truth conditions of sentences of indefinitely increasing complexity, but a theory of truth, the account of "satisfaction" of the basic sentences of *L,* remains unavailable.

Moving again to the material mode, we can see the strong Kantian-Hegelian sympathies of the theory, particularly in Quine's version of it (op cit.). Just as the universe of individuals which satisfies the sentences of *L* must be circumscribed by the Logician in Tarski's theory, the *facts* which make our beliefs true must be "determined" or "constituted" according to Kant and Hegel's epistemologies. And again, this is not to say that we make all of our beliefs true, any more than Tarski makes all of the sentences of *L* true. Rather we set up the conventions according to which a belief or a sentence is made true (or false). To which Hegel adds that there is nothing personally creative in this "determination." The concepts by which I determine the world are not *my* concepts, but *ours* (writ large). I do not choose my concepts, but *we* do. None of us can play Tarski with the world, but *all* of us, mankind or "consciousness in general," (i.e., *Geist*) can and do so.

Thus Austin was correct in pointing out the conventional nature of the correspondence between statements and facts, but he was wrong, as Strawson argues, in thinking that the conventions involved are those governing the "speech-episode" and that the facts are independently existing conditions which make our statements true.

And that is why a hippopotamus is called a "hippopotamus," not because Eve expressed a Lockean association between word and object, but because she was, as we are not, in the cosmic Tarskian condition, able to employ convention *T* to set up a convention, "*x* is a hippopotamus" is true if and only if *x* is a hippopotamus.

5

The problem of truth is the problem of the "truth" about truth, that is, what it is for our beliefs to be true. But now, the awkward question arises: What conception of truth are we to assume in rejecting certain theories as inadequate, and defending another as "true"? In other words, how does one develop a theory of truth without presupposing a criterion according to which that theory is true? Tarski has proven, following Gödel, that any system which includes the claim "This system is true" is formally inconsistent. We need a larger context within which we can judge the truth or falsity of a particular system of beliefs. But in philosophy, of course, there is no larger context, and so the philosopher always finds himself tugging at his own bootstraps. The correspondence theorist seems to argue that his theory corresponds with "the facts" (our ordinary usage of "is true," perhaps); the coherence theorist argues that his theory is consistent and coherent; the pragmatist presumes that his theory is the most practical. Is there a way out of this circle?

What is the standard according to which we evaluate a theory of truth? That it corresponds to the facts of ordinary usage? That it be coherent and consistent? That it not be "impractical" at least (in the sense in which skepticism, for example, is "impractical")? Of course, *all* of these are our standards, plus another, that an adequate theory of truth be *complete,* that is, that it leave no loose ends or unaccountable distinctions, that it be a single theory which covers mathematical and historical truth and philosophical truth (the truth about truth). And, Hegel argues, it must cover nonepistemic predications of truth as well. A *satisfactory* theory of truth, we can now say, is one which satisfies all the demands which we place upon it. But this is not yet enlightening. What demands do we place upon a theory of truth?

It is a mistake to think that we begin with a problem of truth, to which the various theories of truth are attempted solutions. There is no problem of truth, there are only theories of truth, whose inadequacy causes problems. We said earlier that the correspondence or common-sense conception of truth did not become a theory of truth until it was already under fire (as a synergetic community will not pass laws until there are transgressions of the principles which will become the laws.) Thus the problem of truth is a problem of resolving the inadequacies created by the various theories of truth, and there we have our criterion of completeness: A satisfactory philosophical theory of truth is one which resolves all of the inadequacies of the other theories without adding new inadequacies of its own. This is why Hegel always insists (throughout the preface of the *Phenomenology,* in the *Logic,* chs. I–V, and *History of Philosophy* introduction) that a philosophical theory presupposes other philosophical theories, that philosophy is necessarily the history of philosophy as well, and that philosophical systems are not to be thought of as true or false and met "with agreement or contradiction," but are rather to be viewed as "the progressive evolution of the truth" about truth (*Phenomenology,* p. 68). This is also why a philosphical theory cannot be stated as an "abstract formula" or as a "naked result," a "lifeless universal" (ibid., p. 69), because the adequacy and significance of a philosophical theory can only be measured in the philosophical context within which it is a response. John Dewey was arguing something parallel in his "pragmatic" theory. A satisfactory philosophical theory is one which grows from and is a resolution of the theories of other philosphers. The "truth" about truth is that truth has been made into a problem by the philosophers, and it can now be solved only by another philosopher, by more philosophy.

From Tarski, let us borrow the technical notion of "satisfaction," but expand it considerably beyond the limited context of "satisfaction of sentences in L" to include the satisfaction of *beliefs* formulated in L. We can now return to our dis tinction between belief-ψ and belief-ϕ in section 3 and insist that the beliefs satisfied in this context are beliefs-ϕ. Consider a case before a magistrate, in which what is in question is the belief-ϕ (whose instantiation in the magistrate's belief-ψ is, in this instance, authoritative), that the accused is innocent of any wrongdoing. On the basis of the case presented, the magistrate concludes that the evidence is "satisfactory." Satisfactory for what? Not only to satisfy the magistrate (one could satisfy *him* with a bribe), but the belief-ϕ. This is not to deny that truth can also be ascribed to the magistrate's statement that the man is innocent, nor is it to deny, though it is to purposively avoid, the ascription of truth to impersonal ontological or lexical entities (propositions or sentences.) The advantages of our notion of belief-ϕ is that it makes truth explicitly person-relative, but yet not relative to particular persons.

What will satisfy a belief-ϕ that-p? Of course, *the-fact-that-p* will satisfy it, make it true, but this limiting and perfect case is "unilluminating," as James objected, and "inadequate as a philosophical conception," as Hegel insisted. Moreover, it is misleading, as Strawson argues, because it leads us to countenance the existence of a peculiar entity in the world, the-fact-that-p. But the satisfaction of the belief-ϕ that-p does not require the existence of a fact-that-p. "It is a fact that -p" is but a misleading way of accounting for the truth of the belief that-p. It is as if some bureaucrat were to respond to my query, "What will satisfy the Texas residency laws?" with the answer, "A Texas residency."

The triviality of the correspondence theory (and the apparent triviality of Tarski's "convention T," baldly presented), is due to its providing a limiting and unilluminating criterion for the satisfaction of a belief-ϕ based on the misleading phrase "the fact that. . . ." But beliefs are not satisifed by "facts." Our common belief-ϕ that the sum of the angles of a triangle equals 180 degrees is not satisfied by a fact, but by our having seen proof of that theorem. Our common belief-ϕ that the current prime minister of England is a woman is satisfied by our having read about her in the Times and having seen her on television. Thus a theory of epistemic satisfaction and truth becomes a framework of a theory of *evidence*. Or, because the English philosopher's use of that term restricts "evidence" to empirical evidence, perhaps we could use the German term favored by Husserl, *Evidenz,* which includes within its scope considerations of coherence and a priori considerations of "essence" as well as empirical data. Joining Hegel and Heidegger, we can refer the theory of truth to a theory of *reasons*. But just as we distinguished beliefs-ψ from beliefs-ϕ, we must distinguish reasons-ψ from reasons-ϕ. As some recent British philosophers have formulated this distinction, it is the difference between *his* reasons (for holding a certain belief) and *the* reason (or at least *a* reason) for holding it. Thus his reason-ψ for believing the accused to be innocent is that the man is his brother. But *a* or *the* reason-ϕ for believing him innocent is that the man was in Tulsa at the time the crime occurred in Denver. Thus what satisfies beliefs-ϕ are reasons-ϕ.

A reason-ϕ or several reasons-ϕ for a belief-ϕ may not be sufficient to satisfy the belief-ϕ. Truth as satisfaction requires *conclusive* reasons. As Quine says (*PL,* ch. 3), "truth is the one limiting case of satisfaction." Now it may be that we lack conclusive reasons, and so a belief-ϕ may not be satisfied, which is to say that we may not know the truth. For example, Caesar crossed the Rubicon either by foot, or chariot, or horse, or in some other way. But, even with reports from the times, even from Caesar himself, we do not have and shall never have conclusive reasons for believing one alternative or another. Yet we would still say that, on the basis of the reasons we do have, we are justified in believing or we can *rationally* hold the belief-ϕ that Caesar crossed the Rubicon on horseback. Thus, we can distinguish rational belief-ϕ (belief with reasons) and true belief-ϕ or knowledge (belief with conclusive reasons). True belief-ϕ is optimal satisfaction.

The problem of truth typically begins with questions about the "way the world is" and, after several attempts at metaphysics, finds itself trapped in questions about one's own abilities to know the world as it is. Thus an adolescent confused about his love life will first ask, "What's wrong with *them?*" but later, after a few sour affairs, will turn to "What's wrong with me?" But with "maturity," he learns Hegel's absolute, and the question is neither "them" nor "me" but rather "What do I expect (of them and of myself)?" Similarly with Truth: our beliefs are satisfied by the world or not depending on what we expect of the world.

> To ask if a category is true or not must sound strange to the ordinary mind; for a category apparently becomes true only when it is applied to a given object, and apart from this application it would seem meaningless to inquire into its truth. But this is the very question on which everything turns. We must however in the first place understand what we mean by Truth. In common life, truth means the agreement of an object with our conception of it. We thus presuppose an object to which our conception must conform. In the philosophical sense of the word, on the other hand, truth may be described, in general abstract terms, as the agreement of a thought content with itself. This meaning is quite different from the one given above. At the same time the deeper and philosophical meaning of truth can be partially traced even in the ordinary use of language. Thus we speak of a true friend; by which we mean a friend whose manner of conduct accords with the notion of friendship. In the same way we speak of a true work of art . . . (Hegel, *Logic,* pp. 51–52.).

Ultimately, Truth is self-satisfaction, the optimal satisfaction of the categories which we have imposed upon our world.

6

It is clear that the "Hegelian" theory of truth sketched above will account for our nonepistemic predications of "true" and "truth" as well. The notion of satisfaction is ideally suited to this purpose, for not only can our statements and beliefs be satisfied, but so can our desires, intentions, expectations, needs, predictions, hopes, sense of honor, resentment, and love. We satisfy our hunger as well as our thirst for knowledge, and we "demand satisfaction" from shopkeepers and enemies as well as from our studies. We try to satisfy our moral ideals, and we seek out others who satisfy them. Our true friends are those who satisfy our demands as friends, and true butter satisfies our standards for butter. A marksman with true aim satisfies his intention to hit the target. Jesus is the Truth insofar as he satisfies our religious needs. And Keats found that he could be satisfied ultimately only by beauty. Thus we can understand the peculiar mixture of epistemology, moral philosophy, and historical analogy in the *Phenomenology* in terms of

Hegel's expanded notion of Truth. The *truth* of an endeavor is what will *satisfy* its goals or purposes; an endeavor is true when its goals or purposes are satisfied. The truth of science is knowledge, or conclusively rational belief; the truth of ethics is morality or right action; the truth of art is beauty; the truth of religion is God; and the truth of philosophy is the truth about truth.

The point behind this expansion is not only Hegel's desire for a single all-embracing theory of truth, one that will breach the barriers between Kant's *Critiques* and handle science, ethics, religion, and art in a single unified system. The argument of the *Phenomenology* is rather that the epistemic notion of truth *requires* the nonepistemic notions. And here Hegel anticipates the pragmatic theory of truth: purely epistemic satisfaction will not give us a sufficient account of true belief.

In our account of true belief, we have relied on the concept of *reasons.* A belief is a demand for satisfaction by reasons. Reasons make a belief rational: conclusive reasons make a belief true. Some of these reasons will be, or will be based upon, other beliefs (e.g., those involving evidence, proof, and "reasoning"). But the concept of reasons, like the concept of "satisfaction," is perfectly suited to include nonepistemic as well as epistemic considerations. Pascal's famous wager, for example, can be taken as the defense of a belief-ϕ (that God exists) on nonepistemic grounds. One must distinguish carefully here: the rewards and punishments of the wager are personal, but the reasons are reasons-ϕ, that is, they are reasons *for anyone* to adopt the belief in question. The belief in the accused man's innocence may be based upon utilitarian considerations as well as matters of evidence. And a scientific theory may be justified in part by quasi- or nonepistemic considerations, for example, its elegance or simplicity, its conformity to common sense or to religious creed. But of course, no scientific theory can ever be justified *solely* on the basis of such reasons, and here is the failure of the pragmatic theory, literally construed. It correctly points out that *some* of the reasons for holding a belief are nonepistemic. But it is essential to insist that *some* of the reasons for holding any belief must be exclusively epistemic, that is, depending upon such notions as evidence and proof.

One of the more mysterious transitions in the *Phenomenology* is the transition from the purely epistemic chapter on "Understanding," in which the topic under discussion is Newtonian forces and various problems in the philosophies of Leibniz and Kant, to a discussion of "life" and "Desire" (op cit. pp. 218/ff.). I think there is a simple and reasonable account of this transition: the three chapters on "Consciousness" have been exclusively epistemological; the last of these has presented us with the view, which is retained for the rest of the book, that consciousness supplies the concepts which determine, or, in Kantian terms, "constitute," the objects of our experience. But then, what determines which of a number of mutually exclusive alternative sets of epistemic concepts will be employed? No further epistemic considerations, for the concepts chosen will themselves determine what is to count as an epistemic consideration. These considerations must therefore be the *concerns* of consciousness, in other words, *pragmatic* considerations, desires, practices, and social determinations. Historically, Kant would not have agreed to the idea of "a number of mutually exclusive alternative sets of concepts." This idea came to Hegel, and to every other philosopher of the period, through Fichte, who held that the choice of categories "depended on the kind of man you are." And Hegel, who accepts the idea of alternative sets of categories, builds this Fichtean pragmatic criterion (which was later to influence the American pragmatist, C. I. Lewis) into his dialectic. Understanding attempts to be purely epistemic. But truth is essentially tied to desire and pragmatics just as much as it is tied to questions of evidence and proof. Thus in a broader sense Truth is always (Absolutely) self-satisfying.

Beliefs-ϕ are satisfied by reasons, some of which are epistemic, some of which are not. The nonepistemic reasons will involve desires and expectations, hopes and intentions, and these too fall under our notion of satisfacton. What satisfies a desire, however, is not a reason, but rather its "object," which Hegel also calls its *truth*. As we leaf through the *Phenomenology*, we find many very different phenomena marked as the Truth, the "true man" (pp. 98–99; cf. *Logic* 52), in "Master and Slave" the recognition of the other, and the Stoic finds his truth in thought (pp. 243ff.). "Reason's truth" is our first glimmer of the "truth about truth (p. 272). The truth of an organism is its continued life (p. 297), and "the ethical life of a nation" is the truth of "objective spirit" (p. 460). Duty, in Kantian ethics, is truth (p. 615), while "conscience" is truth for Fichte (p. 644). There is truth of culture (p. 645), religion (p. 692), and, of course, the Absolute truth of "Spirit" and "philosophy" (pp. 792ff.). The relationship of this final "absolute" truth to the others is that it includes a true (that is, satisfactory) account of their truth. The goal of philosophy (its "truth") is to comprehend the varieties of truth. And that comprehension is that truth is self-satisfaction, the satisfaction of our own demands.

NOTES

1. Alan R. White, e.g., in *Truth,* (New York: Macmillan, 1970) who at least discusses these at length, discards all such senses in the first chapter.

2. Hegel, *Phenomenology of Mind,* trans. by J. B. Baillie, (Macmillan, 1931) *"(Phen.")* with some necessary changes in translation.

3. "Moore took the lead in the rebellion, and I followed with a sense of emancipation. . . . We believed that grass is green, that the sun and stars would exist if no one was aware of them. . . . The world which had been thin and logical now became rich and varied." In "My Mental Development," in Schlipp, ed., *The Philosphy of Bertrand Russell* 3 ed. (New York: Tudor Publishing Co., 1951).

4. A. N. Prior, "The Correspondence Theory of truth," in *Encyclopedia of Philosophy,* Edwards, ed. (New York: Macmillan, 1968).

5. Hegel often uses the notions of "object" or "particular existence" here, which makes it unclear whether he thinks that the worldly elements of correspondence are things or facts.

6. I have argued this thesis in detail in "Hegel's Epistemology," *American Philosophical Quarterly,* vol. 2, no. 4 (November 1974), pp. 277–89 [chapter 2 in this collection].

7. All references to Hegel's *Logic* are to the *Logic* of the *Encyclopedia,* trans by W. Wallace (Oxford, 1892). Numbers are section numbers.

8. As J. L. Austin gracefully puts the matter, "*In vino,* possibly, *veritas,* but in a sober symposium, '*vcrum*'." But given Hegel's celebrated descripton of truth as "the Bacchanalian revel, in which not a member is sober" (*Phenomenology,* p. 105) we may, in defending his theory, feel entitled to return to "the Truth" as well.

9. Reprinted in Pitcher, G., ed., *Truth* (Englewood Cliffs, N.J.: Prentice-Hall, 1964).

10. Cf. Frege's "The Thought," trans. by A. Quinton, *Mind,* vol. 65, no. 259, (July, 1956), pp. 289–311; and Husserl's "the essence of a judgment," *Ideas* (New York: Macmillan, 1931), ch. 6.

11. Ramsey, in Pitcher, op. cit., 17f. See also Quine, op. cit., p. 12.

12. Alan White (op. cit.) begins by insisting that he is interested only in the truth of what is said, then distinguishes between what is said and what is "expressed" in the saying of it (e.g., beliefs, hopes, fears) and then concludes that what is expressed is not what is true. But what is said is, in the case of belief, what is true. White later adds, without argument, that the truth of belief depends upon the truth of what is said.

13. See John Cook in "Wittgenstein on Privacy" in Pitcher, G., ed. *Wittgenstein* (Doubleday, 1970), pp. 286–323.

14. "True to the Facts," *Journal of Philosophy* (1970).

15. Of course, Tarski is immediately responding to certain logical paradoxes and problems suggested by Gödel, Grelling, and others. We need not worry about that here.

16. Thus Davidson suggests ("Truth and Meaning" in Rosenberg, ed., *Readings in the Philosophy of Language* [Englewood Cliffs, N.J.: Prentice-Hall, 1970], p. 457), that the fact that the "framer of a theory will as a matter of course avail himself when he can of the built-in convenience of a meta-language with a sentence guaranteed equivalent to each sentence in the object language . . . this ought not to con us into thinking a theory any more correct that entails '"Snow is white" is true if and only if snow is white' than one that entails instead; '(S) "Snow is white" is true if and only if grass is green . . . '.

4

The Secret of Hegel
(Kierkegaard's Complaint):
A Study in Hegel's Philosophy
of Religion

"The Secret of Hegel."[1] With that provocative title, James Stirling launched his extravagant pioneering study of Hegel in English (1865). It has since been commented, often and wryly, that it has been a secret well kept. But Stirling claimed to have divined the secret, and most British commentators[2] claim to have learned it with him: *Hegel is a Christian,* "the greatest abstract thinker of Christianity,"[3] and the aim of his difficult works is to "restore our faith, faith in God, faith in Christianity as the revealed religion,"[4] The "secret" is that "the universe is but a materialization, externalization, of the thoughts of God."[5] So would MacTaggart argue at the turn of the century,[6] and only a few years ago, J. N. Findlay held that

> [Hegel's] whole system may in fact be regarded as an attempt to see the Christian mysteries in everything whatever, every natural process, every form of human activity, and every logical transition.[7]

For the reader who has troubled to read through Hegel's two-volume *Science of Logic,* or worse, through Stirling's two-volume *Secret,* this conclusion must be a bitter disappointment. To the contrary, Hegel's Christian apologetics would appear to be one of the best-known "facts" about him, well known even to those who would not think of reading him. Hegel took great pains, at the cost of great obscurity, to remind us of his ultimately religious intentions. The beginning of

This work has been supported in part by the National Endowment for the Humanities and the University of Texas Research Institute. I have been greatly encouraged by Charles Kahn, The American editor of *Archiv Für Geschichte der Philosophie.*

the *Logic,* for example, makes this difficult work all the more so with its abstruse suggestion that the truth of logic is nothing other than God. ("God and God only is the truth."[8]) Similarly, the *Phenomenology* (and the later *Encyclopedia*) is peppered with references to Divinity in the most unlikely places. The sections on "Religion" appear to have been gratuitously and inappropriately but prestigiously placed at the penultimate stage of the dialectic (somewhat like Napoleon's mother in the chronicles of the coronation). Hegel insisted until his death that he was a good Lutheran, and in his lectures he apparently defended the traditional doctrines of the Christian faith. One might say that Christianity is as much of a secret in Hegel as class conflict is in Marx.

But is Hegel "the greatest abstract thinker of Christianity"? There is good reason to think otherwise. Let us first consider an unsolved and often unrecognized puzzle; in the years 1793–99, Hegel wrote but did not publish a set of manuscripts on Christianity. Some are virulently anti-Christian, with Nietzschean contempt for the Church and its priests, for Christian doctrines and authority, for Christendom and even for Christ himself. These essays have been well known in Germany for half a century, and in this country for several decades. They have been argued to be of great importance for understanding the "mature" Hegel [e.g., by Dilthey (1905)[9] Kaufmann (1954)[10]]. Yet it is generally agreed that Hegel underwent an abrupt shift in his attitude toward Christianity about 1800. Even Kaufmann, who has been most responsible for familiarizing English readers with these essays and their import for Hegel's later work, refers to them as "Hegel's anti-theological *phase.*"[11] But why this abrupt shift? What explains the radical difference between the young and the "mature" Hegel? ("Maturity" signifying, as usual, the more conservative position.) The answer I should like to pose to this puzzle (and several others) is unusual, for I believe that Hegel really did have a secret, and that it has been well kept. The secret, abruptly stated, is that *Hegel was an atheist.* His "Christianity" is nothing but nominal, an elaborate subterfuge to protect his professional ambitions in the most religiously conservative country in northern Europe. Hegel had seen Spinoza's *Ethics* condemned in Germany. He had seen Kant, whom he considered to be unquestioningly orthodox, censured and censored by the narrow-minded regime of Frederick Wilhelm II. He had seen Fichte dismissed from the University at Jena for views that were (incorrectly) construed as atheistic. Is it only coincidence that the year of Hegel's "great conversion" (1800) is also the beginning of his professional philosophical career, and that the writing of the *Phenomenology* (1806) is simultaneously the time of his first professorship? Hegel may have been a champion of the truth, but he knew how to look out for himself. He may have stuck to the letter of Christianity, but in "spirit" he was anything but a Christian. He was not the great abstract thinker of Christianity at all, but rather the precursor of atheistic humanism in German philosophy. While holding a series of lucrative and powerful professorships under state auspices and with church approval, Hegel formulated the very doctrines which would soon bring Christianity to its knees, preparing the way for Marx, Nietzsche, and Freud. But the "secret" was a prudential necessity for Hegel, much as we might think of Plato burying his Pythagorean formulae in anagrams to escape the fate of his illustrious teacher, or of Descartes, struggling in double-meanings to pass church censorhip with his *Meditations.*

The poet Heinrich Heine, once a student of Hegel, confessed,

> I was young and proud, and it pleased my vanity when I learned from Hegel
> that it was not the dear God who lived in heaven that was God, as my grand-
> mother supposed, but I myself here on earth.[12]

Heine, a Jew, felt little of the usual timidity in calling a spade a spade. There is
no God, only man. But to defend that conclusion in a respectable way, Hegel used
religion and religious vocabulary as his instruments, as if the last logical consequence to be drawn from Christian doctrine is humanism, and the final meaning
to be given to theological terminology is a meaning which refers strictly and
exclusively to man's conception of himself. In other words, to solve our puzzle,
there is *no* change in Hegel's attitude to Christianity, only in his sense of prudence
and his ability to use what he rejects as the tool for its own rejection. What he
hated in the early manuscripts, he still despises in the *Phenomenology* and his
late lectures on religion. What was false is still false, and what was repulsive, still
repulsive. There is no turn from the "young" Hegel to the "mature" Hegel, except
in style. Hegel may have despised Christianity, but he recognized its social power.
Heine tells us of an incident:

> One beautiful starry-skied evening, we two stood next to each other at a win-
> dow, and I, a young man of about twenty-two who had just eaten well and had
> good coffee, enthused about the stars and called them the abode of the blessed.
> But the master grumbled to himself: 'the stars, hum! hum! the stars are only a
> gleaming leprosy in the sky.' For God's sake, I shouted, then there is no happy
> locality up there to reward virtue after death? But he, staring at me with his
> pale eyes, said cuttingly: 'So you want to get a tip for having nursed your sick
> mother and for not having poisoned your dear brother?—Saying that, he
> looked around anxiously, but he immediately seemed reassured when he saw
> that it was only Heinrich Beer, who had approached him to invite him to play
> whist.[13]

The idea that Hegel was a humanistic atheist was briefly defended after
Hegel's death by the "left" Hegelians (e.g., Bauer and Marx), who saw him as a
subtle subverter of Christian faith, against the "right" Hegelians, who took Hegel
at his word as a Lutheran and as a defender of the faith. But this essentially religious dispute between the "left" and the "right" had political overtones, and soon
the antagonism moved from the theological to the political arena, where it
remains today. The atheistic Hegelians, including the young Marx, were far more
concerned with changing the world than haggling with academic theologians.
Accordingly, they left Hegel's religious position to the right, who retained domination within the small circle of scholars who cared one way or another, at least
until recently.[14] Using Hegel's own public declarations, his explicit celebration of
"revealed religion," and his consistently religious vocabulary, any theologian
with a first degree in pedantry can prove that Hegel was a Christian. What is more
difficult, however, is to understand just how limited the "religious dimension" of
Hegel's thought really is, how nominal and how ironic.[15] By the nature of the case,
our thesis can have no public declarations to rely upon, and must argue against
the explicitly religious doctrines and unquestionably exalted position of "religion" in Hegel's dialectic on the basis of conjecture and indirect evidence. But

there are many clues, not the least of which are to be found in Hegel's curious statement of those doctrines and his structuring of those positions.

It is Hegel, before Nietzsche, who uses the phrase, "the death of God." It is a phrase that far better summarizes Hegel's philosophy of religion than all the claptrap about "the externalization of thought" and the divinity of spirit. In an early published essay ("Faith and Knowledge") Hegel invokes the image of "the good Friday of speculation," which replaces the naïveté of Christianity with "the cheerful freedom of Godlessness."[16] And readers of the *Phenomenology* have long been puzzled by its closing imagery, "the Golgotha of Absolute Spirit,"[17] But what is Golgotha other than the death of God? But where the New Testament Golgotha murders a man, returning him to God, Hegel's Golgotha murders God and returns him to man. A bizarre image, if the *Phenomenology* were in fact a religious treatise, but a fitting image for an elaborate and elusive defense of humanism. With a touch of perversity, Hegel uses the language and imagery of Christianity to establish the blasphemous position for which Spinoza was condemned and Fichte fired. It was as if a perverse Menshevik had published John Locke's *Second Treatise* using Marxist terminology and the pen name of "Karl Marx," then laughed for decades as pedantic Bolsheviks attempted to integrate its doctrines with their own. If there is any comedy to Hegel's work, as Joshua Lowenberg[18] has so long argued, then surely it is here. Hegel's secret has been well kept. Only a few suspected—particularly one eccentric in Copenhagen who discovered the secret early on, but found the joke not at all amusing.

Hegel's Philosophy of Religion

Hegel's interest—and his writings—in the philosophy of religion span his career. He studied theology in Tübingen, and his first known writings are the early "theological" (or "antitheological") manuscripts of the years 1793–99, the years of his fascination with Kant's *Religion innerhalb der Grenzen der blossen Vernunft* (1793). In 1802, he published his essay *Glauben und Wissen* ("Faith and Knowledge") in the second volume of the journal he edited with Schelling. In 1807, the *Phänomenologie des Geistes.* (*Phenomenology*) appears, with "revealed religion" *("offenbare Religion")* standing conspicuously at the end of a long historical "dialectic" of religious forms. In his *Encyklopädie der philosophischen Wissenschaften (Encyclopedia of the Philosophical Sciences),* Hegel omits the historical dialectic, mentioning only "revealed religion" *("Die geoffenbarte Religion")* (again at the end of the development,[19] 564–71), but adding a polemical attack on alternative contemporary religious conceptions. Finally, there are Hegel's lectures on the *Philosophie der Religion,* delivered and reworded in 1821, 1824, 1827, and 1831 (the year of his death), collected together by his students.[20] From the *Phenomenology,* in fact from "Faith and Knowledge," until the *Lectures,* the content, structure, and strategy of Hegel's arguments change remarkably little. And though the structure and strategy of argument are surely different in the early manuscripts and the published work, it can be argued that the content remains the same.[21]

Underlying the polemical "antitheology" of the manuscripts of the 1790s and the alleged rationalization of Christianity that are to be found in the *Phenome-*

nology, the *Encyclopedia* and the *Lectures* is a continuity which must not be overlooked.

The early manuscripts are decidedly anti-Christian, sometimes viciously so (e.g., "the system of the church can be nothing but a system of contempt for human beings," which provides "debasing monuments of human degradation.").[22] This opinion of the church never varies, but the strategy changes. In his *Lectures on the History of Philosophy,* Hegel argues that in the Middle Ages

> thought begins within Christianity, accepting it as absolute presupposition. Later, when the wings of thought have grown strong, philosophy rises to the sun like a young eagle, a bird of prey which strikes down religion. But it is the last development of speculative thought to do justice to faith and make peace with religion.[23]

And Hegel does make peace, but only that peace which emerges after a decisive battle and a devastating victory, the peace that *followed* the destruction of Troy. Enemies alive are objects of scorn, but enemies defeated are not only accepted but may be safely celebrated in their praise. The *Phenomenology* constitutes such a thorough victory over the forces of Christian theology that Hegel can easily afford to allow its emaciated veterans to sit at the foot of Absolute Truth, honoring them only so that he may be seen merciful as well as victorious.

In the early manuscripts, Hegel had attacked Christianity "from the outside," from the side of the Enlightenment (even though Kant, with those same Enlightenment instruments of intellectual warfare, had served the church without serious complaint). But the church had long weathered such attacks, and the priests were well fortified against them. In the *Phenomenology,* however, Hegel no longer challenges the stony walls of theology, but rather enters these walls as a gift, offering his philosophy to the battle-weary theologians. (Later we will hear the cry of Kierkegaard's *Laokoon.*) Not looking their gift horses in the mouth, the theologians accepted, and theology falls, its terminological walls remaining, but the inside burned and gutted and decidedly pagan.

In the *Phenomenology* (and also in the *Encyclopedia* and the *Lectures*), Hegel argues that the short step from "revealed religion" to absolute truth consists in the simple alteration of form, the content remaining the same:

> The Spirit manifested in revealed religion has not as yet surmounted its attitude of consciousness as such. . . . Spirit as a whole and the moments distinguished in it fall within the sphere of figurative thinking, and within the form of objectivity. The *content* of this figurative thought is Absolute Spirit. All that remains to be done now is to cancel and transcend *(aufheben)* this bare form.[24]

Faith has true content; still lacking in it is the form of thought.[25] And in his *Lectures on the History of Philosophy,* Hegel tells us that "Religion and philosophy have a common object, God in and for himself," but that these have different "modes of appropriation." What are these different modes? Religion occupies itself with images and representations *(Vorstellungen)*—unsystematized, quasi-empirical spatio-temporal imagery. Philosophy abandons such mythology and restricts itself to what is essential to thought, that is, the Concept *(Begriff)*. Thus the step from "revealed religion" in *Phenomenology* VII to the "Absolute Knowledge" of VIII is accomplished by "simply" replacing *Vorstellungen* by the *Begriff.*

Throughout his works, Hegel warns us of the dangers of such glib distinctions as "form" versus "content." Let us be suspicious, therefore, of the glib suggestion that the difference between religion and philosophy is one simply of form, while their contents are identical. What is the "content" that remains the same? *Absolute Spirit,* or *God in and for himself.* But Hegel has told us throughout the *Phenomenology* that Spirit is actual or "in and for itself" only when it has *comprehended* itself as a Spirit, and that the object or content of consciousness *changes* with its different forms (or "modes of appropriation"). The difference between Spirit as a represented *object* of awareness and spirit aware of itself is not merely a difference of form; it is the most essential difference of the *Phenomenology,* the difference between Otherness and alienation, negativity and inadequacy, on the one hand, and absolute harmony and total comprehension on the other. God as object is the fateful disharmony of the early essays; God as subject is a conception which is out of reach of orthodox Christianity. So it is clear that this "mere" alteration in *form* must be far more than a simple "mere." The replacement of religious *Vorstellungen* with philosophical *Begriffe,* even while retaining *something,* is in fact the rejection of everything significant to Christianity.

What is Christianity, "revealed religion," divested of its "figurative thought"? It is a faith without icons, images, stories, and myths, without miracles, without a resurrection, without a nativity, without Chartres and Fra Angelico, without wine and wafers, without heaven and hell, without God as judge and without judgment. With philosophical conceptualization, the Trinity is reduced to Kant's categories of Universality (God the father), Particularity (Christ the Son) and Individuality (The Holy Spirit).[26] The incarnation no longer refers to Christ alone, but only to the philosophical thesis that there is no God other than humanity.[27] Spirit, that is, humanity made absolute, is God. This is in fact *all* that is left of religion, the conception of humanity as God, which is to say that there is nothing other than humanity;

> One may have all sorts of ideas about the Kingdom of God; but it is always a realm of Spirit to be realized and brought about in man.[28]

God and incarnation become nothing more than the human community. Original sin becomes human moral responsibility,[29] and immortality, heaven and hell, are reduced to nothing more than the survival of the human spirit in others after our individual deaths, a sense in which any animal is immortal insofar as it is survived by its species.[30] What is left after the philosophical conceptualization of religion? To the orthodox Christian, *nothing* is left, save some terminology which has been emptied of its traditional significance. From Hegel's gutted Christianity to Heine and Nietzsche's aesthetic atheism is a very short distance indeed. Even McTaggert, who takes such considerable pains to save Hegel's Christianity for Christendom, is forced to concede,

> Hegel supports Christianity against all attacks but his own, and thus reveals himself as its most deadly antagonist.[31]

And Findlay, who elsewhere remarks that Hegel's exegeses "catch the very spirit and savour of the New Testament," finds it ncessary to say that Hegel

> has defined religion . . . in a manner to suit himself, his main motive being to secure for the difficult theses of his philosophy the approval normally accompanying the words "religion" and "religious" . . . Hegel, it may be claimed, is simply "cashing in" on this widespread approval, and securing its advantages for his own system.[32]

There is a vital difference, of course, between mere atheism and irreligion, and it is to Hegel's credit that he constructs a humanist position transcending both. Similarly, there is a difference between not being a Christian and not being religious in some broader sense. It must not be thought that Hegel was not religious because he was not a Christian. In fact, his atheism was bolstered by his religiosity, the same religiosity that sustained him through the cynicism of his theological studies at the Stift, the same striving for *übermenschliches* status that characterized Goethe's Faust and Nietzsche's Zarathustra. They too might be called "religious" thinkers, but surely there was little that was Christian about them. For Hegel too, "religion" is an appeal to what is "above," but not what is better *than* man, rather what is potentially best *in* man: he tells us throughout his writing that every man brings into the world not only the right to a mere animal existence but also the right to develop his capacities, to become a human being, a position that might have come directly out of Goethe or Schiller. (Compare Schiller's remark: "Every individual human being carries within himself, as his potential and his destiny, the pure ideal image of man.") By "religion," Hegel means a striving for the infinite, not the "bad infinite" of endless Faustian dissatisfaction but the "genuine infinite" of rational autonomy and freedom. Thus Hegel's concept of religion fits squarely into the French Enlightenment of Voltaire and Rousseau as well as into the German *Aufklärung* of Lessing, Herder, and Kant. Religion is mankind's impulse to a better life, not the "otherworldly" afterlife of Christian heaven and hell, but the "thisworldly" aspirations of great artists, philosophers, statesmen, and truly religious men. Anticipating Neitzsche, Hegel tells us that religion is a "reconciling Yea" to the world, not an escape from it.[33]

Our evidence for this thesis can be summarized by five more-or-less distinct considerations, although a thorough defense would have to examine in detail and as a whole the entirety of the Hegelian corpus. There are: (1) the now well-known anti-Christian diatribes of the early unpublished manuscripts; (2) the discussion of "Religion in General" in both the *Phenomenology* and the *Lectures;* (3) the bewildering configuration of religious *Vorstellungen* of the *Phenomenology* and the more carefully developed dialectic of religions of Hegel's *Lectures;* (4) the appearance and rejection of Christianity at least twice in the early chapters of the *Phenomenology;* and (5) the demonstrably areligious interpretation he gives to what he calls "revealed religion" (both in the *Phenomenology* and in the later *Lectures).*

1. The Early Manuscripts[34]

We can best appreciate Hegel's conception of religion by examining the first full essay he wrote about it, the early manuscript "Folk-Religion and Christianity" (probably written in 1793).[35] In this essay, Hegel shows that he shares with his friend Hölderlin an almost worshipful fascination with the ancient Greeks. Against the gloom of northern "disharmony," he celebrates the harmony of the ancient South; with Christian mourning, he contrasts the "excesses of the bacchanals"; against Jesus, he idolizes Socrates; and against "the mysteries that impress only the ignorant and the credulous,"[36] he defends wisdom and reason. Religion is a striving for harmony; Christianity, which sets doctrine against doctrine, sect against sect, soul against flesh and desire against faith, is the very antithesis of such harmony.

Greek folk religion differed most from modern Christianity, however, in its dominant stress on community practices and shared feelings. Christian salvation is an essentially solitary affair; what Hegel admired in Greek folk religion was its sociability and its appeal to man's "better" instincts, not just his fear of divine punishment and the promise of comfort in misfortune. Religion deserves its coveted place in Hegel's dialectic because it is essentially the ultimate *social* (that is, "spiritual") bond between men. In his later *Lectures,* he will tell us that "Cult," in one form or another, is the mark of every true religion.

The substance of these early manuscripts is now well known to every reader of Hegel. At the basis of each of them is the Kantian doctrine that religion must serve morality and be "within the limits of (practical) reason alone." But Hegel, unlike Kant, argues that Christianity does *not* fit this ideal, is at its very foundations "positive" or authoritarian, opposed to reason and cultural harmony. It is on this charge that the young unpublished Hegel rests his most vitriolic and blasphemous comments. But these "antitheological" salvos are already familiar to us; what must be shown is that the attitudes which they express continue to define Hegel's philosophy of religion throughout his published and nominally Christian works.

2. The Nature of Religion in General

Hegel's strategy in the *Phenomenology* is comparable to that of Kant. He first seeks a general account of the nature of religion in order to formulate a criterion according to which different religions may be shown to be more or less adequate or "rational." But morality as such is no longer the criterion. In several (published and unpublished) essays in the interim, Hegel has repeatedly argued for a conception of social or "custom"-morality *(Sittlichkeit)* against Kant's more formal conception of morality by principle *(Moralität).* Accordingly, the criterion in the *Phenomenology* is the "completion of the life of Spirit,"[37] not any longer the innocent sociability of Greek folk religion but now a far more sophisticated metaphysical sense of harmony and self-realization, as required by an infinitely more sophisticated and complex modern world.

What should strike us from the first in reading Hegel's introduction to "Religion in General" in the *Phenomenology*[38] is that he does not speak of "God" or "Divinity" but only of "Spirit" and "Absolute Being," terms which apply not only to nontheistic religions but to nonreligious metaphysics as well. "Religion," he tells us, "is consciousness of Absolute Being in General," "a consciousness of the supersensuous," "self-consciousness of Spirit."[39] In fact, he informs us that *all* forms of consciousness are religious in nature, which should once and for all prevent us from confusing Hegel's enthusiasm for religion with any particular respect for theism or Christianity. Religious consciousness is not *a* form of consciousness but the motivating impulse behind all the varous forms that make up the *Phenomenology*. Religion is nothing other than the demand for total comprehension, the harmony and completeness of soul that Hegel had so admired in the Greeks, "the striving for absolute self-knowledge" that he learned from Aristotle and Spinoza and, not least, from Goethe. Quite the contrary of the worship of mystery and the search for salvation through an external judgment in Christianity, religion for Hegel is wholly a striving for self-realization. Terminology aside, the religion of the *Phenomenology* is no more Christian than Aristotle's metaphysics, *sans* Aquinas.

The *Phenomenology* provides us with but a brief analysis of "Religion in General." (We remember that Hegel was in a desperate hurry to finish the manuscript at that point of his writing.) Fortunately, the later *Lectures* correct this situation admirably, and there Hegel offers us a nearly two-hundred page account of "Religion in General," employing the same terminology and defending much the same theses that we found in the early manuscript on folk religion, except that Christianity, of course, is treated far more respectfully—or should we say, prudently. What is there said to be of primary importance in religion is *feeling (Gefühl),* a feeling of awe, of worship, of respect. But, against some of his contemporaries (notably Schleiermacher), Hegel insists that feeling alone is not enough (commenting wryly that feelings of dependency alone would make a dog the best Christian), that these feelings must have an *object* and a *representation (Vorstellung),* and that, ultimately, the object of religious feeling must be *spiritual,* which is to say, both infinite and human. But the tension between infinite and finite requires resolution, and this resolution cannot consist of individual thought alone. (The "Unhappy Consciousness" is just such an attempt so to resolve this tension.) What is required, is a return to Hegel's ideal of Greek folk religion and his Kantian conception of religion as *practical* reason, as communal ritual or "cult." It is this tripartite conception of religion as feeling, representation, and cult that constitutes *faith* in general. But where Kant rationalized faith as a postulate of practical reason, Hegel makes faith a matter of community spirit. Faith is a shared feeling for the symbolically represented infinite.

In moving from religion to philosophy, the transition most in contention here, Hegel retains the ideas of feeling and community, but gives up representation. This means giving up image and icon, *Vorstellungen* and biblical stories; but these were only temporary vehicles for religious "truth" until philosophy showed its strength. (Hegel, like Nietzsche's despairing soul in the *Gay Science,* insists repeatedly that Jesus' audience and most men still are simply *not ready* for philosophy—that men needed and still need the mythology and mystery of miracles and stories.) But what earns religion its high status in the dialectic of the *Phenomenology* is its sense of cult, not its metaphors and otherworldly representations. It is the sense of universal community that is religion's ultimate contribution to human consciousness. Particular religions, with their concepts of "chosen people," "the Way" or "the Righteous," only turn us against each other and disrupt the harmony that is religion's ultimate goal. And Hegel makes it clear to us that religion, despite its penultimate position, *must* be transcended for philosophy, and that means to give up all those particular doctrines and metaphors that would allow us to defend any particular religion. However close in pagination Christianity may appear to Absolute Truth, the two are not identical; in fact, the latter, in its very formulation, makes acceptance of the former impossible.

3. The Dialectic of Religions

Of course, the chapter of the *Phenomenology* entitled "Religion" is dialectical in form, but what must strike us about this dialectic is that, unlike any other in the book, it takes as its scope the whole of the *Phenomenology,* reconstruing each of its "forms of consciousness" as a religious form. (The first "form," for example, *das Lichtwesen,* is explicitly paired with "sense-certainty," the second to "perception," and so on.) Thus Hegel's insistence that "religious consciousness" is not a particular form of consciousness is brought home in the very structure of the dialectic itself. Moreover, each of the entries in this dialectic is an ancient religion, sometimes grossly mischaracterized and ill fitting. This should disturb us. A moment's reflection, however, coupled with a reading of the introduction to the *Lectures,*[40] shows that this is not merely a play-off of historical forms at all, but that each has an identifiable modern counterpart. Thus it is not at all difficult to show the applicability of Hegel's arguments to contemporary conceptions (and rejections) of Christianity: Jacobi's latter-day "intuitionism," Enlightenment "Deism," Schelling's glorification of God as a superartist, Laplace's scientific atheism, and the Kantian characterization of religion in terms of morality and practical reason. Once again, this deceptiveness cannot be overlooked as mere "obscurity."

If all of the different forms of (religious) consciousness are now to be viewed by us as aspects (*Seite*) of one and the same Reality, there can be no single-minded defense of any single religion. But neither can there be a reduction, as the French Enlightenment philosophers had attempted, of all religions to one; this, Hegel sees, would be no religion at all, only philosophy. And while he is demonstrably a child of the Enlightenment, it is the German *Aufklärung* that commands Hegel's allegiance. His model is not Voltaire's glib "Deism," that minimal form of "scientific" Christianity, but Lessing's elegant concept of a progression of religious stages, each supplanting the other in a spiritual metamorphosis that can now finally dispense with their services.[41]

4. Christianity in the Phenomenology

The defense of our original claim—that Hegel is not a Christian and his philosophy is only a pretense of Christian theology—must ultimately take account of the at least superficial similarity between Hegel's conception of "Revealed Religion" and orthodox Christian theology. To do this, we must show that "Revealed Religion" is *not* Christianity but that Christianity appears and is rejected in two preceding sections of the *Phenomenology.* Furthermore, we must show that the key doctrines of Christian theology—the Trinity and the Incarnation—are utterly devoid of religious content in Hegel's analysis.

The first appearance of Christianity in the dialectic of the *Phenomenology* is not, of course, "Revealed Religion." If orthodox Christianity is to be located there, there can be no doubt that its proper identification is with the "Unhappy Consciousness."[42] The several "triplets" in the chapter make the recognition of the Trinity unmistakable.[43] Within the complex "logic" of that chapter (though we cannot defend this claim here), Hegel traces not only the metaphysical doctrines of the Trinity but the development of Christianity itself, from Catholicism to Protestanism to the new forms of radical Christian thought that were so pervasive in the Enlightenment. (Here we can clearly see the argument of Lessing's *Education of Mankind* at work, and the same progress we will find a century later in Nietzsche's *Genealogy of Morals*.) And while it is impossible not to identify the "Unhappy Consciousness" with Christianity, it is equally impossible to deny that, both by virtue of its early place in the dialectic and by virtue of the arguments Hegel raises against it, Christianity, as "Unhappy," represents a failure— and surely not the ultimate achievement—of human consciousness. (Moreover, Hegel's buried sarcasm here is often a match for the youthful vitriol of his early manuscripts; see "the discordant clang of ringing bells, a cloud of warm incense, a kind of thinking in terms of music,"[44] and his Nietzschean critique of the ascetic life, in which an agent "ceases to be the author of his own act" and "thinks and speaks what is senseless."[45]

Because Hegel thought far more of Jesus than he did of Christianity,[46] Jesus himself appears long after we have left behind the "Unhappiness" of Christianity. This is a historical Jesus, not a divinity, a "Beautiful soul" *(schöne Seele)* who teaches ethics by example. Again, we must save the detailed analysis of this controversial section of the *Phenomenology*[47] for another place. But what is clear here is that this historical Jesus, taken as an example, is also relegated to that bulk of the dialectic which is transcended, both by way of its juxtaposition (though it is important to notice just how far into the dialectic this "beautiful soul" does appear, at the end of the chapter on "Spirit," and behind only the long and problematic chapter on "Religion"), and by the way of the arguments Hegel advances against Jesus' peculiar metamoral preachings of withdrawal and abstention from judgment.[48]

5. "Revealed Religion"

From the beginning of our reading of "Revealed Religion"[49] we must be careful not to place too much emphasis on the quasi-religious concept of "revealed," which provides Hegel with a convenient equivocation between the clearly religious sense and the epistemic sense in which it means merely "evident" or "manifest." (Heidegger abuses the same equivocation in his philosophy.) And though the doctrines of the Trinity and the Incarnation pervade the discussion[50] we must be careful to distinguish mere mention from serious use. We may take as our guiding suspicion the fact that, where traditional Christianity has placed its stress upon the Father and the Son, leaving the "Holy Ghost" as the mysterious white dove or the ray of light in a Massacio Trinity, Hegel gives the Holy Spirit top priority, reducing God the Father to pure thought and Jesus the Son to no-one-in-particular. This blasphemous pseudo-theology is disguised under some very obscure theological prose, and to the impatient reader who notices only the usual New Testament grammar, "revealed religion" might indeed appear to be very Christian.

"Revealed Religion" consists of a rambling and hurriedly written yet unusually single-minded *rejection* of the traditional ideas of Trinity and Incarnation, preparing us for the following chapter on "Absolute Knowledge" and purging us of the mythological thinking that Christianity has forced upon us. Hegel once again stresses that God is not to be conceived in anthropomorphic terms, yet neither is he to be conceived as *other* than man. God is not the jealous personality or the transcendent Judge of the Old and New Testaments (respectively), nor is he the physical Creator of the universe. (Voltaire's Deism, Hegel argues, suffers from the concept of the "impersonal Being of the World.") God "is spirit," is "attainable in pure, speculative knowledge alone, is merely that knowledge, for he is Spirit." In other words, God is human thought, not to be distinguished from the human.

> Finite consciousness knows God only to the extent to which God knows himself. Spirit is nothing other than those who worship him.[51]

> Man knows God only insofar as God knows himself as man. The Spirit of man, whereby he knows God, is simply the spirit of God himself.[52]

What then does Hegel's conception of God admit which any atheist would not? To say the God exists is no more than to say that humanity exists. That is atheism.

It is the "middle term" of the Trinity that most exercises Hegel, for his concern is to show that the notion of "incarnation," which "contradicts all understanding"[53] is but another myth, if also one from which we have something essential to learn. The incarnation itself should not be conceived as "God appearing as a particular man," but rather, in Goethe's terms, as an allegory, "a particular considered only as an illustration, as an example of the universal" *(Maxims and Reflections).* All men are incarnations of God, and God is *nothing other* than all men. It is not the life of Jesus that is of religious significance, but his *death.* And the significance of his death is not his resurrection but rather an "abstract negativity," in which

> death ceases to signify what it means directly—the death of this individual— and becomes transfigured into the universality of the spirit, which lives in its own community and daily dies and rises again.[54]

Here is Hegel's answer to another puzzle inherited from Lessing: "How is it that Christianity can base the whole of its faith upon a historical accident?"[55] It is not a historical event that matters at all—and Hegel takes great pains to insist that the "historical representation of the incarnation . . . is something dead and devoid of knowledge," a "degradation" and a "reversion to the primitive."[56] Jesus was not a special case, but only "one of us";

> the dead Divine Man or Human God is implicitly self-consciousness; he has to become explicitly so.

Jesus as *another* is an "excluding unity," and the incarnation must be the self-knowledge of spirit as "equally universal self, as *all* self, the universal self-consciousness of a religious community, . . . not the individual by himself."[57] Hegel derides those representations of the "Father and Son"[58] and the Trinity and sarcastically muses whether it should perhaps be a "Quaternity, a four in one, . . . or perhaps even a Quinity."[59] But "counting is useless" since there is "indeterminateness regarding number" where "what is distinguished is truly one and single."[60] Hegel also rejects the "figurative" images of the "creation,"[61] the expulsion from paradise,[62] and the devil.[63] All of this is but an "imperfect form in which the immediate (i.e., ourselves as God) gets mediated and made universal,"[64] mere *"Form des Vorstellens"* which has not yet thrown off its mythological baggage to realize the "simplicity of the *Begriff.*"

What emerges from "Revealed Religion," not surprisingly, is the primacy of the "Holy Spirit," its mystery removed. For this Spirit is nothing other than Community *(Gemeinde),* a "brotherhood" of mutual human love, differing from state and society only in its lack of finitude in space and time. Not that this universal brotherhood is a reality yet, but, with the Enlightenment, the French Revolution, and Napoleon, it has appeared for the first time as a real possibility. The Holy Spirit, far from the mysterious images of orthodox theology, is our concrete and everyday ideal relations with the others, the disappearance of mutual distrust and hostility, and, as Hegel insists in the preface, it is the "individual forgetting himself, . . . expecting less from himself, and asking less for himself."[65]

Conclusion

Hopefully our impatience with theological niceties will be excused as an antidote for the excessive apologetics that have so long been forthcoming from the Hegelian "right." How long have we tolerated the benign sophistry exemplified by McTaggart when he argues at great length that "the orthodox Christian doctrines are not compatible with Hegel's teaching, but they are far closer to that teaching than the doctrines of any other religion known to history,"[66] or by Findlay when he argues that they finally confess—and it is now time for us to admit and to do so without apology or euphemism—that Hegel was no Christian.

This is not, again, to deny that Hegel (like Spinoza, for example) might be considered a man of reverence in some other sense. In his "lesser" *Logic,* for example, he tells us that "Speculative Truth means very much the same as what in special connection with religious experience and doctrines used to be called Mysticism."[68] But Hegel's "mysticism" is emphatically without mystery and his reverence is without God. Hegel has an undeniable reverence for thought, for reason, for life, and, above all, for Humanity. But he is not, in any sense, a defender of Christianity, much less its "greatest abstract thinker." He was, perhaps, the first great atheistic humanist of German philosophy (excepting possibly only Fichte). That was Hegel's secret. It was also the justified source of Kierkegaard's famous complaint.

NOTES

1. J. H. Stifling, *The Secret of Hegel,* 2 vols. (London, 1865).
2. But not only British commentators: cf. Emile Brehier, in his *Histoire de la philosophie;* "What is religion for Hegel? It is essential Christianty with its dogmas of the incar-

nate Word and the remission of sins." (vol. IV, p. 167) See also, Pannenberg in *Hegel Studien* (1970) and of course, B. Croce, *Cio che vive e cio che e morto della filosofia di Hegel* (Bari Laterza, 1927).

3. Stirling, op. cit. 78.

4. Ibid.

5. Ibid. 85.

6. J. M. E. M. McTaggart, *Studies in Hegelian Cosmology* (Cambridge: Cambridge University Press, 1901).

7. J. N. Findlay, *Hegel: A Re-examination* (New York: Colliers, 1962), p. 130. Reprinted as *The Philosophy of Hegel* (New York: Oxford University Press, 1977).

8. *Logic* (vol. 1 of the *Encyclopedia*), trans. by W. Wallace (Oxford University Press,) 1892: sect. 1, p. 3.

9. Dilthey, "Hegels Theologische Jugendschriften," [Berlin, 1905], ed. by Nohl, (Tübingen, 1907).

10. W. Kaufmann, *From Shakespeare to Existentialism* (New York: Doubleday Anchor, 1959), ch. 8.

11. "Where he had previously condemned Christianity for its irrationality, Hegel later celebrated Christian dogmas as ultimate philosophical truths in religious form. Instead of achieving a crowning synthesis, he unwittingly illustrated his own dialectic by overreacting against the views of his youth, and by going to the opposite extreme." Ibid., p. 161.

12. In Kaufmann, *Hegel* (New York: Doubleday Anchor, 1966), p. 366.

13. Heine, in Kaufmann, Ibid., p. 367.

14. See, for example, the variety of essays in D. Christensen, ed., *Hegel and the Philosophy of Religion* (The Hâgue: Nijhoff, 1970). The atheistic interpretation is scarcely mentioned, much less defended there. The Hegelian "left" has had its modern promoters, however, principally in Kojeve's lectures *(An Introduction to the Reading of Hegel)*, trans. James Nichols, Jr., ed. Allan Bloom [Ithaca N.Y.: Cornell University Press, cf. 1969], and in *Dieu est mort; Etude sur Hegel.*

15. E. Fackenheim, *The Religious Dimension of Hegel's Philosophy* (Bloomington, Ind.: Indiana University Press, 1967).

16. "Faith and Knowledge" ("Glauben und Wissen") was published in the *Critical Journal,* edited by Hegel and Schelling in the year 1802.

17. *Phen.* last page. All references to the *Phänomenologie des Geistes* will be abbreviated *"Phen."* and will refer to the J. Schulze edition of 1832 (Berlin: Duncker and Humblot, 1832). The translations are adapted from J. B. Baillie's *Phenomenology of Mind* (New York Harper and Row, 1966). Reference numbers are first to Schulze, then to Baillie (e.g., "509/685").

18. For example, in his much-read introduction to his Scribner's *Hegel: Selections* and in his own dialogal book on the *Phenomenology, (Hegel's Phenomenology).*

19. *Encyclopedia of the Philosophical Sciences* (abbreviated *"Encyclopedia'*) 564–71. Trans. by: W. Wallace, (Oxford: Oxford University Press, 1975). Reference numbers refer to paragraphs, not pages.

20. Translated and edited by E. B. Spiers and J. Burdon Sanderson (New York Humanities Press, 1962), 3 volumees (from Schulze, vols. 11 and 12). Abbreviated *"Lectures."*

21. The notion of "content" raises well-known problems in this context. I will clarify what I mean in the following discussion.

22. Quoted from Kaufmann, *Hegel.*

23. *Lectures on the Philosophy of History,* introduction, published separately as *Reason in History,* trans. R. S. Hartmann, (New York Bobbs-Merrill, 1953), p. 21.

24. *Phen.,* "Absolute Knowledge," 594/789.

25. *Lectures,* vol. III, 148.

26. See, e.g., *Encyclopedia,* 567–71.

27. I will use the neuter "humanity" wherever possible. Hegel uses "man," like most of his contemporaries.

28. *Lectures in the Philosophy of History,* trans. by R. S. Hartman, p. 20 (Schulze vol. 9, p. 20).

29. Lectures, vol. II, 45–48.

30. Cf. *Logic* II, 24.

31. op. cit. 251.

32. op. cit. 131.

33. See ch. VII, C. 592/783.

34. Scholars sometimes object to the use of unpublished manuscripts in establishing a thinker's overall intentions. Fackenheim, for example, derides the "idolizers of these Early Theological Writings" (op. cit. p. 156). But if our suspicions are correct regarding Hegel's covert atheism, we should trust his imprudent unpublished assertions at least as much as we trust his published works. (E. Fackenheim, *The Religious Dimension of Hegel's Philosophy* (Bloomington: Indiana Univ. Press, 1967).

35. All references to Hegel's "Theologische Jugendschriften" are to Nohl's edition (Tübingen, 1907) followed by an English translation reference; "WK"—W. Kaufmann, *From Shakespeare to Existentialism* (New York: Doubleday, 1959), ch. 8; "Knox"— *Hegel: On Christianity,* trans. by T. M. Knox (Philadelphia: University at Pennsylvania Press, 1971). A very different sort of account is argued by H. S. Harris, *Hegel's Development,* (Oxford: Oxford University Press of *Hegel's Development* 1972), who also provides a translation of this first essay.

36. 33. WK 135.

37. *Phen.* 513–690.

38. Ibid., 509–17/685–94.

39. Ibid., 509/685.

40. Especially vol. I, pp. 6–48: "The Relation of the Philosophy of Religion to Its Presuppositions and to the Principles of the Time."

41. Lessing's *Education of Mankind* is Hegel's text here. The idea that "there can be no religion, only religions" gives rise to obvious paradoxes for any given believer, for insofar as he believes his own religion is not the true religion, he is not a believer, but if he does insist upon the truth of his own faith, he cannot open himself up to the co-validity of opposed faith. Emil Fackenheim (op. cit.) exercises himself considerably over this paradox.

42. *Das unglückliche Bewusstsein* in ch. IV (pp. 158–73/251–67).

43. E.g., 160–253; cf. Findlay, op. cit., p. 99f.

44. *Phen.* 164/257.

45. Ibid., 171–265.

46. Consider the second of his early essays, "The Life of Jesus," which represents a crude attempt to salvage the image of Jesus by separating him from the religion that bears his name.

47. "Die Schöne Seele: das Böse und seine Verzeihung;" pp. 495–508/665–97.

48. Cf. the *Early Manuscripts,* p. 289/Knox 239.

49. *"Die Offenbare Religion"* (Phenomenology), pp. 561–93/750–85; *Encyclopedia* VII, sect. III, sub-sect. B, para. 564–71; *Lectures,* vol. III, p. III, pp. 1–151 (vol. II, pp. 192–356).

50. *Phen.,* 569ff/758ff.

51. *Lectures* II, 327.

52. *Lectures* II, 496.

53. *Lectures* III, 76; another agreement with Kierkegaard.

54. *Phenomenology* 587/780.

55. Kierkegaard's *Concluding Unscientific Postscript,* trans. by Lowrie and Swenson (Princeton, N.J.: Cf. Princeton University Press, 1941) bk. II, pt. 1, ch. ii, p. 3.

56. *Phen.*, 578, 573/763, 763.

57. Ibid., 573/763.

58. Ibid., 577/767 and 581/771.

59. Ibid.

60. Ibid., 581–2/772 I have used a simlar "indeterminateness" argument concerning Hegel's concept of *Geist*. ("Hegel's Concept of *Geist*" *Review of Metaphysics,* 1970) [chapter 1 in this collection].

61. Ibid., 579/769.

62. Ibid., 580/770–1. Compare *Logic* II, 24, "Now while we accept the dogma, we must give up the setting."

63. *Phen.*, 582f./773.

64. Ibid., 573/763.

65. Ibid., 58/130.

66. Op. cit., 349.

67. Op. cit., 349.

68. *Logic* VI sect. 82.

5

Kierkegaard and
Subjective Truth

Kierkegaard said of Hegel: He reminds me of someone who builds an
enormous castle but lives himself in a storehouse next to the construction. The mind, by the same token, dwells in the modest quarters of the
skull.

—Adam Zagajewski

Viewed in the context of the history of philosophy, Søren Kierkegaard strikes a
paradoxical pose. He attacks philosophy in general and Hegel in particular; yet
his attack on philosophy is a philosophical attack, and his central argument
against Hegel is a gift from Schelling, Hegel's one-time friend and colleague
turned jealous critic. Kierkegaard viciously attacks Christianity, but does so in
the defense of "becoming a Christian." He assails the "public," and in so doing
becomes a public celebrity. He decries anonymity, but in works which are typically written—not quite anonymously—but pseudonymously, with an aim of dis-
guising his opinions, if not his authorship. And yet the paradox is never without
purpose, Kierkegaard keeps reminding us. The individual is a paradox, and if the
whole of philosophy and what presents itself as Christianity tries to do without
that paradox, so much the worse for them. Indeed, the whole of Kierkegaard's
career might be partially construed as an attack on the supposed clarity and rationality of philosophy and theology, an attack on the notion of "objective truth"—
truth that is common, true for anyone and everyone. Kierkegaard had little regard
for such a promiscuous theory of truth, and he came to have contempt for much
that was defended under the banner of objectivity and rationality, philosophy and
theology in particular. He would make no such claims for his own philosophy. It
was enough that his truths were true *for him*—and for an undetermined legion of
individual readers.

Subjective and Objective Truths

The concept of "objective truth" and its complement, subjective truth," have a
rich but confused ancestry. Kant ambiguously uses the contrast between "objec-

tive" and "subjective" to mark the distinction between the physical and the mental, on the one hand, and, on the other, between what is universal and necessary in contrast to what is merely believed or "felt" by the individual. Between the two distinctions lies the confusion whether "objective truth" means independent of any *particular* subject or rather independent of *any* subject. Hegel resolves the ambiguity; "objective truth" is independence from any *particular* subject. Moreover, "objective truth" is ambiguously treated in Kant to signify any "scientific" *fact,* including empirical facts, and alternatively to include only necessary or a priori truths ("thought"). Again, Hegel answers Kant, objective truth"—that is, philosophical truth—can lie only in the "concept" or "the idea." "Objective truth" as it emerges from Hegel's philosophy, is truth that is suprapersonal, necessarily (conceptually) true and universal. "Subjective truth" is belief that is not necessarily true, not universally acceptable, and perhaps "objectively false." Every objective truth also might be said to be subjective in that it is held by an individual, but "subjective truth" has a stronger meaning, according to which a truth is subjective only if it is not objective. In Kierkegaard's writings, this does not mean that it is objectively false; it may simply be objectively *uncertain.* Objective truth is truth for anyone; subjective truth is truth for an individual.

Hegel was obsessed with the demand that his philosophy should be more than merely true *for him,* or even merely true from a perspective that he shared with many others. If a proposition were one-sided, prejudiced, or based upon presuppositions, it could not be a truth in his philosophy. Kant refused to accept his analysis of the forms and concepts of consciousness or merely the forms and concepts of *his* consciousness; they were the a priori forms and *categories* of "consciousness in general." Hegel eliminated the individual from philosophy altogether through introduction of a literally general consciousness or *Geist.* Philosophical or "objective truths" are true for anyone; the role of the philosopher who discovers or defends them is strictly "accidental." Objective truth has nothing to do with particular individuals. Kierkegaard agrees with this characterization of "objective truth" or "abstract thought." It is "thought without a thinker." Abstract thought ignores everything except the thought, and only the thought is, and is in its own medium.

> The way of objective reflection makes the subject accidental, and thereby transforms existence into something indifferent, something vanishing. . . . It leads to abstract thought, to mathematics, to historical knowledge of different kinds, and always it leads away from the subject whose existence or non-existence, and from the objective point of view, quite rightly, becomes infinitely indifferent. Quite rightly, since, as Hamlet says, existence has only subjective significance.[1]

But suppose a thinker is not interested in "abstract thought" or "consciousness in general."

> What I really lack is to be clear in my mind *what I am to do,* not what I am to know, except insofar as a certain understanding must precede every action . . . the thing is to find a truth which is true *for me,* to find *the idea for which I can live and die.*[2]

And what can objective truth provide?

> What would be the use of discovering so-called objective truth, of working
> through all the systems of philosophy ... to construct a *world in which I do
> not live* but only hold up for the view of others.[8]

Accordingly, Kierkegaard restricts his attention to "subjective truth" or
"concrete thought," "thought with a relation to a thinker." Whereas objective
thought focuses on the concept, the idea, the abstract thought, subjective truth
focuses upon the individual thinker.

> When the question of truth is raised in an objective manner, reflection is
> directed objectively to the truth as an object to which the knower is related.
> Reflection is not focused on the relationship, however, but upon the question
> whether it is the truth to which the knower is related. If only the object to
> which he is related is the truth, the subject is accounted to be in the truth.
> When the question of truth is raised subjectively, reflection is directed subjec-
> tively to the nature of the individual's relationship; if only the mode of this
> relationship is in the truth, even if he should happen to be thus related to what
> is not true.[4]

Thus, subjective truth is true even if what is believed is objectively false. In
fact, Kierkegaard goes so far as to argue that it is true *because* it is objectively
false or objectively uncertain:

> When subjectivity, inwardness, is the truth, the truth becomes objectively a
> paradox; and the fact that the truth is objectively a paradox shows in its turn
> that subjectivity is the truth.[5]

And so, for Kierkegaard, "subjective truth" is not an inferior form of truth at all,
but *the* truth. "Truth is subjectivity."

Is "Subjective Truth" Unintelligible?

Does the notion of "subjective truth" make sense? The usual view is that the truth
is necessarily independent of anyone's accepting it as truth. What is believed to
be true varies from time to time, place to place, person to person, but what is true
does not. Perhaps we can never know what is true, or perhaps—even if we do
believe the truth—we shall never have any way of knowing that we know it. But
truth, according to this strong argument, is independent of any and all persons'
acceptance of that truth. If "subjective truth" is "truth for an individual," that
can only mean "it is true and this person believes it." If a person believes what
is not true, there is no truth at all.

One might weaken this argument by relating truth to rationality, as in Kant
and Hegel, such that truth is independent of any *particular* person's acceptance
of it but not of all possible persons. On this account, it is impossible that no one
could ever know the truth, but it must always be possible for more than one person to accept the same truth. But Kierkegaard says that subjective truth is truth
for one and one alone. On this view, " subjective truth" might be interpreted to

mean "believed by S. K. but has not *in fact* been accepted by anyone else (although it would be if they listened to him)." But there cannot be a truth which *could not* be for anyone else. "Subjective truth" cannot be truth.

Perhaps we can save Kierkegaard's notion in this way: "Subjective truth" does not claim to state a truth about the world, but to state a truth about S. K. Thus, Kierkegaard's claims that he is writing autobiography should be taken seriously. A "subjective truth" is a psychological truth about the author. The object of the author's belief may be false, but it is true that the author has that belief. This account could also explain how it is that "subjective truth" is for only one person. Only one person can "have" his own psychological states, and so only he can ("directly") know them. On this account, subjective truth becomes a mere species of objective truth, and, consequently, the central distinction between "objective" and "subjective" truth is lost. No doubt the "subjective truths" of Kierkegaard's writings—in some but certainly not all cases—can be recast as true statements about Kierkegaard's beliefs. But to say that "subjective truths" are truths *about* the author is not yet to say that they are true *for* the author and the author *only*. And this is the characterization of "subjective truth." Nor are they truths (like psychological reports) whose *objects* are available only to the author. The objects of subjective truths, for example, could be God or principles of morality, which are available to others besides the author. And, as Kierkegaard's characterization of subjective truth has told us, subjectivity does not lie in *what* is believed in any case, but in the *relationship* between the individual and what he believes. Subjective truth cannot be merely "psychological" truth.[6]

Whether "truth" is independent of persons or independent of any particular persons, it would appear that there can be no such truth as "subjective truth." Any analysis of truth adequate to the explication of the truth of principles like, "it is more than ninety million miles from here to the sun" or "the square of the hypotenuse of a right triangle is equal to the sum of the squares of the other two sides" will yield an analysis upon which the notion of "subjective truth" is a self-contradiction. Whether it be a correspondence, coherence, semantic, or phenomenological analysis of "truth," there can be no truth solely for an individual.

Accordingly, Kierkegaard's theory has been dismissed by many philosophers who have agreed that "objective truth" is as redundant as "five-cornered pentagon." Bertrand Russell, for example, simply dimisses all "subjectification of truth" as not only wrongheaded but as a dangerous perversion. Alasdair MacIntyre—a sympathetic commentator—leaves Kierkegaard with the accusation:

> If I hold that truth is subjectivity, what status am I to give to the denial of the proposition that truth is subjectivity? If I produce arguments to refute this denial I appear committed to the view that there are criteria by appeal to which the truth about truth can be vindicated. If I refuse to produce arguments, on the grounds that there can be neither argument nor criteria in such a case, then I appear committed to the view that any view embraced with sufficient subjective passion is as warranted as any other in respect of truth, including the view that truth is not subjectivity. This inescapable dilemma is never faced by Kierkegaard and consequently he remains trapped by it.[7]

What can Kierkegaard respond to all of this? It is true, as MacIntyre claims, that Kierkegaard never faced this dilemma. But it is not true that he remains trapped by it. What has not been understood is the scope and the nature of the concept of "subjective truth." What makes the problem more difficult is the fact that Kierkegaard appears to be perfectly willing to accept all such arguments at face value but simply dismiss them as irrelevant. His strategy is not to defend his notion of subjective truth against the claim that "truth is objective," but to always shift the locus of the argument from "logic" to "life," from science to ethics. "Objective truths," he argues, are simply "indifferent": they make no difference *for me:* "In the case of a mathematical proposition the objectivity is given, but for this reason the truth of such a proposition is also an indifferent truth."[8] Elsewhere, he simply denies the reality of the knowing subject, as if with the shift in emphasis he could thus eliminate the reality of his critics and dissolve the arguments against him.

> The real subject is not the cognitive subject . . . the real subject is the ethically existing subject.[9]

Against the persuasive claim that "truth is objectivity," Kierkegaard complains that "objective truth" is not interesting, is not personal, does not tell us how to live, and is of no particular concern for me. Against the philosophers of "objective truth" (notably Hegel), Kierkegaard hurls his bitterest ad hominem attacks. He argues, for example, that philosophers who talk about "objective truth" "don't know how to live" and "exist in quite different categories for everyday purposes from those in which they speculate." But the problem remains. What sense is there in speaking of "subjective truth" if such a notion is openly self-contradictory? Why not rather call them "false but edifying personal maxims to live by," or simply, after Kant, "subjective maxims"? I would like to argue that "subjective truth," in its appropriate context, can be interpreted with a good deal of literal sense.

Toward a Broader Sense of Truth

I think we can open up a way of defense for Kierkegaard if we begin by deflating the bloatedly epistemological notion of "truth" that is operating here. In Hegel's philosophy, "truth" covers far more ground than the subject matter of Kant's first *Critique.* There is truth in morality, art, and music as well as in natural science and mathematics. Truth is practical as well as theoretical. (In fact, some commentators, e.g., Josiah Royce, have interpreted Hegel's entire *Phenomenology* as an exercise in "practical" Reason.) Truth is the *goal* of a human endeavor. Scientific truth is one kind of truth. But morality, religion, art, and music have their truths as well. This is not merely to say that there are truths *about* morality, religion, art, and music. In morality, truth is right action and wisdom; in religion, the truth is a relationship with God; in art and music, truth is beauty. In Kierkegaard's philosophy, "truth" is used in this extended sense.

The truths of morality, religion, art, and music are very different from the truths of science and mathematics, and not only in the sense that the enterprises and consequently the goals are different. Kant had drawn sharp distinctions between theory and practice, theoretical reason and practical reason, knowledge and action. Not only are theory and knowledge different from practice and action, but they are inhabitants of different "worlds." In Kant's theory, theory and knowledge are definitive of a "sensible world," the subject of which is a "transcendental" or "knowing" ego. Practice and action are definitive of an "intelligible world," the subject of which is a willing agent. Although it would seem that in some sense the self that knows ought to be identical to the self that acts, this identity is never established in Kant's philosophy. And though it would also seem that the objects that I know are in some sense identical to the objects I act upon, this identity is never established either. Instead, Kant instructs us that we are operating from two distinct "'standpoints," each exclusive of the other. Hegel, Fichte, and Kierkegaard's teacher, Schelling, had attempted to break down these sharp distinctions, return to a single conception of "Reason" and "consciousness" and formulate conceptions embodying both knowledge and action. Kierkegaard returns to the Kantian position and draws an equally sharp distinction between theoretical (purely intellectual) and practical (personal) contexts. But he also accepts the expanded Hegelian notion of "truth." Thus he distinguishes, as Kant does not, two kinds of truth. Perhaps he might better have called them "theoretical truth" and "practical truth," or perhaps "right knowledge" and "right action." But Kierkegaard called them "objective truth" and "subjective truth." He does not reject objective truth, or science, mathematics, and abstract theory in their proper domain (or "medium"). He rejects only the idea that they provide the only kind of truth. ("I always say: all honor to the sciences, etc. But the thing is. . . .") In his defense of subjective truth, however, Kierkegaard cannot avoid the polemical push of the pendulum the other way, and so he often talks as if there is no objective truth or as if objective truth is of no interest whatsoever. Typically, he presents the two standpoints as an exclusive choice:

> Is he a human being, or is he speculative philosophy in the abstract? But if he is a human being, then he is also an existing individual. Two ways, in general, are open for an existing individual: *Either* he can do his utmost to forget that he is an existing individual, . . . *Or* he can concentrate his entire energy upon the fact that he is an existing individual. It is from this side, in the first instance . . . that objection must be made to modern philosophy; . . . its having forgotten, in a sort of world-historical absent mindedness, what it means to be a human being.[10]

But this extreme application of Kant's theory is not consistently argued by Kierkegaard, nor could it be, since even he sees that "a certain understanding must precede every action." In spite of his *Either/Or* philosophy, Kierkegaard is committed to the Kantian model in which you must have *both* knowledge *and* action. But there can be no doubt which is to be master and which is to serve in Kierkegaard's philosophy. "To exist" for him is precisely to act: to know—*separated from action*—is precisely to avoid "existing."

Kant's distinction between theory and practice combined with Hegel's extended notion of "truth" gives us a basis for understanding Kierkegaard's notion of "subjective truth." But the distinction between "theory" and "practice" is surely not parallel to the distinction between "objective" and "subjective" in Kant's writings. For Kant, "objectivity" encompasses both theory and practice in

the form of Reason. Where Kant would want to share the responsbility for objectivity between theoretical and practical Reason, Hegel would delegate it to Reason simply. For both philosophers, "objectivity" is not confined to what we
know, and what we do is not merely "subjective." For Kant and Hegel, practice
as well as theory is constrained by rules of Reason, impersonal or at least suprapersonal criteria that make no reference to any particular agent. For Kierkegaard,
"subjective truth" applies only in the absence of such rules, and so practice—in
Kant and Hegel's sense—cannot be "subjective."

Kierkegaard accepts the voluntaristic Kantian tradition according to which
moral principles (and values in general) are determined by choice (or by "the
Will") and not by appeal to "the facts." But he rejects the Kantian idea that there
are "rational" or "objective" constraints upon what can be chosen. It was Kant,
not a Dostoyevsky, who taught Kierkegaard that a human being was unique in
that only he could "posit any end whatsoever." And Kierkegaard takes this
"could" to be not only the "could" that separates the standpoint of action from
the deterministic standpoint of knowledge but the "could" of "without rational
constraint" as well. We know that it is the realm of practice in which Kierkegaard
seeks to apply his notion of "subjective truth." What he does, therefore, is accept
the rigid Kantian distinction between theory and practice, but then he rejects the
Kantian distinction between "objectivity" and "subjectivity." Only knowledge is
objective: and so it is true, for knowledge, that "truth is objective." But "objectivity" is limited to knowledge contexts. Practice is subjective. (Compare Hegel;
in his very first written essay, "Folk Religion and Christianity" (1795), Hegel also
forces an equivalence between "practice" and "subjectivity.")

The parallels between objectivity and subjectivity and knowledge and action
appear to lead us towards an initial understanding of Kierkegaard's insistence
that objective truth focuses on *what* is held to be true while subjective truth
focuses upon the *manner* in which it is held to be true (or elsewhere, the *relationship* between the individual and what is true). In knowledge contexts, we are
interested in what is known—in the idea, the concept, the hypothesis, the theory.
In action contexts, we are interested in what is done. But this cannot be quite
right, for Kierkegaard as well as Kant and Hegel insist that action be action on
principle and not whimsical or imitative. Although Kierkegaard often states that
choices are "arbitrary" or "irrational," it is not to be thought that they are such
in the sense that they are not on principle. One does not simply choose an action
or a course of action. One chooses a way of life ("a sphere of existence," a "mode
of existence"). What distinguishes true existence from "so-called existence" (that
sense of "existence" which is similar to the sense of "driving" in "he was driving
the wagon while he slept") is action on self-chosen principle. But this means that
the action, the course of action and the entire "sphere of existence" are *what* is
chosen and not the manner of choice. Therefore, the distinction between knowledge and action is not yet sufficient to explain Kierkegaard's insistence on the
distinction between the *what* of objectivity and the *how* of subjectivity. But Kierkegaard does not rest his analysis of choice-contexts ("Existence") with an analsis
of *what* is chosen or *what* is done. For Kierkegaard as for Kant, what is ultimately
good is not *what* is done but a "good will." Of course, for Kant the will was good
only if it chose the correct (i.e., rational) principle. But for Kierkegaard, one could
speak of a good "choosing" independently of any concern for what was chosen.

To be an individual, to exist, is to choose, and it is the choosing, not the choice, that needs further analysis.

Subjective Truth as Performative

If we leave nineteenth-century Europe and move a century, a continent, and light-years in philosophical temperament away from Kierkegaard, I believe that we can find a vehicle for understanding Kierkegaard's notion of "subjective truth" which fills in the gaps of the rough sketch we have formulated in Kantian Hegelian terminology. In recent British philosophy, J. L. Austin has drawn a now celebrated distinction between functions of statements which corresponds in an interesting and profound way to Kierkegaard's distinction between "objectivity" and "subjectivity." Austin distinguishes the "constantive" or "descriptive" functions of statments or "speech acts" and the "performative" functions. Against the long-standing philosophical prejudice that all statements are statements of description and the truth of statements is a function of their "truly" describing, Austin argues that many statements do not describe and are neither true nor false.

> We have not got to go very far back in the history of philosophy to find philosophers assuming more or less as a matter of course that the sole business, the sole interesting business of any utterance—that is, of anything we say—is to be true or at least false.[11]

On the basis of this "assumption," the logical positivists had dismissed the entire corpus of those "subjective" interests which preoccupy Kierkegaard as "meaningless" or "nonsense." In their strict sense of "description," propositions of ethics, aesthetics, and religion do not strictly describe anything. But Austin, against the positivists, suggests that many speech acts—including those which state Kierkegaard's "subjective truths"—are not descriptive at all; their "meaning" lies in a different direction. In such acts, "a person is *doing* something rather than merely *saying* something. For example, in the course of a marriage ceremony one says "I do." But "When I say 'I do,' I am not reporting on a marriage, I am indulging in it."[12] Kierkegaard's view of marriage as a whole is remarkably parallel to what Austin says of the speech aspect of the ceremony. Getting married is not coming to *know* or describe anything new about oneself or one's situation; it is *doing* something. What makes marriage "subjective" is that it involves a doing—a commitment. It is true, of course, that one can know that he is getting married, just as it is true that others can know that one is. Austin is perfectly aware that "I take this woman as my lawful wedded wife" entails certain descriptions, and that "he takes this woman to be his lawful wedded wife" is clearly a description. But what must be pointed out is that "I take . . ." cannot be thought of as *mere* description. Because he maintains such a rigid distinction between knowing and doing, Kierkegaard separates the "descriptive" from the "performance" aspects of marriage and minimizes the former while exaggerating the latter. Getting married is something one *does,* not something one *knows* about. Planning to get married (becoming engaged) is making a commitment, not making a prediction.

Similarly, the statement, "I promise . . ." is not a description of my promising. It is the making of a promise. It would be inappropriate to ask how I *know* that I have promised. In the logical positivist's sense, "I promise . . ." does not describe anything that could be verified or falsified, so the statement would be meaningless. But the meaning of such statements, Austin argues, does not lie in their descriptive content, but in the acts they are used to perform. Again, "I hereby vow to give up drinking for a month" is not a prediction about my future behavior. If I begin drinking after a week, it does not show that my vow was false or that I did not vow at all. "I hereby vow . . ." is the making of a vow. It is not a prediction and cannot turn out to be either true or false.

It is peculiar that Austin's own theory of truth remained so primitive and un-Hegelian. As a matter of fact, he held truth to be correspondence to statements of fact (descriptions), which is odd because he so clearly saw that the functions of statements far exceed that simple "mapping" function. Austin freely extended the meaning of "meaning " beyond the restrictions of the positivists, but he left the concepts of "true" and "false" where they were. But we can easily see how a Hegelian conception of "truth" could be applied to Austin's theory to yield notions of "descriptive truth" and "performance truth" to parallel the notions of "descriptive act" and "performance act." Furthermore, we can place the Austinian theory in a nineteenth-century post-Kantian context such that what is true is no longer limited to statements and "act" is no longer limited to "speech act." What is descriptively true would then be Kant's "thoughts" or Hegel's "Ideas"; the "act of knowing" (an awkward expression) would be understanding and reason (i.e., the application of concepts to experience). What is performatively true would then be intentions ("The Will"); the act would be the forming of the intention, a volition, or an act of Will. Hegel himself would refuse to draw these distinctions, since he would maintain that every "form of consciousness" is *both* descriptive and performative, or, in a sense, both "in itself" and "for itself." (From these notions Martin Heidegger and Jean-Paul Sartre will restage Kierkegaard in a phenomenological setting with the notions of "facticity" and *"Existenz"* or "transcendence" replacing the notions of "descriptive truth" and "performative truth.") For Kierkegaard, of course, what we are here calling "descriptive truth" will turn out to be his "objective truth"; what we are calling "performative truth" will turn out to be his "subjective truth."

Descriptive or objective truth has impersonal or at least suprapersonal criteria of "correctness." "The earth is more than ninety million miles from the sun" is not true because I say it is, regardless of who I am, how firmly I believe it, or what I might have done to demonstrate it. This proposition is true because it is a fact that the earth is more than ninety million miles from the sun. Similarly, the Pythagorean theorem is not true because *Pythagoras* proved it, but because the Pythagorean theorem is provable at any time and any place by anyone who has the ability to do so. *It is true* that the earth is so far from the sun, and the Pythagorean theorem is true. Particular individuals are irrelevant to descriptive truth. The distance from earth to sun is independent of astronomers. The Pythagorean theorem has no dependence upon Pythagoras.

Performatives, on the other hand, cannot be impersonal or suprapersonal. *My* marriage is *mine* in a sense in which *the* Pythagorean theorem cannot be mine. This is not to say that my wife is mine, or even that the relationship between my wife and me is mine (although, to be sure, I am an essential part of it). What is mine is the commitment of marriage. Of course, one can speak abstractly of "the commitment of marriage," and one can describe me as "married." But *my* commitment of marriage is not an instance of *the* commitment of marriage in the sense that the theorem on *this* piece of paper is an instance of *the* Pythagorean theorem. While there is the fact that I am married, that is never merely a fact *for me.* Of my marriage, I must always say, "This is *my* choice."

The case of marriage is complicated by the fact that it is a legal contract as well as a personal commitment. Kierkegaard, of course, took the personal commitment of marriage to be its significance, not the legal aspect. If we ignore the legalities, then what is true of performative truth in marriage is that "thinking makes it so." If *I* decide to cancel my commitment, I am *ipso facto* not married. If *I* promise . . . , I am *ipso facto* promised. This is not to say, of course, that I similarly cancel out the consequences of my having been married. And if I decide to abandon my commitment to keep a promise, I have not cancelled the promise. But performative truth is distinguished from descriptive truth in that the former is always personal and involves what I do while the latter is always impersonal and has nothing to do with what I or any other subject happens to do. If I do nothing, there is no performative truth; descriptive truth is *there* even if I do nothing to find it. Someone else can tell me a descriptive truth: I must create my own performative truth. It is only in the extraordinary case (involving a long time lag and amnesia) that it makes sense to say of me that "I found out that I was married" or "I found out that I had promised. . . ." Of course, if one looks not at the performative truth but at the descriptive truth that one is called "married" in this society if he says "I do" in the appropriate circumstancs, then of course we can imagine a case in which an ignorant visitor "finds out" that he is married. Or if we make a rule that a person has made a promise whenever he states an intention, then of course we will catch someone making a promise unwittingly. But "performative truth" is a first-person notion, not only in the sense that a person can only perform for himself (marry for himself, promise for himself) but in the sense that the person himself must be able to identify the act he is performing. In the performative sense, a man is not married if he does not recognize that he is married: a man has not promised if he does not recognize that he has promised. Of course, this point demonstrates as well the impossibility of keeping knowledge claims (descriptive truth) out of the very heart of performative truth. But we have already admitted Kierkegaard's (and perhaps Austin's) overreaction on this point: there is no need to press it further.

Descriptive truth depends upon *what* is true; that much is clear. In what sense can we say that performative truth depends upon "*how* a truth is held" or "the relationship of the individual to the truth"? Of course, it is simply false to talk as if performative truth has no object: an action, a course of action, a way of life—all these function as *what* is chosen, and it is gross falsification of Kierkegaard's philosophy to suppose that these are unimportant to him. But what is true with respect to performative truth is the relative importance of the manner of choice, "relative" not to the object of choice but to the small importance allotted to the manner of discovery in descriptive truth. (One can still ask of Karl Popper whether there is a "logic" of scientific discovery as well as of explanation). Of course, one can criticize a scientist's laboratory techniques, his bad mathematics, his failure to keep up a remote interest in his colleagues' work—all this has nothing to do with the (performative) truth.

Of "performatives," Austin says that they are not to be characterized as "correct" and "incorrect," "true" or "false," but as "happy" and "unhappy," "appropriate" and "inappropriate," "sincere" and "insincere," "successful" and "unsuccessful."[13] The "manner" of an utterance—that is, the circumstances surrounding it—are definitive of the "success" of the act. Sometimes, inappropriate circumstances cause a "misfire"; for example,

> Suppose that, living in a country like our own, we wish to divorce our wife. We may try standing her in front of us squarely, in a voice loud enough for all to hear, and saying,"I divorce you." Now this procedure is not accepted.[14]

> Or consider the case in which I say "I appoint you consul," and it turns out that you have been appointed already— or perhaps it may even transpire that you are a horse.[15]

But Kierkegaard is least interested in these cases in which there is some social or legal convention which is not fulfilled. More important for him is the class of "utterances gone wrong" which Austin characterizes as lacking certain requisite beliefs, feelings, or intentions:

> . . . there is insincerity.
> Take for example, the expression "I congratulate you." This is designed for use by people who are glad that the person addressed has achieved a certain feat, believe that he was personally responsible for the success and so on. If I say "I congratulate you" when I'm not pleased or when I don't believe that the credit was yours, then there is insincerity. Likewise if I say I promise to do something without the least intention of doing it or without believing it feasible. . . . We should not say that I didn't in fact promise, but rather that I did promise but promised insincerely.[16]

Of course, I must take into some account what I have promised or whom I have married, but I must first of all take into account whether I have promised or married. If I fail to prove the Pythagorean theorem, the theorem is still true. But if I fail to make my promise, there is nothing promised, and if I fail to get married there is no marriage. Performatives are distinguished by the fact that whether there is "truth" at all depends upon the "manner in which one obtains the truth."

Austin's characterization of the "manner" or circumstances of "utterance" illuminates in a clear if slightly dull way the sense in which what we are now calling "performance truth" depends upon the "manner" of performance. Because of his general philosophical temperament, Austin is largely concerned with various conventions that surround performatives in a social context. Kierkegaard, of course, could not be less interested in the "manner" of performance in *this* sense. The "context" of performance for Kierkegaard is strictly an *individual* context. For the purposes of "performative truth," it would not matter whether the individual were at a formal state dinner or lost in a jungle. But then, there is an important difference in emphasis between Kierkegaard and Austin, which might lead to serious misunderstanding. Getting married is surely not merely a matter of saying a few words.

> But the one thing we must not suppose is that what is needed in addition to the saying of the words in such cases is the performance of some internal spiritual act, of which the words are then to be the report.[17]

For Austin, it is the social context that is "needed in addition." But, for Kierkegaard, the social context is irrelevant (except, of course, as it is needed as a context to carry through certain choices, e.g., to get married, to be a Don Juan or a Socrates). Moreover, for Kierkegaard it is precisely "some internal spiritual act" that constitutes performative truth. But this apparent disagreement can be resolved. We have already seen that Austin agrees that—in many acts—the beliefs, feelings, and intentions of the performer are part of the context for the "felicity" and "infelicity" of the act. In general, the *sincerity* for the act is one of its properties. But this would appear to indicate that Austin is not maintaining that a performance is merely action in the appropriate context, but that some sort of "internal spiritual act" is necessary as well. What interests him, however, is that the *words* of the ceremony not be construed as a *report* of this act. Words, feelings, and social context function together to constitute the act of marriage. Our Hegelian interpretation of Austin would make some of these concerns irrelevant, for the Hegelian-Austinian notion of "performative truth" applies indiscriminately to the "words" (the "utterance") and the "internal spiritual act." So interpreted, we should surely agree that the "truth" of a marriage depends as much upon what the two people *feel* and quietly *resolve* to themselves as upon the social context of the marriage ceremony.

One way to interpret "subjective truth," endorsed by Kierkegaard, is to take subjective truths not as beliefs but as emotions. This is what he means, for example, when he insists on "passionate inwardness" as the mark of subjective truth. But without going into detail here, one can argue that a proper understanding of emotions goes quite well with this analysis of subjective truths as performatives.[18] This does not make sense, of course, if one endorses the traditional view of emotions as mere "feelings" of physiological origin. But if an emotion is a certain kind of judgment, a personal way of constituting the world, then we could show how it is that subjective truths—as emotional truths—are performatives in a private sense that is clearly vital to Kierkegaard but inappropriate to the Austinian analysis. The sort of personal resolve demanded by Kierkegaard does have its context, but that context consists mainly of other emotions and commitments as well as beliefs and (less significant) an accurate perception of the surrounding social context. Indeed, the private world of the emotions and the personal judgments that constitute them are so important for Kierkegaard that the objective world in which truth is determined impersonally and apart from the passions fades from view and becomes only a backdrop for the quite dramatic personal performances that give us the truth, the only real truth for "an existing human being"—subjective truth.

Using our Hegelian-Austinian notion of "performative truth," we now have a firm basis for interpretation of Kierkegaard's notion of "subjective truth." A subjective truth is what we have been calling a "performative truth." An objective truth is what we have been calling a "descriptive truth." Objective truth is "impersonal," and evaluated by looking past the knower and his way of knowing to the facts, the evidence, or the proof. Objective truths are anonymous, "thoughts without a thinker." Subjective truth is the success of a personal performance. There cannot be an anonymous performance (although there could be a performance where the identity of the performer was hidden from others). The object of subjective truth can be shared (we can accept the same moral principles, believe in the same God), but the subjective truth itself (the performance) cannot be. Thus we have interpreted Kierkegaard's central notion in a literally intelligible way. Perhaps it is odd that we have had to span an enormous philosophical distance to do so; the theory of performatives is superficially alien to the ninteenth century. The Hegelian notion of "truth" is surely alien to many contemporary philosophers. But the connection between the two seems to give us exactly what is needed to provide us with a conception of "subjective truth" which is not subject to the traditional objections. Subjecitve truths are not objectively true, but that is not to say that they are objectively false. They are performances, not propositions, and therefore neither true nor false (in the sense in which propositions are true or false). Russell's fears for the dangers of the "subjectification of truth" are unfounded in the case of Kierkegaard. Subjective truth is not intended to *replace* objectivity.

MacIntyre's "inescapable dilemma" is not a dilemma at all. The proposition that truth is subjectivity is itself not presented as a subjective truth. It is argued for and defended as objectively true, that is, true for everyone. (It is argued to be true, for instance, for Hegel, who would not accept it as true.) "Truth is subjectivity" does not mean that every proposition (including this one or its negation) is true subjectively. Subjective truth is not to be contrasted with either subjective or objective falsity. The contrary of subjective truth is "inauthenticity," not falsity.

Accordingly, it should be clear how "subjective truth," so interpreted, links up with Kierkegaard's other concepts of "commitment," "becoming," "making a beginning," "inwardness," and "passion." And yet it must not be thought that subjective truth is to be characterized as a species of psychological (as opposed to "logical") truth. This popular attempt to save Kierkegaard's notion only succeeds in destroying it. If a subjective truth is a truth about the psychology of the author, then one looses what is most valuable in his analysis. Falling back once again on an "objective" proposition that is either true or false, the central ideas of choice and commitment become nonsensically reduced to truthful reports of "inner" episodes. But a commitment is not a report, and a subjective truth is not a fact of individual psychology. A subjective truth is not a fact of any kind: it is something that one does, not something that one knows.

NOTES

1. Kierkegaard, *Concluding Unscientific Postscript*, trans. by D. Swenson and W. Lowrie (Princeton, N.J.: Princeton University Press, 1941), p. 183. There is always a problem in identifying Kierkegaard with the author of these pseudonymous works. I have taken care in what follows to limit my textual appeals to those theses which do—on the basis of Kierkegaard's other works—appear to be his own beliefs.

2. Kierkegaard, *Journals,* trans. by A. Dru (Oxford: Oxford University Press, 1938), August, 1, 1835.

3. Ibid.

4. *"Concluding Unscientific Postscript"*, p. 178.

5. Ibid., p. 183.

6. This still leaves intact the thesis that Kierkegaard presents "not abstract theoretical philosophial theses but successive moves in a complicated dialectic of therapy" in "efforts to not truth but health." (J. Thompson, *The Lonely Labyrinth* [Carbondale, Ill.: South Illinois University Press, 1967[, p. xiii, 16). It seems clear to me that the road to therapy might well be paved with brilliant philosophical insights. Then, too, his thesis does not contradict, but is similarly compatible with those who would insist Kierkegaard is a "preacher" (e.g., Auden) or a "poet" (e.g., J. L. Mackey) and not a philosopher. If poetry is, as Robert Graves has written, "sense, good sense; penetrating often heart-rending sense", there is no need to argue the various interpretations of Kierkegaard as philosopher, therapist, preacher, poet against one another. (See my review of Mackey, *Kierkegaard: A Kind of Poet,* in the *Philosophical Review* [vol. 82, no. 2 April 1974]).

7. A. MacIntyre, "Existentialism," in *Sartre,* M. Warnock, ed., (New York: Doubleday-Anchor, 1971), p. 8.

8. Kierkegaard, p. 183.

9. Ibid., p. 281.

10. Ibid., p. 108.

11. "Performance Utterances" in *Philosophical Papers,* J. O. Urmson and G. Warnock, eds., (Oxford: Oxford University Press, 1970), p. 233.

12. Ibid., p. 235.

13. Ibid.

14. Ibid., 238.

15. Ibid.

16. Ibid., 239.

17. Ibid., 236.

18. I have developed this view in detail in *The Passions* (New York: Doubleday-Anchor, 1976 [reissued by the University of Notre Dame Press, 1981]).

REFERENCES

Austin, J. L. *How to Do Things with Words.* Oxford: Oxford University Papers, 1962.

————. *Philosophical Papers.* Oxford: Oxford University Press, 1970.

Hegel, G. W. F. *The Science of Logic.* Translated by A. V. Miller. London: Allen & Unwin, 1969.

Kierkegaard, S. *Either/Or.* Vol. 1. Translated by Swenson, Lowrie, and Johnston. New York: Doubleday-Anchor, 1959.

————. *Fear and Trembling and Sickness Unto Death.* Translated by W. Lowrie. Princeton, N.J.: Princeton University Press, 1954.

————. *Concluding Unscientific Postscript.* Translated by D. Swenson and W. Lowrie. Princeton, N.J.: Princeton University Press, 1944.

————. *The Point of View of My Work as an Author.* Translated by W. Lowrie. New York: Harper & Row, 1962.

————. *Journals.* Translated by A. Dru. London: Collins, 1958.

Mackey, L. *Kierkegaard: A Kind of Poet.* Philadelphia: University of Pennsylvania Press, 1971.

Sartre, J.-P. "The Singular Universal." In *Kierkegaard*. Paris, UNESCO, 1964. Translated in J. Thompson, *Kierkegaard*. New York: Doubleday, 1972.

Solomon, R. C. *From Rationalism to Existentialism*. New York: Harper & Row, 1972.

Thompson, J. *The Lonely Labyrinth*. Carbondale, Ill.: Southern Illinois University Press, 1967.

6

Nietzsche, Nihilism, and Morality

1

Friedrich Nietzsche is commonly referred to as a "nihilist" on the grounds that he rejects "morality." Yet Nietzsche does argue for a specific "morality," based upon what he calls the "will to power," with the *Übermensch* as its ideal and the eternal recurrence as its criterion. If Nietzsche is a nihilist, and if he does deny the possibility of rational justification of any set of values, then it would seem that his own "philosophy of power" cannot be justified rationally. But if Nietzsche believes his ethics of power to be justifiable, he cannot consistently be a nihilist.

One might attempt to resolve the apparent inconsistency by denying the central role of either nihilism or the will to power in Nietzsche's philosophy. For example, one might argue that Nietzsche is not a nihilist but only the diagnostician of the nihilism inherent in the "other-worldly" values of his contemporaries. In the early notes of *The Will to Power,* Nietzsche does so refer to nihilism as the problem of his age, as a problem consequent of decadence and the collapse of Christian morality. So construed, nihilism is not a doctrine which Nietzsche endorses but a symptom which he attacks. But "nihilism" has a broader and more important meaning. Nihilism is not only the collapse of traditional values, it is the *demand* for freedom from imposed values. Of course, these motives often appear together—the loss of foundation and faith in traditional values is the

The main problems of this essay have grown from years of discussions with Frithjof Bergmann. I am indebted to Ed Allaire for his criticisms of the present version.

ground for the demand for freedom from their now questionable authority. When Zarathustra urges, "what is now falling, one should also push," he is not giving a diagnosis but a prescription, in the name of freedom, for moral euthanasia. This demand for freedom from imposed values is nihilism in a vital sense, and in this sense, Nietzsche is undeniably a nihilist.

Alternatively, one might deny the will to power its central role in Nietzsche's philosophy, perhaps even as a consequence of his nihilism. In *Beyond Good and Evil* (22), Nietzsche taunts a critic, "Granted that this also is only interpretation—and you will be eager enough to make this objection?—well so much the better." Accordingly, one might suggest that the doctrine of the will to power is itself "only interpretation." Moreover, one can point out that the phrase "will to power" arrives rather late in Nietzsche's thought and that its occurence is confined chiefly to his unpublished notes. But like those interpretations which unwisely limit "Nietzsche's nihilism" to his explicit use of the word "nihilism," this argument misleadingly restricts his conception of the will to power to his explicit use of the phrase "will to power." But the concepts of strength and weakness, health and "overcoming" occupy key positions in Nietzsche's thought from his very first works until *Zarathustra,* where the will to power finally becomes the definiendum of every morality ("A tablet of the goal hangs over every people. Behold, it is the tablet of their overcomings; behold it is the voice of their Will to Power" [*Z* I 15]). In *Beyond Good and Evil* and *The Genealogy of Morals,* the values of strength and weakness are basic to the conceptions of master and slave morality. In *Twilight of the Idols* and *The Antichrist,* the themes of decadence and health are dominant even where the phrase "will to power" does not occur. And surely not to be ignored is Nietzsche's own insistence that the will to power is key to his "revaluation of values," the theme which he took to be the central goal of his entire work.

The themes of nihilism and the will to power occupy approximately the same periods and proportions of Nietzsche's work, and they function together as the key poles of Nietzsche's thought. Nihilism is the problem to which the will to power is the answer. But nihilism, so conceived, is not just the nihilism Nietzsche finds: it is his own insistence upon freedom from imposed values, "ideals," and "morality." Like Albert Camus in this century, Nietzsche wants to *begin* with a temperament of the age and derive a new set of values from it. But where Camus is to make the acceptance of nihilism ("the absurd") this very set of values ("keeping the absurd alive"), Nietzsche uses his nihilism as a foundation for the acceptance of a very different set of values, based upon the will to power.

2

The apparent inconsistency in Nietzsche's philosophy is largely due to his often intentional wordplay with key notions, notably "nihilism" and "morality," and also "foundation" and "reason." We may distinguish, for a start, the following interrelated conceptions of nihilism:

1. The collapse of values. ("Nihilism stands at the door . . . " [*The Will to Power (WP)* 1].[1] "What does nihilism mean? That the highest values devaluate

themselves? [*WP* 2].) References to "collapse," "decline," "decadence," and "degeneration" abound in Nietzsche's writings. Yet this diagnosis of "collapse" appears in many very different accusations: that values are inconsistent, unrealized, no longer taken seriously, without foundation. Regarding the last, we shall see that the notion of "foundation" also admits of several radically different interpretations, and so values can rest upon, or fail to rest upon, very different kinds of "foundations" or justifications.

2. The philosophical diagnosis of the collapse of values. ("The philosopher as the physician of his culture"; "the vivisectionist of the values of the times"; "nihilism represents a pathological transition stage" [*WP* 13]) ("nihilism is the recognition of the long *waste* of strength . . . " [*WP* 12].) In this sense, nihilism is the recognition of the phenomenon of nihilism (1). One might be a nihilist (1) without such recognition (e.g., "Pessimism is a preliminary form of nihilism" [*WP* 9]. "Our pessimism: the world does not have the values we thought it had" [*WP* 32].) To be a nihilist (1) is to be a product—a victim—of nihilism. To be a nihilist (2) is to be the diagnostician—the physician—of nihilism (1). In Nietzsche's case, it is clear that the patient is his own doctor, and that he is a nihilist in both senses, " . . . the necessity of doctors and nurses who are themselves sick" (*GM* III 15).

3. The collapse of a particular set of values—"morality." ("The nihilistic consequence [the belief in valuelessness] as a consequence of moral valuation: everything egoistic has come to disgust us" [*WP* 8].) (" . . . it is in one particular interpretation, the Christian-moral one, that nihilism is rooted" [*WP* 1].) It is debatable whether this should be called a different *sense* from the first conception of nihilism rather than simply its paradigm or even defining instance. If one takes "morality" to mean "the highest values," then the two would be equivalent. But "morality" also admits of manifold conceptions, and if one takes "morality" in the Judeo-Christian sense, as a specific set of principles within a determinate historical tradition, then there will be important qualifications in any discussion of the scope of Nietzsche's nihilism.

4. The diagnosis of the collapse of "morality." ("Skepticism regarding morality is what is decisive" [*WP* 3].) ("A Critique of Christian morality is still lacking" [*WP* 4].) (4) is to (3) as (2) is to (1).

5. The discovery of a lack of foundations or justifications for a particular set of values or a type of value. ("The aim is lacking: 'Why?' finds no answer" [*WP* 2].) (5) might be a special case of (2) and (4). It is worthy of separate mention, however, in order to lay the foundation for a crucial point: that Nietzsche is not simply concerned with a single set of values or a single morality, no matter how focused his attack on Judeo-Christian bourgeois morality may become. He is always interested in foundations, and it is the collapse not just of the foundations of Christian morality, but of all foundations of a certain type (the "otherworldly"), which Nietzsche diagnoses. It is important that such diagnosis is not confined to *moral* foundations. From the aphoristic works (particularly *Gay Science*) to the late notes, moral nihilism is grounded in an epistemological nihilism. ("The most extreme form of nihilism . . . there is no true world" [*WP* 15].)

6. Cosmic purposelessness. ("the eternal recurrence; the extreme form of nihilism [*WP* 55].) ("The whole of history is the refutation by experiment of the principle of the so-called 'moral world order!'" [*EH*].)

7. A particular moral attitude. ("life is no good" [*Twilight of the Idols* "The Problem of Socrates" 1].) A "hostility against life," a "nay-saying" appeal to the "other-worldly." Nietzsche's starting point, as he often states it, is "life." By this, he means to insist—in his epistemology as well as his moral philosophy—that the justification of any value or principle must account for the *function* of that value or principle in *this* life, without appeal to what is "ideal," "divine," or "rational." It is in this sense that nihilism characterizes a type of value, rather than a collapse of values and their justification. Nihilism is a "negation of life" (*A* 7), a symptom of decline:

> It is my contention that all the supreme values of mankind *lack* this will (for *power*)—that the values which are symptomatic of decline, *nihilistic* values, are lording it under the holiest names. (*A* 6)

In this sense of "nihilism," Nietzsche is not a nihilist; rather he is even an *anti-nihilist*. But this is not to say that Nietzsche is contradicting himself, nor is it to say that this sense of "nihilism" is unrelated to the others. Superficially, it might appear that Nietzsche is using "nihilism" to refer both to a set of values and to the rejection of that set of values. But, in Nietzsche's analysis, the former is the cause of the latter. Nihilism, like reason in Hegel's dialectic, evolves through varied stages of development and expression. In Nietzsche's philosophy, nihilism is first a moral attitude, then an attitude that turns on itself and "devaluates its own values," and then, finally, attains that form of self-recognition which is the end (in both senses) of Hegel's dialectic. ("*The Will to Power*: Attempt at a Revaluation of All Values— . . . a movement that in some future will take the place of this perfect nihilism—but presupposes it, logically and psychologically, and certainly can come only after and out of it" [*WP* preface].)

In each of the past seven senses, nihilism is a phenomenon to be analyzed. But now, the point is to embrace this recognition and this phenomenon, to move from patient and diagnostician to one who makes the disease the very basis of his health ("That which does not destroy me makes me stronger" *Twilight* I 8). And so, Nietzsche moves from the diagnostician to the nihilist proper, the one who endorses, not just recognizes, the phenomenon of nihilism (1–7):

> Main proposition. How *complete nihilism* is the necessary consequence of the ideals entertained hitherto. Incomplete nihilism; its forms: we live in the midst of it. (*WP* 28)
>
> That is precisely how we find the pathos that impels us to seek new values. (*WP* 32)
>
> What is falling, one should also push. (*Z* III 12)

8. The demand for freedom from imposed values. Perhaps the best characterization of this embracing spirit of nihilism comes from Ivan Turgenev, who popularized the term "nihilist" for nineteenth-century Europe in his novel *Fathers and Sons*. There, young Arkady describes the friend Bazarov as a "nihilist," as

> a man who does not bow down before any authority, who does not take any principle on faith, whatever reverence that principle is enshrined in.

As it stands, unfortunately, this characterization captures the spirit of the entire Enlightenment from Descartes to Kant as well as the nihilism of Bazarov, Dostoevsky, and Nietzsche. But Nietzsche, unlike Descartes or Kant, will turn to neither God nor reason in his search for values, and so his rejection of "authority" is considerably more radical than theirs. It is in his war against imposed values that Nietzsche conducts his "campaign against morality," urges us to "become who we are" and pursue "our own virtue." The often misunderstood attack on reason and the celebration of the instincts and passions is first of all a reaction against the *"tyranny"* of reason and the authority of church, morality, and "the herd" in their disdain for "the individual" and the "exceptional human being."

> *We ourselves,* we free spirits, are nothing less than a "revaluation of all values," an *incarnate* declaration of war . . . (*A* 13)

9. The demand for freedom from certain values or moral commands, namely, "other-worldy values." (" . . . my brothers, remain faithful to the earth! [*Z* I 3].) The attack on other-worldly values (of which Christian morality is the paradigm) and the attack on imposed values (8) are of a piece, but not equivalent. One of Nietzsche's battles is against the other-worldly foundations and goals of Christianity; but another is against all universal and social morality, the morality of the herd, all morality which places group interests above and opposed to the individual. Ultimately, Christian morality and herd morality are attacked as one, as it is herd morality which is responsible for Christian morality. But the two are distinct. Socrates, for example, is indicted by Nietzsche for his appeal to the other-worldly, but he is admired for his individuality. The "last man" is "contemptible" for his herd spirit, but he is not guilty of being "other-worldly." It is important to remind ourselves that Nietzsche never simply attacks an isolated moral principle: he always attacks a *system* of morality, a connected set of principles, values, foundations, and motivations. And so, while Nietzsche is clearly a nihilist in the sense that he rejects a great many (but surely not all) principles of Christian morality, to so limit Nietzsche's nihilism is to trivialize the depth of his philosophy.

10. The demand for freedom from all moral rules, principles, and "ideals." On one interpretation, this form of nihilism is surely too extreme for Nietzsche, who continuously insists that he seeks "new values": (*BGE* 211; *WP* preface 4, 32). But there is an aspect of Nietzsche's attack on Christian and herd morality and his "revaluation" which is often overlooked. What he seeks is not another set of rules, an alternative set of imperatives to the Ten Commandments. Nietzsche's nihilism is " . . . let me emphasize this once more—*moraline-free*" (*A* 6). ("My philosophy aims at an ordering of rank; not at an individualistic morality." [*WP* 287].) This is the sense in which Nietzsche attacks all "ideals" as well as "the improvers of mankind." To say what man *ought* to be, Nietzsche tells us, is "no small madness, no modest kind of immodesty." This will seem strange only so long as we insist that value consists of principles of right and wrong action (of "good and evil"), and ignore the value of "good character" and "style." ("Giving style to one's character . . . a rare and noble art . . . " *GS*.) There is a moral sense in which a good character is one who has performed good actions and abstained from bad actions, but that is not the sense which Nietzsche has in mind. He is concerned, in terms taken from Greek ethics, with *virtue* and *excellence,*

individual style and character that is not reducible to the actions a man has and has not performed or will perform. The man of character might perform any action—even cruel action—without detracting from his character. This shift from rules to style has opened up Nietzsche to many serious misinterpretations, for example, that he favors cruelty and evil. But his point is not to argue *im*morality, but to seriously go "beyond good and evil" to a conception of good (and bad) which pays less attention to rules and principles and more to individual virtue and excellence of character.

Is Nietzsche a nihilist? In the sense that he is the diagnostician of the "devaluation of the highest values" and the corruption of the foundations of "morality," in the sense that he denies any moral order or purpose to the universe, in the sense that he demands freedom from imposed values, in particular the authoritarian values of the "other-worldly," and in the sense that he rejects moral principles and rules in favor of personal style and character—yes. But Nietzsche is not a nihilist in the sense that he attacks all values, or in the sense that he endorses principles or positions simply because they are antimoral, or in the sense that he adopts those values which he calls "nihilistic," that is, those "hostile to life." To the contrary, Nietzsche ridicules those who would deny all values, he rejects those who would adopt an antimorality, which, after all, retains the foundations of morality but only perverts its substance, and he attacks values—including antimoral values—which are "against life."

Given the Hegelian movement between different yet related senses of "nihilism," we must be very careful in any discussion of "Nietzsche's nihilism" and doubly careful in any attempt to provide a single answer to the question whether Nietzsche is a nihilist or not. With regard to his nihilistic attack upon morality, we must not only keep in mind these various senses of "nihilism," we must also keep in mind an equally complicated dialectic regarding the notion of "morality."

3

The centrality of Nietzsche's attack on morality and his own "immorality" is as much a matter of reputation as intention. It is true that he announces, in *Dawn* (1881) "the beginning of my campaign against morality," that he titles one of his later works "Beyond Good and Evil," and that he frequently attacks morality as "immoral," "detrimental to life," "the work of error," "a disease" (*WP* 266, 273). But his central concern is not attack, but *creation* "of new values."

> [Philosophy] demands that one create values.... the real philosophers are
> commanders and legislators. They say, "it shall be thus!" ... Their instrument,
> their hammer. (*BGE* 211)

Nietzsche's nihilism is but a precondition, a clearing of the ground to make room for a new *conception* of values.

The concept of "value" is the key to Nietzsche's philosophy. It is the *value of value* that he seeks to understand, the *revaluation of values* that he undertakes as the goal of his philosophizing, the *transvaluation of values* that he seeks to unmask as the origin of "morality," the nihilistic *devaluation of the highest values* that he diagnoses as the consequence of Christian morality. "Value" is the general conception of which "morality" is a special instance. A value is any object of desire, any "inclination," motivation, drive, attraction, whether instinctual or acquired, latent or aroused, whether "end-in-itself" or means to another end. "Value" is in the domain of psychology, and so Nietzsche prides himself as being "a philosopher who is also a psychologist." A value is the property of a person; it is what Kant called a "subjective maxim," except that the notion of "maxim" already leans toward an interpretation of a value as a principle, albeit a personal rather than a universal principle. And Nietzsche is interested in other values than principled values, for example, aesthetic and spiritual values, and personal character, which need not result in any specific forms of action. There is much more that is good than a "good will." A good will is good only, contrary to Kant, with serious qualification. For example, one wants to know *whose* will it is: what is *he* worth?

A *moral* value, however, is more than psychological, more than a "subjective maxim." A moral value is an action-guiding principle (just as likely a rule for abstention and resistance as a rule for doing, however; compare Bertrand Russell [1929]: "In all ages and nations positive morality has consisted almost wholly of prohibition of various classes of actions, with the addition of a small number of commands to perform certain other actions"). It is a principle that is *universal,* never the property of an individual; and it is justifiable on the basis of a *rational* foundation. Its relation to the individual, again in Kant's terms, is *categorical,* not conditional on the interests and character of the individual: "reason commands, not advises."

But "morality" allows many different interpretations, and so there are many senses in which one might say that Nietzsche attacks morality in order to leave room for the creation of new values. To make matters far more complicated, "morality," unlike "nihilism," is an everyday concept that had been distorted and played with for several philosophical generations before Nietzsche had his opportunity to do so. Kant, for example, had analyzed a trimmed, perhaps truncated, concept of morality *(Moralität)* which effectively ruled out all psychological influences (of "interest" and "inclination") from considerations of "moral worth." Hegel had then attacked Kant and replaced this trimmed notion of "morality" with a far more generous concept *(Sittlichkeit),* which included within the domain of morality not only the universal rules and principles of reason but also the customs and mores of one's society.

Nietzsche employs several conceptions of morality and often plays them against one another. For example, he remarks in a letter to his friend Paul Rée,

> She told me herself that she had no morality,—and I thought she had, like myself, a more severe morality than anybody.... (1882, translated in Kaufmann, *The Portable Nietzsche,* p. 102)

The clash of uses produces curious tensions and oxymorons such as "morality as the work of immorality" (*WP* 266; compare *WP* 308) and contrasts such as "good and bad" as *opposed* to "good and evil." Occasionally, Nietzsche praises or endorses the work of morality, for example, where he speaks of "healthy morality, dominated by the instinct for life" (*Twilight* "Morality as Anti-Nature"). (Compare "I understand by 'morality' a system of evaluations that partially coincides with the conditions of a creature's life" [*WP* 256].) These uses must be clearly distinguished from those conceptions of "morality" which Nietzsche attacks and rejects as "against life."

Of the various conceptions employed by Nietzsche, those which are most important refer to a more or less specific set of moral principles with their roots in the Judeo-Christian religious tradition, their current practice in the bourgeoisie that Hesse later describes as "that fat brood of mediocrity," their most sophisticated defense in the moral philosophy of Kant, and their psychological genesis, Nietzsche argues, in feelings of *ressentiment*. But these central conceptions of morality can be reinterpreted more broadly and more narrowly. At their extremes, such interpretations become troublesome. For example, one might extensionally interpret "morality" such that morality becomes a distinct list of specific principles, for example, "thou shalt not kill!" "don't break promises!" "treat others as you would be treated yourself!" But Nietzsche is never concerned solely with specific principles but always with the system of which they are a part, the foundation which gives them support, and the psychology within which they serve as a function. To reduce Nietzsche's attack on morality to an attack on a specific set of principles is at least a trivialization of his philosophy. Or worse, it is in some instances a falsification, since at least some of Nietzsche's own values are also values in the Judeo-Christian tradition. ("The good four. Honest . . . courageous . . . generous . . . polite . . ." [*Dawn* 556].) At the other extreme, there is a broad conception of "morality" such that it becomes an equivalent to Nietzsche's conception of "value." Any set of values, on this conception, would be a morality. Given this conception of "morality," however, it is simply false that Nietzsche attacks morality, and so one of the central themes of his philosophy, his "campaign against morality," is lost to us.

In a simple-minded way, one might say that Nietzsche defends *values* in general ("one could not live without valuing"), but attacks *moral* values. But there are many senses in which Nietzsche attacks moral values, for there are many different conceptions of morality that are operative in Nietzsche's work. And the fact that Nietzsche defends values in general is not sufficient to understand why he should believe that some values are of more value than others. To understand Nietzsche's attack on his defense of one set of values—based upon the will to power—we shall have to be far more precise about these various conceptions.

For relative simplicity, I want to restrict the notion of morality to sets of action-guiding principles. There is a sense in which we—and Nietzsche—can speak of moral character (as Aristotle does in his *Ethics,* without reducing moral character to a mere summary of history and propensity for morally right acts) or the morality of art or history. But the focus of Nietzsche's attention is those moral principles which prescribe and proscribe specific actions and types of actions universally, and this sense is sufficient to understand Nietzsche's attack on morality.

Morality may be characterized by virtue of the source of its principles, the justification or sanction for its principles, the form of its principles, the content of its principles, or its relationship to other principles. And morality might be taken to be those principles which are current (as in *Sittlichkeit*) or as any coherent set of principles:

1. If morality is characterized by virtue of the source of its principles, moral rules and attitudes would be those that have developed from the Judeo-Christian tradition. Nietzsche's analysis of this development is brilliantly insightful; he augments this superficial historical tradition with a psychological syndrome, such that Judeo-Christian religion and practices become not nearly so important as the *psychology* of the practitioners. Whether it is the tradition or the psychology that is taken as fundamental, this sense of morality refers to those principles which can be traced more or less directly to this genealogy. "Thou shalt not kill" is a moral principle, therefore, because it is one of the Ten Commandments, whether or not the principle has any justification outside its traditional context.

2. There is no single sense in which morality can be characterized by virtue of justification or sanctions of its principles. In an obvious sense (2a), morality might be characterized as those principles which have their justification and their sanction in the will of God. This would be related to, but still very different from (1). For example, a recent "God is dead" movement *within* the Christian church attempts to hold onto the moral tradition of Christianity while giving up its theological supports. Alternatively, there are radical conceptions of Christian faith (e.g., in Kierkegaard's *Fear and Trembling:* "The Problem of Abraham") such that one might see being a Christian as distinct from (though not necessarily opposed to) acceptance of Judeo-Christian moral traditions. But it is clear that Nietzsche's frequent references to morality as "other-worldly" derive in large measure from the Judeo-Christian conception of a transcendent and divine judge and sanction as well as from Judeo-Christian tradition. "Morality," so conceived, is those principles which are (believed to be) objects to God's will.

2b. But morality has its other, more earthly sanctions. Most evidently, the authority for justification and sanctions might be society itself, through its social customs and laws. Accordingly, morality might be characterized as those principles which receive their validity through societal acceptance and authority. Thus, "Thou shalt not kill," although it has its origins in a religious tradition, is taken to be a moral principle because it is embodied in the mores and laws of society.

2c. There is a third source of authority, however, which is not, in any simple way, reducible to the authority of religion or society. That is *reason.* Kant, for example, had attempted to *define* moral principles as principles of practical reason and justify these principles without appeal to societal authority (one source of Hegel's criticism) and without appeal, in one sense, to the authority of God. (This point is a bit touchy; on the one hand, Kant insists that the validity of morality can depend only on reason and cannot appeal to divine promises; on the other hand, he insists that belief in God as omniscient, omnipotent, all-just judge is a "postulate of practical reason," a "necessary presupposition of morality." The logical distinction here between belief in God as part of the justification of morality and as one of its presuppositions is a matter which never ceased to give Kant serious problems.) Ultimately, Kant insists that reason is the final authority (and that God as well as men are subject to its authority). Reason is the *universal* lawgiver and pays no attention to the particular interests and characters of individual men. Morality, so conceived, is those principles which can be defended by reason alone, whether or not they are derivative of a religious tradition, embodied in religious morality or a social order.

3. I have several times insisted that moral principles are universal principles,

but I have not yet elevated this to a uniquely defining characteristic. In Kant's analysis of "morality," it is the universal *form* of certain principles that makes them moral principles. Moral principles are *categorical* imperatives, universal commands, and the "first formulation" of the categorical imperative demands that one "act such that he would will the maxim of his action as *universal law.*" Kant takes this to be a purely *formal* characteristic of such principles, a matter of their common logic rather than any specific content, consequences, or circumstances of application. Accordingly, morality, so conceived, is that set of action-guiding principles which are universal or categorical in form.

4. So far, I have not even mentioned the specific content of moral principles. I have characterized morality only by appeal to its sources, justifications and sanctions, and forms. But clearly one might wish to argue that the reason that killing is *morally* wrong is not because that proscription happens to be one of the Ten Commandments, not because it is societally unacceptable and illegal or irrational to kill, but because killing itself is immoral. But this characterization is incomplete until we specify by virtue of what killing is immoral. One might insist that the principle proscribing killing is a moral principle simply because it is one of *those* principles. In other words, one might give a straightforwardly *extensional* characterization of morality, such that a moral principle is any principle on a certain list, not a principle of a certain kind. When Nietzsche speaks of "morality," he sometimes means "current morality," those principles which are held to be "moral" principles at that time. But there will quite naturally be dissatisfaction with the suggestion that certain principles are simply *called* "moral," and so one wants to look further for that by virtue of which these principles are called "moral." One might suggest that the content of moral principles is characterized by a social concern, a respect for other persons. This is very different from that earlier characterization (2b) which takes moral principles to be those *authorized* by society. A principle might be authorized by a society which has very little respect for persons, just as principles of respect for persons in general are typically not authorized by a great many societies when they conflict with personal interests and privileges. Thus conceived, morality consists of those principles which, like Kant's "3rd [by one count] formulation" of the categorical imperative, respect persons "always as ends and never merely as means." The interpretation of "respect" and "ends" varies widely, focusing sometimes upon welfare, sometimes on dignity, sometimes on equality of rights. However conceived, such a characterization falls squarely within the realm of what Nietzsche derogatorily entitled "herd morality." It is concern for others that constitutes morality.

5. A morality might be conceived as a set of psychologically efficient principles of action. For example, a utilitarian theory of morality takes the essence of a moral principle to be its efficiency in promoting happiness and/or pleasure. Of course, there are serious questions concerning the status of moral principles in such discussions, whether it is the principle itself which is to be defended on utilitarian grounds or rather only the actions which fall under it. But morality so conceived is very different from our previous conceptions in that it need not give rise to universal principles or to the demand for any sanction or justification rather than the facts of one's own welfare. (Compare Bertrand Russell: " . . . the supreme moral rule: act so as to produce harmonious rather than discordant desires" [*Outline of Philosophy,* p. 234].) As such, Nietzsche himself adopts such

a "morality," but his basic psychological principle is not the desire for pleasure or happiness but *will to power.* Arguing against utilitarianism and all hedonist ethics, Nietzsche attempts to show that the goal of action is rarely pleasure and that pleasure appears only as an accompaniment of increase in power. (Compare Aristotle, *N. Ethics,* bk. X: "pleasure completes the activity . . . as an end which supervenes as the bloom of youth does on those in the flower of their age.")

If morality is conceived as a set of psychological efficient principles whose ultimate goal ("value") is the will to power, then morality in all previous senses would appear to be "immoral." While Nietzsche does employ this apparent contradiction for its shock value ("the immorality of morality"), he argues extensively that "moral" principles, whether conceived in terms of their historical origins, their justification and sanction, or their logical form, are also expressions of the will to power, even where they explicitly disclaim any desires for power. ("When theologians reach out for *power* through the "conscience" of princes (*or* of peoples) we need never doubt what really happens at bottom; the will to the end, the *nihilistic* will, wants power" [*A* 10].) Judeo-Christian morality is the *collective* ("herd") exercise of the will to power by the weak. Incapable of satisfying their own desires (for power), they collectively settle for prevention of similar satisfactions in the stronger. Where the manifestation of the will to power in the powerful is *desire* and *passion,* the will to power in the impotent is *ressentiment* of the powerful. ("One should distinguish well: whoever still wants to gain the consciousness of power will use any means. . . . He, however, who has it has become very choosy and noble in his tastes" [*Dawn* 348].) Accordingly, Nietzsche recharacterizes "herd morality" as "slave morality," for its values are dependent upon a reaction to and *reversal* of ("transvaluation of") the desires of the powerful. The values of the powerful depend upon "Dionysian" frenzy, and so it is necessary to convert this wild and often destructive torrent of passion and desire into an "Apollonian" coherent and "life-enhancing" set of values and virtues. But *morality,* now conceived as the expression of the will to power of the impotent (whatever its nominal formulation and rationalization as "practical reason," "the Will of God," or "the social contract"), tries not to so sublimate and organize the passions but to *deny* them. ("the moralist's mania which demands not the control but the extirpation of the passions. Their conclusion is ever; only the emasculated man is the good man" [*A* 47].)

> Instead of employing the great sources of strength, those impetuous torrents of the soul that are so often dangerous and over-whelming, and enconomizing them, this most short-sighted and pernicious mode of thought wants to make them dry up (*WP* 383).

Thus, Nietzsche's attack on morality is not simply a confrontation of one set of values pitted against another. All values, Nietzsche argues, are based upon the will to power, and his objection to morality is not that its values are not aimed at power or that they are aimed at impotent power through *ressentiment.* The objection is that morality hypocritically and secretly aims at power for the impotent by imposing standards of impotence upon the strong. It is the *universalization* of the impotent will to power to cover the strong that Nietzsche rejects. He does not attempt, despite his reputation and his most frequent interpretations, to deny morality. Nietzsche's elitism commits him to the position that there will always be weak persons; his psychology commits him to the position that all values are expressions of the will to power; consequently, he is committed to the position that morality will always be necessary—for the weak. What he insists upon doing is rather to limit the universal claims of morality to leave room for a different kind of expression of the will to power. But neither can this expression— in art, in philosophy, in saintliness and asceticism—be universalized, for the cardinal principle of Nietzsche's philosophy is that people are different, and so their values, though all expressions of the will to power, must be different as well.

We can already see that Nietzsche's "attack on morality," and thus his "nihilism," must be seriously qualified. He attacks the claims of moral principles to be universal, but he does not deny morality its proper domain. He exposes the hidden motivation of the moralists to be an impotent will to power, but he does not suggest that the impotent could be sensibly commanded to become potent. Nietzsche's "attack on morality," like Kant's defense of morality, might be more accurately reinterpreted as an analysis of morality, its presuppositions, and its proper place.

6. Underlying all of these characterizations of morality is the idea that moral principles are the *highest* principles. Accordingly, one might characterize morality simply as "the highest principles." But this leads to serious problems when one attempts to justify morality. "Why ought I be moral?" Perhaps because it would be amusing, or gratifying, or because I would benefit from the public display of virtue. (Compare Camus' Clamence [before his "fall"] in *The Fall*.) Or perhaps one ought to be moral because it will make him and/or others happier, or perhaps one should simply try to avoid noxious punishments, legal indictments, public disgrace. But if any of these ends are taken to be justifications of moral action, they themselves would become "higher" in value than the "moral" principles in question, since moral action would become a mere means to their satisfaction. Accordingly, either one gives up the idea that morality can be justified, or one moves to a different characterization of morality. Or, taking this characterization seriously, one might become that sort of relativist who takes *any* coherent system of principles to be *a morality*. While there are philosophers who would hold such a concept of morality, Nietzsche is surely not one of them. Although Nietzsche employs varied conceptions of "morality," he is not a relativist, and he does not believe that any set of values, considered apart from their function in the life of a people, can be a morality. He believes that there is a single psychologically justifiable standard, and that differences in the ways of acting upon that standard are not differences in basic moral principles, but only differences in character. The weak cannot exercise their power in the same ways as the strong. Apparent differences in morality are in fact only differences in strength.

7. It might be mentioned, in ending this lengthy list, that there is a final degenerate sense of "moral" which Nietzsche uses not infrequently in his later polemics. "Moral" and "immoral" can function, quite apart from any *conception* of morality, as adjectives of emotional evaluative stress. Without any further argument to fall back upon in an attack, one might desperately or angrily grab onto a "moral" accusation, weight his indictment of an act, principle, or person with the weighty word "immoral." While this nonconception of morality is not

of theoretical interest to us here, it is sometimes necessary to the understanding of Nietzsche's harshest attacks.

This is an oppressive list of distinctions. What do they signify? Different meanings? Different senses? Different conceptions? In *Genealogy of Morals,* Nietzsche offers us an insight: "Only that which has no history can be defined" (*GM* II 13). "Morality" is first of all an extensional concept; it *points* to a list of rules, currently accepted action-guiding principles, a "tablet of virtues" within a specific historical-moral context. These rules and principles are superficially unconnected and perhaps even inconsistent. It is a matter of reflection to find their common threads, perhaps by appeal to a small set of principles which provide the "deep structure" which ties this diversity into a unity. One might point to a common ground or justification. Of course, to show the coherence and common ground of our diverse moral beliefs is not yet to give them a rational justification, but at least it can demonstrate that they are systematic and consistent. But there is no single way to tie diverse moral principles together, any more than there is a single line which can be drawn through any large number of scattered points on a sheet of paper.

In several of his works, Nietzsche instructs us that "there are no moral facts, only moral interpretations." In one sense, however, there are moral facts—the facts of the acceptance of certain principles as moral principles within a given social context (Hegel's *Sittlichkeit*). In this society, even with its inconsistencies and confusions, I can make a moral judgment or decision within particular circumstances for a concrete act. In doing so, I appeal to moral principles which, for the purposes of that judgment or decision, are *given* as fixed criteria. But though I justify the judgment or the decision by appeal to the criteria, that is not yet a justification of the criteria. Moral criteria have their significance in concrete practice, not in philosophical reflection. This early Hegelian–late Wittgensteinian point, innocent as it seems, is the very base of what Nietzsche diagnoses as European nihilism, and it is what he means when he insists, "there are no moral facts." There are only interpretations of morality: only various ways of tying together the diverse facts of our everyday moral life. Perhaps what they have in common is social concern, perhaps it is their universal scope, perhaps it is their Judeo-Christian heritage, perhaps it is just that these are our highest values. But if these all are true, then which or which combination of these common features is uniquely moral? This question might remain academic, unless one has in mind a "revaluation of all values." Then it becomes incumbent upon him to specify just those features of "morality" which are to be rejected, and upon what grounds.

In other words, the above varied conceptions of morality are not different *meanings* or *senses* of "morality."[2] They are different interpretations of a familiar set of moral facts—that is, acknowledged moral prejudices—which have no single principle of unity. Though the moral text upon which each of these interpretations is based is one and the same, these various interpretations can be attacked and defended independently of each other. Accordingly, Nietzsche's "attack on morality" is not simply an assault on a set of principles whose significance is given; it is a battle within a series of interpretations of disconnected prejudices, some of which he wants to reject, some of which he wants to continue to accept, all of which he wants to understand on a psychological basis.

4

Although we singled out types of justification as one basis for interpretation of "morality," it must not be thought that conceptions of morality and theories of justification are separate concerns. For example, Kant's conception of morality as universalizability clearly commits him to a theory of justification such that a moral principle can only be defended by appeal to universal and impersonal criteria. Similarly, the utilitarian's conception of morality as rules of maximum utility ties him to a theory of justification such that acceptance of a moral principle (or act, or type of act) must *in fact* maximize utility. For Nietzsche, it is clear that conceptions of morality and theories of justification are inseparable. In spite of his epistemological atomism, Nietzsche is a monist. Moral principles and their foundations are of a single piece, a single system united and based upon the will to power. Kant's conception of morality as universal principles of duty, his theory of practical reason, and his Christianity are a single complex though brilliant "prejudice." Christian morality and its theology are the same.

(Naivete: as if morality could survive when the *God* who sanctions it is missing! The beyond absolutely necessary if faith in morality is to be maintained.) (*WP* 253)

With this inseparability of conception and justification in mind, we must introduce one further vital distinction which Nietzsche employs as the basis for nearly all his attacks on "morality," and which consequently forms the foundation for his "nihilism." Nietzsche distinguishes two types of "values," that is, two types of systems of values, principles, justifications, and "prejudices" (or simply, motives). The first can be characterized—though misleadingly—as "other-worldly." I say misleadingly because it too graphically appeals to the Christian literally "other-world," while the scope of Nietzsche's attack extends far beyond this. In addition to his attack upon other-worldly concerns as such (i.e., not doing what one wants in this life in order to earn a position in the delights—or at least not in the tortures—of the next one), Nietzsche also attacks appeals to metaphysical conceptions of the "other-worldly" (e.g., the "world of Being" in "The Problem of Socrates" [*Twilight*]), and these are clearly very different, even if, as Nietzsche proceeds to argue, their motivation is the same (i.e., dissatisfaction with *this* life). Furthermore, Nietzsche attacks under the same rubric all moralities that have universal principles, which appeal to universal reason rather than individual desires and "virtues." The connection between Christian morality, Platonic metaphysics, Kant's practical reason, and "herd morality" is their mutual demand for universal and suprapersonal values. But it is misleading to talk as if what Nietzsche hated was simply "the other-worldly." He also hated what was decadent and "nay-saying," and these conceptions are far broader than the specialized metaphysical and theological structures to which they *sometimes* give rise. He hated "herd morality" and personal weakness, but again, though these might lead to metaphysical and theological constructions, they need not. Nietzsche diagnoses "the other-worldly" only as a symptom, not as the source of "life-negating values." It is "danger of life" and the impersonal that Nietzsche attacks.

One more word against Kant as a *moralist*. A virtue must be *our own* invention, *our* most necessary self-expression and self-defense; any other kind of
virtue is merely a danger. Whatever is not a condition of our life *harms* it: a
virtue that is prompted solely by a feeling of respect for the concept of "virtue," as Kant would have it, is harmful. "Virtue," "duty," the "good in itself,"
the good which is impersonal and universally valid—chimeras and expressions of decline, the final exhaustion of life, of the Chinese phase of Königsberg. The fundamental laws of self-preservation and growth demand the opposite—that everyone invent *his own* virtue, *his own* categorical imperative. A
people perishes when it confuses *its* duty with duty in general . . . *anti-nature*
as instinct, German decadence as philosophy—*that is Kant.* (*A* 11)

The contrary of such "other-worldly," "decadent," "impersonal," "herd,"
and "life-threatening" values is, as suggested so often above, "naturalistic" values, life-affirming, personal virtues. Such values are personal needs, desires, aspirations, and "instincts." The source of such values is individual psychology,
depending upon the character and circumstance of the individual. This is not to
say that every felt need or desire is personal or life-affirming, however. Nietzsche
has an operative but never developed conception of true as opposed to false needs
and desires, only the former being "naturalistic," the latter being imposed and
learned through the authority and discipline of church, society, and even "reason." The separation of *our own* values and imposed internalized values lies at
the very heart of Nietzsche's philosophy, and it is one of its serious failings that
it does not provide us with more analysis.

It is the *source* of desires that differentiates naturalistic from "other-worldly"
values, which is not to say that naturalistic values cannot be *learned,* only that
their "value" must be their gratification of an "inner" need. (Compare Nietzsche
on education: "one should give education to only him who needs it.") But this is
tantamount to denying the need for any sanction or justification other than an
appeal to the personal function of those needs and desires, in Russell's Hegelian
phrase, "harmony of desires." In Nietzsche's individualistic naturalistic ethics,
there can be no *reason* for a value other than "I want *x*," except that *x* might be
a means to some other goal *y* (such that "I want *y*" would be a further reason for
wanting *x*), and that *x* must be shown to be a *real* need or desire in its function
in a whole personality. But this is to say that individualistic naturalistic values
do not call for justification, they demand, at most, explanation, a demonstration
of their function. That sense of justification that demands appeal to some outside
criterion or authority (other than personal needs and desires) is out of place here.
This would even include "outside" valuations of psychological states, for example, the "objective" value of happiness or satisfaction. It may be that my artistic
aspirations cause me to be unhappy, but the relative worth of those aspirations
and that unhappiness is a question of my needs and desires, not a question of
appeal to an abstract ideal of "happiness." Similarly, piglike behavior might give
me far more satisfaction than Socratic reflection, but the question is one of my
personality, not of the "quality" of the respective desires in any universal sense.

Naturalistic values are at their basis universal—that is, they are all based
upon the will to power—but they are universal only as a matter of fact and not
as a matter of necessity, as would be Kant's moral imperatives. Though the will
to power is, according to Nietzsche, universal, *people* are different, and because

they are different their "virtues"—their "self-overcomings" in accordance with
the will to power—must be different also.

One final point: Nietzsche's ethics is not, as one finds in Socrates or Kant, a
reflective ethics. This is due, in part, to the stress on "instinct" rather than "reason," but underlying this stress is the recognition, much like that of Dostoevsky
in *Notes from Underground,* of the useless if not harmful or even paralyzing
effects of conscious reflection and deliberation. It is Nietzsche's intention to display the proper grounds for value, but not to insist that to act in accordance with
such value it is necessary to consciously act for the sake of it. This is why I earlier
quipped, against Kant, that there is much that is good besides a good will. For
Nietzsche, the demand for deliberate action gives way to the prereflective harmony of good character, and the crucial Kantian distinction between action in
conformity with duty and action for the sake of duty becomes irrelevant, for every
action, in spite of its apparent "rationale," is but an expression of the will to
power. It is not a question of a good will, but style, and style is, perhaps essentially, practiced but not deliberate, unthinking and not self-conscious.

5

We are now in a position to resolve our initial paradox. Insofar as Nietzsche's
nihilism consists of a diagnosis of a phenomenon developing outside of him—in
society, in the values themselves—it has no bearing on the apparent inconsistency between Nietzschean nihilism and the will to power. It is only insofar as
Nietzschean nihilism becomes a position Nietzsche himself holds that it apparently clashes with his defense of the will to power. Nietzsche does accept nihilism
as a rejection of the ultimate "value of values" and their foundations, but not all
values, only *imposed* values. What marks such "other-worldly" values might be
their source, but it is ultimately their failure to conform to the personal demands
of the individual. In other words, the will to power, far from being inconsistent
with Nietzsche's nihilism, is its *criterion.* Nihilism is an attack upon and rejection
of "other-worldly" values, but the range of otherworldly values is distinguished
by the peculiar expressions they offer of the will to power, through a denial of life
and *ressentiment* of power.

With particular regard to "morality," Nietzschean nihilism consists of the
attack upon and rejection of all those *conceptions* of morality which do not recognize the will to power and personal needs and desires as primary. These would
include all conceptions of morality which find the need to appeal to authority—
whether of God, church, society, or reason—a sure *symptom* of neglect of individual "instincts." They would include every conception of morality which finds
its source in a historical tradition or in a society or group rather than in personal
character. They would include every conception of morality which would insist
that its commands be universal, an explicit rejection of the interests of the individual. And Nietzschean nihilism would need to reject as well those naturalistic
conceptions which, while correctly beginning by appealing only to individual
needs and desires, do not find the will to power as the fundamental drive, but
rather pleasure or happiness. But the disagreement here is "scientific" and empirical, an agreement which might be settled by appeal to the "facts" of human psy-

chology. Nietzsche would also object to those naturalistic conceptions of morality which move from an appeal to individual needs and desires to an abstract standard which no longer appeals to these needs and desires directly. In utilitarianism, most importantly, Nietzsche despises the "shopkeeper mentality" that moves from the alleged need and desire for happiness in each individual to the need and desire for the happiness of all.

Nietzsche's moral nihilism presupposes the will to power as its standard. Nietzsche's nihilism is, put in its basic form, the attack upon and rejection of every conception of morality which does not acknowledge the will to power. Although the term "nihilism" has several senses in Nietzsche's philosophy, and although the standard of the will to power emerges only slowly and rather late in his writings, we can justifiably say, with the above qualifications, that Nietzsche's nihilism and his philosophy of power are one and the same set of doctrines.

6

In closing, it might be helpful to comment upon a second, related paradox which has haunted our discussion from its very beginning. Nietzsche sometimes insists that "philosophers must be legislators" and "creators of value." He himself insists that his intention is to offer us new values and a new type of man (the *Übermensch*). This is hardly consistent with his sarcastic attacks upon the "improvers of mankind" and all those who tell us "what man *ought* to be." The same paradox arises in a more substantial way: Nietzsche claims that all values and all actions are based upon the will to power. But then what is his ethics? If we do in fact act according to the will to power, it is pointless to tell us we *ought* to act accordingly. And, bringing these two formulations together, what is the point of having philosophers who are legislators and creators of value if all values are based upon the will to power?

The paradox begins to resolve itself, however, as soon as we move from a demand for new values to a demand for a new *conception* of values, from the attack on morality to an attack on certain *conceptions* of morality. If we do (psychologically) necessarily act according to the will to power, it makes no sense to formulate an ethics which urges us to do so, and there are no value systems (including "morality") which do not conform to the will to power. But there is a real need for an understanding of "the springs of human action," and there is a real objection—not to morality, but to those *conceptions* of morality which attempt to universalize and impose their will to power upon people very different. In other words, Nietzsche's intent is to give us a new conception of value ("the value of value," "the revaluation of all values") in terms of the will to power, to show us how morality (as a set of particular action-guiding principles) acts as an expression of the will to power in some people, but then to limit the validity of such principles by attacking those *conceptions* of morality which parade these principles as if they were something *more* than personal expressions of the will to power. In this sense, Nietzsche is not after new values after all, nor can we take him completely seriously when he has his Zarathustra announce the advent of a new kind of man. What he urges upon us is not "legislation" of values but to "become who you are." This is far from being a trivial demand; Nietzsche would urge (compare Sartre's nominally similar conception of human consciousness) that none of us "is who he is." The most difficult task is to "overcome ourselves," to overcome that personal timidity which allows us to accept the imposition of external standards of value which are harmful to ourselves. Unfortunately, this most important challenge remains a series of slogans and allegories in Nietzsche's writings. To be totally charitable: perhaps that is his way of urging us to follow ourselves, not him.

NOTES

1. All translations by Walter Kaufmann. *Thus Spoke Zarathustra, Twilight of the Idols,* and *Antichrist* in *Viking Portable Nietzsche* (New York: Viking, 1954); *Will to Power* (New York: Random House, 1967); *Genealogy of Morals* and *Beyond Good and Evil* (New York: Random House, 1966).

2. A current controversy in the now sleepy quarters of "ethical analysis" concerns itself with the *meaning* of "morality." The alternatives generally range between universalizability and social-concern. But if what I have indicated above is correct, "morality" does not have *a* meaning (though it certainly has meaning), and the dispute cannot be settled without appeal to specific goals for which one requires such an analysis.

7

A More Severe Morality:
Nietzsche's Affirmative Ethics

She told me herself that she had no morality,—and I thought she had,
like myself, a more severe morality than anyone.

—NIETZSCHE, in a letter to Paul Rée, 1882.

A mad dog, foaming at the moustache and snarling at the world; that is how the
American artist David Levine portrays Freidrich Nietzsche in his well-known
caricature in *The New York Review of Books.* It is not so different in its malicious
intent, nor further wrong in its interpretation of Nietzsche, than a good number
of scholarly works. This is indeed the traditional portrait: the unconsummated
consummate immoralist, the personally gentle, even timid, archdestroyer. Of
course, Nietzsche himself made adolescent comments about his own destructive-
ness not infrequently—throughout *Ecce Homo,* for example. Nevertheless, these
give a false impression of his intentions as well as of the good philosophical sense
to be made of his works.

In recent years, we have been treated to a rather systematic whitewashing of
Nietzsche. Gone is the foam and the snarl; indeed, what has come to replace the
"revaluation of all values" has become so tame that, a certain impatience for
scholarship aside, one of these new Nietzsches (perhaps not the French one)
would find himself very much at home on most university campuses. This new
Nietzsche, founded by Walter Kaufmann and now promoted by Richard Schacht,
is the champion of honesty against the forces of hypocrisy.[1] Or, more recently, he
is Harold Alderman's benign Californish guru, urging us simply to "be ourselves," preferably by reading Heidegger.[2] This picture is no less false than the
first, but it has the undeniable virtue of welcoming Nietzsche, belatedly, back to
the fold of professional philosophers. Better respectable than rabid, one might
suppose, though I would guess Nietzsche himself would opt for the latter.

The new French Nietzsche, on the other hand, enjoys the *philosophe* at the
extremes, almost beyond the limits of the imaginable, an adolescent implosion of

forces dancing on the edge of nothingness. He is, accordingly, a thoroughly playful
Nietzsche. He is the "anti-Oedipe" as well as the "anti-Christ," a deconstructionist, a Derridaian, a Dada-ian, before his time. He does not destroy but rather
revels in the destruction we have already inflicted upon ourselves. He is a burst
of energy rather than a philosopher, an explosion instead of a visionary. Most of
all, he plays, and reminds us of the importance of dancing and the unimportance
of serious scholarship and Truth. And, we are assured (for example, by David
Allison in his introduction to "The New Nietzsche"[3]) that Nietzsche is wholly
outside of that somber and intellectually fraudulent onto-theological tradition
that he so playfully attacks, but in which we less imaginative and playless scholarly souls are still enmired.

Perhaps. But of all the authors in German history, Nietzsche must surely be
the most historical and even "timely," as well as one of the most solemn (as
opposed to bourgeois "serious"). He was, from all evidence, incapable of even the
uptight version of dancing propounded by his Zarathustra. His playfulness
seemed largely limited to the scholarly joke. Lou Andreas Salomé once described
him (in 1882):

> ... a light laugh, a quiet way of speaking, and a cautious, pensive way of walk-
> ing ... He took pleasure in the refined forms of social intercourse ... But in it
> all lay a penchant for disguise ... I recall that when I first spoke with him his
> formal manner shocked and deceived me. But I was not deceived for long by
> this lonesome man who only wore his mask as unalterably as someone coming
> from the desert and mountains wears the cloak of the worldly-wise ...[4]

Playful, indeed. And as for "the tradition," as it has come to be called, Nietzsche
as philosopher can be understood only within it, despite his unself-critical mega-
lomania about his own "untimely" and wholly novel importance.

It was decidedly *within* that somber philosophical tradition, typically traced
in misleading linear fashion back to Socrates, that I want to try to understand
Nietzsche's ethics. His reputation as archdestroyer and philosophical outlaw has
so enveloped Nietzsche's notorious "reputation," largely at his own bidding, that
the kernel of his moral philosophy—and I do insist on calling it that—has been
lost. There is in Nietzsche, unmistakably, an ethics that is considerably more than
nihilism or academic good fellowship or playfulness, an ethics that is very much
part of "the tradition." It is, however, a brand of ethics that had and has been all
but abandoned in the wake of Kant and the anal compulsiveness of what is now
called rationality in ethics. It is this other brand of ethics, for which Nietzsche
quite properly failed to find a name, that I would like to indicate in this essay.

Nietzsche's Nihilism, and Morality

Nietzsche's novelty is to be found, in part, in his energetic descriptions of what
he calls "nihilism." It is, first of all, a cultural experience, a profound sense of
disappointment, not only, as some ethicists would have it, in the failure of philosophy to justify moral principles, but in the fabric of life as such, the "widespread sensibility of our age" more sympathetically described by Camus half a
century later. It is also, Nietzsche keeps reminding us, a stance to be taken up as

well as a phenomenon to be described. Zarathustra, in one of his more belligerent moments, urges us to "push what is falling" and, in his notes, Nietzsche urges to promote "a complete nihilism," in place of the incomplete nihilism in which we now live. *(WP 28).*[5] Here again we note Nietzsche's self-conscious "timeliness," and his devotion to a tradition dedicated to completeness in ethics.

"Nihilism," obvious entymology aside, does not mean "accepting nothing." Like most philosophical terms, subsequently raised to an isolated and artificial level of abstraction, this one does its work in particular contexts, in specific perspectives, often as a kind of accusation. Some traditional but much-in-the-news Christians use the term as a more or less crude synonym for "secular humanism," on the (false) assumption that a man without God must be a man without Christian values as well. (The dubious argument by Ivan Karamazov: "if there is no God, then everything is permitted.") But note that I say "Christian" values, for the accuser might well allow, indeed insist, that the nihilist does have values,— subjective, self-serving and secularly narrow-minded though they be. (Brother Mitya, perhaps: hardly a paragon if virtue.) Similarly, an orthodox Jewish friend of mine refers to as "nihilists" any people without a self-conscious if not obsessive sense of tradition, assuming that others must lack in their experience what he finds so essential in his own. Marxists use the term (sometimes but not always along with "bourgeois individualism") to indict those who do not share their class-conscious values. Aesthetes use it to knock the philistines, and my academic colleagues use it to chastize anyone with "looser" standards and higher grade averages than themselves. Stanley Rosen attacks nihilism at book length without ever saying exactly what's wrong with it, except that it falls far short of his own rather pretentious search for Hegelian absolute truth.[6]

If Nietzsche made us aware of anything in ethics, it is the importance of *perspectives,* the need to see all concepts and values *in context.* How odd, then, that the key concepts of Nietzsche's own ethics have been so routinely blown up to absolute–that is nonperspectival—proportions. Nihilism is an accusation, in context. Outside of all contexts, it is nothing (which, of course, leads to some quaint and cute Parmenidean wordplay.) As Blanchot has written, nihilism is a particular achievement of a particular sort of society.[7] It becomes a world-hypothesis only at the expense of losing what is most urgent and cleansing in Nietzsche, the attack on the transcendental pretension of understanding the world "in itself" on the basis of our own limited and limiting moral experience.

Nietzsche's nihilism is an accusation *within* the context of traditional ethics (what other kind of ethics could there be?). It points to a tragic or at any rate damnable hollowness in "the moral point of view," which we might anticipate by asking why moral philosophers ever became compelled to talk in such a peculiar fashion. Indeed, it is part and parcel of the whole history of ethics that morality is emphatically *not* just "a point of view"; it is necessary and obligatory. Such talk already betrays a fatal compromise; "perspectivism" and Morality are warring enemies, not complementary theses. What is morality, that it has been forced and has been able to hide behind a veneer of pluralism, to search for "reasons" for its own necessity which—successful or not—leave the acceptance of morality unchallenged?

What is morality? This, perhaps more than any other question, guided Nietzsche's ethics. It is the concept of morals that intrigues Nietzsche: How morals ever became reduced to Morality, how the virtues ever got melted together into the shapeless form of Virtue. But, as I shall argue shortly, there are many meanings of "morality" just as there are many different sorts of morals. (It is the terms themselves—but not just the terms—that is most in question here.) The definition of "morality" that preoccupies Nietzsche, and which I shall be employing here, is the definition provided by Kant: a set of universal, categorical principles of practical reason. "Morals," on the other hand, is a term much less precise, and I shall be using that term much as Hume used it in his *Enquiry*: morals are those generally agreeable or acceptable traits that characterize a good person—leaving quite open the all-important nonconceptual question what is to count (in what context) as a good person. Ethics, finally, I take to be the overall arena in which morality and morals and other questions concerning the good life and how to live it are debated. Morality in its Kantian guise may not be all essential to ethics; indeed, one might formulate Nietzsche's concern by asking how the subject of ethics has so easily been converted into Moral Philosophy, that is, the philosophical analysis of Morality *à la Kant* rather than the somewhat pagan celebration of the virtues *à la Hume* (which is not to say that Nietzsche would have felt very much at home with the Scot either, whatever their philosophical affinities).

In his recent book, *After Virtue*,[8] Alasdair MacIntyre has attacked Nietzsche and nihilism together, as symptoms of our general decay ("decadence" would be too fashionable and thus too positive a term for our moral wretchedness). But in doing so, he has also rendered Nietzsche's own thesis in admirably contemporary form; morality is undone, hollow, an empty sham for which philosophers busily manufacture "reasons" and tinker with grand principles if only to convince themselves that something might still be there. What philosophers defensively call "the moral point of view" is a camouflaged retreat. It serves only to hide the vacuousness of the moral prejudices they serve. Morality is no longer a "tablet of virtues" but a *tabula rasa,* for which we are poorly compensated by the insistence that it is itself necessary. Or, in Hume's terms, morality is the repository of those "monkish" virtues, whose degrading, humiliating effects are disguised by the defenses of reason.[9] For Hume, as for Nietzsche, "some passions are merely stupid, dragging us down with them." And this will be the area where an adequate understanding of morals will emerge, in the realm of passion rather than reason. The good person will emphatically not be the one who is expertly consistent in universalizing maxims according to the principles of practical reason.

Nietzsche, Kant, and Aristotle

Nihilism is not a thesis; it is a reaction. It is not a romantic "naysaying" so much as it is a feature of good old enlightenment criticism in the form of a critical phenomenology or a diagnostic hermeneutics. Indeed, in Germany romanticism and *Aufklärung* were never very clearly distinguished, except in rhetoric, and so, too, beneath the bluster of nihilism a much more profound and, dare I say, reasonable Nietzsche can be discerned. In fact, I want to argue that Nietzsche might best be understood, perhaps ironically, in the company of that more optimistic decadent of ancient times, Aristotle, and in close contrast to the most powerful moral philosopher of modern times—Immanuel Kant. They were hardly nihilists; indeed, they remain even today the two paradigms of morality, the two great proponents of all-encompassing ethical world views. Next to them, the contemporary fiddling with so-called "utilitarianism" seems, as Hegel complained in the *Phenomenology,* rather petty and devoid of anything deserving the honorific name "morality".[10]

It has always seemed to me perverse to read Aristotle and Kant as engaged in the same intellectual exercise, that is, to present and promote a *theory* of morality. They were, without question, both moralists; that is, they had the "moral prejudices" that Nietzsche discovers beneath every philosophical theory. This, of course, would not bother them (except perhaps the word "prejudices"). They were both also, Nietzsche would be the first to argue, *reactionaries,* trying to prop up with an ethics an *ethos*—an established way of life—that was already collapsing. To do so, both ethicists appealed to an overriding (if not absolute) *telos* of reason and rationality, the suspicious status of which Nietzsche deftly displays vis-à-vis Socrates in *Twilight of the Idols.*[11] Both philosophers, too, saw themselves as defenders of "civilized" virtues in the face of the nihilists of their time, though Aristotle displays ample affinity with Protagoras and Kant had no hesitation about supporting Robespierre. But, nevertheless, there is a profound difference between these two great thinkers that too easily gets lost in the need to sustain the linear tradition that supposedly begins with Socrates, ignoring the dialectical conflict that is to be found even within Socrates himself. Aristotle and Kant represent not just two opposed ethical theories, "teleological" and "deontological" respectively, synthesized by the *telos* of rationality. They represent two opposed ways of life.

Aristotle may be a long way from the Greece described by Homer, but the form of his ethics is still very much involved with the Homeric warrior tradition. The virtue of courage still deserves first mention in the list of excellences, and pride is still a virtue rather than a vice. It is an ethics for the privileged few; though Aristotle, unlike Nietzsche, had no need to announce this in a preface. But most important, it is an ethics that is not primarily concerned with rules and principles, much less *universal* rules and principles (i.e., *categorical imperatives.*) Indeed, Aristotle's much-heralded discussion of the so-called "practical syllogism" in book VI of the *Nicomachean Ethics,* in which something akin to principles universal in form (and as ethically invigorating as "eating dry foods is healthy") is quite modest[12]—hardly the cornerstone of his ethics, as some recent scholars have made it out to be.[12] Aristotle's ethics is not an ethics of principles, categorical or otherwise. It is an ethics of *practice,* a description of an actual ethos rather than an abstract attempt to define or create one. Ethos is by its very nature bound to a culture; Kantian ethics, by its pure rational nature but much to its peril, seems not to be. Of course, any philosopher can show how a practice is *really* a rule-governed activity, and proceed to formulate, examine, and criticize the rules.[13] Indeed, one might even show that children playing with their food follow certain rules, but to do so clearly is to misdescribe if not also misunderstand their activity.[14] But what is critical to an ethics of practice is not the absence of rules; it is rather the overriding importance of the concept of *excellence* or virtue (*aretê*). What Aristotle describes is the ideal citizen, the excellent individual who is already (before he studies ethics and learns to articulate principles of any kind) proud of himself and the pride of his family and community. He is

surrounded by friends; he is the model of strength, if not only the physical prow-
ess that was singularly important to Achilles (who was far from ideal in other
virtues). He may have been a bit too "civilized" already for Nietzsche's Homeric
fantasies, but he represents a moral type distinctively different from that
described by Kant, two thousand years later. His ethics are his virtues; his excellence is his pride.

Kant, on the other hand, is the outstanding moralist in a very different tradition. The warrior plays no role and presents us with no ideal; individual talents
and the good fortune of having been "brought up well," which Aristotle simply
presupposes, are ruled out of the moral realm from page one.[15] Kant's ethics is
the ethics of the categorical imperative, the ethics of universal rational principles,
the ethics of obedient virtue instead of the cultivation of the virtues. It is an ethics
that minimized differences and begins by assuming that we all share a common
category of "humanity" and a common moral faculty of reason.The good man is
the man who resists his "inclinations" and acts for the sake of duty and duty
alone. This extreme criterion is qualified in a number of entertaining ways: for
example, by suggesting that the rule that one should cultivate one's talents is itself
an example of the categorical imperative and that one has a peculiar duty to pursue one's own happiness, if only so that one is thereby better disposed to fulfill
one's duties to others.[16]

What I want to argue here should be, in part at least, transparent. Nietzsche
may talk about "creating new values," but—as he himself often says—it is something of a return to an old and neglected set of values—the values of masterly
virtue—that most concerns him. There are complications. We do not have the
ethos of the *Iliad,* nor even the tamer *ethē* of Homer or Aristotle, nor for that
matter even the bourgeois complacency of Kantian Königsberg with its definitive
set of practices in which the very idea of an unconditional imperative is alone
plausible. There is no context, in other words, within which the new virtues we
are to "create" are to be virtues, for a virtue without a practice is of no more
value than a word without a language, a gesture without a context. When
Nietzsche insists on "creating new values," in other words, he is urging us on in
a desperate state of affairs. He is rejecting the mediocre banality of an abstract
ethics of principles, but he has no practice upon which to depend in advancing
his renewed ethics of virtue. No practice, that is, except for the somewhat pretentious and sometimes absurd self-glorification of nineteenth-century German
romanticism, which Nietzsche rebukes even as he adopts it as his only available
context.[17] This is no small point: Nietzsche is not nearly so isolated nor so unique
as he needs to think of himself. Dionysus, like "the Crucified," is an ideal only
within a context, even if, in *Der Fall Nietzsche,* it seems to be a context defined
primarily by rejection.

Nietzsche's nihilism is a reaction against a quite particular *conception* of
morality, summarized in modern times in the ethics of Kant. Quite predictably,
much of Judeo-Christian morality—or what is often called "Judeo-Christian
morality"—shares this conception. It too is for the many, not just a few. It too
treats all souls as the same, whether rational or not. It too dwells on abstractions,
whether such categorical imperatives as "the Golden Rule" or the universal love
called *agapē,* which applies to everyone and therefore to no one in particular.
Hegel was not entirely wrong when, in an early essay, he had Jesus on the Mount

deliver a sermon taken straight from *The Critique of Practical Reason*.[18] Nor was Kant deceiving himself when he looked with pride on his moral philosophy as the heart of Christian ethics, interpreting the commandement to love as well as the desire to be happy as nothing more nor less than instantiations of the categorical imperative, functions of practical reason rather than expressions of individual virtues and exuberance for life.[19]

Aristotle and Achilles versus Kant and Christianity. It is not a perfect match, but it allows us to explain Nietzsche's aims and Nietzsche's problems far better than the overreaching nonsense about "the transvaluation of *all* values" and "Dionysus versus the Crucified." On the other hand, it is not as if Kant and Nietzsche are completely opposed. It is Kant who sets up the philosophical conditions for the Nietzschean reaction, not only by so clearly codifying the central theses to be attacked but also by conceptually undermining the traditional supports of morality. The (*Aufklärung*) attack-on authority ("heteronom") and the emphasis of "automony" by Kant is a necessary precondition for Nietzsche's moral moves, however much the latter presents himself as providing a conception of morality which precedes, rather than presupposes, this Kantian move. It is Kant, of course, who so streses the importance of the Will, which is further dramatized (to put it mildly) by Schopenhauer and which, again, Nietzsche attacks only by way of taking for granted its primary features. (Nietzsche's attacks on "the Will," especially "free will," deserve some special attention in his regard. "Character" and "will to power" are not the same as "will power.") It is Kant who rejects the support of morality by appeal to religion—arguing instead a dependency of the inverse kind—and though Nietzsche's now-tiresome "God is dead" hypothesis may be aimed primarily at the traditional thesis, the bulk of his moral arguments presuppose the Kantian inversion: religion as a rationalization, not the precondition, of moral thinking.

Meanings of Morality

It was Kant too, perhaps, who best exemplified the philosophical temptation to suppose that "morality" refers to a single phenomenon, faculty, or feature of certain, if not all, societies. Moral theories and some specific rules may vary, according to this monolithic position, but Morality is that one single set of basic moral rules which all theories of morality must accept as a given. This is stated outright by Kant, at the beginning of his second *Critique* and his *Grounding of the Metaphysics of Morals*.[20] Every society, one might reasonably suppose, has some "trump" set of rules and regulations which prohibit certain kinds of actions and are considered to be absolute, "categorical." Philosophers might argue whether there is a single rationale behind the variety of rules (a "utility principle" or some principle of authority). Others might challenge the alleged universality and disinterestedness of such principles, but morality everywhere is assumed to be the same, in form if not in content, or in at least intent, nevertheless. Indeed even Nietzsche, in his later works, is tempted by the monolithic image; his pluralistic view of a "tablet of virtues hanging over every people" is explained by his familiar exuberant account: "it is the expression of their Will to Power!" In his repeated "campaign against morality," he too makes it seem too much as if morality is a monolith rather than a complex set of phenomena whose differences may be as striking as their similarities.

What is in question and what ethics is about, according to moral philosophers since Kant, is the *justification* of moral principles, and along with this quest for justification comes the search for a single *ultimate* principle, a *summum bonum,* through which all disagreements and conflicts can be resolved. The question "What is morality?" gets solved in a few opening pages; the search for an adequate answer to the more troublesome challenge, "Why be moral?" becomes the main order of business. The question, however, is not entirely serious. "But there is no reason for worry," Nietzsche assures us (*BGE* 228);[21] "Things still stand today as they have always stood: I see nobody in Europe who has (let alone *promotes*) any awareness that thinking about morality could become dangerous, captious, seductive—that there might be any *calamity* involved." (Ibid.) Thus today we find a nearly total moral skepticism (nihilism?) defended in such centers of Moral Standards as Oxford and Yale, under such nonprovocative titles as "prescriptivism" and "emotivism." But, whatever the analysis, these folks still keep their promises and restrain themselves to their fair share of the high table pie. The quest for justification is not a challenge to the monolith; it is only an exercise.

In fact, it is the phenomenon or morality itself that is in question. More than half a century before Nietzsche issued his challenge to Kant, a more sympathetic post-Kantian, Hegel, attacked the Kantian conception of "morality" in terms that would have been agreeable to Nietzsche, had he been a bit more receptive to the German *Geist*. Hegel too treated the Kantian conception of morality as a monolith, but he also saw that is was surrounded by other conceptions that might also be called "moral" which were, in the *telos* of human development, both superior and more "primitive." One of these was *Sittlichkeit,* or the morality of customs *(Sitten).*[22] It is what we earlier called a morality of *practice,* as opposed to a morality of principles. Hegel proposed not just a different way of interpreting and justifying moral rules (though this would be entailed as well); he defended a conception of morals that did not depend upon rules at all—in which the activity of justification, in fact, became something of a philosophical irrelevancy, at best. The need to justify moral rules betrays an emptiness in those rules themselves, a lack of conviction, a lack of support. Since then, Hegel has mistakenly been viewed as lacking in his concern for the basic ethical question, leading several noted ethical commentators (Popper, Walsh)[23] to accuse him of a gross amorality, conducive to if not openly inviting authoritarianism. It is as if rejecting the Kantian conception of morality and refusing to indulge in the academic justification game were tantamount to abandoning ethics—both the practice and the theory—altogether.

If we are to understand Nietzsche's attack on Morality, we must appreciate not so much the breadth of his attack and the all-out nihilism celebrated by some of his more enthusiastic defenders but rather the more limited precise conception of Morality that falls under his hollow-seeking hammer. We can then appreciate what some have called the "affirmative" side of Nietzsche's moral thinking, the sense in which he sees himself as having "a more severe morality than anybody." In *Beyond Good and Evil* he boasts, "WE IMMORALISTS!— . . . We have been spun into a severe yarn and short of duties and CANNOT get out of that—and in this we are men of duty, we too . . . the dolts and appearances speak against us saying, 'These are men *without* duty.' We always have the dolts and appearances against us." (*BGE* 226) To write about Nietzsche as a literal "immoralist" and the destroyer of morality is to read him badly, or it is to confuse the appearance with the personality. Or, he would say, it is to be a "dolt."

For Nietzsche, as for Hegel, and as for Aristotle, morality does not consist of principles but of practices. It is *doing,* not willing, that is of moral significance, an expression of character rather than a display of practical reason. A practice has local significance; it requires—and sets up—a context; it is not a matter of universal rule; in fact, universality is sometimes argued to show that something is *not* a practice. (For example, sociobiologists have argued that incest and certain other sexual preferences are not sex practices because—on the basis of their alleged universality—they can be shown genetically inherited traits.[14]) Some practices are based upon principles, of course, but not all are; and principles help define a practice, though they rarely if ever do so alone. Hegel and Aristotle, of course, emphasize *collective* social practices, in which laws may be much in evidence. Nietzsche is particularly interested in the "genealogy" of social practices in which principles play a central if also devious role, but he too quickly concludes that there is but one such "moral type" and one alternative "type," which he designates "slave" ("herd") and "master" moralities, respectively. In fact, there are as many moral "types" as one is willing to distinguish, and to designate as "master morality" the historical and anthropological gamut of relatively lawless (as opposed to lawless) societies is most unhistorical as well as confusing philosophically.

The monolithic image of morality, divorced from particular peoples and practices, gives rise to the disastrous disjunction—common to Kant and Nietzsche at least—it is either Morality or *nothing.* If Nietzsche often seems to come up empty-handed and obscurely calling for "the creation of new values," it is because he finds himself rejecting principles without a set of practices to fall back on. If only he had his own non-nihilistic world—something more than his friends and his study and his images of nobility—where he could say, "Here is where we can prove ourselves!" But what he finds instead is the hardly heroic world of nineteenth-century democratic socialism. In reaction, he celebrates self-assertion and "life." This is poor stuff from which to reconstruct Nietzsche's "affirmative philosophy." Add a synthetic notion, "the will to power," and Nietzsche's ethics is reduced to a combination of aggressive banality and energetic self-indulgence. (Would it be unfair to mention Leopold and Loeb here? They were not the least literate of Nietzsche's students.) What we find in appearances, accordingly, is not an "affirmative" philosophy at all. Having given us his polemical typology of morals, the rejection of Morality—misinterpreted as a broad-based rejection of *all* morality (for example, by Philippa Foot, who is one of Nietzsche's more sensitive Anglo-American readers)—seems to lead us to nothing substantial at all.[25] The banality of Zarathustra.

"What is morality?" The very question invites a simple if not simpleminded answer. But "morality" is itself a morally loaded term which can be used to designate and applaude any number of different *ethē* and their justificatory contexts. Nietzsche famously insisted that "there are no moral phenomena, only moral interpretations of phenomena." I would add that there are only moral interpretations of "morality" too. Indeed, I would even suggest that Nietzsche might mean the very opposite of what his aphorism says, that there are *only* moral phenomena, in precisely the sense that Kant denied, especially regarding the supposedly neutral word "Morality" itself.

Areteic Ethics: Nietzsche and Aristotle

In *After Virtue,* Alasdair MacIntyre gives us a choice, *enten-eller:* Nietzsche *or* Aristotle.[26] There is, he explicitly warns us, no third alternative. MacIntyre sees Nietzsche's philosophy as purely destructive, despite the fact that he praises the archdestroyer for his insight into the collapse of morals that had been increasingly evident since the Enlightenment. MacIntyre chooses Aristotle as the positive alternative. Aristotle had an *ethos:* Nietzsche leaves us with nothing. But Nietzsche is nevertheless the culmination of that whole tradition—which we still refer to as "moral philosophy" or "ethics"—which is based on a tragic and possibly irreversible error in both theory and practice. The error is the rejection of ethos as the foundation of morality with a compensating insistence on the rational justification of morality. Without a presupposed ethos, no justification is possible. Within an ethos, none is necessary. (Nietzsche: "not to *need* to impose values . . .") And so after centuries of degeneration, internal inconsistencies and failures in the Enlightenment project of transcending mere custom and justifying moral rules once and for all, the structures of morality have collapsed, leaving only incoherent fragments. "Ethics" is the futile effort to make sense of the fragments and "justify" them, from Hume's appeal to the sentiments and Kant's appeal to practical reason to the contemporary vacuity of "metaethical" theory. Here is the rubble that Nietzsche's Zarathustra urges us to clear away. Here is the vacuum in which Nietzsche urges us to become "legislators" and "create new values." But out of what are we to do this? What would it be, "to create a new value"?

MacIntyre, by opposing Nietzsche and Aristotle, closes off to us the basis upon which we could best reconceive of morality: a reconsideration of Aristotle through Nietzschean eyes. Nietzsche, of course, encourages the antagonistic interpretation. But the opposition is ill conceived, and the interpretation is misleading. MacIntyre, like Philippa Foot, takes Nietzsche too literally to be attacking *all* morality. But quite the contrary of rejecting the ethics of Aristotle, I see Nietzsche as harking back to Aristotle and the still warrior-bound aristocratic tradition he was (retrospectively) cataloging in his *Nicomachean* (Neo-McKeon) *Ethics.* Whatever the differences between Greece of the *Illiad* and Aristotle's Athens, there was a far vaster gulf—and not only in centuries—between the elitist ethics of Aristotle and the egalitarian, bourgeois, Pietist ethics of Kant. Nietzsche may have envisioned himself as Dionysus versus the Crucified; he is better understood as a modern-day Sophist versus Kant, a defender of the virtues against the categorical imperative.

When I was in graduate school an embarrassing number of years ago, my professor Julius Moravscik began his lectures on Aristotle with a comparison to Nietzsche. They were two of a kind, he said, both functionalists, naturalists, "teleologists," standing very much opposed to the utilitarian and Kantian temperaments. Moravscik never followed this through, to my knowledge, but his casual seminar remark has stuck with me for all of these years, and the more I read and lecture on both authors, so different in times and tempers, the more I find the compasion illuminating. Nietzsche was indeed, like Aristotle, a self-proclaimed functionalist, naturalist, teleologist, and, I would add, an elitist, though on both men's views this would follow from the rest. Nietzsche's functionalism is most evident in his constant insistence that we *evaluate* values, see what they are *for,* what role they play in the survival and life of a people. He never tires of telling us about his "naturalism," of course, from his flatly false declaration that he is the first philosopher who was also a psychologist (MacIntyre here substitutes sociology) to his refreshing emphasis on psychological explanation in place of rationalizing justification. Nietzsche often states this in terms of the "this-worldly" as opposed to the "other-worldly" visions of Christianity, but I think that this is not the contrast of importance. Indeed, today it is the very "this-worldly" activity of some Christian power blocks that is a major ethical concern, and there is much more to naturalism (as opposed, for example, to Kant's rationalism) than the rejection of heaven and hell as the end of ethics. (Kant, of course, would agree with that too).

Nietzsche's teleology is at times as cosmic as Aristotle's, especially where the grand *telos* becomes "the will to power." But on the strictly human (if not all-too-human) level, Nietzsche's ethics like Aristotle's can best be classified in introductory ethics readers as an ethics of "self-realization." "Become who you are" is the slogan in the middle writings: the *telos* of the *Übermensch* serves from *Thus Spake Zarathustra* on. Indeed, who is the *Ubermensch* if not Aristotle's *megalopsychos,* "the great-souled man" from whom Nietzsche even borrows much of his "master-type" terminology. He is the ideal who "deserves and claims great things." He is the man driven by what Goethe (the most frequent candidate for *Übermensch* status) called his "daemon" (the association with Aristotle's *"eu-daimonia"* is not incidental).

Aristotle's teleology begins modestly, with the *telos* of the craftsman, the physician, the farmer. Each has his purpose, his own criteria for excellence, his own "good." But such modest goods and goals are hardly the stuff of ethics, and Aristotle quickly turns to "the good for man," by which he means the ideal man, and the "function of man," by which he means man at his best.[27] There is no point to discussing what we banally call today "the good person," who breaks no rules or laws, offends no one and interests no one except certain moral philosophers. There is no reson to discuss *hoi polloi,* who serve their city-state well and honor their superiors appropriately. It is the superiors themselves who deserve description, for they are the models from whom the vision of humanity is conceived. What sort of insanity, we hear Aristotle and Nietzsche asking in unison, can explain the idea that all people are of equal value, that everyone and anyone can serve as an ideal, as a model for what is best in us? With leaders like Pericles, who needs the categorical imperative? ("What are morals to us sons of God?") With leaders like our own, no wonder we are suffocating with laws.

To reject egalitarian ethics and dismiss the banal notion of "the good person" as no ethical interest is not to become an "immoralist." It does not mean breaking all the rules. It does not result in such inability as suffered by Richard Hare, a temporary incapacity to morally censure Hitler for any rational reasons.[28] Or, if we want an "immoralist," he might be at worst the sort of person that André Gide created in his short novel of that name, a man who senses his own mortality and luxuriates in his own bodily sensations, amused and fascinated by the foibles of people around him.[29] This is not, of course, the man whom Aristotle has in mind. The Stagirite was concerned with statesmen, philosopher-kings, the flesh-and-blood *Übermenschen* who exist in actuality, not just in novels and philosophical fantasies and Zarathustra's pronouncements. But Nietzsche too, when it comes down to cases, is concerned not with a phantom but with real-life heroes, the "great men" who justify (I use the word advisedly) the existence of the society that created them—and which they in turn created. But though he may shock us with his military language, the *Übermenschen* more near to his heart are for the most part his artistic comrades, "philosophers, saints and artists."[30] The rejection of bourgeois morality does not dictate cruelty but rather an emphasis on excellence. The will to power is not *Reich* but *Macht* and not supremacy but superiority. Nietzsche urges us to create values, but I believe that it is the value of creating as such—and having the strength and the *telos* to do so—that he most valued. The unspoken but always present thesis is this: It is only in the romantic practice of artistic creativity that modern excellence can be achieved.

Elitism is not itself an ethics. Indeed, I think both Aristotle and Nietzsche might well object to it as such. It is rather the presupposition that people's talents and abilities differ. It is beginning with what is the case. (Compare John Rawls: "It is upon a correct choice of a basic structure of society ... that justice ... depends.")[31] The purpose of an ethics is to maximize people's potential, to encourage the most and the best from all of them, but more by far from the best of them. It is also the recognition that any universal rule—however ingeniously formulated and equally applied—will be disadvantageous to someone, coupled with the insistence that it is an enormous waste as well as unfair (both authors worry more about the former than the latter) for the strong to be limited by the weak, the productive limited by the unproductive, the creative limited by the uncreative. It will not do to mask the point by saying that elitism does not treat people unequally, only differently. It presumes inequality from the outset, and defends it by appeal to the larger picture. Aristotle by appeal to the well-being of the city-state and the natural order of things, Nietzsche by a more abstract but very modern romantic appeal to human creativity. Of course, Nietzsche refuses to be so Kantian as to appeal to "humanity" as such, and so he appeals to a step beyond humanity, to *über*-humanity. But what is the *Übermensch* but a projection of what is best in us, what Kant called "dignity" but Nietzsche insists is "nobility." The difference, of course, is that Kant thought that dignity was inherent in everyone of us; Nietzsche recognizes nobility in only the very few.

What is essential to this view of ethics—let us not call it elitist ethics but rather an ethics of virtue, *areteic* ethics—is that the emphasis is wholly on excellence, a teleological conception. What counts for much less is obedience of rules, laws, and principles, for one can be wholly obedient and also dull, unproductive, and useless. This does not mean that the "immoralist"—as Nietzsche misleadingly calls him—will kill innocents, steal from the elderly and betray the community, nor even, indeed, run a car through a red light. The *Übermensch* character is perfectly willing to act "in accordance with morality," even in a qualified way, "for the sake of duty," that is, if it is a duty that fits his character and his telos. In a much-dehbated passage, Nietzsche even insists that the strong have a "duty" to help the weak, a statement that is utterly confusing on the nihilist interpretation of Nietzsche's ethics.[32] What the *Übermensch*-aspirant does not recognize are *categorical* imperatives, commands made impersonally and universally, without respect for rank or abilities. As a system of hypothetrical imperatives useful to his purposes, however, the *Übermensch* might be as moral as anyone else. (Why Phillipa loves Friedrich, and how the spirit of Sils Maria finally comes to Oxford).

MacIntyre's diagnosis of our tragic fate turns on his recognition that the singular ethos upon which a unified and coherent ethics might be based has fragmented. We no longer have a culture with customs and an agreed upon system of morals; we instead have pluralism. Our insistence on tolerance and our emphasis on rules and laws are a poor substitute, more symptoms of our malaise rather than possible cures. But Nietzsche is something more than the pathologist of a dead or dying morality. He is also the champion of that sense of integrity that MacIntyre claims we have lost. The question is, "How is integrity possible in a society without an ethos or, in more positive terms, in a pluralist society with many *ethē,* some of them admittedly dubious?" Does it make sense in such a society to still speak of "excellence," or should we just award "achievement" and recognize limited accomplishments in cautiously defined subgroups and professions? Or should we rather express the atavistic urge to excellence with an intentionally obscure phrase: "will to power"?

Nietzsche's Problem

In Aristotle, two convening ideals made possible his powerful teleological vision: the unity of his community and the projected vision of the *telos* of man (which not incidentally coincided with the best images of his community). We no longer have that unified community—although those are not the grounds on which Nietzsche rejects bourgeois morality. (Indeed, sometimes it is the small-mindedness of small communities that he most violently reacts against.) It is not difficult to see Nietzsche's provocative ethics as precisely the expression of a rather distinctive if ill-circumscribed community, namely the community of disaffected academics and intellectuals, but this in not an ethos that Nietzsche could recognize as the basis for his rather extravagant claims for a new ethics. Nevertheless, Nietzsche, like Aristotle, held onto the vision of an overriding human *telos,* an enormous sense of human *potential,* a hunger for excellence that is ill-expressed by his monolithic expression, "will to power."

Depending on one's views of Aristotle (some rather priggish Oxford ethicists have called him a "prig"), this view of Nietzsche may or may not be considered another case of Anglo-American whitewash. After all, Aristotle may have retained some of the warrior virtues, but most of his virtues are distinctively those of the good citizen, concerned with justice and friendship and getting along together. There is little of the fire and ice that Nietzsche talks about, certainly no emphasis on cruelty and suffering. Aristotle was hardly the lonely wanderer in the mountains and desert whom Nietzsche sometimes resembled and celebrated in *Zarathustra.* However aristocratic they may be, Aristotle's virtues seem too genteel, too much in the spirit of party life to be comparable to Nietzsche's severe moral strictures (see Zarathustra's "party" in part IV). It would be an unforgivable historical mistake to call Aristotle's virtues "bourgeois," but, nevertheless, they surely lack the cutting edge of Nietzsche's pronouncements.

The problem, however, is that Nietzsche's affirmative instructions are often without substantial content. It is all well and good to talk about the glories of solitude, but Nietzsche's own letters and friendships show us that he himself lived by his friends, defined himself in terms of them. Zarathustra, Biblical bluster aside, spends most of his time looking for friends. "Who would want to live without them?" asked Aristotle rhetorically in his *Ethics.* Surely not Nietzsche. And he was, by all accounts, a good friend, an enthusiastic friend. And if he remained lonely, that is a matter for psychiatric, not ontological, diagnosis. As for the warrior spirit, the cutting edge of cruelty, the fire and ice, there is little evidence that we have that Nietzsche either displayed or admired them, Lou's description of the glint in his eyes notwithstanding. His own list of virtues included such Aristotlean traits as honesty, courage, generosity, and courtesy.[33] (*Daybreak* 556). And, at the end, didn't he collapse while saving a horse from a beating?

One needn't ask whether Aristotle lived up to his own virtues. But Nietzsche leaves so much unsaid, and gives us so much hyperbolically, that an ad hominem hint is not beside the point. One can grasp the struggle with morality that is going on in the man, so readily expressed in the murderous language of adolescence, without confusing the rhetoric with the ideals. There are different warriors for different times. Achilles suited the *Iliad.* Our warrior today is Gandhi.

Nietzsche's problem is that he sees himself as a destroyer, not a reformer or a revisionist. ("On the Improvers of Mankind" in *Twilight of the Idols,* for example).[34] He sees the Judeo-Christian tradition and the Morality that goes with it as a single historical entity, against which there is no clearly conceived alternative. Consequently, he gives us two very different prescriptions for our fate, which includes the moral collapse that has been so systematically described by MacIntyre.

First, he urges us to recapture a sense of "master" morality, a morality of nobility, insofar as this nobility is still possible, after two thousand years of Christianity. The war-torn pre*polis* world of the *Iliad* is gone, and it is never clear what Nietzsche intends to replace it with. Democracy and socialism have rendered the aristocratic virtues unacceptable, even where these coincide exactly with the good bourgeois virtues (courtesy, for instance). The foundation is gone; human equality has become an a priori truth. If "Christianity is Platonism for the masses," then democratic socialism is Christianity for the middle class.

That is on the one side—an impossible nostalgia, not unlike the American (and European) fantasy about the American West, "where men were men" (but were in fact unwashed and hungry refugees eking out a difficult living.) But if there is no warrior ethos to which we can return, then what? "The creation of values!" Nietzsche says. But what is it to "create a value"? Not even Nietzsche suggests one—not even *one!* What he does is to remind us, again and again, of old and established values which can be used as an ethical Archimedean point, to topple the professions of a too abstract, too banal morality that fails to promote the virtues of character. He appeals to weakness of will (not by that name) and resentment—what could be more Christian vices? He charges us with hypocrisy—the tribute that even "immoralists" pay to virtue. He points out the cruelty of Tertullian and other Christian moralists. He chastizes the Stoics for emulating wasteful nature. He attacks Spinoza for being too in love with "his own wisdom." He attacks Christianity as a whole as a "slave" morality, a "herd instinct" detrimental to the progress of the species as a whole. New values?

Ethics is an expression of an ethos. There is no such thing as "creating new values" in Nietzsche's sense. It is not like declaring clam shells as currency and it is not, as in MacIntyre's good example, Kamehameha II of Hawaii declaring invalid the "taboos" whose function had long ago been forgotten. Nietzsche does not reject morals, only one version of Morality, which has as its instrument the universalizable principles formalized by Kant, the ancestries of which go all the way back to the Bible. But, as Scheler says in defense of Christianity, the diagnosis is not complete. Indeed, it would not be wrong (as Lou Salomé observed) to see Nietzsche as an old-fashioned moralist, disgusted with the world around him but unable to provide a satisfactory account of an alternative and unable to find a context in which an alternative could be properly cultivated.

None of this is to deny that Nietzsche is, as Kaufmann calls him, a moral revolutionary, or that he has an affirmative ethics. He is indeed after something new and important, even if it is also very old and something less than the creation of new values. He is, as MacIntyre puns, after virtues, even if he would prefer to think of them in Homeric rather than Aristotelean form. And in his writings and his letters, the focus of that alternative is as discernible as the larger concept of Morality he attacks. It is Aristotle's ethics of virtue, an ethics of practice instead of an ethics of principle, an ethics in which *character,* not duty or abstract poses of universal love, plays the primary role. "To give style to one's character. A rare art."[35] In that one sentence, Nietzsche sums up his own ethics far better than in whole books of abuse:

> One more word against Kant as a *Moralist.* A virtue must be *Our Own* invention, *Our* most necessary self-expression and self-defense; any other kind of virtue is a danger . . . "Virtue," "duty," the "good in itself," the good which is impersonal and universally valid—chimeras and expressions of decline, of the final exhaustion of life, of the Chinese phase of Königsberg. The fundamental laws of self-preservation and growth demand the opposite—that everyone invent *his own* virtue, his *own* categorical imperative. A people perishes when it confuses *Its* duty with duty in general . . . *ANTI*-Nature as instinct, German decadence as philosophy—*THAT IS KANT. (A* 11)[36]

NOTES

1. Walter Kaufmann, *Nietzsche: Philosopher, Psychologist, Antichrist,* 4th ed. (Princeton, N.J.: Princeton University Press, 1974).

2. Richard Schacht, *Nietzsche* (London: Routledge and Kegan-Paul, 1983).

3. David Allison, ed., *The New Nietzsche* (Columbus: Ohio University Press, 1980).

4. Lou Salomé (1882) quoted in Karl Jasper's *Nietzsche* (Tucson: University of Arizona Press, 1965) pp. 37-B and in R. C. Solomon, ed., *Nietzsche* (New York: Doubleday, 1963) p. 8.

5. Nietzsche, *The Will to Power,* trans. and ed. by Walter Kaufmann (New York: Random House, 1968). All references are to paragraph numbers.

6. Stanley Rosen, *Nihilism.* Cf. his more recent *G. W. F. Hegel: An Introduction to His Science of Wisdom* (New Haven, Conn.: Yale University Press, 1974).

7. Maurice Blanchot, "The Limits of Experience: Nihilism," *L'etretien infini,* reprinted in Allison, op. cit., pp. 121–8.

8. Alasdair MacIntyre, *After Virtue* (Notre Dame, Ind.: University of Notre Dame Press, 1981).

9. David Hume. *A Treatise of Human Nature* (Oxford: Oxford University Press, 1978). bk. II, esp. pp. 297ff.

10. G. W. F. Hegel, *The Phenomenology of Spirit,* trans by A. W. Miller (Oxford, Oxford University Press, 1977). See esp. paras. 559–62 and Hegel's attack on the enlightenment emphasis on "the Useful" ("an abomination" and "utterly detestable").

11. Nietzsche, *Twilight of the Idols,* trans., Kaufmann in *The Portable Nietzsche* (New York: Viking, 1954). pp. 473–79 and 479–84.

12. See, for example, G. E. M. Anscombe in *Intention* (Oxford: Oxford University Press, 1957). esp. pp. 58–66, and John Cooper's rebuttal in his *Aristotle.*

13. E. g. William Frankena, *Ethics,* 2d ed. (Englewood Cliffs, N.J.: Prentice-Hall, 1973). pp. 62–67.

14. The delightful use of this example is in MacIntyre, op. cit., contrasting descriptive reports of practices with prescriptive rules.

15. Immanuel Kant, *Grounding for the Metaphysics of Morals* (Indianapolis, Ind.: Hackett, 1983). pt. 1, p. 7.

16. Ibid, pp. 12.

17. E.g., "At first, I approached the modern world . . . *hopefully.* I understood . . . the philosophical pessimism of the nineteenth century as if it were the symptom of a greater strength of thought, of more daring courage, and of a more triumphant fullness of life . . . What is romanticism? Every art and every philosophy may be considered a remedy and aid in the service of growing and struggling life, but there are two kinds of sufferers: first those who suffer from an *overfullness of life* . . . and then there are those who suffer from the *impoverishment of life* . . . To this dual need of the *latter* corresponds all romanticism . . .
The will to *eternalize* also requires a dual interpretation. First, it can come from gratitude and love . . . But it can also be that tyrannic will (i.e. *ressentiment*) of one who is seriously ailing, struggling, and tortured . . . (*Gay Science,* 370).
Cf. Novalis: "The world must be made more romantic. Then once more we shall discover its original meaning. To make something romantic . . . the lower self becomes identified with the higher self."

18. G. W. F. Hegel, *The Life of Jesus,* (1975) trans. by Peter Fuss (Notre Dame, Ind.: University of Notre Dame Press, 1984).

19. Kant, op. cit. pp.12.

20. Kant, op. cit, and the second *Critique,* trans. by L. W. Beck (Indianapolis, Ind.: Bobbs-Merrill, 1956).

21. Nietzsche, *Beyond Good and Evil,* trans. by Kaufmann (New York: Random House, 1966). All references are to paragraph numbers.

22. Hegel, *System der Sittlichkeit* (1802) and *The Phenomenology,* pt. C (AA), Ch. VI ("Spirit"), esp. paras. 439–50.

23. Karl Popper. *The Open Society and Its Enemies* (London: Routledge and Kegan-Paul, 1954). W. H. Walsh, *Hegel's Ethics* (New York: St. Martin's, 1969).

24. Edward O. Wilson toys with this argument, for example, in the infamous twenty-seventh chapter of his *Sociobiology* (Cambridge, Mass.: Harvard University Press, 1978).

25. Philippa Foot, "Nietzsche: The Revaluation of Values," in Solomon, ed., op. cit., pp. 156–68.

26. MacIntyre, op. cit., pp. 103ff.

27. Aristotle, *Nicomachean Ethics,* trans. by H. Rackham (Cambridge, Mass.: Harvard University Press, 1946). bk. 1, ch. ii.

28. Richard Hare, *Freedom and Reason,* (Oxford: Clarendon, 1963), e.g., p. 172.

29. André Gide, *The Immortalist* (New York: Vintage, 1954).

30. Alexander Nehemas has completed one long-needed bit of empirical research in this regard: in *Beyond Good and Evil,* he has found that better than three quarters of the candidates for *Übermensch* are writers. See his forthcoming *Nietzsche: Life as Literature* (Cambridge: Harvard University Press, 1986).

31. John Rawls. *A Theory of Justice* (Cambridge, Mass.: Harvard University Press, 1971).

32. "When the exceptional human being treats the mediocre more tenderly than himself and his peers, this is not mere courtesy of the heart—it is simply his duty." Nietzsche. *The Antichrist,* trans., by Walter Kaufmann in *The Portable Nietzsche* (New York: Viking, 1954), para. 57.

33. Nietzsche, *Daybreak,* trans. by R. J. Hollingdale (Cambridge, Mass.: Cambridge University Press, 1982). References are to paragraph numbers.

34. Nietzsche, *Twilight of the Idols,* trans. by Kaufmann in *Portable Nietzsche,* op. cit.

35. Nietzsche, *The Gay Science,* trans. by Kaufmann (New York: Random House, 1974), para. 290.

36. *The Antichrist,* op. cit.

8

Sex and Perversion

Sexuality is often said to be one of the appetites, like thirst and hunger—an instinctual drive, the animal lust that invades the ego from the subconscious "id" and that is without logic, morality, scruples, and often without taste. But if sexuality were merely an appetite, it would be inexplicable that our lives should be so complicated, so threatened, so secretive and repressed, so ritualized and obsessed by a desire that has so little survival value and so many dangers. Like the appetites, sexuality admits of failures of both deficiency and excess, although it is understandably only the former that is common cause for grievance. Sexuality also admits of infinite variations for the sake of sociability, elegance, taste, and diversion, once its most primitive demands have been met, and here again it resembles thirst and hunger. But sexuality, at least in this and many other societies, is thought to have a dimension that hunger and thirst surely lack, a moral and interpersonal dimension that is essential to our very conception of sexuality. This is nowhere more evident than in the notion of "sexual perversion," for which there are no plausible analogues in the appetitive realms of food and drink.[1]

Perversion

"Perversion" is an insidious concept. It presents itself as a straightforward descriptive term, but carries with it an undeniable connotation of moral censure. To describe a person or an activity as perverse is not yet a full-blown moral condemnation, for it need not entail that one *ought* not to indulge in such activities.

Yet such censure may be more offensive than open moral condemnation, for it suggests that the person in question is "sick" or an inferior human being or that the activity is depraved. Freud, for example, while resisting all moral evaluation of perversions, does not hesitate to characterize them as matters of "arrested development." Similarly, moralists find an easy refuge in such apparently descriptive and quasi-moral categories, for it provides them with an arsenal of weapons for self-righteous abuse of others that is made all the more effective by its ability to disavow moral intent and to draw on the researches of science. Accordingly, I want to begin by noticing how the very idea of "sexual perversion" forces many of our attitudes about ourselves and our relationships with other people on the defensive, and, in so doing, places what we might call "straight sex" above criticism by making it the criterion by which other sexual activities are judged. What I should like to argue, perhaps perversely, is that the very idea of "sexual perversion" is itself perverse.

It is worth insisting from the outset that perversion has nothing to do with statistics. Perversions cannot be identified or condemned just because they happen to be activities that are engaged in by a small number of people. But neither, then, can these same activities be defended on statistical grounds. Kinsey's early figures, which suggest that 95 percent of American adult males engage in "perverse" activities, prove nothing. Nor does the current popularity of pornographic movies and the consequent porno-business boom constitute a case for the defense or redefinition of sexual perversion. It is a symptom of our logical incontinence that we so typically appeal to statistics to defend our personal prejudices, when we would reject the same appeal were the figures turned against us. The same sexual activities that were once defined and attacked on the basis of their infrequency are now typically defended by appeal to the large number of "respectable" middle-class couples who enjoy them. But the fact that thousands of middle-aged, middle-class New Yorkers paid five dollars each to watch the swallowing of the giant genitalia in *Deep throat* does not constitute a statistical or an economic defense of fellatio, or voyeurism, or pornography. But, insofar as perversion is a quasi-moral concept, the defensive traditionalists are in the right: the topic of perversion is not subject to argument by numbers. It could be, in fact, that "straight sex," once we get straight about sex, could itself be a "perversion" of sexuality.

"Sexual perversion" indicates deviation from a norm, but not from a statistical norm. Perversion is an *abuse* of an established function, a corruption, not simply a diversion or a deviation. Sexuality, like all human activities, serves some natural purpose, some end that we can recognize as a reason for putting up with considerable anxiety and aggravation in a lifelong rabbit-race that only occasionally meets our expectations and is too infrequently satisfied at all for the most people. It is the *importance* of sexuality in our lives that cries out for explanation, and such explanations are typically in terms of the fact that sexuality is a "natural" activity, that it is an instinct, part of our animal nature, a biological need, and so on. Acordingly, the idea of sexual perversion is derivative of this idea of natural purpose, and perverse activities are those that deviate from this purpose taken as a norm. Sexual perversion is acting at cross-purposes with nature. But then, what is "natural sex"?

It is fair enough to try to provide an account of "natural sex" by an appeal to "nature." And sex does serve an obvious biological function, that of reproduction (or, moving from the biological to the pious, "procreation"). As such, not only human adults but animals of most kinds and many plants engage in sexual activity or, at least, are "sexual beings" in a familiar technical sense. Natural sex, accordingly, is that which aims at reproduction (although there is a serious ambiguity here of whether it is nature that aims or rather those engaged in sexual activity who aim at reproduction).

I take it to be beyond argument that human sexuality is more than this. In fact, one might argue that most human sexual activity not only is not aimed at reproduction but is practiced *in spite of* the threat of reproducing. (This is true even of those who would argue that contraception and abortion are wrong.) This pervasive interest in nonreproductive sexuality is not a matter of widespread sexual perversion, although doubtless there are still those who would argue so. Rather it is due to the very nature of sexuality itself. Arguments to the contrary, whether derived from personal neuroses or high-level theological doctrines (or both), exemplify a profound disregard for the realities of human life, and reality is all that interests us here. Our starting point will be that human sexuality has its own "natural purposes," its own "nature," apart from any *further* purposes attributed to our creator, and apart from any biological function of increasing the numbers of an already too numerous natural kind.

Natural Sex

What is "natural sex"? It seems reasonable to look to nature for an account, but it is clear from the history of the philosophical concept of "nature" that this is not what has been intended. The concept of "nature" is our inheritance from Aristotle and then from the Enlightenment, and as such it betrays the familiar sophistries of those pervasive forms of Western thinking. When the philosophes of eighteenth-century France and their counterparts in England and America appealed to "nature," it was rarely biological nature that they had in mind. Rather, "nature" served as a particularly solid and incontrovertible court of appeal, beyond the reach of the dogmas and practices of particular traditional and typically outdated societies. However, "nature" is not the natural world, but man's "natural reason." "Nature" is what is rational, not what is biological, and has a decided moral edge. When philosophers sought a "natural religion" or "natural justice," for example, they were not appealing to a "return to nature," to nature worship or animal faith, nor to the "law of the jungle." They were appealing to *reason,* to rational faith and rational law. And so, too, "natural sex," as part of this tradition, is not a call for bestiality or rear-entry intercourse, but to "rational sex." Thus we should not be surprised that most talk of "natural sex" carries with it a decided moral overtone. And, since sex is generally considered to be a paradigm of *ir*rational human activity, we should not be surprised that "rational sex" tends to emerge as *minimal* sex.

Even after sexuality has been severed from its reproductive consequences, the obsession with quick, efficient heterosexual intercourse—the two-minute emissionary missionary male-superior ejaculation service[2]—remains. Even with the traditional biological and theological arguments defused, the conclusion—the equation of male-evacuation lust with sexuality—persists.[3] Whenever the appeal to "natural sexuality" arises, it is necessary to balance the account by reference to the perverse wisdom of the notorious Marquis de Sade, who was a genius at twisting "arguments from design" to justify his own tastes. He argued and profusely illustrated the proposition that any possible human sensuous activity, whether buggery or impassioned murder could not help but be "natural." Against the horror of the pious concerning the "wasting of seed," in onanism and masturbation, de Sade wryly comments that nature herself seems to have arranged generously for such "spillage." Against the "natural design" arguments for genital intercourse, de Sade argues with vengeance—turning the Enlightenment against itself—that the relative sizes of the various apertures and protrusions of the human body could only have been so fittingly designed in order to be employed accordingly. If "nature" is to be the standard, argues de Sade, we can find much in nature that is cruel and destructive, surprisingly little that is truly creative; and so cruelty and rape are at least as "natural" as reproductive intercourse. Of course there is a second thread of argument that pervades de Sade's thesis: that this indifference of the universe and nature is an outrage to us. Much as Camus was to argue a similar thesis above the belt more recently, de Sade argues that nature's indifference to waste and cruelty is a cause for contemptuous assault and scorn on our part. But if the arguments seem at odds with each other, the upshot is the same—any act humanly possible is as natural, or as unnatural, as any other.

Freud's Reinterpretation of Sexuality

The breakdown of this "rational" and quasi-moral, pious view of sex owes much to Sigmund Freud, the single most important theoretician in the modern fight for sexual liberation.[4] It was Freud, primarily in his "Three Contributions to the Theory of Sex," who changed our conception of sexuality from reproduction to sex-for-its-own-sake, to personal satisfaction. (Although it is necessary to stress that Freud took the new concept, as well as the old one, to be a *biological,* and thereby a "natural," conception.) It was Freud who argued that sexual activity is aimed at release of tension or "discharge" (which he called, misleadingly, "pleasure") and as such aims at no further goals. So conceived, the paradigm sexual activity might be thought of not in terms of heterosexual intercourse but in terms of scratching an itch. Of course the activity that releases tension also serves to increase the tension to be released (the greater the "pleasure"). So conceived, genital sex is but a single possibility for sexual activity, based on the *contingency* that the genitals of an adult generally provide the most prominent erogenous zone; that is, it itches or can be made to itch more than any other place on the body and thus feels better when appropriately scratched. Freud's theory, although based on painstaking empirical observations, clearly marks a conceptual or philosophical revolution as well as a scientific one. According to this conception of sex, heterosexual intercourse loses both its logically and its biologically privileged position in the repertoire of human sexual response. It is no longer *logically* privileged because sex is now conceived in terms of discharge (or "pleasure"), and it is at most a contingent fact (and probably not even that) that most people gain the greatest release of tension (or "pleasure") from intercourse alone. It is no longer biologically privileged because sex as sex is no longer conceived in terms of the further purposes it serves but rather in its own terms. It should be noted that sexuality, so conceived, is no longer "an aspect of," but is the contrary of, reproductive sex: it is defined as an activity that, as sex, has no further aims. Accordingly, intercourse with the explicit intention to conceive children is no longer pure sex, but sex plus something else.

We might also make note of the fact that sexuality, so conceived, can be used to serve other, ulterior, purposes as well. In fact sex aimed at reproduction is probably the least frequent, and also philosophically the least interesting, of the varieties of "impure sex," that is, sexuality not for its own sake, sex for pleasure. People use sex as an expression of power, or as an expression of impotence (the one often parading as the other), as a way of going to sleep, as a way of getting even, as a way of getting ahead in careers, as a way of distracting themselves, as a way of demeaning themselves, and so on. On Freud's account, these various extrasexual aims, however commonly they might be conjoined with sexual desire and activity, are not themselves sexual, and sexuality is not to be identified with any of them. Once sexuality is so conceived, the road is opened to a new interpretation of its extent and domain. Under the old pious and puritanical conception, sex was for strictly ulterior purposes, and pleasure was at most a by-product: excess pleasure was condemnable as "unnatural." And under the old conception, sexual activity was limited to being a means to an end. Its paradigm accordingly was male "evacuation lust" (coupled with female submissiveness). A sexual perversion, then, was any alteration in this basic function, even prolongation beyond the minimum requisite time for ejaculation of the male, any alteration in position, and needless to say, any attempt or desire on the part of either for equal enjoyment on the part of the female. It is with Freud that this horror story loses its grounds, for sex as release of tension or "pleasure" or "satisfaction" is not related to any particular social or sexual roles, nor aimed at serving any function beyond the release of tension (which, Freud also realizes, is intentionally created for the sake of releasing it), and so the old restrictions melt away. Sexual release need not be through intercourse alone, nor need it even involve intercourse; it need not be heterosexual, nor need it even involve more than a single person. Here is the "Copernican revolution" of our sexual liberation. It always strikes me as unfair, if not insulting or embarrassing, that Freud is so often dismissed for his sexual conservatism and blamed for enforcing the attitudes that have encouraged male repression and female oppression. But Freud is the revolutionary who, like most revolutionaries, was unable to free himself of the old prejudices, now seen as weaknesses, that he was instrumental in overcoming. Without Freud, the questions that now appear as accusations against him could not even be asked. It is with him that former "sexual perversions," including enjoyment, can now claim legitimacy as full-blooded, "natural" sexual activities.[5]

It is well known how Freud extended the scope of sexuality far beyond its traditional limitations. From his account of sexuality as "release of tension," we can easily see how he did this, and how it became possible for him to account for the rich empirical findings of child psychology with his revised and expanded notion of sexuality. As release of tension, oral and anal sexuality are literally sexual although they need not involve any use or association with the genitals or with the reproductive functions. Oral sexuality, for example, is sexuality because appropriate stimulation of the lips, tongue, and mucous membranes of the mouth is "satisfying." Yet oral sexuality maybe distinguished from other forms of oral satisfaction, notably eating and drinking, by the fact that it appears as an end in itself (even if, as Freud insists, the erogenous functions of the mouth may be consequent to associations with the satisfactions of eating). In other words, oral sexuality, like genital sexuality, must be (on Freud's account) satisfaction of an automonous sort, not satisfaction of anything else. Yet, again, this is not to say that it cannot be used to achieve some further goal, nor is it to say that sexual satisfaction cannot accompany some other satisfaction. Eating might be conceived as a sexual activity, but not as a pure sexual activity, such as, for example, thumb-sucking or pipe-smoking. Again, the new conception of sexuality is release of pleasure for its own sake. It follows that any part of the human body has an equal biological and logical claim as an "erogenous zone" and that any human activity has an equal claim as a "sexual activity."

Freud's own account of sexuality becomes inconsistent precisely at the moment he abandons this radical conclusion and returns to the primacy of evacuation lust, supported by questionable genetic arguments that suggest that all the sexual perversions, although admittedly "normal," are cases of regression and "arrested devlopment." But Freud's own reconception of the sexuality undermines both evacuation lust and his quasi-moral conception of the maturity of pleasures. There is no a priori or scientific way to determine the maturity or preferability of one erogenous zone or activity over another. (Again, statistics and even universal practices have no weight here.) Evacuation lust and heterosexual intercourse might themselves be conceived as an early stage in sexual development at which the bourgeosie of turn-of-the-century Vienna had become fixated.

It is clear that Freud's account of sexuality and sexual perversion is inadequate as it stands, as well as inconsistent. If there were no limitation whatever on the scope of sexual activities, then every motivated human activity, insofar as it released tension or gave pleasure, would count as sexual. But this "pansexualism" is clearly nonsense. Freud himself continually repudiated it, even if his own position seemed to commit him to it nevertheless. Pansexualism has been best described by John Barth:

> The dance of sex: If one had no other reason for choosing to subscribe to Freud, what could be more charming than to believe that the whole vaudeville of the world, the entire dizzy circus of history, is but a fancy mating dance? That dictators burn Jews and businessmen vote Republican, that helmsmen steer ships and ladies play bridge, that girls study grammar and boys engineering all at behest of the Absolute Genital? When the synthesizing mood is upon one, what is more soothing than to assert that this one simple yen of humankind, poor little coitus, alone gives rise to cities and monasteries, paragraphs and poems, foot races and battle tactics, metaphysics and hydroponics, trade unions and universities? Who would not delight in telling some extragalactic tourist, "On our planet, sir, males and females copulate. Moreover, they enjoy copulating. But for various reasons they cannot do this whenever, wherever, and with whomever they choose. Hence all this running around that you observe. Hence the world"? A therapeutic notion![6]

But even if any activity *might* be a sexual activity in an appropriate (that is, a sexual) context, it is surely false that every motivated human activity *is* in fact sexual. If sexuality were merely release of tension for its own sake, the paradigm of sexuality would remain, as I suggested, the scratching of an itch, and if that itch happened to involve the genitals, sexuality would take as its paradigm masturbation. But this concept of sexuality, which agrees with the traditional conceptions in accepting as its paradigm the sexual "union" of two people, surely is not our concept. And, given Freud's account, the appropriate question is why we bother, given the enormous amount of effort and the continuous threats to our egos and our health, to attempt to engage in sex mutually instead of in solitude and in the safety and convenience of our own rooms. On this account it would seem that our sexual paradigm ought to be masturbation, and sexual release with other people an unnecessary complication. And before he backslides into heterosexual evacuation lust, Freud appears to hold just this view, insofar as sexual release to bodily tension remains for him the "primary process." But clearly our sexual paradigms are to be found elsewhere, in our attraction for and enjoyment of other people, in what Freud calls the "secondary processes." According to Freud it is not just the body that seeks release, but the "psychic apparatus," and the tension from which it suffers is not due to "inner" tensions alone, but to relations and identifications with sexual "objects," that is, other people.[7]

In insisting that the paradigm of sexuality involves a relationship with other people, let me quickly point out that this is as far as can be from the pious linkage of sex and love. One may love another person with whom he or she is sexually involved, but there are any number of attitudes he or she might take toward the person to whom he or she is sexually attracted, among which, unfortunately, hate, fear, resentment, anger, jealousy, insecurity, mastery, and competition are probably far more common and more powerful than the rare and delicate threads of love and respect.

Freud's revolutionary breakthrough, though incomplete, was also too radical. In focusing our attention on the autonomous tension-releasing function of sexuality he freed sexuality from its former religious and moral restrictions, but at the expense of completely cutting it off from all other human activities. This newfound autonomy of sexuality, the source of our sexual freedom, has now become our main sexual problem. As more of us enjoy more sexual activity, sex itself has become less satisfying and more "meaningless." We now have to see once again that sexual tension and its release is not the whole of sex, nor even its major aspect. Rather it is Freud's "secondary" aspect of sexuality, the "psychical" aspect, that explains its nature and its overwhelming importance in our affairs. For sex is primarily for us a way of relating to other people and only secondarily and in a primitive way a matter of release of "sexual tension."

The belief that sexuality is primarily a matter of enjoyment has become commonplace since Freud; in fact it is often suggested that sexual activity is the closest we can come to "pure pleasure." But this emphasis on pleasure, like Freud's stress on release of tension (these were equivalent for him), fails to explain the enormous stress we put on these activities. (Man is basically *not* a pleasure-seeking animal.) It fails to explain why sex for us is *essentially* with other people, why our own enjoyment in sex is so bound up with the pleasure of someone else. Aristotle, in his attack on the hedonists of his day, insisted that pleasure was not an activity itself but rather an accompaniment of gratifying activity. In sex, we are not satisfied by our enjoyment, but rather we enjoy ourselves because we are satisfied. But then, once again, what is the activity that we satisfy in sexuality?

The problem still with us is the predominantly male paradigm of "evacuation lust," once rationalized as the "natural" means to reproduction, now justified by appeal to the "natural" enjoyment it involves. Sexuality typically involves discharge of tension (both physical and psychological), but Freud's "primary process" is not the essence of sexuality, and evacuation lust is not its paradigm. One might say that evacuation lust plays a role in sex similar to swallowing in wine tasting. It is typically the "end" of the activity, but surely neither its goal nor its essence (it is even frowned upon in professional circles). I take our obsession with evacuation lust, in the post-Freudian as well as pre-Freudian mentality, to be a symptom of our sensual and aesthetic deprivation, like the lusty and excessive need of a wino who swallows without tasing a glass of delicate white Burgundy. If there is a category of sexual perversion, of abusive and demeaning, sex, what often passes for "normal" or "straight" sex surely deserves a place on the list. And what is essential to sex will remain hidden from us so long as we remain fixated on the wonders of the genital orgasm.

One might suggest that what properly characterizes sexuality is not the narrow conception of pleasure entailed by the evacuation-lust model but rather the broader conception of pleasure as sensuousness. And, of course, this would be reasonable enough. It reinstates Freud's important demand that sexuality may involve any part of or the whole body, as well as the genitals. And sexuality, whatever else it may be, is surely a bodily conception. (One may be forced to stretch this demand slightly to include purely verbal or visual sexual activities—for example: telephone sex, anonymous or not; and pornography, where the body is only referred to or represented rather than actually touched. But I think it is somewhat of a tautology that no desire or activity can be sexual if it does not involve the body as a center of focus. I take it that this is what Sarte intends by his awkward phrase, "incarnation of oneself as flesh.") Which parts of the body are paradigmatically sexual varies considerably, of course, from society to society, and so do the roles of the various nontactile senses in sexual activities. In our society female breasts have acquired a somewhat bizarrely exaggerated sexual role; the sense of smell, a mysteriously diminished and even taboo sexual sense. Because of this variation it is not easy to distinguish those bodily activities that are essentially sexual from those that are not. Wrestling and dancing, acrobatics and athletics, for example, involve considerable bodily contact; yet we would not want to say that they are in every instance sexual. Teenage petting and dancing may differ from these other activities only in minute details yet be clearly sexual. And the wrestling scene from *Women in Love,* for example, is surely more than "symbolically" sexual. A furtive glance across the room may be highly sexual in spite of the fact that it involves the most minute movements. We may agree without controversy that sexuality is essentially physical. Yet bodily focus is not sufficient to distinguish sexuality. What else would be sufficient?

An additional component of sexuality, also to be found in Freud, is tension and the expectation of its release. "Arousal," on this account,[8] is not merely a preliminary to sexuality but part of its essence. (Even boring sex is exciting, insofar as it is sex at all.) The fact that excitement is essential to sexuality explains how it is that many people find danger "highly sexual" and why many sexual relations can be improved if they are made a bit more daring or dangerous (short of terror, which understandably kills enthusiasm). The same equation allows us to understand the confused medley of reactions we find to cinematic violence. It also allows us to understand one of the apparent anomalies of our sexual behavior, the fact that our most satisfying sexual encounters are often with strangers, where there are strong elements of tension—fear, insecurity, guilt, anticipation. Conversely, sex may be least satisfying with those whom we love and know well and whose habits and reactions are extremely well known to us. It ought to strike us as odd that we can be upsettingly attracted to a stranger who is not particularly attractive, who shares little in common with us, and who presents us with an evident set of personal and perhaps moral and medical threats. At the same time, married couples who find each other most attractive, compatible, nonthreatening, and comfortable often find intercourse more of a routine or a repetitive ritual, or as evacuation lust, to be completed efficiently and without fanfare, or perhaps as a battlegound, with only a minimum of sexual desire or excitement.

But tension, arousal, and excitement, together with bodily sensuality, still add up to something much less than sexuality. Enthusiastic acrobatics or dancing is still less than sexual, and a gentle touch on a finger or cheek cannot be understood simply in the above terms. Moreover, the concepts of "tension," "arousal," and "excitement" tells us far less than they might at first appear to. We might think that such tension is uniquely sexual, but it is not. Arousal is arousal, whether it is found in reactions of fear, anger, hatred, anxiety, love, or desire. As far as excitement itself is concerned, making love, dancing, a cold shower, a Librium, a fistfight, or a two-mile jog might be equally effective. What makes tension, arousal, and excitement sexual is the nature of its object, what the tension is *about*. And it is not mere sensuality that is aroused, and it is not merely a human body (one's own or someone else's) that excites us. But to understand this "something more" that is essential to sexuality we shall have to leave the safe and well-explored confines of sensuousness and the variety of bodily activities and modes of coupling. We need a new theory in which sensuality and bodily activities and excitement might be mentioned in passing, but only as "but of course. . . ."

Sex as Language

Sexuality is primarily a means of communicating with other people, a way of talking to them, of expressing our feelings about ourselves and them. It is essentially a language, a body language, in which one can express gentleness and affection, anger and resentment, superiority and dependence far more succinctly than would be possible verbally, where expressions are unavoidably abstract and often clumsy. If sexuality is a means of communication, it is not surprising that it is *essentially* an activity performed with other people. And, if it is our best means to express what are often our dominant and difficult-to-verbalize feelings and relationships, it is not surprising that sexuality is one of the most powerful forces in our lives.

It is also evident, though not obvious, that any bodily contact and any human activity, including genital contact and the physical activity of intercourse, both might and might not be sexual. (It is difficult, but not impossible, for gentle genital contact and intercourse not to be sexual, just as it is difficult, as Wittgenstein said, to say "It is cold" in English and not mean by that that it is cold. But in a suitable context, for example, speaking in code, one might mean almost anything by "It is cold." Similarly, in suitably asexual contexts, for example, on a movie set or in a Masters and Johnson experiment, genital contact and intercourse may not be sexual, for then they would not be plausible instances of body language.)

There are other body languages, of course, and most of them can be more or less distinguished from sexual body language. Aggression, for example, while often sharing a body vocabulary with sexuality, is surely distinct. Fear is also expressed in body language, sharing some of its vocabulary with sexuality, but its bodily expression is not sexual as such. Defense, insecurity, domination, and self-confidence, and any number of various desires (including particular sensuous pleasures) are also expressed in body language. Sex is basically a nonverbal language that takes bodily movements, postures, and sensations as its form, whatever content it expresses. Now, in a sense there is but one body language, since we have but one body; but there can be different body languages, much as there are different verbal languages, in different societies. Edgar Rice Burroughs imagines a people who laugh to express sadness and cry to express amusement. More within reality, Chinese open their eyes to express anger, whereas we narrow them; so we can imagine, and find, peoples whose sexual expressions vary considerably from ours. Body languages must be publicly learned and will vary between different groups, although there are obviously biological restrictions that supply the depth grammar of all human body languages. Not all body language is sexual, and not all people need have a sexual language. (There are societies in which intercourse serves a purely reproductive or ritualistic function, or even à la Freud, the pure function of providing pleasure. Such a society, however, ours is not.

The basic vocabulary of body language is the gesture, which might be an activity but is usually an expression or a stance. The gesture is the bodily equivalent of a sentence. Particular movements (for example, the lifting of an arm) and touches have meaning only as part of a gesture.[9] Body languages, like verbal languages, are born and grow in a societal context, as means of communication. They are, to use J. L. Austin's term, *"performances"* (the notion of "constative" or "descriptive" makes only minimal sense here), and they are learned and have meaning only in context. Of course, once one learns the body language, one can employ it, so to speak, alone. But in body language, as in verbal language, there can be no strictly private language. (Autoeroticism, far from being our sexual paradigm, is at best considered a borderline case.) Having learned the body language, one who travels for the sake of "adventure" to a paradisical island or to a radically different society will be grossly misunderstood. Or one can conscientiously, as does a dancer, learn new expressions and new forms of expressive elegance. But one first needs a language to vary, a given language in order to learn another. Body language, again like verbal language, is the realization of a capacity that is not equally shared by everyone. Some people are inarticulate, even retarded, others brilliant and creative. Sexual "losers" are often people who suffer more from bodily inarticulateness than verbal inability, and impotence is more often a matter of aphasia than physical damage. There are those whose body language is forceful without being either articulate or graceful. And there are those who, perhaps forceful, perhaps not, are elegant and even creative in their use of body language. An athlete might be forceful, but not articulate, and in spite of his skills of physical enunciation and projection and his large bodily vocabulary, have nothing to say. A dancer might be highly elegant, but ultimately be a solipsist. Most people, needless to say, here as in speech, know only those features of the language that are most common, most easily articulated, least committal, and least personal. Some people, including dancers by profession, articulate their body language with such perfection that every gesture is an exact and perfect expression.

Whatever else sexuality might be and for whatever purposes it might be used or abused, it is first of all language. When spoken it tends to result in pregnancy, in scandal, in jealousy and divorce (the "perlocutionary" effects of language, in Austin's terminology). It is a language that, like verbal language, but sometimes more effectively, can be used to manipulate people, to offend and to ingratiate oneself with them. It can be enjoyable, not just on account of its phonetics, which are neither enjoyable nor meaningful in themselves, but because of *what* is said. One enjoys not just the tender caress but the message it carries; and one welcomes a painful thrust or bite not because of masochism but because of the meaning, in context, that it conveys. Most sexologists, one might add, commit the McLuhanesque fallacy of confusing the medium with the message.

Sexuality, while having a certain structure that confines it, can take any number of forms. It is a language we first learn on the borderlines of sex, in shaking hands, standing with our hands on our hips, letting a cigarette droop from our lips in Junior High School, scratching our forehead or our thighs in public, looking at each other, kissing, smiling, walking, and eventually, petting and making love. Like dancing, sexuality is an extension and fine development of everyday movements, capable of open-ended refinement and individual variation, as poetry of the body. But where dancing takes its audience to be anonymous and its message impersonal, sexuality is always personal and deeply revealing. One might argue that sexuality is much less refined, much less self-consciously an "art" than dancing; but this, I would counter, is a mark of our general vulgarity and lack of self-consciousness in all things important. Nothing can or ought to be more human an art form than intimate communication.

We can now see what is wrong with "pansexualism," the idea that all human activities are sexual. Not all human activities are linguistic activities, for not all activities are intended to communicate or express either desire or interpersonal feelings. Athletic activity, acrobatics, and much dancing, for example, may be concerned with the precise performance of the body, but those activities themselves are not intended to communicate or express personal desire or feelings. And of course there are many activities that are communicative and expressive that are not essentially sexual, for example, writing poetry or philosophy, signaling a right-hand turn, or sending a telegram. But any human activity *can* be sexual insofar as it involves the use of the body as an expression of interpersonal desire. (Stances and postures need not involve touching. Consider, for example, a "provocative" appearance.) But unlike verbal language, body language is not well adapted to addressing large audiences and consequently can only appear vulgar when removed from a more intimate setting. Similarly, sex, as language, is predominantly reciprocal. And that is why mutual touch and intercourse must remain our paradigm.

Sexual Perversion Reinterpreted

If sexuality is a form of language that can be used to express almost anything, it follows that the use of sexuality admits of any number of creative as well as forced variations. As a language it also admits of breaches in comprehension, and it is here that we can locate what little is left of our conception of "sexual perversion." It should now be clear that this is not a moral term but more a logical category, a breach of comprehensibility. Accordingly, it would be advisable to drop the notion of perversion altogether and content ourselves with "sexual incompatibility" or "sexual misunderstanding." It is not always easy to distinguish abuses of the language from abuses expressed by the language, or to separate nonsense from sophistry, sexual fanaticism from sexual "politics." It is not always clear what is to count as a literal expression, a metaphorical usage, an imaginative expression, a pun, a solecism, or a bad joke. And so what might be taken as incomprehensibility and perversion by a sexual conservative would be taken as poetry or pun by someone else. Perversion, then, is a communication breakdown; it may have general guidelines but ultimately rests in the context of the bodily mutual understanding of the people involved. Quite the contrary of a moral or quasi-moral category, "sexual incompatibility" is strictly relativized, within the language, to the particular people involved.

If sexuality is essentially a language, it follows that masturbation, while not a perversion, is a deviation and not, as Freud thought, the primary case. Masturbation is essentially speaking to oneself. But not only children, lunatics, and hermits speak to themselves; so do poets and philosophers. And so masturbation might, in different contexts, count as wholly different extensions of language. With Freud, we would have to distinguish masturbation as autoeroticism from masturbation as narcissism—the first being more like muttering to oneself, the latter more like self-praise; the first being innocent and childlike, the latter potentially either pathetic or selfish and self-indulgent. Masturbation is not "self-abuse," as we were once taught, but it is, in an important sense, self-denial. It represents an inability or a refusal to say what one wants to say, going through the effort of expression without an audience, like writing to someone and then putting the letter in a drawer. If sexualtiy is a language, then it is primarily communicative. Autoeroticism, therefore, along with Freud's primary process, is not primary at all, but conceptually secondary or derivative, similar to a young child's early attempts at language, which can be interpreted as phonemes only within the context of the language his parents already speak. But any language, once learned, can be spoken privately. Masturbation is the secondary, private use of sexual language—minimal rather than primary, the Archimedean standpoint of sex, essential as an ultimate retreat, but empty and without content. Masturbation is the sexual equivalent of a Cartesian soliloquy.

It is clear that between two people almost any activity *can* be fully sexual when it is an attempt to communicate mutual feeling through bodily gesture, touches, and movements. But this requires serious qualification. Expressions of domination and dependence are among the most primitive vocabulary items in our body language. But these may go beyond mere expressions and gestures to become a kind of "acting out"; and there is a difference, if only of degree, between gestures and full-blooded actions. When expressions of domination and dependence turn into actions, they become sadism and masochism, respectively. If these feelings are not complementary, they can only be interpreted as a communication breakdown, as sexual incompatibility. When sadistic actions are not expected, they are to sexuality as real bullets in a supposedly prop gun are to the stage. Again, the possible extension of sexual language depends mutually upon the participants. The subtlety and explicitness of a language depends upon the perceptivity of the conversationalists. For the articulate and the quick, sadism and masochism may consist of an apparently minor change in sexual position, a slight but degrading change of posture that is ample expression of mutually negative or hostile feelings or of complementary dominance and submission. For the more dense or uninitiated, such expression may require outright infliction of pain or discomfort, a painful pinch or punch. In many cases we might want to say that, as Billy Budd was inarticulate, and violent as a result, sadism and masochism may be matters of inarticulateness and lack of interpersonal perception as well as products of the hostile feelings to be expressed.

There is no reason, apart from traditional squeamishness, to suppose that the employment of parts of the body other than the genitals in sexuality is perverse or need result in a breakdown of communication. Not only are these not perversions in themselves, but it may well be that those who would call them perversions are somewhat perverse themselves. The cry of perversion with regard to body language is very much like that of censorship with regard to the written word. To judge something tasteless is often itself a sign of bad taste, as in the case of the judges who banned *Ulysses* or *Lady Chatterley's Lover*. They did not prove abuses of language by the authors they condemned but rather, by attempting to castrate the language and expel some of its finest moments, displayed themselves as illiterates. Similarly, sexuality conceived as a language of intimacy and feeling that calls for ever new variation and inventiveness has as its worst violators those who, unimaginative and illiterate themselves, attempt to force others to accept their limited and impoverished vocabulary. But it might also be admitted, though it rarely is, that the common sexual variations are not for the sake of variety and pleasure alone. Oral sex and anal sex, for example, carry unavoidable expressions of domination subservience, though these surely need not be considered degrading (as they are treated in some of Norman Mailer's writings) and may be exceptionally expressive of tenderness and trust.

Vulgarity, in this as in any art form, can be a charm in small doses but an offense when overdone. It is because sex is a language that demands subtlety and artfulness that over-frankness and vulgarity are, if not perversions, at least gross abuses of the language, as very bad poetry might still be considered poetry. This explains, for example, why overt propositions and subway exhibitionism are generally offensive, which is a mystery if one considers sex, as most people do, one of the "appetites." There are, for example, no acceptable sexual expressions that are parallel to the straightforward expression of hunger in "Let's eat" or "When is dinner?" or "Dinner is ready." Eating, of course, can be much more than the satisfaction of hunger; it can become an elegant social (and thereby also, some-times, sexual) activity as well. But sexuality, far from being the "animal" instinct in us, appears only in those human activities where considerable refinement is possible. Sexuality permits of vulgarity only because it is itself a matter of refine-ment. It is therefore not at all one of those physiological functions that well-mean-ing sexual pedants often describe. Thus blatant sexual propositions and subway exhibitionism are offensive, not because they deviate from some "normal sexual aim" (the former, at least, being an unusually direct approach to the "normal sexual aim"), but because they are vulgar, the equivalent of an antipoetry poet who writes an entire poem consisting of a single vulgar word, or a comedian who, unable to handle condensation and understatement, has to spell out his obscene jokes explicitly. Similarly, sexuality lies in subtlety. There is sometimes nothing less appealing or satisfying, even when one is in a fully sexual mood, than a too-straightforward sexual encounter, "unadorned" by preliminary conversation—both verbal and bodily.

To other so-called perversions the same considerations apply, and the degree of the breakdown in communication is not always clear. Sexual activities them-selves are not perverted; people are perverted. Fetishism in general might be a product of stupidity, poor vocabulary, or fear of communicating, but it might be extreme ingenuity in the face of an impoverished sexual field. A voyeur might be someone with nothing to say, but the voyeur might count as a good listener in those cases in which he makes himself known. Sexual *in*versions, as Freud calls them, are not deviations of *sex* (acording to the theory developed here, homosex-uality is not such an inversion), but relations with children or animals would be like carrying on an adult conversation with a child who does not have the vocab-ulary to understand or a dog who nods dumb agreement to every proposal. Mul-tiple sexual encounters are surely not in themselves perversions; quite the con-trary, languages are not designated for exclusive two-party use. But it is clear that such multiple relationships, like trying to hold several conversations at once or working on several books at the same time, can be distracting, confusing, and ultimately disastrous. There is some difference—but only in manageability—between Don Juanism, or serial multiplicity, one on hand, and group sex, on the other. In the first case one risks carrying over from one conversation gestures that are appropriate to another, but such relationships offer the compensation and reward of being always fresh and novel, without the immediate danger of falling into the bodily equivalent of a Harold Pinter conversational rut. (Here, too, we can appreciate the attractiveness of strangers over those whom we already know well.) Group sex, on the other hand, makes the matter of gesture and response immensely complicated, and while it creates the serious danger of simultaneous incoherent polylogues, it offers the rare possibility of linguistic forms unavailable with fewer voices, much as a larger group of musicians, after protracted training, can create movements impossible for small groups and soloists. Therefore, whether or not Don Juanism and group sex are satisfying depends, as before, not on the nature of the activity but on the skill and performance of the participants.

There is, however, still room for a concept of sexual perversion. It does not involve any deviation of "sexual aim or object," as Freud insisted, nor does it involve any special deviation in sexual activity, peculiar parts of the body, special techniques, or personality quirks. As a language, sex has at least one possible per-version: the nonverbal equivalent of lying, or *insincerity*. And, as an art, sex has a possible perversion in *vulgarity.* Given the conception of sexuality as the art of body language that I have defended, we are forced to see the brutal perverseness of our conception of sexuality, in which insincerity and vulgarity, artificial sexual "roles" and "how-to" technology still play such an essential and generally accepted part.

NOTES

1. Thomas Nagel, in "Sexual Perversion," *The Journal of Philosophy,* vol. 66 (January 16, 1969), suggests some such analogues, for example, smearing an omelet on one's face. But however rude, vulgar, or humorous such a performance might be, it surely does not display the moral repugnance that sadism and pederasty are commonly agreed to have.

2. Cf. John Barth, *Giles Goat-Boy* (New York: Fawcett World Library, 1974), p. 235: "there is no term for 'service' that is not obscene, clinical, legalistic, ironic, euphemistic, or periphrastic." For the sake of brevity, I will henceforth refer to this obsession, borrowing a term from a poem by D. H. Lawrence, as "evacuation lust." From "Sex and Trust," in *Collected Poetry,* (New York: Viking, 1964), vol. 2, p. 197.

3. What makes many of Norman Mailer's literary sexual exploits so offensive is not an excessive sense of perversity so much as an enduring and brutally unsubtle obsession with biology and male-dominated traditional "evacuation lust." See, for example, *An American Dream* (New York: Dial Press, 1965), ch. 1.

4. Scientifically, Freud owed much to his predecessors. Krafft-Ebing and Havelock Ellis, among others. But it was Freud who used these findings so dramatically, not only to increase our knowledge but to change our very conception of sexuality.

5. Freud lays the groundwork for the argument that any sexual activity is "natural," but he is still caught in Enlightenment and Victorian morality. It must be admitted that Freud's notion of "discharge" bears too strong a resemblance to a male perspective of sexuality. He does fall into embarrassing lapses in commenting on "the culture stunting and . . . the convention reticence and insincerity of women," and there are telling metaphors ("piercing the tunnel from both sides") that betray a defensive male posture. Regarding intercourse, he is still caught in the paradigm of "evacuation lust," and considers as perversions "anatomical transgressions of the bodily regions destined for sexual union or a lingering at the intermediary relations to the sexual object which should normally be rapidly passed, on the way to the definite sexual aim." With regard to his own revolutionary thought Freud must be considered something of a frightened reactionary. But we should give full weight to Lou Andreas-Salomé's comment in her *Journal:* ". . . confronted by a human being who impresses us as great should we not be moved rather than chilled by the knowledge that he might have attained his greatness only through his frailties."

6. *End of the Road* (Garden City, N.Y.: Doubleday, 1967), p. 93.

7. Of course, fetishists are attracted primarily to people parts, rather than to people as such. But a moment's reflection is sufficient to realize that fetishists are attracted to people parts—a breast, a calf, or even a shoe—just because they are in fact parts of people to whom they are attracted. Of course, there may be persons who are in fact attracted to people parts that are detached, but we would not consider them fetishists or perverts, but rather ghouls.

8. Nagel takes such "arousal" as central to his analysis, too.

9. Cf. Gottlob Frege on words and sentences, in, for example, "On Sense and Nominatum," in *Readings in Philosophical Analysis,* ed. by Herbert Feigl and Wilfred Sellars (New York: Appleton-Century-Crofts, 1949), pp. 85–102.

9

Freud's Neurological Theory of Mind

Sigmund Freud began his medical career as a neurologist. But this familiar fact is too often treated either as an irrelevancy or as a threat to Freudian theory. It is argued that Freud's genius lay in his acute and even brilliant clinical observations and that these observations were obscured and even subverted by his dangerous tendency to return to speculative neurology. Freud's materialist presumptions, his dedication to the "unity of science," and his desire for a systematic theory of both mind and brain are dismissed as disruptions to psychoanalytic theory. The consequence of this mixture of psychology and neurology is presumed to be a series of confusions and category mistakes. And so, in defense of Freud, psychoanalytic theory is typically separated from neurology, and Freud himself is quoted from those appropriate passages in the later works where he does appear to separate psychology and neurology and endorse a type of psychophysical dualism. This causes some problematic discontinuities: for example, the severing of the quasi-physicalistic notion of "energy" from its materialist moorings. But even such conceptual incoherence is welcomed by analysts who insist upon isolating concepts original to psychoanalysis from similar notions derived from other fields. Accordingly, Freud's lapses into neurological theory and his neurological background are treated as unimportant digressions and influences which can be eliminated without loss of comprehension or theoretical completeness.

Research for this study was supported by The Research Foundation of the City University of New York, faculty grant number 1477. My thanks to Bernard Gendron for his helpful comments.

Against such objections and interpretations, I want to argue that Freud's "speculative" neurological theory is central to his work from the very first studies to the last summaries and that the basic claims of his entire theory are dependent upon his neurological observations and speculations. Furthermore, I want to argue, with reference to current philosophical theories of mind and body, that Freud's theory does not thereby become a series of category mistakes. Freud is often criticized for his philosophical naïveté, largely on the basis of his "confusing" mentalistic and biological categories and remaining ignorant of the complexities of psychophysical dualism. I will argue that Freud was not only aware of these problems, but that he was one of the very few psychologists or philosophers of his time (another being William James)[1] who began to see the serious problems in the linguistic and metaphysical conservativism that provided the inertia of Cartesian dualism in psychology. Accordingly, I want to use this occasion not only to explicate an interpretation of Freud's work, but to show how I believe that some ideas which are still rejected in that work can be used to answer a number of long-standing and currently pressing problems in philosophy.

Freud's theory of mind, which he was already formulating in systematic form in 1895, begins with an explicit acceptance of a neurophysiological and partially neuroanatomical model. (This distinction is often ignored by philosophers and psychologists. I shall argue that Freud never gives up his neurophysiological model, but he does give up the neuroanatomical commitments of that model.) In an unpublished, untitled "pre-psychoanalytic" project,[2] Freud writes a "psychology for neurologists."[3] One might begin by claiming that Freud presents a "theory of mind" which is based on the form of, or is isomorphic with, a neurological theory. But the *Project* is more than this. Psychophysical isomorphism, as we find it, for example, in the Gestalt psychology of Wolfgang Köhler,[4] is essentially dualistic. It is of the essence of Freud's theory, I shall argue, that it is not dualistic, and does not even depend upon what is now glibly referred to as the "correlation" of mental and bodily processes.[5]

I have said that Freud's neurology is "speculative." This is not to say that it is unrelated to evidence or that it is wild or unconfirmable. Rather, it is to say that there was little knowledge of the nervous system and its physiology, and consequently most of the hypotheses and theories advanced by Freud were to be investigated and confirmed in dissection and experiment only years later. Karl Pribram, a contemporary psychophysiologist who is one of the few scholars to write a serious study of Freud's *Project,* says of the work, "I found that the *Project* contains a detailed neurological model which is, by today's standards, sophisticated . . . The *Project* is very much alive and not just of historical importance."[6] The neurone as the basic unit of the nervous system had just been discovered and named (W. Waldeyer, 1891). The locus of interaction between neurones (Freud's "contact barriers," now known as "synapses" since Sherrington) was just becoming known anatomically and remained a complete mystery physiologically. Most importantly, the nature of the impulses was not known (although Helmholtz had established their approximate speed of transmission), and the relations between anatomical arrangement, physiological processes, conscious occurrences, and behavior were, apart from a few crude correlations, a matter of speculation. It was known, for example, that the "higher levels" of human intelligence were "located" in the cerebral hemispheres, but the neurological theory of mind for Freud (and, we might add, for James) was based more upon an enthusiastic confidence in the rapid development of these new sciences and upon the ultimate heuristic principle of the "unity of science" than upon concrete discoveries of neurological functions.

The absence of nearly all information regarding the mechanisms of stimulation and conduction, and the localization of physiological or psychological processes in the central nervous system left huge gaps which, in Freud's time, could only be filled by sophisticated guesswork, as often as not supported by theories borrowed wholesale from physics, chemistry, and biology as well as common-sense notions of psychology. The rapid advance of neurology fed Freud's speculative enthusiasm. But as the complexity of the problems became more apparent, Freud recognized the deficiencies in his early *Project* and saw that neurology would not provide the sought-after details in his lifetime. For these reasons, Freud discouraged psychoanalytic theorists from guessing prematurely at neuroanatomical functions. He did not publish and rarely referred to the *Project,* and he apparently attempted to destroy it.[7]

Yet the neurological theory remains as what Thomas Kuhn has called a *paradigm* of psychoanalytic theory.[8] Even where it is not mentioned as such, it provides the model of explanation, it circumscribes the data and their interpretation, and it gives form to the psychoanalytic model which is typically but wrongly supposed to be derived from clinical observation and description. As the editors of the Standard Edition tell us,

> But in fact the *Project,* or rather its invisible ghost, haunts the whole series of
> Freud's theoretical writings to the very end. [290]

The "Psychology for Neurologists"

What defines the temperament of the *Project* is its Newtonian demand that "psychology shall be a natural science,"

> that is, to represent psychical processes as quantitatively determinate states of
> specifiable material particles . . . [295]

The "specifiable material particles" are the neurones; the theory is explicitly a neuroanatomical model. Then, "what distinguishes activity from rest is to be regarded as Q, subject to the general laws of motion" [295].[9] The theory is a working out of the relationship between the neurones and Q. But the emphasis on the newly discovered neurone must not mislead us. The subject matter of the study is ultimately not the neurone but the (central) nervous *system* (*Nervensystem,* not *Neuronensystem*). Freud says, "a single neurone is thus a model of the whole nervous system . . ." [298]. But this is misleading, since it is transmission of Q between neurones which is central to Freud's theory, it is always systems of neurones and not individual neurones which are the subject matter. We shall see that there are important properties of the system which could not be properties of the single neurone.

The first "theorem" is what Freud calls the "principle of *neuronal* inertia,"[10] "that neurones tend to divest themselves of Q. On this basis the structure and development as well as the functions [of neurones] are to be understood" [296].

The cell's divesting itself of Q is "discharge"; "this discharge [of $Q\acute{\eta}$] represents the primary function of the nervous system" [296]. Reflex movement is the primary mode of discharge; "the principle [of inertia] provides the *motive* [my italics] for reflex movement" [296]. The principle of inertia is a form of what biologists refer to as *homeostasis,* the maintenance of steady physiological states of a system through self-regulating mechanisms. On the one hand, Freud traces the law of inertia to the general irritability of protoplasm of any living cell. But, more importantly, he stresses that the tendency to discharge Q manifests itself in *"flight from the stimulus"* [296]. Notice that the neurological model thus rests from the start on a behavioral model. Notice also that the model incorporates from the start purposive or teleological explanations in terms of "tendency," "motive," "flight." These notions, like the "principle of inertia" itself, are ambiguous between mechanistic and purposive models: we shall see that Freud's "hydraulic model" of mind deliberately persists in this ambiguity.

But the principle of inertia requires serious modification. The human nervous system is so complex that it is stimulated not only by "external stimuli," but by "internal" or "endogenous stimuli" (later, "instincts"), from which the organism cannot flee. Accordingly, "the nervous system is obliged to abandon its original trend to inertia . . ." [297]. "It must put up with a store of $Q\acute{\eta}$ sufficient to meet the demand for a specific action . . ." [297] and "endeavor at least to keep the $Q\acute{\eta}$ as low as possible . . . and keep it constant" [297]. Freud refers to the tendency to reduce the level of $Q\acute{\eta}$ to zero as the "primary function," the maintenance of a low and constant level of Q to cope with the "exigencies of life" (hunger, respiration, sexuality) as the "secondary process."[11]

It is noteworthy that Freud first distinguishes the primary and secondary processes on the basis of the behavioral distinction between those stimuli that one can flee from and those that one cannot. In fact, his definitive reason for making this distinction is also psychological, but with a physiological basis. It is one of the peculiarities of the nervous system, Freud tells us, that it can both retain and remain capable of receiving stimuli [302]. In psychological terms, we might say that the reflex model so far introduced as the primary process cannot account for memory and learning. In neurological terms, it was already known that excitation might increase or decrease in nerve tissue without discharge. Freud refers to this retention of nondischarged Q as *cathexis.*[12] To account for the psychological data of learning and memory, Freud incorporates the neurological discovery. He distinguishes between two systems of neurones, ϕ and ψ, the former entirely "permeable" (allowing free flow of Q), the latter to some degree "impermeable" (restricting or resisting the free flow of Q). Freud notes with some concern that there is no histological basis for this psychologically based distinction. But he does not maintain, as his language and his interpreters suggest, the existence of two types of neurones in addition to two types of neurone systems. (He attacks, for example, the then current distinction between "perceptual cells" and "mnemic cells"— "a distinction . . . which fits into no other context and cannot itself appeal to anything in its support" [299].) Rather, the difference between neurones is a *functional* difference depending upon their location in one of the two systems. Furthermore, the distinction between ϕ and ψ systems does have neurological support—the distinction between the gray matter of the spinal cord (with its sensory and motor attachments to the "external world") and the gray matter of the brain ("to which the development of the nervous system and the psychical functions are attached" [303]).

The distinction between two systems of neurones can be used to explain learning, memory, and coping with instincts by appeal to the two central activities of the nervous system discharge and cathexis. Cathexis is the unique ability of the ψ, or impermeable, neurones. The source of the resistance to discharge which allows for cathexis, Freud tells us, is the "contact barrier" (or "synapse"). The contact barriers of the ϕ neurones offer no resistance; the contact barriers of the ψ neurones resist discharge and allow buildup or cathexis of Q$\dot\eta$. Again, Freud warns that this distinction has "an unfortunate tinge of arbitrariness" [303], but that it does explain how "the secondary function . . . is made possible by the *assumption* [my italics] of resistances which oppose discharge" [298]. Learning and memory can thus be explained by appeal to the distinction between the ϕ and ψ systems. The resistance of the ψ neurones to discharge varies according to both the amount of Q passed to them from the ϕ system and the number of previous stimulations. The result is facilitation of certain neurone pathways (James's *habit*, the neurological analogue of learning). Through differentiated facilitation of different pathways, Q can follow different courses to discharge. Learning is the development of such differentiation of the ψ neurones, but always leaving the ϕ neurones free of Q and ready for new stimulation.

The notion of "neurones" seems clear enough—the neurone is, as Freud insisted, a "specificable material particle." But what is Q (Q$\dot\eta$)? What is it that "flows" through the neurones? Today we know that the nerve impulse within the neurone is an electrochemical charge at the nerve-cell membrane which results from the movement of ions across the membrane, while the nerve impulse which is transmitted across the synaptic space (between the axon of the transmitting neurone and the dendrite of the receiving neurone) is a release of a chemical "transmitter substance" upon impulse within the first neurone, which stimulates the second neurone. But Freud had no way of knowing any of this. For him, the evidence pointed to the transmission of an unknown substance which could be stored in a cell or passed between cells. Were he the thoroughgoing materialist he is sometimes claimed to be (as he poses in the opening paragraph of the *Project*), he might have pursued his suggestion that what flows is a quantity (thus "Q") of material particles is undetectably tiny amounts within and between neurones. But Freud's thought aims in a different direction with a notion of "energy," and this is clearly borne out in the later theoretical works where "psychic energy" becomes the central variable of the theory. Accordingly, Q is the energy utilized and released by the neurones. Of course, Freud could have no way of specifying what *kind* of energy this would be (i.e., electrical or chemical or mechanical or some peculiarly "psychic" energy). In *Studies on Hysteria*, Breuer had commented that the potential energy of the cell was known to us as chemical but was unknown to us in its state of discharge and in the "tonic excitement of the nervous system."[13] It is, according to Freud, "a quantity—although we possess no means of measuring it—a something which is capable of increase, decrease, displacement and discharge, and which extends itself over the memory traces of an idea like an electric charge over the surface of the body. We can apply this hypothesis in the same sense as the physicist employs the concept of a fluid electric current."[14] Accordingly, Freud's Q has been typically interpreted as electrical current. (Pribram [op

cit.], explicitly interprets it so.) But the editors of the Standard Edition reject any
such interpretation:

> nowhere in the Project is there a word to suggest that any such idea was present
> in Freud's mind. On the contrary, he repeatedly emphasizes the fact that the
> nature of 'neuronal motion' is unknown to us. [393]

The editors are surely correct in reminding us that the notion of Q is speculative.
Yet there is no point in overstressing its unknown quality. While Freud did not
narrowly intend "Q" to signify "electrical energy," it must not be supposed that
his notion of Q is to be interpreted differently from notions of energy in the physical sciences. The notion is essentially a borrowed notion, and to divorce the
Freudian notion of "Q," and, later, "psychic energy," from its physicalistic origins is to rob the concept of its substantial meaning. Freud did not have evidence
that Q was distinctively electrical energy; but he did have evidence that Q was
some combination of energies (electrical plus chemical), as we now know it to be.
So long as the notion of "Q" (or "energy") is tied up to the neurophysiological
model, there is ample evidence for the existence of Q. But if the model of the
"psychic apparatus" is divorced from the neruophysiological model, the central
notion of "energy" becomes little more than a metaphor.[15] It has been argued that
the concept of "energy" cannot be more than a metaphorical and ultimately
unjustifiable attempt to construct psychoanalytic theory on a physicalistic basis.[16]
In defense, the psychoanalytic concept of "energy" has been often distinguished
as an autonomous explanatory concept which does not require conceptual ties to
other sciences.[17] Both these objections to and defenses of the concept of "energy"
ignore the intentionally ambiguous status it holds in Freud's theories. It is the
neurophysiological model that gives conceptual anchorage to the concept. The
evidence for calling Q "energy" is exactly identical with the justification for identifying any form of energy, discovery of detectable electric current, and detectable
change in activity with addition of chemical substance or electric charge. What
Freud could not know was only what kind(s) of energy were involved in the cathexis and transmission of the nervous impulse. This does not mean—cannot be
allowed to mean—that Q, or "psychic energy," was a form of energy different (or
different in "level of abstraction" [Colby, op. cit., pp. 25f.] from "physical
energy." The mistake is to think that "physical" restricts us to Newtonian physics
and mechanical energy.[18] The concept of "energy" in Freud's theories comes
directly from the biological sciences (specifically neurology) and only indirectly
from physics. Since Q, or "energy," is clearly not mechanical energy, it may be
admitted from the first that there are serious dissimilarities with the quantitative
concept of "energy" in Newtonian physics. (Here the "hydraulic model," taken
literally, breaks down.)

Freud knew of the physical existence of neurones and postulated, with ample
evidence shared by many scientists of that period, that these neurones collected
together as nerves provided pathways for impulses to and from the "higher centers" in the brain. The nature of these impulses was unknown, but not completely
unknown. The notion of Q, or "energy," is a theoretical construct borrowed from
other sciences to explain both these impulses and their similarities with processes
in other sciences.[19]

In a later section, we shall analyze the notion of Q in the *Project* and "energy" in the later works in more detail. Even at this stage, however, we may appreciate how ingeniously these notions bridge the conceptual-theoretical gap between teleological theories of psychology and mechanistic theories of neurology. "Energy" holds a respectable role in Newtonian science while holding at the same time a tradition-honored role in the philosophy of the mind.[20] It is thus that Freud will be able to transcend the crude distinction between the human body as mere "mechanism" and the human person as goal-directed and conscious.

The Psychological Model

Where in this apparently neurological model are we to find *consciousness*? It is with this question that Freud's psychological monism fails him just when he needs it most. On the one hand, Freud realizes that the value of his theory is that it does not limit us to a mere description of consciousness in the style of the old empirical psychologists, and that it allows us to treat psychic phenomena as "natural" phenomena and not as mysterious Cartesian substances.

> We at once become clear about a postulate which has been guiding us up till now. We have been treating psychical processes as something that could dispense with this awareness through consciousness, as something that exists independently of such awareness. We are prepared to find that some of our assumptions are not confirmed through consciousness. If we do not allow ourselves to be confused on that account, it follows, from the postulate of consciousness providing neither complete nor trustworthy knowledge of the neuronal processes, that these are in the first instance to be regarded to their whole extent as unconscious [*unbewusst*] and are to be inferred like other natural things. [308]

What appears above is not only the germ of the concept of "unconscious psychic processes" which will form the radical foundation of Freud's later theory. We can also see in the *Project* the recognition of a crucial philosophical or methodological point—the separation of a scientific and "naturalistic" account of psychological functions and the very different sort of account that emerges from introspection or phenomenological description. It is only the first that interests Freud. Emphatically, this is not to deny that people "have" feelings and sensations, but only to deny that these have any role as data in a causal theory of psychology. As Freud often stresses, (e.g., in "The Unconscious"), the model of the psychic apparatus is essentially a theory of the *Other*. Accordingly, psychological predicates are not first-person observation reports, but rather theoretical terms that serve a function in an overall theory of human behavior and psychology. This is not to reject all dualism, but rather to replace the troublesome metaphysical dualism of mind and body with a methodological dualism between science and empirical phenomenology.

But Freud is not satisfied with methodological dualism, and he consequently makes himself vulnerable to the plague of metaphysical dualism throughout his career. Early in the *Project,* he tells us:

> Hitherto, nothing whatever has been said of the fact that every psychological theory, apart from what it achieves from the point of view of natural science,

must fulfill yet another major requirement. It should explain to us what we are aware of, in the most puzzling fashion, through our 'consciousness'; since this consciousness knows nothing of what we have so far been assuming—quantities and neurones—it should explain this lack of knowledge to us as well. [307–8]

He insists that his theory find "a place for the content of consciousness in our quantitative psychic processes." The *"quality"*[21] (of sensations) must be accounted for. But how? In the neurones, there is only quantity. And so it must be that "quality" is not "in" the nervous system but yet determined by it. And here, of course, we return at once to Cartesian dualism.

The "problem of quality" never gives Freud satisfaction. From the beginning, he recognizes that consciousness cannot be accounted for as an effect of either the ϕ or the ψ system of neurones, and so, he insists,

> We summon up the courage to assume that there is a third system of neurones—ω perhaps—which is excited along with perception [ϕ] but not along with reproduction [ψ], and whose states of excitation give rise to the various qualities—that is to say, are—*conscious sensations.* [309][22]

Freud is never sure whether $Q\acute{\eta}$ *is* consciousness, or whether $Q\acute{\eta}$ rather "generates" consciousness. Nor is it clear to Freud *where* in this neurological model the ω-neuronal system is to be located. In desperation, he is forced to abandon any attempt to solve the dualistic "problem of quality" in the context of his monistic model:

> No attempt, of course, can be made to explain how it is that excitatory processes in the ω neurones bring consciousness *along with them* [my italics]. [311]

But if Freud had remained faithful to his own philosophical demands, he might have seen that there was no need to "explain consciousness," and consequently no need for an ω system of neurones.

Yet Freud is not, and need not be, a behaviorist. Motives, memories, pains, and pleasures play an essential role in his theory. They cannot be eliminated or "reduced" to behavioral formulae of any complexity. The remainder of the *Project* consists of a sketch of a general theory of mind, not behavior. It includes a theory of the ego, an analysis of cognition and thought, a dream psychology that remains intact in *The Interpretation of Dreams,* an analysis of hysteria,[23] and attempts to analyze sensation, judgment, motivation, and rationality in neurological terms. It may seem as if there are two separate psychological models operating in the *Project* (and later works) which are confused together and with the third neurological model. The first is what contemporary psychologists call a "drive-reduction model,"[24] a neo-behaviorist nonteleological Stimulus-Response theory which takes "drive"—a state of "arousal"—as an intervening variable and attempts to explain "goal-oriented behavior" according to Thorndike's "Law of Effect" (Hull's "Law of Reinforcement"); that is, a reaction followed closely by diminution of need or drive will increase the tendency or similar stimuli to evoke a similar reaction. Insofar as Freud's *Project* stresses learning as facilitation of neural pathways following previous discharge and reduction of tension, it parallels such theories. Thus even the editors of the Standard Edition comment,

> it may be an alluring possibility to see him as a precursor of latter-day behaviorism. [293]

Freud also employs a purposive or *teleological* model of explanation in which intentionalistic notions such as "goal," "wish," and "expectation" play a central role. But the definitive conceptions of the teleological model are identical to those of the "drive-reduction model," such as the concepts of "tension" or "urgency to discharge." The notions of perception and memory correspond to the ϕ and ψ systems respectively. From his teacher Brentano, Freud takes the notion of an "intentional object," and the operations of the psychic apparatus are explained in terms of satisfaction and frustration of wishes by such objects. A wish is a motive or urgency directed towards a particular object or type of object. Satisfaction is the congruence of perception and wish. Thinking emerges from an "incongruity" between memory and perception. Dreams are distorted wish fulfillments. A defense mechanism is a memory disconnected from its associated wishes. In primary processes, the object is simply the stimulus, and the wish is either for continuation or cessation. In the more sophisticated secondary processes, the object is an intentional object in a more literal sense, an object in "the outside world."

This synthesis of teleology, cybernetics, and neurology has often been reproached as "naïve." Critics have delighted in pointing out inconsistencies and "category mistakes." Those who would "save" Freud's theory have accordingly attempted to squeeze it into one of the three models. For example, R. S. Peters and A. MacIntyre have attempted to argue that Freud has only extended the teleological model and not provided alternative (causal) explanations at all; B. F. Skinner has argued that Freud should be purged of all "psychological concepts" in favor of terms of the "explicit shaping of behavioral repertories."[25] And Pribram often appears to be interpreting at least the early Freud as a primarily neurological theory. But Freud is none of these, or is rather all of these, and the charge of "naïveté" presupposes the incompatibility of the three models. Before Freud's early theory is dismissed, it must be demonstrated that there cannot be a single psychological model which is both "drive-reductionist" and teleological as well as neurological, a model which can provide us with what Pribram appropriately calls a "psychobiological Rosetta stone."[26]

The Persistence of the Paradigm

At first appearance, it might seem that Freud abandoned the *Project* and its neurological model. He never published it, rarely referred to it, tried to destroy it, and evidently turned increasingly towards psychophysical dualism. Thus we find the editors of the Standard Edition writing,

> And after all, we must remember that Freud himself ultimately threw over the whole neurological framework. Nor is it hard to guess why. For he found that

his neuronal machinery had no means of accounting for what, in *The Ego and the Id* he described as being 'in the last resort our one beacon-light in the darkness of depth-psychology'—namely, 'the property of being conscious or not.' [293]

Again,

> He believed it should be possible to state the facts of psychology in neurological terms and his efforts to do so culminated in the *Project*. The attempt failed: the *Project* was abandoned and in the years that followed little more was heard of a neurological basis of psychological events. . . . Nevertheless, this repulse did not involve any wholesale revolution. The fact was, no doubt, that the formulations and hypotheses which Freud put forward in neurological terms had actually been constituted with more than half an eye to psychological events; and when the time came for dropping the neurology, it turned out that the greater part of the theoretical material could be understood as applying, and indeed applying more cogently, to purely mental phenomena. [1894a, III, 64]

The editors, it appears, are not unsympathetic to dualism themselves. Of course Freud did construct his theory with "more than half an eye to psychological events," and of course it is much easier to formulate a theory of psychology which simply neglects the difficult questions concerning the relationship of psychology to neurology. What Freud attempted in the *Project* was a monumental effort, an attempt to overcome the dualism that plagued and still plagues psychology and neurology. But the idea that Freud abandoned the *Project* because of a return to dualism is common. Pribram, for example, tells us that

> . . . the results of behavioral observations as well as the inferences drawn from them were often couched in neurological terms. These confusions between the behavioral and neurological levels of discourse made these early attempts so 'difficult' that Freud finally abandoned the explicit neuropsychological approach. [Op. cit., p. 443]

Again, we have to appreciate the "difficulty" of such attempts, but we are not willing to admit that they are "confusions." It is true that Freud abandoned the "explicit" neuropsychological approach. But it is also true that he retained an "implicit" one. Or rather, he retains the neurophysiological "hydraulic" model of energy, resistance, discharge, inertia, storing, urgency, and primary and secondary processes. What he abandons is only the neuroanatomical model, the attempt to locate these physiological processes in specifiable anatomical positions in the central nervous system. It is only the "specifiable material particles" that are given up. This is not to say, of course, that Freud supposed that he could apply neurological predicates to anything other than a nervous system. But it is to the nervous system in general, viewed not as an isolated system within a person but as equivalent to something slightly less than a person (e.g., a "patient"), that these predicates apply. Freud no longer hopes that neurology will progress sufficiently in his lifetime for completion of the neuroanatomical model. As his youthful hopefulness gives way to the urgency of advancing age, Freud replaces the anatomy-dependent model of the *Project* with a noncommittal quasi-spatial "psychic apparatus" which provides us with—in contemporary terms—a functional localization of psychic processes without committing us to a mapping of this apparatus onto the brain.[27]

Yet Freud's metaphors are persistently spatial—and these are not, as he sometimes claims, "only pictorial" or "merely expository." The *paradigm* of his theory remains, from the *Project* to the final *Outline,* a neurophysiological model which makes sense only if understood on the basis of a neuroanatomical system, whether or not the "spatial arrangement" of its components has the same spatial (as opposed to functional) localizability in the brain. Freud remains aware of this peculiar modeling procedure. For example, in *The Interpretation of Dreams,* he writes,

> I shall entirely disregard the fact that the mental apparatus with which we are here concerned is also known to us in the form of an anatomical preparation, and I shall carefully avoid the temptation to determine psychical locality in any anatomical fashion. . . . Accordingly, we will picture the mental apparatus as a compound instrument, to the components of which we will give the name of 'agencies,' or (for the sake of greater clarity) 'systems.' It is to be anticipated, in the next place, that these systems may perhaps stand in a regular spatial relation to one another . . . Strictly speaking, there is no need for the hypothesis that the psychical systems are actually arranged in a *spatial* order. It would be sufficient if a fixed order were established by the fact that in a given psychical process the excitation passes through the systems in a particular *temporal* sequence . . .
>
> The first thing that strikes us is that this apparatus compounded of ψ-systems, has a sense or direction. All our psychic activity starts from stimuli (whether internal or external) and ends in innervations . . . The psychical apparatus must be constructed like a reflex apparatus. Reflex processes remain the model of every psychical function.[28]

This sort of noncommital spatial modeling is familiar to us. "Flowcharts," for example, showing functional relations within a computer, a business or political organization, a complex biological process (e.g., photosynthesis, Krebs cycle), are spatially committed in the abstract (to the physical components of the computer, to the individuals and/or offices of the organization, to the biological organism). Yet there need be no mapping onto the physical structure. (The computer circuits need not be arranged in the same physical-spatial order as the flowchart; the president's office might be on the ground floor; the arrangement of structures in the cell or the organism need not correspond to the mapping of the biosynthetic cycle.) Thus Freud retains the crude functional mapping of the *Project,* but gives up hope of locating the components of this map in the physical structure of the brain.

The "theoretical" seventh chapter of *The Interpretation of Dreams* retains virtually every feature of the *Project* except for the commitment to specific neuronal pathways. The distinction between ϕ and ψ neurone-systems is reintroduced as two psychic systems:

> But, as already has been pointed out elsewhere, there are obvious difficulties involved in supposing that one and the same system can accurately retain modifications of its elements and yet remain perpetually open to the reception

of fresh occasions for modification. . . . We shall distribute these two functions on to different systems.[29]

In this work, Freud distinguishes between the system *Pcpt* (perception), which is "at the front of the apparatus [and] receives the perceptual stimuli," and the system *Pcs* (Preconscious), which is "the last of the systems at the motor end" which allows "the excitatory processes occurring in it [to] enter consciousness without further impediment. . . ." There is no clear analogue to the ω system of the *Project*. Freud's work from 1895 until 1915 is generally acknowledged to retain some hope of neurological support. But I want to argue that the "change" so often pointed out that then appears is not an abandonment of the neurological model but only an abandonment of that hope for neuroanatomical support. When, for example, he later refers to his entire *Jokes and Their Relation to the Unconscious* as "economic" (as when, e.g., "one laughs away, as it were, this amount of psychic energy"), it is clear that the hydraulic model was still with him. After 1915, there is a nominal change, most often pointed out in Freud's own claim in his meta-psychological essay "The Unconscious" that "our mental topography has nothing to do with anatomy." But the complete statement in this essay simply bears out our interpretation, that Freud held on to the neurological model (or "paradigm") and gave up, and only *"for the present,"* the hope that the systems of his psychic apparatus could be localized in the brain. A precise conception of psychic topography, he writes,

> touches on the relations of the mental apparatus to anatomy. We know that in the roughest sense such relations exist. Research has given irrefutable proof that mental activity is bound up with the function of the brain as it is with no other organ . . . But every attempt to go on from there to discover a localization of mental processes, every endeavour to think of ideas as stored up in nerve-cells and of excitations as travelling along nerve-fibres, has miscarried completely. The same fate would await any theory which attempted to recognize, let us say, the anatomical position of the system *Cs*—conscious mental activity—as being in the cortex, and to localize the unconscious processes in the subcortical parts of the brain. There is a hiatus here which at present cannot be filled, nor is it one of the tasks of psychology to fill it. Our psychical topography has *for the present* nothing to do with anatomy; it has references not to anatomical localities, but to regions in the mental apparatus, wherever they may be situated in the body.[30]

About the same time he writes, in "Instincts and Their Vicissitudes" that his postulate is

> of a biological nature, and makes use of the concept of 'purpose' . . . and runs as follows: the nervous system is an apparatus which has the function of getting rid of the stimuli that reach it, or of reducing them to the lowest possible level.[31]

It has pointed out (e.g., by K. Colby, op. cit., p. 12) that Freud summarizes his own work as a dualism in his final *An Outline of Psychoanalysis.* But what Freud there denies is, once again, only the *present* knowledge of localization and the idea that *understanding* of psychic processes can be afforded by knowledge of anatomical localization:

> Psychoanalysis makes a basic assumption, the discussion of which is reserved to philosophical thought, but the justification for which lies in its results. We know two kinds of things about what we call our psyche (or mental life): firstly, its bodily organ and scene of action, the brain (or nervous system), and, on the other hand, our acts of consciousness, which are immediate data and cannot be further explained by any kind of description. Everything that lies between is unknown to us and the data do not include any direct relation between these two terminal points of our knowledge. If it existed, it would at the most afford an exact localization of the processes of consciousness and would give us no help towards understanding them.[32]

On the same page Freud restates his theory again in spatial terms without apology or justification:

> We assume that mental life is the function of an apparatus to which we ascribe the characteristics of being extended in space and of being made up of several portions.

And towards the end of the same work, he talks of

> The hypothesis we have adopted of a psychical apparatus, extended in space, expediently put together, developed by the exigencies of life, which gives rise to the phenomena of consciousness only at one particular point and under certain conditions.[33]

Now, why does Freud so persistently pursue these spatial notions? They are not confined to the *Project,* but continue and proliferate into his later work. In, for example, *The Ego and the Id* we again find clearly spatial notions, "interior of the apparatus," "advance toward the surface," "displacement" (of mental energy). If Freud occasionally protests that these are metaphorical and not spatial, it is perhaps only to avoid having his functional localizations confused with anatomical commitments. Otherwise, how can we explain why a gifted writer and brilliant theoretician should have been plagued for forty years by a metaphor, a *façon de parler?*

What persists, I suggest, is the neurophysiological model as the foundation of the so-called "psychic apparatus" with its essential connection to the brain even in the absence of specific localizations. As Freud increasingly despairs of confirmation of his structural model by neuroanatomical research, he separates his models from neurology, but only in a formal gesture (like the apologetic and humble comments in the preface of a book) which he never really accepts.

The Structure of the Model

What persists throughout Freud's work is a neurophysiological model of mind with its neuroanatomical commitments suspended. This is not to say, of course, that there could be neurophysiological processes without a brain and nervous system. It is rather to admit ignorance—along with Freud—of the exact localizability of those physiological processes in the brain and nervous system. What can be maintained with some certainty is that psychological processes are functionally equivalent to some physiological processes without assuming that the arrangement of such processes corresponds in any specifiable way to the anatomical structure of the central nervous system.

The key to this physiological model is the notion of energy, its sources, aims, objects, and obstacles in "the hydraulic model." While the notion of energy cannot be further specified as electrical, chemical, mechanical, and so on, it is clear that this notion can only make sense when still grounded in the neurophysiological model. It might be noted that this conceptual demand has not changed with the dramatic advances in neurology since Freud's work. We can not specify the nature of neural transmission, cathexis, and resistance in terms of the properties of an ion-sensitive polarized cell membrane and a chemical substance released in transmission. But an adequate description of the nervous system as a whole, whether in terms of "energy" or not, in specifiable anatomical terms is still not available to us. Whether or not such an adequate description could or will be available is a question which a wise neuropsychologist—like Freud—will abstain from answering. Sufficient changes in our knowledge of the nervous system may very well change the concepts and models we will use to describe and account for both the workings of that system and human behavior and thought in general. With Freud, I want to maintain that, for the present, our understanding of the "psychic apparatus" can neither rely upon nor rule out a correlative neuroanatomical model.

The problem facing Freud is to bridge the conceptual-theoretical abyss between the concepts and principles of psychology and those of neurophysiology. Several problems are involved, not the least of which are those dilemmas which surround the traditional dualism of mind and body. But, before we tackle those dilemmas, there is another set of problems which we have already encountered. I argued that Freud combines teleological, drive-reduction, and neurological models of his "psychic apparatus." The first model is straightforwardly purposive, as defined by Charles Taylor (op. cit., p. 6), and "invokes the goal for the sake of which the explicandum occurs." The last model is mechanistic or causal, explaining its occurrences by appeal to antecedent conditions and general laws according to a (more-or-less) Hempelian-type model. The drive-reduction model holds a somewhat debatable position, and when regarded as successful (e.g., by Clark Hull or Edward C. Tolman), is taken to be an example of the latter model, but, when rejected (e.g., by Taylor), is taken as a disguised version of the former model. Because Freud repeatedly points to the "mechanistic" nature of his model [e.g., 295, 308, 322, 360] it might appear that his model shares the controversies of the drive-reduction model. It is not unreasonable, however, to view Freud's appeal to "mechanism" as little more than verbal appeal, once again, to a Newtonian paradigm of science. But, at this point, it is necessary for us briefly to examine this appeal, for Freud's prejudice that only the "mechanical" is truly scientific is a prejudice shared to this day.

I have several times mentioned the "unity of science" as Freud's working hypothesis. If this precise phrase has come into prominence only in recent philosophy, Freud had a similar if not identical hypothesis in mind. In his *New Introductory Lectures,* Freud says of psychoanalysis,

> As a specialist science . . . it is quite unfit to construct a *Weltanschauung* of its own; it must accept the scientific one . . . the *uniformity* of the explanation of the universe . . . the intellect and the mind are objects for scientific research in exactly the way as any non-human things.[34]

This scientific *Weltanschauung,* Freud insists, requires "objective" explanation of phenomena by subsumption under general (causal) law. But then, as now, this Hempelian claim has been augmented with the demand that all entities, concepts, laws, and theories of every science be *reducible* to basic physicalist or materialist entities, concepts, laws, and theories. Psychological explanation is thus thought to be a threat to the unity of science hypothesis because its entities, concepts, laws, and theories are thought not to be so reducible. But, without argument, I want to stress only the first part of this requirement, not the second. Freud's model of mind must explain public phenomena by subsuming them under general law. The "bogey of mechanism" (as Ryle and others have attacked it) is not sufficiently clear, nor is the need for reduction to materialism or mechanism sufficiently sharp, to trouble our account at this stage. Freud's scientific outlook does *not* commit him, despite his frequent nominal appeals to Newtonian science, to a mechanistic or materialist outlook.

To fill the gap between teleological and causal models of mind, Freud ingeniously employs the concept of "energy." "Energy" serves this purpose in at least two vital ways. First, "energy" is an accepted concept in causal explanations in the natural sciences, yet it does not consist solely of "specifiable material particles" and need not itself be spatially extended or precisely localizable in space. As it is one of the obvious (not to say essential) attributes of mental events that they are, as Descartes characterized them, "not extended in space," it is the energy of a neurological system—and not the anatomical system—to which psychic processes are directly related or identical. Our picture of "nervous energy" has changed, of course, but the principle remains the same. Over and above the specifiable anatomical components of the nervous system, there is nervous activity, the system and its properties, and this activity can be sensibly interpreted as psychic activity. Secondly, "energy" plays more than a causal role in neurological theory. It also manifests a direction, has tendencies, and serves functions in the system as a whole.[35] Thus the notion of energy fits well in teleological explanations. What is essential to this idea of teleological explanation is the idea of function. An event is explained by appeal to its function in a system. What is not essential, but is typically confused with or even the paradigm of such explanation, is reference to consciousness. It is here that Freud's separation of the psychic from the conscious is most important. To say that energy fits into teleological explanations and thereby functions in laws which are isomorphic with psychological laws is not to say that energy—or psychological functions—are essentially conscious. (Compare Kant's *Zweckmässigkeit ohne Zweck.*)

In Freud's *Project,* the activities of the nervous system, for example, are accounted for in terms of a teleological or functional model—"The *function* of the system is to discharge Q." In psychological explanations, Freud offers the same sort of account: for example, in terms of the function of a desire, of a hysterical attack, or repression and defense. Of key importance is the fact that consciousness need play no role whatever in this account. Moreover, this stress on teleological explanation in no way supposes that teleological explanations are opposed to causal explanations. In psychology as well as neurology, any teleological explanation can be replaced (but not strictly reduced to) causal explanation. (On this thesis, Goldman, passim.)

We are now in a position to see how Freud's model in the *Project* can be both a teleological and a "mechanistic" neurological model of mind. One and the same set of concepts can be used to signify both the functions of the "psychic apparatus" and the nervous system. This set of concepts will be the concepts of the "hydraulic model," "discharge," "cathexis," "hypercathexis," "repression," "resistance," and so on. It is the always quasi-material notion of energy that allows Freud the theoretical freedom to draw this equivalence. It is the neurophysiological hydraulic model that defines the concepts of his psychic apparatus throughout his works, even after he had given up hope of neuroanatomical localizations of physiological-psychic processes. It should not surprise us, then, as it does most commentators, that Freud's emphasis upon the notion of "energy" increases in his later work just as his confidence in the ability of neurology to localize processes decreases.

Mind and Body

I have already indicated that I believe that Freud's theory can best be interpreted as a psychophysical *monism*. Of course, traditional dualist tendencies threaten him throughout, from the problem of "quality" in the *Project* to the apparent dualism in the *Outline of Psychoanalysis*. But the thrust of Freud's theory is essentially to deny the distinction between a concept of the mental which is essentially conscious and a concept of the brain and nervous processes which are "correlated" with mental events and states. Where he loses hold of this radical monism, his theory suffers as well, as in the treatment of consciousness in the *Project* and in his perennial struggles to defend the notion of "unconscious mental process" as more than a mere *façon de parler*. It is ironic that most of Freud's critics attack his "philosophical naïveté" in his attempted monism, but not his dualism. The *identity* of mind and body is his most radical and problematic insight.

We have seen in some detail how Freud attempts to derive a theory of the mind and a neurophysiological theory which are identical in *form*. This is not yet to say, however, that mind and the nervous system themselves are identical. What is the relation between the body—or the brain and nervous system—and the mind (i.e., certain primitive or basic mental events, e.g., sensations)? The metaphysical dispute surrounding this question since Descartes appears formidable, but there really are a small number of proposed solutions and variations, only one of which seems to be the subject of raging controversy at the present time.

Either mind and body (sensations and brain processes) are ontologically distinct, or they are not. If they are distinct, there is the question of whether they *merely* parallel each other—an intolerable proposal which dismisses the unity of science hypothesis from the outset—or whether there is causal interaction between them. But causal interactionism raises its problems also, since the nature of such causal connections is at best obscure. Moreover, there is the traditional Cartesian problem of how such different "substances" could possibly causally interact with each other. For those materialists who are not yet willing to abandon dualism, there is epiphenomenalism, the suggestion that bodily processes cause mental events but not the converse. But this leaves those entities or laws to which J. J. C. Smart and Herbert Feigl have respectively referred as "nomological danglers," entities or laws which are impervious to further scientific explanation. Thus epiphenomenalism, although it reduces the importance of mental entities to a minimum within the context of dualism, still remains an obstacle to the unity of science. This leaves the (nonempirical) hypothesis that mind and body (sensations and brain processes) are not merely correlated but *identical.* And "identical," in this context, usually means identical to brain processes (since the idea that certain brain processes are nothing but mental events, though this follows from the thesis, would appeal only to an overzealous idealist). It is the identity theory which is the center of the current mind-body controversy, whether it be thought that mind and body (sensations and brain processes) are but different aspects or modes of one and the same x, or different features of one and the same x, or x described from two different standpoints in two different languages. In one sense, Freud agrees with the monism of the identity theory. But in another, philosophically more important sense, he rejects it. Traditional mind-body monism has always been an awkward affair. The nagging presence of pains and sensations haunted those materialists who denied their independent existence. And there were awkward questions, "Does losing an arm entail losing a part of your mind?" Moreover, most mental events were recognized to be—following Brentano— intentional: that is, ideas which are true or false and which might refer to objects which do not exist. Surely there could be no comparable events or states in the body. Consequently, the current dispute over the identity theory does not concern mind and body as such, but carefully restricts itself to the possible identitiy of certain brain processes on the one hand and sensations (nonintentional mental events) on the other.

We cannot possibly do justice to the intricacies of argument that now populate philosophical journals, but we can localize the two primary points of dispute. First, if the identity thesis is correct, then every property of sensations must also be a property of brain processes and vice versa. According to Leibniz's law, if $p = q$ then every property of p must be a property of q, and vice versa. (This is not to say that we now speak this way, or that sentences about sensations are synonymous with sentences about brain processes—only that they are about the same entities.) Second, the defense of the identity thesis rests upon heuistic considerations of simplicity and parsimony, for the sake of the unity of science. It must be pointed out that there is no more *evidence* for the identity thesis than there is for mere psychophysical parallelism or epiphenomenalism; the difference between these "hypotheses" lies in their ontological and heuristic appeal. Yet it is not at all clear that the identity theory is any more "simple" than its rivals. It only replaces a duality of entities with a duality of aspects, features, or descriptions.[36]

We cannot enter into these disputes as such, but we can enter the problem at a level where these disputes have not yet begun. The particulars to be identified in the current controversy are sensations and brain processes. But here is where

Freud can be forced into the mind-body problem. Freud's *Project* is always a *systematic* analysis (as are his later theoretical writings). It is not individual brain processes that concern him, but the nervous *system*. Similarly, he is not concerned with individual psychic processes, but processes of the psychic apparatus. Particular processes, either neurological or peculiarly psychological, always play a systematic role. Using Freud's model, we make what at first appears to be an innocent modification of the identity thesis.[37]

Rather than take sensations as isolated particulars, we will take sensations as a function of Freud's "psychic apparatus." And rather than presumptuously suppose that we have identified specifiable brain processes (which we surely have not) we shall take brain processes to be a condition of the nervous system. But now the identity thesis is not the identity of sensations and brain processes any longer, but the identity of the psychic apparatus and the nervous system and their respective functions. This is, of course, exactly what Freud has argued. But what sort of identity is this? At first, we might say that both the psychic apparatus and the nervous system are nothing less than a *person,* that persons are the particulars that have both minds and nervous systems, sensations and brain processes. But this will not quite do. A nervous system is not a person, nor is a psyche a person. We need something less than a person for our locus of identity. Wilfrid Sellars has suggested a slightly grotesque model of a "core person," "a person defleshed and deboned, but whose nervous system is alive, intact and in functioning order."[38]

I wish to adopt a less gruesome but similar conception, what I shall call a *neuroid*—the person as viewed through the theory of a neurologist. He need not be defleshed and deboned, but the flesh has only the function of protecting the nervous system, the bones of holding it up, the sense organs of providing it with stimuli, the heart and blood of giving it nutrition and oxygen and so on. Now, while the neuroid is something less than a person, we can see that it is precisely the unspecified organism which is the subject of Freud's *Project*. It is at once the subject of both neurological and psychological predicates. In other words, it is both a nervous system and the psychic apparatus. Now, it might be argued that we have only replaced a dualism of entities, features, and descriptions with a new dualism of properties and descriptions of the neuroid. But it is at this point that the substance of Freud's *Project* becomes crucial. The properties of the neuroid can be referred to with the concepts of the *Project* without distinguishing—in sense or reference—neurological from psychological predicates. The basic concepts of the *Project*—"discharge," "cathexis," "tension," "hypercathexis," "resistance," "quantity," or "psychic energy" and the like provide the beginnings of the "topic neutral language" demanded by J. J. C. Smart and others. Freud's descriptions in terms of "tension" and "facilitation" refer indiscriminately to psychological and neurological processes; or, more accurately, they refer to one set of processes as functions of the psychic apparatus which are neither peculiarly psychological nor neurological. The Cartesian distinction between the mental and the mechanical can find no expression in such a language.

Freud's monism differs from current versions of the "mind-body identity thesis" in its insistence that both psychological and neurological processes are *essentially* functions of the overall *system* and cannot be treated—even in theory—as isolated processes. Notice that this is in part an empirical hypothesis, but one that has been well confirmed in recent neurological studies. There is no "one-one correlation" between mental events and physical events, for it is now understood that there is no satisfactory way to individuate such events in any way that makes such a correlation intelligible. But such a correlation thesis is not necessary to defend either psychological monism or the unity of science hypothesis. For such purposes, the *functional equivalence* of Freud's precocious model is sufficient; psychophysiological monism and the unity of science do not need *specific* neuroanatomical correlations.

Karl Pribram has praised Freud's *Project* for its sophistication even by today's standards in neurology. I would like to add that it is sophisticated by today's standards in philosophy as well. As in so many other instances, a work of this outstanding genius of our century has been abused for "naïveté" only because it was too radical to be appreciated in its own time.

NOTES

1. "Our first conclusion, then, is that a certain amount of brain physiology must be presupposed or included in psychology . . . the psychologist is forced to be something of a nerve physiologist." William James, *The Principles of Psychology* (New York: Dover, 1950), vol. 1, p. 5.

2. All page references to the *Project* will be to the Standard Edition and these will be included in brackets in the text.

3. Letter to Wilhelm Fliess, April 27, 1895.

4. See, for example, W. Köhler, *Gestalt Psychology* (New York: Liveright, 1947), and his *Dynamics in Psychology* (New York: Liveright, 1940).

5. Cf. The "psycho-physical parallelist theorem" attacked by Sandor Ferenczi in his *Further Contributions to the Theory and Technique in Psychoanalysis,* (London: Hogarth, 1926), pp. 16f.

6. K. Pribram, "The Neuropsychology of Sigmund Freud" in *Experimental Foundations of Clinical Psychology,* ed. by Arthur J. Bachrach (New York: Basic Books, 1962), p. 443.

7. Ernest Jones, *The Life and Work of Sigmund Freud* (New York: Basic Books, 1953), vol. 1, ch. 13, pp. 316–18.

8. See Thomas S. Kuhn, *The Structure of Scientific Revolutions,* 2d ed. (Chicago: University of Chicago Press, 1962), pp. 10ff. A paradigm need not itself be explicitly stated as theory. More typically, it is presupposed by the theory. Often the paradigm is openly expressed only in an author's early writings and then remains implicit in his later works. One might compare the relationship between Freud's *Project* and his later work to the relationship between some of Hegel's early manuscripts and his later philosophy. Hegel never published these, and considered them a source of embarrassment. Yet they provide one of the best available clues to the intentions and origins of his mature philosophy.

9. Q is "quantity of excitation in flow" or, occasionally, "current" or "impulse" or "stimulation." Freud distinguishes, but we need not, Q and $Q\dot{\eta}$, the latter being of an "intercellular" and "lesser order of magnitude," not measurable (at that time). It might be noted that Freud's talk of "activity and rest" and "motion" here represent deliberate and perhaps gratuitous appeals to Newtonian science. Cf. also " . . . only matter in motion" [327].

10. Attributed by Freud to Fechner, later called "the Constancy Principle."

11. Perhaps it would be wise to caution the reader against confusing the primary and secondary processes that appear in the *Project* with the processes that carry the same names in the later works. The secondary processes of the *Project* encompass *both* primary and secondary processes in the later theory of the instincts and their "vicissitudes."

12. Concerning Freud's notion of "cathexis" *(Besetzung),* Pribram comments, "This emphasis on cathexis is one of those strokes of luck or genius which in retrospect appears uncanny, for only in the past decade have neurophysiologists recognized the importance of the graded nonimpulsive activities of neural tissue . . ." (op. cit., p. 445).

13. 1895d, II, 193.

14. 1894a, III, 60.

15. It is on this basis that K. Colby attacks what I shall be calling "the hydraulic model," of "the psychic apparatus as a series of pipes or passageways in and out of which energy flows like a fluid." But, because he separates the model of the psychic apparatus ("PA") from the neurological model, his central concept of energy begins to look exactly like this metaphorical fluid flowing through a "cyclic-circular" structure that looks not unlike the heating system of a New York tenement building. K. Colby, *Energy and Structure in Psychoanalysis* (New York: Ronald, 1955), pp. 18, 79ff.

16. E.g., by L. Kubie, "The Fallacious Use of Quantitative Concepts in Dynamic Psychology," *Psychoanalytic Quarterly* vol. 16 (1947), pp. 507–8, and, more recently, by R. K. Shope, "Physical and Psychic Energy," *Philosophy of Science,* vol. 38 (1971), pp. 1–11.

17. E.g., K. Colby, op. cit.; and D. Rapaport, "On the Psychoanalytic Theory of Motivation," *Nebraska Symposium on Motivation,* 1960, ed. by M. Jones (Lincoln University of Nebraska Press, 1960), and "The Conceptual Model of Psychoanalysis" in *Theoretical Models and Personality Theory* (Durham, N.C.: Duke University Press, 1952).

18. Cf. Shope's argument that "the concepts of *energy, work* and *force*" in psychoanalysis and physics are "quite dissimilar" (op. cit., p. 2).

19. Freud was well aware of the problematic status of these theoretical concepts. So in "Instincts and Their Vicissitudes," he begins with the recognition that no science, not even the most exact, begins with "clear and sharply defined basic concepts. . . . Even at the stage of description it is not possible to avoid applying certain abstract ideas to the material in hand, ideas derived from somewhere or other but certainly not from the new observations alone" (1915c, XIV, 117). This recognition surely places Freud far ahead of his interpreters and critics alike, who wrongly suppose that the distinction between theoretical and observation concepts is clear, exact, and valid independently of a concept's role in a particular theory. Freud's anticipation of the Kuhnian thesis is evident here: we need only repeat that the "abstract ideas" of central importance here are of biological (neurological) origin.

20. We recall, for example, a dispute between Plato and Aristotle concerning the relationship between tragedy and catharsis some two thousand years before Freud.

21. This notion of "quality" (of sensations) is common in German thought since at least Kant (see, e.g., his *Critique of Pure Reason,* 2d ed. ("B"), trans. by N. Kemp-Smith, [London: Macmillan, 1929] pp. 182ff.), and it is still evident in the works of recent phenomenologists (see, notably, E. Husserl, *Ideas,* vol. 1, trans. by W. R. Boyce Gibson [New York: Macmillan, 1931], sec. 12, 15).

22. The use of ω involves a slight pun; it resembles a small w for *Wahrnehmung* (Perception). Cf. "Perception-system" in later works.

23. *Studies on Hysteria* had just been published that year. The main theoretical study in that work, however, was by Breuer, not by Freud. While Breuer concerned himself with a primitive "excitation theory" not unlike the *Project,* and also introduced (before Freud, at least in writing) a notion of "the unconscious," Freud restricted his attention to problems of psychotherapy. See 1895d, II, ch. 3 and 4.

24. See, e.g., Clark Hull, *The Principles of Behavior* (New York: Appleton, 1943); and J. W. Atkinson, *Introduction to Motivation* (Princeton, N.J.: Princeton University Press, 1964). For a devastating critique of all such theories, see Charles Taylor, *The Explanation of Behavior* (London: Routledge, 1965), pp. 236ff.

25. See R. S. Peters, *The Concept of Motivation* (London: Routledge, 1958); A. MacIntyre, *The Unconscious* (London: Routledge, 1958); B. F. Skinner, "Critique of Psychoanalytic Concepts and Theories" in *Minnesota Studies in the Philosophy of Science,* vol. I, ed. by Herbert Feigl and Michael Scriven (Minneapolis: University of Minnesota Press, 1956).

26. On these issues, see Charles Taylor, op. cit.; Alvin Goldman, "The Compatibility of Mechanism and Purpose," *Philosophical Review,* vol. 78, no. 4 (October 1969), pp. 468–82, and *A Theory of Human Action* 1970).

27. Cf. James, " . . . in *some* way, it is true, our diagram [of the association of ideas] must be realized in the brain; but surely in no such visible and palpable way as we first suppose" (op. cit., p. 81).

28. 1900a, V, 536–38.

29. 1900a, V, 538.

30. 1915e, XIV, 174–75 (my italics).

31. 1915c, XIV, 120.

32. 1940a, XXIII, 144–45.

33. 1940a, XXIII, 196.

34. 1933a, XXII, 158–59.

35. Cf. R. R. Holt, "Beyond Vitalism and Mechanism: Freud's Concept of Psychic Energy" in *The Historical Roots of Contemporary Psychology,* ed. by E. Wolman, (New York: Harper, 1968), pp. 196–226. One can also say of a charged particle that it has a direction, tendencies, and serves systematic functions.

36. See, e.g., J. Kim "On the Psycho-Physical Identity Theory," *Amer. Phil. Quart.* vol. 3, no. 3 (July 1966), pp. 227–35, reprinted in *Modern Materialism: Readings on Mind-Body Identity,* ed. by John O'Connor (New York: Harcourt, 1969).

37. One anticipated by T. Nagel, "Physicalism," *Philosophical Review* vol. 74, no. 3 (July 1965), pp. 339–56, reprinted in *Modern Materialism: Readings on Mind-Body Identity.*

38. Wilfrid Sellars, "The Identity Approach to the Mind-Body Problem," *Review of Metaphysics* vol. 18, no. 3 (March 1965), pp. 430–51, reprinted in *Philosophy of Mind,* ed. by Stuart Hampshire (New York: Harper, 1966), and in *Modern Materialism: Readings on Mind-Body Identity.*

10

An Introduction to
Phenomenology

Jean-Paul Sartre is the best known of the many philosophers who have referred to their work as "phenomenology." He is also the most articulate spokesman for the popular philosophy of "existentialism." As a result, commentators on recent European philosophy have bonded phenomenology and existentialism together in a common-law marriage of association. But on first examination, no two philosophies could appear more different. Phenomenology is often characterized as a philosophical method whose goal is to establish a "science" of philosophy and to demonstrate the objective validity of the foundation principles of mathematics and natural science, epistemology, and ontology. Phenomenology was christened if not wholly initiated by Edmund Husserl, a German philosophy professor who has left us volumes of austere and difficult academic lectures and manuscripts, most of which are still not published and few of which are easily understood even by professional philosophers who have not immersed themselves in Husserliana.

In contrast, the existentialists have rejected academic and professional philosophy, have rejected the idea that philosophy could ever become a science, have illustrated their ideas in novels and plays as often as arguing them in philosophical essays, and have ignored and even denied the importance and even the possibility of proofs of the "objective validity" of science and mathematics. Existentialism has its roots in the nineteenth century in the individualistic, irreverent, and "untimely" writings of Kierkegaard, Nietzsche, and Dostoyevsky. Existentialists have produced some of the most sensational literature, some of the most influential changes in Christian thought, and some of the most controversial moral doctrines of the twentieth century. Because of their scandalous reputations and their dramatic celebration of the human condition, existentialists are still ignored and even repudiated by many professional philosophers, including some well-known phenomenologists.

Thus it must appear that Sartre has sanctioned an impossible marriage of professions. But he is not the only philosopher who has joined together phenomenology and existentialism. Martin Heidegger before him, and Gabriel Marcel, Maurice Merleau-Ponty, and Paul Ricoeur, his contemporaries, have also been self-avowed phenomenologists and have been called, with good reason, existentialists as well. The coupling of phenomenology and existentialism is not a historical accident; there is a "logic" here that too-technical descriptions of phenomenology and too-popular characterizations of existentialism tend to obscure. Both movements have their basis in traditional European philosophy, the tradition following Descartes that established the framework within which Husserl, Heidegger, Sartre, et al. support each other and disagree. It is what we shall describe as the Cartesian starting point that defines the position from-which all theories, analyses, objections, and methods derive their validity. Both phenomenology and existentialism are concerned with the relationship that we may, gingerly at first, call "the relationship between human consciousness and the world," and with the "foundations" or "essences" or "existential-structures" that support this relationship. In the work of Heidegger and Sartre, phenomenology becomes support for an existentialism derived from Nietzsche and Kierkegaard. This support is not, as it is often described, simply the support of a set of philosophical doctrines by a philosophical method. (We shall show that it is a serious mistake to see phenomenology merely as a philosophical method.) Phenomenology supports existentialism as an epistemological and ontological thesis that is used to support a theory of human action and freedom. Both begin with a special kind of description of human consciousness. But while Husserl remains concerned with human *knowledge* and *belief,* Heidegger and Sartre turn their attention to problems of human *practice.* All remain within respectable reach of traditional Cartesian philosophy, whatever the radical departure from this tradition that over-zealous defenders have so repeatedly claimed. Both movements can only be understood in the context of the problems and ambitions of Western philosophy as a whole, and the seemingly vast differences between the two movements can only be appreciated in a perspective from which the similarities and mutual dependencies are evident.

What Is Phenomenology?

Phenomenology is a philosophical movement that received its most persuasive impetus, formulation, and defense from the German philosopher Edmund Husserl during the first three decades of this century. Husserl views Descartes and Kant as his most important philosophical predecessors, and his phenomenology takes the Cartesian attention to the primacy of first-person experience and the Kantian search for basic a priori principles as its modus operandi. Phenomenology begins with the study of human consciousness; it is an attempt to define the "structures" that are essential to any and every possible experience. Phenomenology is ultimately a search for "foundations." Husserl's own interest in philosophy began with an attempt to explain the validity of the fundamental laws and concepts of arithmetic. As his interests developed he came to seek not only the foundations of arithmetic but the a priori principles of all human "cognition" (i.e., all knowledge and belief). Ultimately Husserl's phenomenology took the ambitious range of concerns that occupied Kant in his *Critique of Pure Reason*—the identification and defense of the basic a priori principles of all human experience and understanding.

The existential phenomenologists also begin from Descartes and his "first-person standpoint," but they shift their attention away from the foundations of knowledge to the foundations of human *action*. According to the variations of phenomenology advanced by Heidegger, Sartre, and Merleau-Ponty, "consciousness" is not to be interpreted primarily as a *knowing* consciousness but as an acting, "willing," deciding consciousness. It is not those experiences relating to knowing and reasoning that are the paradigm to be examined but rather the experiences of doing, participating, and choosing. For the existentialists, it is the Kant of the *Critique of Practical Reason* that serves as a historical model, for it is the nature of human freedom and not the nature of human knowledge that poses the fundamental problem. For Husserl, the study of consciousness is essentially an epistemological study; for the existentialists, it is a means to understanding what it is to be a *person*. Of course, there are very important disagreements among the existentialists as they carry this analysis through, but their heretical deviation from Husserl can best be appreciated by understanding that Heidegger, Sartre, and Merleau-Ponty are only tangentially interested in the foundations of mathematics and science but fundamentally interested in the universal ("a priori," "essential," "existential," "ontological") presuppositions of human action.*

Although phenomenology, both Husserlian and existential, has a Cartesian starting point, there is no easy way to define this general philosophical approach. The details of method employed by Descartes himself—a rigid distinction between mind and body coupled with the presumption that we know the mind better than the body, and the tentative methodological supposition that everything we believe is false—these are all repudiated by every phenomenologist. Husserl characterized his phenomenology as a "return to the things themselves," where the things in question are phenomena or intuitions. But it is not immediately clear how "phenomena" or "intuition" are to be analyzed. Phenomena are not to be identified with natural phenomena, and intuitions are not to be identified (in general) as "experiences." Husserl insists that phenomenology begins with a "suspension of the natural (everyday) standpoint." We must begin with the *ego cogito* instead of nature and take up the standpoint of "transcendental subjectivity." But not only do all of these technical phrases need accounting for, some of them would be rejected as a fair characterization of phenomenology by a great many phenomenologists. Perhaps the most general characterization possible is the thesis that the phenomenologists begin with an analysis of "one's own con-

---

*The existentialists are *not* to be characterized by their interest in the individual and their rejection of the universal, nor by their attention to the concrete and neglect of the concept, nor by their focus on *life* and their neglect of the transcendental. These glib and popular characterizations might be reinterpreted as the shift from knowledge to practice, from *Denken überhaupt* to individual perspective, but more often they simply provide a poor ground for wild claims about existentialism. In the readings from the existentialists, it will be quite clear that they are making universal conceptual claims about all (possible) human beings.

sciousness of the world"; but the complex concept "consciousness of the world" is analyzed in radically different ways by different phenomenologists. One is rightly warned by practicing phenomenologists that one needs to develop a taste for phenomenology and some feeling for its workings before one can be in a position to say what it is. This is not meant to make phenomenology sound mysterious; it is simply to remind us that phenomenology is a very loose-knit system of problems, philosophers, and philosophies, all of which are brought together only by the slack and ultimately vacuous insistence that a first-person description, without theoretical bias, of one's own consciousness of the world must precede all philosophical theorizing. Although we may expect phenomenology to emerge from our readings as a more or less distinct approach to philosophy, we must not demand too rigid a summary or definition of the phenomenological approach.

The Presuppositions of Phenomenology

Among the strongest claims for phenomenology made by Husserl and his followers is that phenomenology is "presuppositionless" and without theoretical bias—that the results of phenomenology, if properly attained, are unconditionally, or "absolutely," true. But Husserl characterized himself as a "perpetual beginner," by which he meant that no concept in his philosophy was immune to further criticism. He insisted that phenomenology consists solely of descriptions, and that it neither presupposes nor advances any philosophical theories (a claim made more recently by Ludwig Wittgenstein in his later work). Husserl denied that a philosophical theory is possible: theories always assert something more than their data, and this "something more" has no place in philosophy. (As with Wittgenstein, it is some of Husserl's closest followers who ignore this basic denial.)

Phenomenology is said to be presuppositionless and theory-free. Here we may distinguish two separate claims: Phenomenology is presuppositionless because it demands that any concept and any proposition can be reassessed at any point; it may also be said to be presuppositionless in the much stronger sense that its descriptions neither presuppose nor involve any philosophical theory.

The demand that philosophy be without presuppositions (in both senses) is an attempt to guarantee that a philosophy will not be one more system of dogmatic assertions without ultimate philosophical support. Husserl is suspicious of the axiomatic philosophical systems of Descartes and Spinoza, and at the same time he is intolerant of the relativist claims of philosophers like Dilthey and Marx, who would deny any philosophy the claim of being absolutely true outside of a particular socio-intellectual context. Against the temptation to be dogmatic, Husserl demands that every philosophical proposition be constantly open to question. Against the temptation to give up the demand for absolute truth, Husserl insists that a presuppositionless philosophy will admit only those propositions which will be true and acceptable in any intellectual environment. Wary of having his philosophical vision distorted by preconceptions, Husserl devises a series of disciplines to assure that phenomenological descriptions are not philosophical theories in disguise. (His famous *epoche* is one of these disciplinary techniques.) For example, a description of consciousness is constantly endangered by the many metaphors and traditional philosophical theories that present an image of the mind as a mysterious container or stream ("all in your mind," "introspect," "stream of consciousness"). A philosophy that begins by taking these metaphors and theories seriously has, according to Husserl, based itself on presuppositions instead of pure description. Phenomenology must limit itself to reconfirmable descriptions of experience.

These good intentions give rise to problems and paradoxes. The two senses of "presuppositionless" which have been praised as the greatest merit of phenomenology have been roughly paralleled by two widespread and often persuasive criticisms of phenomenology. First, the demand that phenomenology continuously reassess all of its own concepts and propositions leads to the objection that the phenomenological enterprise is unavoidably circular. The concepts and claims of phenomenology can only be criticized and evaluated in terms of the concepts and claims of phenomenology. Secondly, the demand that phenomenology undergo constant reexamination leads to the objection that phenomenology will always be so obsessed with itself as method that it can never be productive. Hence a frequent challenge from both critics and proponents of phenomenology is to stop *talking about* phenomenology and to start *doing* phenomenology.

If we are to understand Husserl's phenomenology, we must first understand what is so very wrong with these objections. We must appreciate both the extent to which the demand is valid that phenomenology be presuppositionless and the extent to which it is hopelessly extravagent. The weaker demand for presuppositionless philosophy (that every concept and proposition be always open to reassessment) lies at the very heart of Husserl's philosophizing. This is not only evident in what Husserl says about his work; it is more persuasively obvious in what Husserl does. His writings are a remarkable model of philosophical integrity, whatever else one might say about them. Every idea is worked and reworked, altered, and even rejected as his philosophy develops. If phenomenology appears to be presented dogmatically in Husserl's formidable writings, that is surely not the nature either of the discipline itself or of Husserl as philosopher.

But to defend Husserl's phenomenology as presuppositionless in this sense is not to accept it in the stronger sense, which may amount to a claim that phenomenology is the *only* correct approach to philosophy. What one does see is that phenomenology is a *distinct* philosophical approach. It employs concepts that other philosophies do not employ; it defends claims that other philosophies would reject. But if phenomenology is distinct as a philosophy, there must be something that distinguishes it from other philosophies. We have called it the "Cartesian starting point." Most likely we would not want to call this starting point a "theory" or even a "presupposition" in any ordinary sense. But isn't any such starting point or position already a delimitation of what a philosophy can describe, explain, or argue? It may be that no philosophical principle is presupposed, whether formal, logical, material, or epistemological, and yet certain methodological procedures are employed from the outset. What is mistaken, of course, is the assumption that methodological procedures cannot prejudice results (as if an axiom is a presupposition but a rule of inference is not). It is clear that for Husserl, starting with "phenomena" does dictate certain results and deny others. Otherwise there would be no dispute between phenomenology and alternative philosophical approaches. But this separation of method from results raises more serious dangers, especially because of the frequent talk of phenomenology as a philosophical *method*. To distinguish methodological principles from doctrines in philosophy is to establish a set of principles that are immune to criticism. The role of this set of principles will go unchallenged during the production of a philosophy (e.g., Descartes' or Sponoza's "mathematico-deductive" methods and the empiricists' exhaustive distinction between "truths of reason" and "matters of fact"). But this is a flagrant violation of Husserl's insistence that there be no privileged principles, and Husserl's own works made it clear that those principles which might be called "methodological" are the very ones that are rethought and recast most often. There can be no distinction between method and result in Husserl's philosophy, and the acceptance of the weaker demand for presuppositionless philosophy entails a rejection of the stronger demand.

There is an apparent paradox in our introduction to Husserl. Very simply, it appears that we have presented phenomenology as a distinct philosophical approach while insisting that its every concept and proposition is always open to revision. In removing this paradox we can also show that the circular nature of phenomenology is not "vicious," and that it is simply false that phenomenology has become obsessed with method.

The solution to the paradox—and the answer to these two objections—is that there is no distinction in Husserl's philosophy between method and result. The claims that Husserl makes about the nature of consciousness, experience, and knowledge cannot be the results of any method that does not already have something to say about the nature of consciousness, experience, and knowledge. It does not make sense to call these claims "methodological" because these are the very claims that are generally recognized as the *fruits* of Husserl's phenomenology.

Deprived of any distinction between method and result, the objection that phenomenology has become obsessed with its own method is simply foolish. Phenomenologists have indeed continuously recast their propositions about the nature of consciousness, experience, knowledge, truth, and intentionality, but now we see that this is not a struggle with method, it is simply doing philosophy.

If phenomenology cannot analyze its concepts and defend its propositions except by appeal to its own concepts and principles, then it is in a dilemma no different from any other thoroughgoing philosophy. Because philosophy, unlike specific scientific disciplines, has no methodology to be distinguished from its substantial content, and because a philosophy presents itself as the source of ultimate appeal, there can be no escape from circularity. An empiricist insists that all knowledge comes from experience, but how does he defend *that* claim? He either defends it from experience or he gives up his claim as a piece of *knowledge*. Linguistic philosophers claim that philosophical insights can be obtained through an investigation of language, but the very notions central to the development of this claim, "meaning," "synonymy," "convention," "statement," and so on, have become central to their investigations. Yet it is not the case that these philosophers have become obsessed with their *method*. Instead, certain important initial insights generated a family of new philosophical problems, and not surprisingly, these problems turned out to be inseparably interrelated. Similarly, phenomenology has no alternative but to defend its claims and analyze its concepts in its own terms. It is in no worse and no better a position in this regard than any other philosophy.

Does this "turning back on itself" reduce phenomenology (or any other phi-losophy) to triviality? We might briefly answer this by appealing to a metaphor used by W. V. O. Quine. Doing philosophy is like repairing a boat on the high seas. It is not a matter of formulating a method with clear concepts and then applying it, but a matter of keeping afloat. We may build and tear apart, but we must always keep the entire structure sufficiently intact. Phenomenology starts with the crude insight that philosophy must examine consciousness. Slowly it builds a theory of consciousness, all the while keeping the initial insight as its framework. When the theory is sufficiently developed, even the initial insight can be reworked, torn apart, and possibly even rejected. This is the course of Husserl's philosophy. It is ever self-contained and self-referring and yet it is neither trivial nor dogmatic. There are doctrines in Husserl's thought that remain more or less invariant throughout, for example, the demand that philosophy pay attention to "phenomena." But his analysis of "phenomenon" changes continuously, as do his analyses of the central concepts of "intentionality," "constitution," "con-sciousness," and his theories of the role of the ego in consciousness. What distin-guishes phenomenology from alternative philosophies, for example, from tradi-tional empiricism or from linguistic philosophy, is its use of this family of concepts, its general insistence on the role of intuition—special kinds of intui-tion—in knowing. At the same time, it neglects or denies a similar role to (empir-ical) experience and to language. There are no clear head-on confrontations between phenomenology and other philosophies, but neither do they differ only in vocabulary and learned societies.

The "Foundations" of Knowledge

Phenomenology has been referred to as both a "rationalism" and a "radical empi-ricism." Husserl's philosophy is rationalistic in that he believes there are a priori principles or "truths of reason"; but he does not agree with traditional rationalists that there is a faculty or special power of reason that will identify these truths. Rather, these a priori truths are to be located and defended in terms of a special sort of "seeing," and it is in this sense that Husserl claims to be a sort of empi-ricist. But his empiricism is not the traditional empiricism of Locke, Berkeley, Hume, and Mill. He maintains what they would never allow: that there are *nec-essary* truths which can be established *through intuition*. The fundamental doc-trine of Husserl's phenomenology is the doctrine that he summarizes in the phrase "intuition of essences." With the rationalists, he maintains that we can and do have knowledge which is neither empirical nor trivial; with the empiri-cists, he maintains that all knowledge comes from intuition. But contrary to both traditional movements, he insists that intuition itself gives us necessary truths, that the empiricist notion of "experience" must be supplanted with a more gen-eral notion of "intuition" such that it is possible not only to have intuition of empirical facts ("the cat is on the mat") but to also have intuition of necessary truths ("$2 + 3 = 5$").

The "foundations" of knowledge are those necessary and a priori principles which constitute the presuppositions of any knowledge whatever. For example, the existence of the ("external") world is a presupposition of every law, theory, and hypothesis of every natural science. Similarly, a naturalized version of the principle of sufficient reason ("there is a sufficient natural explanation in terms of antecedent conditions and natural laws for everything that happens") is a presupposition for every attempt at scientific explanation, and the basic principles of arithmetic and geometry are presupposed in every act of measuring, counting, calculating. But it is not enough to demonstrate that these presuppositions are necessary to carry out the endeavor in question (i.e., it is not enough to show that belief in the world is necessary to do physics and chemistry, and not sufficient to show that acceptance of arithmetic is necessary to count and calculate); it must also be demonstrated that these principles are necessary in that one could not but accept them. "Rationalist" philosophers from the ancients to Descartes, Leibniz, and Spinoza attempted to prove that reason assured us the truth of such principles; "empiricist" philosophers have attempted to show that such principles could be firmly anchored in experience. Some philosophers, notably David Hume, concluded from the failure of both of these approaches that no justification for these principles could be found, and while the fact of our belief in them had to be admitted, our *right* to them could not be defended. Subsequently, Kant made an elegant list of the fundamental a priori principles necessary for mathematics and science and attempted to prove their legitimacy by arguing that they were not only necessary to do mathematics and science but basic to the very nature of human consciousness. The existence of human consciousness alone was sufficient to establish their validity.

Before we examine Husserl's "radical" claim that the foundations or a priori principles he seeks to identify and defend can be found in an examination of a special sort of "intuition," we should look at the alternative attempts to provide the "foundations" of knowledge that Husserl rejected. Foremost among these is the doctrine referred to as *psychologism,* which is a species of a general philosophical approach called *naturalism.* According to the naturalist, all concepts are abstractions from experience and all knowledge of the world is empirical knowledge; the only necessary truths are trivial and conventional truths, for example, "every cat is an animal," or "a rose is a rose." According to the psychologist, all nontrivial but apparently "necessary" truths are not necessary at all, but merely well-confirmed psychological truths, principles governing the way in which we do, as a matter of fact, think. The naturalist presses allegedly a priori principles into one or the other of these two categories: either they are abstract and very general empirical truths or subtle linguistic or logical conventions. Modern empiricists tend to push most of the problematic a priori principles, including all of mathematics, logic, and geometry, as well as the basic principles of natural science, into the class of conventions and linguistic truths. But the naturalist-psychologists of Husserl's time (including Husserl himself in his earliest works), tended to defend most of these a priori principles, including all of mathematics, logic, geometry, and most philosophical principles, as well-confirmed empirical generalizations. Thus the psychologist would argue that the laws of elementary arithmetic are empirical laws formulated on the basis of our experience of counting, and that the principle that every event has sufficient natural cause is an empirical law different only in its level of abstraction from "bronze statues turn green because copper is oxidized in the open air." The psychologist would explain the apparent necessity of mathematical proof and logical validity solely by appeal to psychological laws: The proof of the Pythagorean theorem would be translated from a list of axioms, postulates, previously proven theorems, and intermediate steps into a series of psychological laws to the effect that "if someone believes these axioms and postulates, then he will accept these intermediate steps and accept the Pythagorean theorem." Similarly, the logical law that states "if 'if P then Q,' is true and P is true, then Q is true" would be "justified" psychologically by establishing that if anyone believes both "if P then Q" and that P is true, then he will believe that Q is true.

As a student of Franz Brentano and an enthusiast for John Stuart Mill, Husserl had endorsed psychologism and written his dissertation and a book *(Philosophy of Arithmetic)* applying psychologism to the foundations of arithmetic. But Husserl's enthusiasm for psychologism was utterly destroyed by a review of his book by the great German mathematician Gottlob Frege. Frege argued that mathematical concepts are not abstractions and mathematical laws are not generalizations. Psychological laws say what people in fact do think; mathematical laws state what is necessarily true whether or not anyone happens to think it. Psychological laws are at best probable; they are revisable every time we find someone who happens not to believe the law. But mathematical laws are necessarily true: a proof of a theorem by one person is a proof of that theorem for all persons. What is established in a mathematical proof is not a truth about people's having certain thoughts, but a truth about the thoughts themselves.

Husserl's reaction to this onslaught was admirable. He was so impressed with Frege's critique that he altered the entire direction of his philosophy and tried to understand how a priori principles could be possible.

The attack on psychologism and naturalism is the best known of Husserl's attacks against alternative philosophies, but it must be seen as one aspect of his general concern to understand necessary truth. It is not sufficient for him to argue that necessary truths are not psychological or empirical truths. Frege also asserted this, but went on to insist that necessary truths are *conventional* truths. There were other mathematicians too, who agreed with the attack on psychologism, but they went on to insist that mathematical truths were merely *formal* truths—truths concerning the manipulation of signs. Husserl's rejection of these two alternatives marked his most important deviation from the linguistic direction of philosophy influenced by Frege. Husserl rejected "linguisticism" and "formalism" along with psychologism, and in place of these current alternatives he suggested a thesis reminiscent of scholastic philosophy. What makes necessary truths true, he said, is the very structure of human consciousness and a peculiar class of objects called essences, which are not to be discovered in a study of psychology or in a study of the syntax and semantics of the language of necessary truth. The discovery of essences would demand a new and special discipline, and this discipline is, of course, phenomenology.

Phenomena and Phenomenological Description

What is described in phenomenology? The most obvious characterization of that which is described by phenomenologists is simply *phenomena*. But what are phenomena?

"Phenomena" are best characterized as that which can be described from the phenomenological standpoint, and the "phenomenological standpoint" is best characterized as that standpoint from which phenomena are described—but obviously we would have to bring in some other concepts to avoid vicious circularity. We have already pointed to those concepts, of course, in the phenomenological study of consciousness in general and intuition and in our mention of the Cartesian or first-person standpoint. We can give an independent characterization of "phenomena" by further characterizing the phenomenological description of consciousness. Then we can give an independent characterization of the "phenomenological standpoint" by characterizing the Cartesian standpoint and the nature of phenomenological reflection. The two studies will provide us with complementary analyses of both "phenomena" and "phenomenology."

It would not be correct to say that phenomena are experiences, even if we were to qualify this by adding that phenomena are *essential* experiences. The problem with all such "experience" talk is that it reinforces traditional philosophical dualisms that distinguish between experiences and the objects themselves. But Husserl's phenomenology and the phenomenology of the existential phenomenologists both reject this distinction. The concept of the "phenomenon" represents *both* something that is "in" experience and something that is the object itself. Perhaps we can begin by stating that the phenomenon is an object as it is experienced. One might say that the phenomenon is what is *directly evident* or what "immediately presents itself." To say that a phenomenon is directly evident is to say that the only justification for the proposition identifying that phenomenon is that one is conscious of the phenomenon. As Husserl says, "If we ask why the statement is justified, and ascribe no value to the reply 'I see that it is so,' we fall into absurdity." *(Ideas)*. Descartes tells us that "there is an earth" is a dubitable proposition because it is possible that I should believe there is an earth when in fact there is not. But, he insists, "I *think* there is an earth" is indubitable because I cannot think there is an earth and not think it. Descartes' distinction between what is indubitable and what is dubitable is a crude ancestor of the distinction between what is phenomenon and what is not. We must not put much stress on the clumsy notion of "indubitability" here, but the idea of "self-confirming" propositions will be a helpful approach to the analysis of phenomena.

It is still not clear to what extent a phenomenon is and is not an experience. Descartes' distinction is often cast in the form of a distinction between my knowledge of experience and my knowledge of physical objects. The phenomenon that Husserl talks about is not something other than a physical object, but it is not something other than experience either. To understand this complex analysis, we shall have to understand what Husserl calls the *"intentionality"* of experience, and we shall have to understand what he calls the *"constitution"* of objects in consciousness."

A characterization of the phenomenological standpoint in terms of Cartesianism and reflection might appear at first to be simply a return to the Cartesian insistence that one first examine one's intuitions. But talk of intuition need have no place in the characterization of the phenomenological standpoint. One of the disputes that most sharply distinguishes the existential phenomenologists from the Husserlian phenomenologists is the rejection by the existentialists of the idea that one can talk about intuitions or phenomena at all without at the same time talking about existent objects. The nature of this disagreement is too subtle to go into at this point, but it forces us to separate a characterization of phenomenology in terms of an examination of consciousness from a similar characterization in terms of the phenomenological standpoint. What makes the existentialists phenomenologists is their acceptance of the standpoint in spite of their rejection of key Husserlian doctrines concerning the nature of consciousness.

The phenomenological standpoint is marked by an insistence that one describe one's *world* (*not* one's experience) without any presumption that it is either real or imagined, or that it is shared with other persons or is private. This may sound like just another way of repeating the demand that phenomenology limit itself to describing phenomena. But since for Husserl these two characterizations are complementary, we should expect that the characterization of "phenomena" and the characterization of the "phenomenological standpoint" would complement each other. The misleadingly simple characterization of the phenomenological standpoint as the insistence that one simply describe the world is not the same as an insistence that one examine *consciousness*. Underlying this simple characterization is a complex of doctrines about the "world," about the sense in which one is "conscious" of the world, and about the extent to which some description of experience is involved in the description of the world. It is not altogether clear in what sense this Cartesian standpoint can be said to be a *first-person* standpoint. Husserl, like Descartes and Kant, usually argued that there must be a self or ego that "inhabits" consciousness and is in some sense responsible for consciousness of the world. According to his doctrine, the first-person standpoint might be characterized as a "self-examination," or as "egology" as Husserl sometimes put it. But some phenomenologists—notably the existential phenomenologists and even Husserl himself in one of his important early works—deny the existence of any such "inhabitant" of consciousness. There is no ego; there is just "consciousness-of-the-world." And this consciousness must be "impersonal"—not mine ("my ego's") or yours or ours. Thus it becomes puzzling how the phenomenological standpoint can be called a "first-person" standpoint—or for that matter, any "standpoint" at all.

Husserl's phenomenology is the investigation of the nature of human consciousness with a view toward disclosing certain special intuitions that yield necessary truths. These special intuitions are called *"eidetic"* or *"essential"* intuitions and are to be distinguished from the traditional notion of "experience" which is limited to what Husserl calls *factual* or *empirical* intuition. Essential intuition is also identified as intuition of the universal, while empirical intuition is sometimes called *individual* intuition. Because Husserl seeks the a priori conditions of all experience and knowledge, his interest in empirical intuition is not an interest in the (empirical) contents of these intuitions but rather in their essential forms. Thus there are two questions here: "What is essential intuition?" and "What is the essential form of any experience?"

These questions are not equivalent, but pertain to different "realms" of consciousness. The first question is directed toward necessary truths of an "ideal" sort, such as the truths of mathematics. The second question is directed toward the nature of empirical experiences; it is the search for necessary truths regarding perception, like the Principles of Understanding in Kant's philosophy. Having mentioned before the marked similarities between Husserl and Kant—particularly in the search for a priori foundations of all experience and knowledge—we might point out the very important differences between the two. Kant distinguishes between phenomena, which are given in intuition, and noumena, which lie "behind" intuition. Husserl collapses this distinction and insists that the phenomena *are* the things themselves. Moreover, Husserl rejects Kant's view of the "faculties" of sensibility and understanding. Not only does he reject the presupposition that there are any such distinct faculties, but more importantly, he holds that Kant's distinction between sensibility and understanding already precludes the basic thesis of phenomenology—namely, that what Kant called the a priori principles of understanding are given in intuition. Husserl's concept of "intuition" includes parts of *both* what Kant divided into sense and understanding.

Husserl's insistence that phenomena simply be *described* is directed at eliminating the philosophical constructions that all philosophers impose upon their experience. This is not to deny that experience itself has structures that are imposed upon it by consciousness, but only that the theories philosophers use to explain their experience may not be an accurate description of these structures. How can one distinguish between those structures that are "given" in any experience, those structures that are learned and imposed upon experience, and those structures that are imposed by philosophical reflection upon experience? For example, it seems to be "given" that we see objects in Euclidean three-dimensional space. To what extent is this an essential feature of any experience? There are non-Euclidean geometries which have been developed by mathematicians, and hypothetical many-dimensional worlds which have been described by writers. To what extent is the Euclidean world one that we have all learned to see and which now seems to us as the "natural" way of seeing the world? To what extent is the Euclidean view actually imposed by centuries of philosophical thought? Husserl demands: Describe phenomena, don't superimpose theories on them and don't populate an imaginary "behind-the-phenomena" stage with unknowable "things-in-themselves." The description of phenomena must be one that is devoid of theory, devoid of prejudice or presupposition. But whether such a description is in fact possible is a major problem for phenomenology.

Intentionality and Intentional Objects

Two of the problems we encounter in any attempt to explain the notion of "phenomena" is the temptation to reduce it to the empiricist notion of "experience" and the dialectically opposed compulsion to interpret the phenomena as if they are not to be distinguished from things-in-themselves, as whatever natural *objects* we experience. Analogously, the traditional philosophical analysis of "consciousness" has often either fallen into a treatment of consciousness as some mysterious and autonomous realm or substance (Descartes and the British empiricists) or it has come to deny consciousness altogether and simply talk in a persistently third-person if not behaviorist manner (e.g., Spinoza and Wittgenstein). Husserl criticizes the empiricists for their "naturalization" of consciousness, which means, first, that they mistook a priori truths about consciousness for empirical truths about consciousness. Even so, they treated consciousness as a medium or "stream" separate from nature and natural objects, and at the same time incorporated into their analysis of consciousness a great many naturalistic concepts. The criticism that empiricists separated consciousness from the world and yet confused the two has the effect of a two-pronged attack on the naïve view of consciousness that gives rise to many of the epistemological problems of the Cartesian tradition.

Descartes spoke seriously of the distinction between mental and physical *substance,* and philosophers following him took equally seriously the metaphorical distinction between "in the mind" and "in the world." The views of the mind as a container of ideas, as a stream of floating impressions, and as a blank tablet that passively receives sensations, are at the very heart of the epistemologies of many modern philosophers. Husserl argues that such theories of mind are simply the product of careless phenomenological description—a failure to look at what consciousness really is like.

From his teacher Brentano, Husserl borrowed his central thesis: Consciousness is *intentional.* This tell us, in a phrase, that consciousness always takes an object. An act of consciuosness is always directed towards something. When we love, we love something; when we are afraid, we are afraid of something; when we know, we know something. The object of an intentional act need not be a real material object. One can be afraid of Communists under the bed when there are no Communists under the bed; one can imagine a golden mountain when there is no golden mountain; one can believe that there is no prime number between 3 and 11 when the proposition that there is no prime number between 3 and 11 is false. The intentional object can be a material object, but it may also be an "unreal" object, a proposition, or an "ideal object," (e.g., a number).

The thesis that consciousness is intentional requires that we distinguish between an *act* of consciousness and the intentional *object* of consciousness. Intentional acts are of many kinds: loving, thinking, feeling, imagining, perceiving, calculating, asserting, doubting. There is a correlation between acts and objects: every act takes at least one object; every object is the object of at least one possible act.

We can see now what is wrong with traditional philosophical talk of "experience" or "consciousness" by itself, and we can understand our difficulties in understanding the notion of "phenomenon." "Experience" is equivocal between the intentional act (the *experiencing*) and the intentional object (the *experienced*). To say "experience is 'in' consciousness," or "we experience only experiences, not objects themselves," or "only I can have my experience," is to speak ambiguously. If we are talking about the *act,* it makes some sense to say that the act is "in" consciousness (i.e., it is an act of consciousness), and to say that only I can perform my *acts,* while it makes no sense at all to say "I experience nothing but my acts of experiencing." If we are talking about the intentional *objects,* all three statements are false or senseless. What I experience may or may not have existence apart from my experiencing of it, may or may not be experiencable by other people. If the object is a tree, it is an open question whether the object of my experience is an object of a perceptual act or an object of a hallucinatory act. If the object is the number 5 or the proof of the Pythagorean theorem, it is surely available to anyone else. The number 5 is not an idea of mine, but a number, and if my proof is a proof at all, it is a proof for everybody. If the object in question is a proposition, for example, "the cat is on the mat," it may be certain that I believe it, but it is an open question whether or not it is true.

Insofar as the phenomenon is an intentional object of consciousness, therefore, it is not correct to say that it is simply an intuition, nor is it correct to say that it is simply an object. The phenomenon is an *object as intuited*. Whether the phenomenon is real or unreal (if it is the sort of object that can be perceived), whether it is true or false (if it is the sort of object that, like a proposition, can be asserted or denied), or whether it exists or not in some other sense (e.g., in the sense that a prime number between 7 and 13 exists) is a question which the analysis and description of the phenomenon itself (i.e., the intentional object) need not determine. Thus we can see how there is no distinction to be drawn between the phenomenon and the object-in-itself. If I perceive a real tree, then the tree as a phenomenon and the tree-in-itself are one and the same. But at the same time the phenomenon is inseparably connected to experience, for it is a phenomenon because it is an object as experienced. Thus we can also see how it will be possible to develop a phenomenology such that no mention at all need be made of *experience*; there are experiencing acts or act of intuition, and there are experienced objects or phenomena. If one wishes to insert an intermediate term such as "sense data," "sense," "immediate nonobjective experience," or "sensation appearances," this is something additional to the basic phenomenological project. (Husserl does supply us with an equivalent term of this sort, but he continuously argues that it has a merely secondary place in this analysis; he calls it *hylé*, the "matter" of experience. Merleau-Ponty's *Phenomenology of Perception* contains the best detailed phenomenological account of the concept of the "sensation" in perception.)

Phenomenology may thus be separated once again into two distinct but yet complementary investigations: there is the investigation of the conscious *act*, and the investigation of the intentional *object*. While the two cannot be completely separated, it is the latter investigation that will occupy most of our attention.

Phenomenological Reduction

Husserl takes the phenomenological reduction or *epoche* (literally, *abstention*) to be his greatest "discovery." The nature of this reduction (or these reductions, as a number of them may be distinguished) can be stated summarily, provided that we keep in mind that the reduction is among the most controversial of all of the issues raised by Husserl's philosophy. Sartre and Heidegger explicitly reject the reduction in all of its forms; Merleau-Ponty reinterprets it beyond recognition; and Husserl and other phenomenologists have offered several different and sometimes incompatible descriptions of it.

The purpose of the reduction is to satisfy the demands that we have described as central to phenomenology: to guarantee the "purity" of description and to aid in the discovery of the essences that are the key to Husserl's analysis of necessary truth. The reduction assures us that the object described by phenomenology will be the phenomenon, or intentional object of experience, and not something else—especially not a construction made by philosophers or scientists, or a transexperiential object that "common sense" teaches us to see. The reduction forces us to look at what we simply *see*, without the presupposition of interpretations *imposed* upon what we see. If I am asked to give a phenomenological description of the setting sun on a smogless night, for example, I cannot say that I see a gaseous ball of fire some ninety-three million miles away which appears red because of the refraction of light through the earth's atmosphere. What I describe is a red disk, which might just as well be two hundred yards away. In other words, my knowledge of the solar system and of the behavior of light in the earth's atmosphere is irrelevant to the description of what I *see*. The phenomenological reduction does not deny any of these scientific facts, it only suspends them so that we begin our philosophy only with what we see.

The reduction guarantees us purity of description by forcing us to describe only intentional objects or phenomena and forbidding us to describe "natural objects." A different way of putting it in Husserl's philosophy is to say that the reduction or *epoche* forces us to describe consciousness and its objects rather than the world and its objects. This can be misleading if we take this distinction to mark off the traditional realms of nature and mind. But this is not the purpose of the distinction. Rather, we want only to distinguish between objects as seen and objects as interpreted. There is only one world and one (indefinitely large) set of objects, but it can be seen from two viewpoints, the natural viewpoint and the phenomenological viewpoint. Phenomenology, we might say, is always a describing of objects *for consciousness* (i.e., as one sees them) rather than for science or for common sense.

The phenomenological reduction also guarantees that we see essences and not just individuals. Husserl reminds us that our description of consciousness must be a description of the essence of consciousness, and our description of objects—either objects in general or particular kinds of objects—must be a description of essences of objects. The phenomenologist is not interested in the fact that he now sees a red-x; but he is interested in what it is to see a material object. He is not interested in the fact that he now sees A cause B, but he is interested in what it is to see something cause something. The purpose of the phenomenological reduction is to "reduce" descriptions to descriptions of essences, to focus attention on the *meaning* of phenomena rather than on the peculiarities of particular experiences.

Finally, the reduction is intended to eliminate from philosophical investigation a number of puzzles that have plagued philosophers since Plato, problems that might be summarized as problems of existence. What is it for a material object to exist? Is there a difference between one hundred real dollars and one hundred nonexistent dollars? Is the number 5 as real as my typewriter? Does the concept of "cat" exist over and above all existent cats? Although Husserl has been indicted as a Platonist on several counts, he rejects not only Plato's postulation of a superworldly realm of Being but also the philosophical questions that lead Plato to make such a postulation. According to the phenomenological reduction, we do not ask whether something exists or not, is real or not. When we describe the essence of something, its existence is irrelevant. We can describe the essence of the minotaur without asking whether there are such beasts. We can ask the essence of the number 5 without puzzling ourselves whether numbers exist like mushrooms. We do not mean to say that the phenomenologist is not interested in the analysis of what it is for a material object or a number to be an object for consciousness—to exist in that sense. But a main function of the reduction, according to Husserl, is to "bracket out existence" for the purpose of phenomenology, to abstain from asking, "Does this thing exist?"

Husserl often talks of *the* phenomenological reduction, as if a single methodological technique will assure us of all these ends. But there are several different reductions to be distinguished in Husserl's philosophy. These reductions perform different functions and raise different issues.

The reduction does not appear in Husserl's philosophy until his mature works, and then it appears as the simple *epoche,* the "suspension of the natural standpoint" or "the bracketing of existence." In Husserl's *Ideas,* the *epoche* instructs us that we should "put out of action" our belief in the independent existence of the world we see. In the same work, we are introduced to a number of specific "phenomenological reductions": the suspension of our beliefs in the existence of our ego, in the existence of God, in the validity of the laws of logic, in the laws of natural science, and even in the existence of the phenomenologist himself. All of this is strongly reminiscent of Descartes' thoroughgoing methodological doubt, but with a most important difference. Where Descartes seriously (or mock-seriously) doubts all of those things and then insists on a proof of their derivation from some indubitable self-evident truth, Husserl does not doubt, and does not seek a proof, but only seeks to describe *what it is* to believe these things. In other words, the *epoche* is not a universal doubt, but a demand that we stop simply believing and start looking at our belief to see what it is for one to believe in his own existence, in the existence of the world, and in God.

In the same work again, Husserl introduces an *eidetic* reduction. As we may see in the very name, this is a reduction to *essences.* It is to be more or less distinguished from the *epoche,* or what is there called the "phenomenological reduction." The *epoche* assures us that we will describe only "pure consciousness"; the eidetic reduction assures us that we shall describe only the essence of consciousness and its objects.

In his later works *(Cartesian Meditations),* Husserl continues to use the phrase *"phenomenological reduction,"* but in this period the reduction becomes a *transcendental reduction.* There is a difficulty in that Husserl uses his old terminology to describe something new, but it is clear that the transcendental reduction is not meant to be added to the other reductions as much as to replace them all. The transcendental reduction represents a step back toward Descartes, for it is no longer a reduction to pure consciousness so much as a reduction to the transcendental ego and a transcendental "realm." In the earlier works, the *epoche* was a temporary methodological device to allow us to perform our phenomenological tasks more securely; in the later works the reduction becomes a permanent performance, and the phenomenological standpoint is not a new way of looking at things so much as a "new realm of transcendental subjectivity." With such drastic changes in the conception of the reduction, we must avoid general claims abut what it does or does not do. But since it is surely a key feature of Husserl's phenomenology, these wildly different conceptions of the function and results of the reduction will also lead to radically different conceptions of the phenomenological project.

Meaning and Constitution

The central concept of "meaning" in Husserl's philosophy is not to be identified with the linguistic analysts' notion of "meaning." Husserl is concerned with the meaning of phenomena and the meanings of intentional acts; the meanings of words and sentences, and what a person means when he says something, are special instances of this more general concept of meaning.

According to Husserl and most phenomenologists, the object of consciousness *is* its meaning. This *locution may sound* strange to those who are unfamiliar with Continental philosophy, but is used to convey a two-way implication: If an *act* has any meaning, that meaning is its object, and if an act has any object, that object is its meaning. Thus acts of perception, imagination, and feeling have their meanings in the objects perceived, imagined, and felt. Acts of speech, of doubting, thinking, and believing have their meaning in the propositions expressed, doubted, thought, and believed. For phenomenologists, the analysis of meaning and the analysis of what it is for there to be an object are one and the same.

As we said before, talk about acts and talk abut intentional objects must always be correlated. The analysis of the meaning of the intentional act and of that meaning as the intentional object must be carried out together. But this is not because of the simple equivalence between an act's having meaning and an act's having an object. It is not as if the object itself can be understood apart from the act that intends it. In Husserl's terminology, it is the intentional act that *constitutes* the object. Without the act there would be no object.

The idea that the intentional object is constituted in the intentional act has become the central confusion in Husserl's entire philosophy. On the one hand, Husserl does insist, particularly in his early works, upon the possibility and the necessity of investigating objects without regard for the activities that reflect upon them or whatever activities may have "produced" them. This insistence is central to his refutation of psychologism, and the idea of the "investigation of phenomena" lies, almost tautologically, at the heart of phenomenology. Accordingly, Husserl's works carry the persistent theme (but more clearly in the earlier works again) that objects (phenomena) are *given* in intuition, that objects can be described independently of intentional acts but only *understood* in such acts. Phenomenological reflection contributes nothing to the meaning or unity of the phenomenon or object, but describes it as it is. But there is a second picture of the nature of constitution which emerges throughout Husserl's writings and becomes dominant in his later works. Husserl continuously stresses the nature of the act of consciousness as "meaning-bestowing" or "signifying." His later works, for example, *Cartesian Meditations,* stress the notion of the active constitution of objects by the ego. According to this second theme, constitution is not an already completed process that is *given* to the phenomenologist, but an always ongoing *production* of the object. Quite literally, it is the act of consciousness that produces a phenomenon. As such, it is impossible for the phenomenologist to identify those aspects of the object which he creates in his reflection, and those aspects of the object which are produced by other acts simultaneous with the reflection, as distinct from those aspects of the object (if there are any) which are simply given. It is not to be supposed, however, that these two themes are completely separable: as in Kant's philosophy, the question of whether an object is given or not is a one for which there is no clear answer. The nature of the concept of "constitution" changes throughout Husserl's writings, and the contrast between constitution and intuition changes accordingly. Husserl is always trying to reconcile the two, and his conceptions of the reduction, the transcendental ego, and the key notions of "phenomena" and "reflection" change as he attempts to reconcile these two theses. It is on the basis of this uncertainty about the possibility of distinguishing phenomenon from the reflective act, and the problem of ascertaining to what extent the object or phenomenon is given and to what extent it is literally produced, that most of the subsequent problems of phenomenology are born. The question whether phenomenology is a "realism" or an "idealism"—whether it maintains that consciousness simply finds objects before it or whether it actively creates these objects—is a manifestation of this unresolved attempt at synthesis throughout Husserl's works. The split between Husserl's transcendental phenomenology and the existentialists' phenomenology largely revolves around this intuition-constitution dispute. If one interprets Husserl as placing his emphasis wholly upon the production of phenomena by consciousness or by the ego, one has the picture of a total split between phenomenology and existentialism that one finds in Sartre's writings on Husserl. But if one focuses rather upon Husserl's notions of "intuition," the "giveness" of phenomena, and the notion of "intentionality," then the split between Husserl and existentialism appears to be one of minor points of interpretation. It is such a reconciliation that one finds, for example, in Merleau-Ponty's reflections on Husserl.

Essences and Necessary Truth

The phenomenologist is concerned with the description of what is essential in phenomena—what is necessary for there to be any experience whatever. He is concerned not only with essential aspects of empirical consciousness but also with the peculiarities of nonempirical consciousness. In his analysis of empirical consciousness, he separates the essential form of experience from the particular content of experience. But in his examination of certain kinds of intuition, for example, the intuitions of a mathematician (*qua* mathematician) he finds no empirical content because the contents of those intuitions are themselves essential. The objects of such intuitions are "ideal" objects, *essences.*

In one sense, we might say that essences are the sorts of things that other philosophers have called "concepts" and "propositions." (Husserl, like many philosophers of that time, talked about words and sentences, concepts and propositions, without always distinguishing between them.) Husserl warns us, however, against interpreting this equivalent sense of "concept" in a psychological fashion. Concepts are different from people's having concepts, as propositions are different from people's believing propositions. If we neglect this difference, we fall back into psychologism, the rejected thesis that items of logic are reducible to psychological entities. Concepts and propositions are what give meaning to all experience, what make it possible for us to see objects. For every particular object we see, we also intuit an essence. Every time I see a dog, I see *that* it is a dog (or if I misperceive, at least I see that it is an animal, or that it is an object). Essences are what make a thing "what it is." The essence of a dog is what makes it a dog; the essence of the number 5 is what makes "it" the number 5.

The nature of an essence can be illustrated very simply by an appeal to a proof of geometry. If I prove that the interior angles of a (Euclidean) triangle are equal to 180 degrees, I have proven this of all triangles, those that have never been or never will be drawn or imagined as well as all actual triangles. I may perform the proof by using a hastily sketched-out triangle on a blackboard, but the precise nature of that triangle is irrelevant to the proof. In fact, it is probably empirically false that the triangle drawn on the board has angles that total 180 degrees. My proof of the theorem is not an observation about this particular triangle, but a proof about triangles in general. The triangle we have drawn is purely an instance of essential being, and "in accordance with the rubric *'in general'*" *(Ideas)*. Husserl is concerned with such objects "in general," for they are the subject of philosophical investigation and the objects that lie at the foundation of the a priori disciplines such as mathematics, logic, and geometry.

Propositions that take essences as their subject matter are necessary (essential) truths. "The interior angles of a triangle total 180 degrees" is an essential truth because it is a proposition about the essence of triangle, not a proposition about a particular triangle. It is not even a proposition about *all triangles,* but about every possible triangle. Propositions that take essences as their subject matter must be distinguished from propositions *about* essences; for example, "'triangle' means three-angled figure" is a proposition about essences, but its status as a necessary truth is much more debatable than "triangles have three angles." Our concern for essences and essential or necessary truths will be limited to propositions that take essences as their subjects. Essences are what make necessary propositions true and what make any experience at all possible. The problem Husserl faces is a Platonic one: How is it that we not only see particular objects but that we also see *kinds* of particular objects and *ideal* objects? Husserl rejects the Platonic solution that what we see as particulars are but shadows of Ideas or Forms that we do not see. Plato thought that essences occupy a peculiar world of Being and are separate from the particulars, which only "participate" in them. Aristotle then objected on the ground that essences are inseparable from objects themselves—they are to be found in the forms of objects and in the world. Scholastic philosophers (e.g., William of Ockham), argued that the existence of essences was only in consciousness. But Husserl will take no sides in this classical dispute over "universals." To a phenomenologist who has already broken down the traditional distinctions between "'in' consciousness" and "in the world," the Platonic-Aristotelean-Scholastic dispute makes no sense. Essences or Ideas (after Plato) are to be found in phenomena through phenomenological reflection. And this means that essences are neither "in" consciousness nor in the world nor anywhere else. The *epoche* assures us that such bizarre questions of ontology can be avoided, and that one can describe the nature of essences and essential truth without dealing with the ontology of universals at all.

Existential Phenomenology

The existential phenomenologists shift the emphasis away from Husserl's question, "What is knowledge?" to the very different question, "What is it to be a person?". It is not to be thought that the existentialists leave Husserl far behind, however. His phenomenology is always the foundation of their investigations, and the existentialists' primary interest in what people are and do rather than what they can and do know is not a rejection of Husserl so much as a redirecting of his philosophy. In fact, Husserl's last work, *Crisis,* is already an anticipation of many of the major theses developed by existentialist philosophers.

The existentialists, like Husserl, are concerned with *foundations,* not the foundations of knowledge (essences) but "existential foundations," the a priori principles regarding what it is to be human. This does not mean, as is so often suggested, that existentialism is concerned with the individual and the particular instead of the universal and the conceptual. Existential phenomenology is looking for the universal conceptual features that are necessary for anything to be a human being. The ability to think and to know is, as would be expected, one such set of features, but not the most significant. Equally important human characteristics, according to the existentialists, are man's abilities to act, to plan, to use language, to evaluate, and perhaps most important of all, to ask who he is and what he ought to *do.* Heidegger's early formulation of the "question of Being" begins, if not ends, with this question of self-identity. Heidegger's notions of "authenticity" and "inauthenticity" (or "ownness" *(eigentlichkeit)* and "un-own-ness") as well as Sartre's central concepts of "bad faith" *(mauvaise foi)* and "sincerity" are wholly concerned with the question of who one is.

The question of self-identity, which is fundamental to existential phenomenology, is directed both to the general problem, "What is it to be a person?" and to the particular question, "As a person, who am I?" One might think that both questions could be answered in the form, "A person is something that has the following characteristics:———" and "I am the person who has———characteristics." For example, we might say that a person is, first of all, a slightly hairy biped, and that Charles is identifiable as having brown hair and being 5 feet 8 inches tall. But the existentialists' answer to the general question of self-identity rejects this formulation. They answer that the nature of man is such that there is no nature of man (compare Sartre's celebrated slogans "man makes himself" and "human existence precedes essence.") In other words, to be a person is to be in a position to raise the question of who one is. But this is not a question of *knowledge*; one does not *find out* who he is. He decides, and acts upon his decision. He does not find that he is selfish; he makes himself selfish. He does not find mankind to be pitiful or glorious; he makes a decision that men are pitiful or glorious. In other words, the existentialist answer to the question "Who is man?" is, roughly, "Whatever he decides to be." And the answer for each of us to the question "Who am I?" is: "Whatever I make of myself." And since we *are* what we *do,* according to this philosophy, the questions of phenomenology, ontology, and ethics merge into a single set of problems.

Although existentialism is best known for these ethical theses, the existentialist philosophers have not considered their own work as "ethics." Sartre does not take *Being and Nothingness* to be a work of ethics and he has never written

the treatise on ethics that he promises at the end of that work. Heidegger has gone
so far as to have claimed that ethics is impossible. But this incredible divorce
between the popular conception of existentialism as an ethics and the existentialists' own rejection of ethics is only apparent. Because their answer to the question "What is it to be a person?" is that a person is whatever he makes of himself,
they cannot possibly go on to give a detailed account of specific principles that
men ought to live by. They argue that there is no possible "given" answer to the
question "Who am I?" and so they must refuse to treat any ethical principles as
"givens." But the existentialists have a great deal to say that bears on the nature
of evaluation, action, freedom, choice, and reasons for choice. Although they do
not and cannot dictate choices or courses of action to their readers, the existentialists do outline a theory of choice and action, one which sets the parameters
for any possible choice and actions. It is this theory and the phenomenological
analysis that supports it that make the existentialists important philosophers. The
ethical conclusions themselves (e.g., "man makes himself") could be no more
than trite grandmotherly "wisdom" unless viewed in the perspective of their
foundations. And these foundations begin with what at first appear to be innocent
and merely technical variations on Husserl's phenomenology.

But Heidegger, Sartre, and Merleau-Ponty hardly confine themselves to a
point-by-point critique of Husserl's work. Quite the opposite, they ignore Husserl's warnings against systematized philosophy and return in style to the ambitious systematic philosophy of Hegel. Heidegger's *Being and Time,* Sartre's *Being
and Nothingness,* and Merleau-Ponty's *Phenomenology of Perception* each
attempt a remarkable construction of a system of phenomenological descriptions.
The key deviations from Husserl are not always presented as such and often are
left implied as presuppositions for an analysis. Thus it would be highly misleading to isolate one or two points of disagreement with Husserl and mark them as
the seeds from which these existentialist systems grew. It is also impossible for us
to reconstruct in miniature a model of the theses, analyses, and systematic structures which they share with Husserl. Still there are some clearly identifiable elements in the existentialist revolt within phenomenology, and a brief mention of
them should suffice as an introduction to existentialist thought.

1. Human Action

The existential phenomenologists are as concerned as Husserl with the nature of
our consciousness of the world. But they disagree with his description of consciousness. Fundamentally, we do not *know about* objects in the world; we *use*
them, and the problem for the phenomenologist is to explain how it is that we
can withdraw ourselves from our tools in order to look at them as *things.* Phenomenology cannot describe the objects of our world without paying attention to
what we do with them as well as what we know about them. Husserl's mistake,
according to the existentialists, was to suppose that our primary commerce with
things was to know them, that our distinguishing and most essential ability was
reflective thought, and that our relationship to the world was not first to *live* in
it. The ideal of description of the "things themselves" must not be mistaken for
a description of intentional objects without regard for the *person* who is conscious
of them, and this means paying attention to those intentional acts which are not

merely cognitive but also involve caring, desiring, and manipulating, and are tied up with moods, emotions, and simple feeling.

2. The Epoche Reconsidered

The existential phenomenologists reject Husserl's phenomenological reduction in all its forms (although Merleau-Ponty attempts to reinterpret it in a harmless way). It is not possible, according to them, to suspend our belief in the world, nor is it possible to place oneself in any "realm" other than the natural world. This does not mean that they reject the phenomenological standpoint; what they reject is a particular technique supposedly applicable within that standpoint. A man is not a detachable consciousness who can abstract himself from the world around him. He is essentially "being-in-the-world"—an expression whose hyphenation indicates that its morphemic parts are not separable. The most important link among the existential phenomenologists—the philosophical key to their calling themselves "existential"—is their insistence that it is not possible to abstract oneself from involvement in the world. One cannot "bracket existence" as the *epoche* requires; our existence and the existence of the world around us are given together as the starting point of all phenomenological description.

It might be questioned to what extent this celebrated difference between Husserl and the existentialists is a real difference. Husserl starts out by describing intentional objects or phenomena *as if* they were nothing more than objects *for* consciousness, but he soon argues that one cannot but describe them as natural objects; epistemological skepticism is absurd because the very nature of phenomena makes it necessary for us to interpret intended objects as the objects-themselves. Similarly, Merleau-Ponty tells us that the "most important lesson which the reduction teaches us is the impossibility of a complete reduction." In some of Husserl's later work (e.g., *Cartesian Meditations*), he does maintain that the *epoche* is more than a reductio ad absurdum way of establishing the necessary nature of our knowledge of the "external" (transcendental) world. But in his earlier and his very latest works, his position is not so far from the existentialists—as Sartre, at least, has claimed.

The rejection of the *epoche* leads Heidegger, followed by Sartre and Merleau-Ponty, to equate the practice of phenomenology with ontology. In other words, the study of phenomena and the study of the kinds of things in the world are not separable enterprises. Once again, it may be questioned whether this in fact marks a more than technical difference with Husserl, since Husserl himself had argued that ontology could only be based on phenomenology and that phenomenology could not properly dispense with ontology.

But the rejection of the *epoche,* even if itself not a serious departure from Husserl, leads the existentialists to conclusions that are antithetical to Husserl's phenomenological outlook. Heidegger's introduction of the notion of "being-in-the-world" is not simply a clever Germanic neologism but one of the most radical moves in modern philosophy. What he rejects is not only the Husserlian *epoche* but the entire tradition of epistemological dualism for which Descartes is ceremoniously blamed. Husserl had rejected one traditional dualism between consciousness and nature—the one which began by distinguishing between objects of consciousness and objects-in-themselves—but he readily accepted another dualism, that between consciousness and its intentional objects. Heidegger rejects all such dualisms, and demands that philosophy begin with a single concept of "Being-in-the-world" which is not separable into consciousness on the one hand and objects (whether intentional or 'in-themselves') on the other. Sartre also begins with the existential concept of man-in-the-world, but then he distinguishes between pure consciousness ("being-for-itself") and objects ("being-in-itself")— the pair of terms coming from Hegel. Merleau-Ponty rightfully accuses Sartre of falling back into the traditional dualistic traps. He remains more faithful to Heidegger's radical notion of "Being-in-the-world" by developing in detail a concept of "bodily consciousness" that further breaks down all traditional attempts to isolate consciousness from concrete worldly existence.

3. Prereflective Consciousness

The existential emphasis on human practice and the rejection of the *epoche* come together in the recognition of an entire realm for investigation that Husserl neglected if not ignored. Husserl, like Descartes, began his philosophy from a *cogito,* an "I think," and took this *cogito* to be a basic starting point for phenomenological description and philosophical argument. The existentialists point out that the starting point of phenomenological description need not be this self-reflection or the reflection on our consciousness of objects. We can describe what we are doing as well as our *knowledge* of what we are doing, our knowing *how* to do something rather than our knowing *that* something is the case. Thus Heidegger distinguishes between *ontic* and *ontological* structures: that is, between those that exist before we are aware that they exist, and those that come into existence only with reflection. Similarly, Sartre distinguishes between "prereflective" and "reflective consciousness," and Merleau-Ponty distinguishes "preconscious" and "conscious (i.e., knowing) intentionality." We have already observed that the existentialists pay attention primarily to description of human action rather than human knowledge. To this we may now add that they describe our preconscious or prereflective involvement in our actions rather than our reflections on our actions and our actions as they become reflected upon. Self-conscious reflection is not a detached observer of our actions but an active participant that changes what it "observes."

4. The Rejection of the Self

Among the most treacherous distortions induced by description of *self*-consciousness is the idea that consciousness is *essentially* self-conscious. The *cogito* of Descartes, Kant, and Husserl falls into just this trap. Sartre argues that while it is always possible for us to reflect on our experiences, we do not *in fact* always do so. Consciousness is not always self-conscious.

But the idea of "self-consciousness" is itself suspicious. What is this "self" of which we are conscious? In Descartes and Husserl, it appears as if the "self" is a peculiar internal object that "inhabits consciousness" or "lies behind it." But the self is no such peculiar object, argues Sartre, nor is it a transcendental or formal principle that unifies our experience, as Kant had argued. The self does not exist in prereflective consciousness, and it is only *created* in reflective consciousness. We become "selves" by looking at ourselves as other people look at us. The self is "an object in the world, like the self of an Other," according to Sartre. Similarly, Heidegger tells us that the self is not primitive (not necessary to consciousness) but develops only in the company of other persons.

5. The "Ambiguity" of Human Existence

In our introduction to Husserl, we argued that he never resolves a conflict in his philosophy between the claim that objects are "given in intuition" and the opposing claim that objects are "constituted by consciousness." According to the first thesis, consciousness is at the mercy of whatever is given to it; according to the second thesis, consciousness creates its world. Husserl could never be satisfied with either thesis alone. He maintained an uncomfortable if not inconsistent attempt to hold the two together. The existentialists, influenced much more than Husserl by the dialectics of Hegel and Marx, saw this conflict but did not think it necessary to resolve it. They accepted it as a necessary peculiarity of human existence. This is not to say that they held inconsistent theses or that existentialism condones the occurrence of contradictions as such. It is rather to say that it is the nature of being a person that one can never ascertain with confidence which features of our "situation" are given to us and fixed from without *(facticity)* and which features, of our situation are created by us *(transcendence,* or *possibility).* One can never tell how much of what we see is there independently of us, and how much of what we see is created by our viewpoint, by our language, our prejudices and presuppositions. This is not offered solely as a thesis about our perception of objects, however; it is more importantly applied to our evaluations and conceptions of ourselves. The questions "What is it to be a person?" and "Who am I?" receive strange and disturbing answers. To be a person is to be in a position of never being able to *know* what is given and what one can produce, and this means there can be no answer for a living person to the question "Who am I?" To accept any answer to this question would be to accept a characterization of oneself as a "given," to make oneself inauthentic or put oneself in bad faith. When Sartre offers his famous slogans "man makes himself" and the "man's existence precedes his essence," he means to make just this point. One cannot give a characterization of oneself or of people generally, except to say that we are that kind of being who have to decide who we are.

6. Absolute Freedom

This begins to give us a clear view of the celebrated existentialist notion of "absolute freedom." Because one can never know what is given (one's facticity) and what is up to him to decide (one's transcendence), one can never settle for any characterization of oneself or of people generally. "Absolute freedom" means that nothing is ever simply "given." But the existentialists do not mean, as is often argued by unsympathetic critics, that a person is always free to do anything he or she likes. It means at most that a person has freedom to *decide* to do anything, though even this must be tempered with Sartre's thesis that a person can decide to do only what he believes he can actually try to do. I can decide to climb the mountain, for example, even though I can't do it; but I cannot decide to levitate, since I do not have the faintest belief that I could succeed if I tried. It is wrong, however, to concentrate only on the freedom or transcendence half of the existentialist ambiguity. One is always unsure about the limits of his situation and the restrictions on his freedom. In Heidegger's dramatic terms, man is *thrown* into a world and into a particular situation. Absolute freedom, Sartre tells us, is free only within the confines of one's situation. But one never knows where his situation stops and his freedom begins. This is the source of the existential anxiety derived from Kierkegaard's philosophy. Existentialism insists that people are always in a position such that they must make choices; but we must not forget that existentialism also insists that people are always in a position such that there are any number of choices that they do *not* have. And to make the entire thesis more problematic, they can never know which is which.

7. *Existential Ethics*

It should be evident by now why the existentialists cannot provide us with an ethics. Our situation consists not only of tools for us to act with and physical obstacles for us to act against, it consists also of any number of seemingly "given" values—given by parents, society, God, conscience, and by nature. But we are in the same ambiguous position with regard to values: One can never tell whether a value is truly a given value, or whether it is something that one has chosen to accept. There is always the temptation to proselytize a value as given (by God, by "Reason") when in fact it is a value that one has simply chosen and for which one has constructed a rationalization. Or one might try to shut his eyes to the problem and claim to be a "nihilist" (e.g., as does Camus' Sisyphus), and refuse to accept any values at all. But this Oedipal refusal to see is but one more version of "bad faith," for as Sartre reminds us, "not to choose is to *choose* not to choose."

> There is nothing that gives rise to knowledge of any object which does not even more certainly lead us to know our thought.
> —RENÉ DESCARTES, *Discourse on Method*

> All our knowledge relates, in the end, to possible intuitions, for it is by them alone that an object can be given.
> —IMMANUEL KANT, *Critique of Pure Reason*

> ... everything depends upon grasping and expressing the ultimate truth not as substance but as subject as well. At the same time we must note that concrete substantiality implicates and involves the universal or the immediacy of knowledge itself, as well as the immediacy which is being, or immediacy *qua* object *for* knowledge ...
> —GEORG WILHELM FRIEDRICH HEGEL, *Phenomenology of Mind*

> Phenomenology denotes a new, descriptive, philosophical method, which, since the concluding years of the last century, has established (1) an *a priori* psychological discipline, able to provide the only secure basis on which a strong empirical psychology can be built, and (2) a universal philosophy, which can supply an organum for the methodological revision of all the sciences.
> —EDMUND HUSSERL, *"Phenomenology"*

The expression "phenomenology" signifies primarily a *methodological conception*. This expression does not characterize the what of the objects of philosophical research as subject-matter, but rather the *how* of that research. . . . Thus the term "phenomenology" expresses a maxim which can be formulated as "To the things themselves!" It is opposed to all free-floating constructions and accidental findings; it is opposed to taking over any conceptions which only seem to have been demonstrated; it is opposed to those pseudo-questions which parade themselves as "problems," often for generations at a time.

—MARTIN HEIDEGGER, *Being and Time*

"It was in reaction against the inadequacies of psychology and psychologism that about thirty years ago a new discipline was constituted called phenomenology. Its founder, Husserl, was struck by this truth: essences and facts are incommensurable, and one who begins his inquiry with facts will never arrive at essences. . . . However, without giving up the idea of experience (the principle of phenomenology is to go to "things themselves" and the basis of these methods is eidetic intuition), it must be made flexible and must take into account the experience of essences and values; it must even recognize that essences alone permit us to classify and inspect the facts."

—JEAN-PAUL SARTRE, *Emotions*

What is phenomenology? It may seem strange that this question has still to be asked half a century after the first works of Husserl. The fact remains that it has by no means been answered. Phenomenology is the study of essences; and according to it, all problems amount to finding definitions of essences: the essence of perception, or the essence of consciousness, for example. But phenomenology is also a philosophy which puts essences back into existence, and does not expect to arrive at any understanding of man and the world from any starting point other than of their 'facticity'. . . . It is the search for a philosophy which shall be a 'rigorous science', but it also offers an account of space, time, and the world as we 'live' them.

—MAURICE MERLEAU-PONTY, *Phenomenology of Perception*

Taken alone the term "phenomenology" is not very illuminating. The word means science of appearances or of appearings. Thus any inquiry or any work devoted to the way anything whatsoever appears is already phenomenology. . . . Phenomenology becomes strict when the status of the appearing of things (in the broadest sense of the term) becomes problematical. . . . Phenomenology is a vast project whose expression is not restricted to one work or to any specific group of works. It is less a doctrine than a method capable of many exemplifications of which Husserl exploited only a few.

—PAUL RICOEUR, *Husserl*

11

Husserl's Private Language

"(What do you see when you turn out the light?)
I can't tell you but I know it's mine."
—LENNON-MCCARTNEY,
"With a Little Help From My Friends."

When I refer to "Husserl's private language," I am not referring to the opaque style of his philosophical writings, nor to the fact that most of his work continues to be inaccessible to the general public, nor to the fact that his ideas are still too often the possession of small protective groups of philosophers. What I am worried about is the peculiar sorts of entities and states-of-affairs to which those opaque and sometimes inaccessible writings *refer*. In brief, they refer to *phenomena*—objects of experience—to "the immediate data of experience," to "pure consciousness," to "the predicative sphere of receptive experience."

However, just about the time of Husserl's death, another philosopher, Ludwig Wittgenstein, was beginning to raise questions about the very intelligibility of talk of such objects. Wittgenstein is now credited with the repudiation of the idea of a "private language," one that refers to "private objects." And since phenomenologists after Husserl have taken the phenomenological return to "subjectivity" as their major triumph, I should like to consider whether Husserl's "phenomena" are "private objects" in any sense that would place them in jeopardy from Wittgenstein's so-called "private-language argument."

In his early *Logical Investigations,* Husserl describes his embryonic method as the description of the "constitutive elements" of experience, "the immediate data of experience," and "thought-and-knowledge experiences." In his later *Ideas I*, phenomenological investigation commences with a number of "reductions," the purpose of which is to insure that the objects of phenomenological description are objects of "pure consciousness":

> ... What can remain over when the whole world is bracketed, including our-selves and all our thinking? ... We proceed in the first instance by showing up simply and directly what we see; and since the Being to be thus shown up is neither more nor less than that which we refer to on essential grounds as "pure experiences," "pure consciousness" with its pure "correlates of consciousness" and on the other side its *"pure Ego,"* we observe that it is from *the Ego, the* consciousness, *the* experience as given to us from the natural standpoint, that we take our start.[1]

> We disconnect the whole natural world and all eidetic spheres of the transcen-dent order, and should thereby reach a 'pure consciousness.'[2]

It is clear that Husserl's *epoche* fills at least one role in his philosophy that Descartes' method of universal doubt filled in his philosophy. (Husserl points this out in the sections of *Ideas* immediately preceding the above quotations, esp. 31, 32, and again in the introduction to *Cartesian Meditations.*) For both philoso-phers it is supposed that what one knows "directly" or "immediately" is "in" one's own consciousness, and it is argued that philosophical certainty ("apodic-ticity") can be obtained only if philosophy begins from the data of "pure con-sciousness." In *Cartesian Meditations,* Husserl gives us

> " ... a *first methodological principle.* It is plain that I, as someone beginning philosophically ... must neither make nor go on accepting any judgment as scientific that I have not derived from experience, from 'experiences' in which the affairs and affair-complexes in question are present to me as 'they themselves.'[3]

Husserl's writings are attempts to carry out this Cartesian program through the execution of various phenomenological reductions, reflections, and descrip-tions. What is being reduced, reflected upon, and described in these writings, we are told, are the acts, objects, and contents of (Husserl's *own*) consciousness. It might seem that the addition of *"his own"* to this characterization is superfluous, for it can be presumed that the consciousness one is capable of examining "directly" can only be "one's own." Yet this addition will serve us well by focus-ing our attention on certain aspects of the "phenomenological method" which have received too little attention from both phenomenologists and analytic phi-losophers. If it seems like a trivial step to move from "reflection on consciousness or experience" to "reflection on *one's own* consciousness," then the step from this to "reflection on *only* one's own consciousness" will probably also seem trivial, as will the step to *"private* reflection on one's own consciousness."

But the proposition that Husserl's phenomenological investigations are pri-vate reflections upon his own and only his own consciousness and its objects ("correlates") is disastrous to his Cartesianism. Husserl emphatically rejects such a proposition, and insists that although phenomenology begins with a description of one's own consciousness, it also demands that

1. Phenomenological descriptions are *"essential"* ("eidetic") descriptions. In Kantian terms, they are descriptions of the "conditions for any conscious-

ness whatever." In other words, phenomenological descriptions are not, despite their origin, autobiographical, but statements of what is "essential" to one's (Husserl's) and any possible consciousness.

2. Phenomenological descriptions are *"intersubjective."* What is described as a phenomenological "datum" by one person must be recognizable and describable by any other. Phenomenological descriptions can be understood by anyone else.

3. Phenomenological descriptions are *"reiterable."* What one (Husserl) describes must be recognizable and describable at any time by him and by anyone else who reflects on his consciousness.

It is clear that these three demands are essentially one: the demand that phenomenological reflection and description is *not* concerned with one's own consciousness but with "the experiences that can be grasped and analyzed in intuition in their essential generality" *(Logical Investigations)*. But this demand for "essential generality" and "objectivity" raises problems that are not identical to the problem of the alleged "subjectivity" or "privacy" of the phenomenological reflection. Husserl spent most of his career trying to show that one could validly move from a description of (one's own) consciousness and its objects, acts, and contents to judgments about physical objects, other people, and other people's experiences. But, even prior to that effort, it is necessary to make intelligible the very idea of reflecting upon and describing (one's own) consciousness, its acts, objects, and contents, without already making essential reference to physical objects, other people, and other people's experiences. If the idea of phenomenological reflection (or, more generally, the idea of a Cartesian starting point) is unintelligible, then the problem of proving the "essential generality" and "objectivity" of phenomenological description does not even arise.

In the past two decades, many prominent Anglo-American philosophers have formulated a variety of "private-language arguments," based upon a number of paragraphs from Wittgenstein's later writings, which argue that the very notion of a "private object" is unintelligible. One cannot, according to these philosophers, reflect upon and identify and describe consciousness and its objects because it is not possible to have a language which is capable of referring to such "private objects." And, it is easily added, if there can be no such language, it makes no sense to talk about any such objects.

If any such "private-language argument" is sound and valid, the Cartesian project and Husserl's phenomenology would be unsound. If one cannot intelligibly reflect upon and describe one's own consciousness without reference to physical objects, other people, and other people's experiences (in other words, without disregarding the *epoche* and returning to the "natural standpoint"), then the question of whether one can move from description of one's own consciousness to statements about the world and other people and their experiences need not even be asked. Yet most efforts in phenomenology have been directed to the defense of the claim that phenomenology can and will yield "objectivity" and not to the defense of the claim that it makes sense *to begin from one's own consciousness* ("one's own case" as the Wittgensteinians have put it). But if we take both Husserl and Wittgenstein seriously, we may arrange a direct confrontation between two often incommunicative major philosophical "movements." If Husserl's project is intelligible, he must show how a private language is possible; if

Wittgenstein's argument is sound (if what has been attributed to Wittgenstein is sound), he must show why phenomenology is not possible.

The existing literature on this major confrontation is scanty at best. Although many studies have been done comparing Husserl and Wittgenstein, there has been no concerted attempt to force them to do battle on this very basic point. Gilbert Ryle published one of the only major critiques of phenomenology from a still undeveloped Wittgensteinian viewpoint in 1932. Moritz Schlick attacked the Husserlian notion of a "factual a priori" from a positivist point of view. But for all the many volumes that have been written both on the private-language argument and on Husserl's "subjectivity," it has not been argued (although it has frequently been supposed) that the two doctrines are mutually incompatible.

We have said, however, that Husserl is a Cartesian; his phenomenological starting point is one with the egocentric starting point of Descartes. There have been a number of more or less explicit applications of Wittgensteinian arguments to Cartesianism: from these, we shall be able to construct a Wittgensteinian attack upon Husserl's phenomenology. Of course, not all the objections to Descartes' philosophy will be applicable to Husserl, but certain basic objections regarding the intelligibility of Descartes' initial claim that "one knows one's own mind better than anything else" will hold equally for Husserl, who similarly argues that

> At this point, following Descartes, we make the great reversal that, if made in the right manner, leads to transcendental subjectivity: the turn to the *Ego Cogito* as the ultimate and apodictically certain basis for judgments, the basis on which any radical philosophy must be grounded.[4]

and

> If I . . . refrain from doing any believing that takes 'the' world straightforwardly as existing—if I direct my regard exclusively to this life itself, as consciousness *of* 'the' world—I thereby acquire myself as the pure ego, with the pure stream of my *cogitationes.*[5]

Husserl's Starting Point

Husserl's phenomenology presumes to be a description of (one's own) consciousness with an eye to obtaining certain, objective, intersubjective, reiterable truths. This ambition is not original to Husserl, of course; it is decidedly Cartesian, despite the many reservations expressed by Husserl concerning the subsequent direction of Descartes' thinking. Similarly, Husserl openly marks Locke and Hume as proto-phenomenologists, and his own studies were inspired and structured by later empiricists, notably Brentano, Stumpf, and J. S. Mill. And again, Husserl has much in common with nineteenth-century pragmatists, idealists, and positivists, all of whom are at some points briefly praised for their "contributions" to the "possibility of phenomenology." But Husserl clearly distinguishes himself from all of these movements: he considers empiricism, idealism, pragmatism, positivism, traditional Cartesianism all "absurd."[6] Thus, the basic insistence that phenomenology begin with an examination of experience is not sufficient to distinguish it from any number of competing philosophical movements.

It is often insisted that what distinguishes Husserl from traditional empiricist-minded movements is his *conception* of consciousness and experience. After Brentano, Husserl considered consciousness as consisting of *acts*—a quasi-metaphorical defense against traditional passive-receptive analysis of consciousness—and, also following Brentano, he considered consciousness as fundamentally *intentional,* not an entity or a realm of entities but essentially a set of *relationships* with objects. Furthermore, he rejects the traditional empiricist identification of truths based on experience as empirical truths, and insists that the knowledge gained from certain facts—eidetic facts—of consciousness are necessary truths. But this conception of consciousness is *not* definitive of Husserl's departure from traditional empiricism and positivism; behind this conception of consciousness is the *standpoint* from which he commences his phenomenology. And here, the description of consciousness as acts, as intentional, as eidetic, is consequent of what we may call the phenomenological standpoint.

This standpoint is independent of these claims; one need not talk about consciousness at all (Heidegger), and one need not accept Husserl's idea of "intuition of essences" (Merleau-Ponty), to do phenomenology, that is, to adopt the "phenomenological standpoint." Husserl's "discovery" of the phenomenological standpoint (as opposed to Brentano's "empirical standpoint"), is imitated in a dispute with Frege concerning the foundations of arithmetic and the nature of necessary truths. Husserl had argued a causal psychological account of the concept of number after the fashion of J. S. Mill; Frege had convinced Husserl that no such account could be adequate to account for the concepts of arithmetic or necessary truths. And so, in a repudiation of his own earlier work, in the Prolegomena (vol. 1) to his *Logical Investigations,* Husserl insists that no causal, and consequently no psychological, account of necessary propositions would do. While retaining an empiricist's bias, Husserl also became a rationalist, insisting that truths based on experience need not be empirical, and that an account of the essential structure of experience could not be a causal account.

Thus, in spite of an initial agreement between Husserl's phenomenology and traditional empiricism, there are important differences—differences which render inapplicable at least some objections to traditional empiricism. But rather than begin by attempting to characterize this phenomenological standpoint—an enterprise which has typically gone on interminably and taken the place of vital discussions about and within that standpoint—I shall simply mention four key points which I shall later use in defending Husserl against the Wittgensteinian private-language argument:

1. From the phenomenological standpoint, we can describe *only* consciousness: its acts, contents, and objects. The phenomenological standpoint is first to be distinguished from what Husserl calls the "natural standpoint." The difference between the two is often said to be captured by the phenomenological *epoche:* a "bracketing or disconnecting of the natural standpoint" or a "bracketing of existence." But for our purposes here, the *epoche* is not definitive of the phenomenological standpoint, but is at most an instrument to assure us of a proper transition from standpoint to standpoint. One can talk of "experience" and "consciousness" in the natural standpoint, but, from the natural standpoint, it is not *only* experience and consciousness that is discussed. In the natural stand-

point, I "naturalize consciousness," talking of it in causal terms, in relationship to the body, and it is the other person's experience as well as mine that is subject for description. In the phenomenological standpoint, I can speak only of my own experience, and I do not talk of my experience in relationship—particularly not in causal relationship—to anything else.

What is vitally different between the phenomenological and natural standpoints is the appropriateness of causal accounts: these are essential to "natural" description; they are systematically excluded from phenomenological description. It is often said that the objects of description in the natural standpoint are natural objects, while the objects of description in phenomenology are "reduced" objects: intentional objects or objects of experience. But this is not sufficient to distinguish phenomenology from traditional empiricism; both phenomenalistic sense-datum theory and Lockean representationalism (as well as other recent movements, e.g., C. I. Lewis's pragmatism) share with phenomenology the move from talk about natural objects to talk about experiences of objects. What is at stake is rather the kind of description, specifically, the appropriateness of introducing the notion of "causality" into these descriptions. Descartes is rejected by Husserl, for example, not for failing to turn his attention to the *ego cogito,* but because Descartes

> introduced the apparently insignificant but actually fateful change whereby the ego becomes a *substantia cogitans,* a separate human, *"mens sive animus,"* and the point of departure for inferences according to the principle of causality— in short, the change by virtue of which Descartes became the father of transcendental realism. . . . [7]

Husserl frequently argues that causal accounts are inappropriate to philosophy because the notion of "causality" must itself be "clarified" and defended philosophically (phenomenologically). But this is a singularly bad argument for Husserl; logical inferences must also be "clarified" and defended philosophically (phenomenologically), but Husserl makes it quite clear that this does not require that we cease employing logically valid arguments or logical notions in our philosophizing. But there is a second, more powerful argument, one which Husserl ably defends in his early *Logical Investigations:* namely, causal theories cannot account for necessary truth. Truths of arithmetic, for example, cannot be established by an account of how one learns these truths, for example, by counting (compare Husserl's earlier *Philosophie der Arithmetik*). Husserl's phenomenology, even in his early work, is a strictly *transcendental* phenomenology, at least in the sense that its truths are necessary truths about how we *must* experience objects (e.g., numbers). The expulsion of causal accounts from philosophical analysis applies both to causal explanations of phenomena and causal relationships among phenomena. The former excludes all "causal theories" of perception, from Descartes' theory of ideas and Locke's "representationalism" to Carnap's physicalism. The latter excludes all naturalistic and, specifically, psychologistic accounts of knowledge, based, for example, on associations among ideas.

Causal theories of perception, Husserl remarks, are not always announced as such (e.g., in Descartes and Hume), and they occasionally lie presupposed even in philosophies that explicitly repudiate them (e.g., in Kant's faculty psychology

that underlies his transcendental idealism).[8] Such specifically causal theories had
been under heavy attack from Nietzsche—himself a strict "psychologist"—several years before:

> What? And others even say that the external world is the work of our
> organs? But then our body, as a part of this external world, would be the work
> of our organs! But then our organs themselves would be—the work of our
> organs. It seems to me this is a complete *reductio ad absurdum* assuming that
> the concept of a *causa sui* is something fundamentally absurd.[9]

Husserl's departure from naturalism can be illustrated by a brief comparison
with Carnap's "physicalism." Both philosophers share the ambition to construct
an account of knowledge in general on the basis of immediate experience. But
Carnap feels threatened by those considerations which are later to loom so large
in "private-language arguments." If the elementary propositions ("protocol sentences") are "direct records of one person's experiences," then "every statement
in any person's protocol language would have sense for that person alone. . . .
Every protocol language could therefore be applied only solipsistically;. . . ."[10] In
order to show how it is possible for people to understand each other, Carnap
argues that the protocol language is but a part of physical language, and that protocol sentences are logically equivalent to statements about persons' behavior,
brain physiology, and so forth. But, according to Husserl, it is just this physicalist
language that stands in need of justification, so Carnap's position is "absurd."
And, since statements like "knowledge is based upon experience," and "other person's experience (as well as their behavior and physiology) is similar to mine,"
are insisted to be *necessary* truths, the contingent similarity of brains and behavior and the questionable inference by analogy to the similarity of experience are
surely not sufficient here.

Phenomenological descriptions must be "pure," according to Husserl; they
must be "neutral" with regard to any "theories," and since every causal notion
and every ontological commitment is, for Husserl, the acceptance of a "theory,"
all such notions must be expunged from phenomenological descriptions. The
descriptive terms must be epistemologically "neutralized" ("reduced"). Experience and consciousness are not to be considered within the context of the natural
standpoint, and it is here that Husserl rejects Descartes, traditional empiricism,
and all such moves as Carnap's attempt to *explain* the nature of experience in
terms of behavior, physiology, and the like. Phenomenology insists on being a
"first" philosophy, and by this is meant that its descriptions must be entailed by
all naturalistic descriptions, but that it must not entail any naturalistic
descriptions.

2. Husserl not only rejects causal theories of perception; he also rejects one
of the key ideas in many such theories—the idea of "raw experience" or "sense-
data." The "phenomena" described in phenomenology are not unconceptualized
experiences (though Husserl insists that they are "pre-predicative" experiences),
but objects of experience or *intentional* objects. While it is important not to confuse intentional objects with natural objects (i.e., the phenomenological and the
natural standpoints), it is equally important not to think of these as numerically
distinct. Whether or not the intentional chair of my experience is the same as the

natural object upon which I rest my body, and whether you can be said to see the same intentional object that I see (as opposed to the same natural object that I see) is a very difficult question which we shall have to postpone. But, for now, it is sufficient to point out that intentional objects are not the sorts of things (like sensations) of which it is logically true that "they can be experienced by one and only one person."

For Husserl, "intentional objects" or "phenomena" share many properties and confusions with Roderick Firth's "ostensibles." It is simply left unclear to what extent these are to be described as experiences and to what extent they are to be described as objects-proper ("the things-themselves"). Of course, Husserl does introduce a notion which plays a sense-datum-type role, the preinterpreted "matter" of experience or "hyletic data," but this conception plays but a small role in his phenomenology and is not part of his conception of the "original" or "essential" data for phenomenological description. Therefore, many traditional objections to the role of "sensations" as the basic elements of experience will not apply to Husserl's conceptions of "phenomena" and "intentional objects."

3. Because Husserl rejects the Cartesian distinction between experience and the "things-themselves," and because he insists that it is the objects of experience that are described, traditional ontology—that is, attempt to describe kinds of objects as they exist *independently* of consciousness—has no place in Husserl's philosophy. Husserl mistakes this claim, however, with the claim that he is not interested in ontology (i.e., in "the existence of objects") at all. I believe this to be a falsification of his phenomenology, however, one to which the classical description of the *epoche* as "a bracketing of existence" has contributed heavily. What does happen, I shall argue, is that Husserl is forced by his talk of intentional acts and objects to break down the distinction between the meaning and the reference of phenomenologically grounded expressions. Yet Husserl still retains this Fregean distinction in his analyses, and peculiarities result. I will also argue that Wittgenstein similarly rejects this Fregean distinction while continuing to utilize it, with similar oddities in his philosophy.

4. With the rejection of sense-datum theory, phenomenology also frees itself from the traditional Cartesian claim that our recognition and description of our immediate experiences is incorrigible. Now, it is true that a phenomenologist *may* go on to make this claim, and it is also true that Husserl claims a sort of certainty for phenomenological description. But the "apodicticity" claimed by Husserl applies only to phenomenological description *in general* (as a defense against all-inclusive skepticism) and not to particular descriptions. This means that phenomenological descriptions are not essentially free from error, and it means that phenomenological description can be corrected in the light of other descriptions. (At this point, Husserl's phenomenology is far closer to Goodman's *Structure of Appearance* than to traditional sense-datum-theory) in view of the fact that it is a kind of incorrigibility or immunity to self-correction that supplies the main support for the central formulation of the private-language argument, this point will become of major importance in our defense of Husserl.

I began this paper by distinguishing two very different problems facing the Husserlian phenomenologist: a problem of establishing the "objectivity" of phenomena, and a *prior* problem of making sense of the notion of "phenomena," "phenomenological standpoint," and "pure consciousness." We are concentrating upon the prior problem, and want to insist that it is different and independent of the "problem of objectivity." The difference between Husserl and Wittgenstein, we must remember, is not their attitude toward skepticism. Both reject skepticism as "logically possible but absurd." The difference is rather that Husserl attempts to follow Descartes and Kant in developing a sort of transcendental proof that our experiences are also objective. Wittgenstein rejects not only skepticism but the statement of the problem which drives Descartes, Kant, and Husserl.

If one cannot distinguish at the outset objects of experience from objects of nature, then the skeptical problem cannot even be stated. But even here, the differences are less than they first appear. What Husserl tries to do is to show that one cannot but describe his experience as objective, thus destroying the Cartesian base for skepticism in a similar way. But yet, if it is true that Husserl insists from the outset that the data of phenomenological descriptions are in some sense experiential, objects of consciousness *as opposed to* natural objects, then it would appear that crucial affinities persist between Husserlian phenomenology and traditional Cartesianism. And so, if "private" does not mean "necessarily private" (in the sense in which sensations are said to be "necessarily private"), "phenomena" or "intentional objects" may yet be "private objects" in the sense attacked by Wittgenstein.

Private Languages and Private Objects

The private-language argument now attributed to Wittgenstein surfaces in more than twenty paragraphs of the first part of his *Philosophical Investigations*[11] as a sequence of suggestions, parables, and queries. There is no clearly formulated argument; it is a matter of debate not only whether there is an argument but even whether there is a thesis—and so there is ample room for creative interpretative reading. Accordingly, there are many interpretations of both the thesis and the argument (and denials that there are either). Given the volume and variety of literature, an unrestricted discussion of "Wittgenstein's private-language argument" is as unnecessary as it is tedious. For our purposes, we can restrict the field of confrontation between Husserl and Wittgenstein with the following clarificatory remarks.

1. Wittgenstein introduces the "idea of a private language" in *PI* 243: "The individual words of the language are to refer to what can only be known to the person speaking; to his immediate sensations. So another person cannot understand the language." But this "idea" has two aspects:

a. A private language is one that refers to objects that only one person can know.

b. A private language is one that only one person can understand.

The "so" makes it appear that the move from (a) to (b) is an argument: a private language refers to private objects and *therefore* no one else can understand. Or, the same passage has been taken as a single definition, and so it is taken as a matter of *definition* that only one person can understand a private language.

According to the second interpretation, the nature of the referents of the words of the language are irrelevant to the argument. Now it has already been made clear that Husserl is not attempting to formulate a language that no one else can understand; he does not deny the possibility of someone else understanding his phenomenological identifications and descriptions; quite to the contrary, he insists that they must be understandable and "reiterable." Privacy here is only a *methodological* privacy, a stipulation that publicity cannot be *presupposed*. It is of the essence of Husserl's efforts that the language is not defined by its privacy; rather Husserl gives us a version of Malcolm's *reductio ad absurdum:* suspend your belief that the language you use to describe your experiences is understandable by anyone else, and then demonstrate that it *must* be understandable by anyone else.

Thus, to define a private language as one that no one else can understand is to drop the applicability of Wittgenstein to Husserl from the outset. Husserl is more than willing to say he is not arguing for a private language in *that* sense; he wishes to argue that one must begin in philosophy by describing his own experiences without supposing that these descriptions apply to anything other than one's own experience and can be understood by anyone else. And so, a "private language" for us will have to be identified by the privacy of the objects it refers to. Whether such a language can be understood by others is a problem that must be argued and not taken as a simple conceptual truth based on the definition of "private language."

2. Wittgenstein's own "postulation" of a possible private language centers upon the stipulation of a single sign *("E")* for a single "object" (a sensation) in the context of a public language ("it is within public language that sensation gets its meaning"). Husserl's descriptive language is neither restricted to a single sign (his 50,000 pages of tedious description is evidence for this); nor is it introduced in the context of "public" language; at the level of phenomenological description there is no "public." This means that Husserl's language must be a *systematic,* grammatically complete (not semantically complete) language. I mean to put aside certain formulations of the private language against those narrow conceptions of private language which would not allow the language to be grammatically complete.[12]

It may well be that no one could speak such a language, but that is not yet an argument against Husserl. Similarly, Husserl's language, insofar as it is a "private" language, is what Casteñeda has called a *strictly* private language, a language *all* of whose terms (i.e., all of whose referring terms) refer to private objects. Again, arguments against the incorporation of some peculiarly private sensation terms into a "mixed" language will be independent to the confrontation between Husserl and Wittgenstein. Even if English does include sensation-terms and refer to private objects, this is not yet a defense of phenomenological description.

3. The idea of a private language is often qualified as the idea of a *necessarily* private language. Norman Malcolm clearly takes a private language to be by definition a language only one can understand: "Let us see something of how Wittgenstein attacks what he calls the idea of a private language. By a "private" language is meant one that not merely is not but cannot be understood by anyone other than the speaker."[13]

Malcolm then goes on to describe his own argument (taken from Wittgenstein) as a reductio ad absurdum: "postulate a private language, then deduce that it is not a language."[14]

The idea of a necessarily private language has been the object of some confusion. Many commentators fail to see that there are two claims to necessity regarding private languages. First, that a private language *by definition* ("is meant") can be understood by only one person. Secondly, Malcolm means to insist that the sense of "can" here is itself a logically necessary "can." In other words, his interpretation of Wittgenstein's "idea of a private language" looks like the following:

PL = df N (only one can understand)
N (PL = N (only one can understand))

To deny that a private language ought to be *defined* as one that only one person can understand is only to reject the first necessity modality, not the second. Thus we will deny that a private language is necessarily private only in the sense that we shall first deny that it is a matter of definition to say that no one else can understand a private language. It may still be that it can be argued that no one can (logically) understand a private language, and that no one can (logically can) have such a language.

What does the second "necessity" in Malcolm signify? It has been argued that the notion of "logical necessity" here is unintelligible[15]; it has also been argued that there is simply no point in distinguishing between

(1) only one can understand L

and

(2) logically only one can understand L.[16]

We need not depend on "logical" here, since it can be stressed what theses are not being argued. Malcolm's insistence on the *cannot* is used to reject purported counterexamples by Ayer, Strawson, and to show that the thesis in Wittgenstein is not open to certain sorts of objections. Wittgenstein's paragraph 243 surely shows that he allowed for "private" languages in the uninteresting sense in which only a small number of people can speak Latin, or that the few members of a club can develop a secret code, or that a husband and wife can make it a practice to speak Flemish between themselves at dinner parties so that no one else can understand. But the esoteric cases cited by philosophers in which every speaker of Urdu save one is savagely done away with or in which Robinson Crusoe on a desert island develops his own system of notation for his diary are no more interesting than this. That there is a language which one and only one person happens to speak is not to show that there can be a private language in any sense relevant here.

The question at stake for Wittgenstein is whether Robinson Crusoe *could* show anyone else his diary. And it is here that one wants to bring in some sense of "logical necessity" to stress that the mere fact that Crusoe is alone on the island is not relevant to what is meant by "could show the diary to someone else." Malcolm wants to say that no one else could understand the diary even if they were on the island and if Crusoe took every possible step to teach them his style of notation. The idea is that Crusoe *could not* teach them no matter what. But here the argument becomes meaningless if it is said the reason he cannot teach them his private language is because it ceases to become private as soon as they learn it (which is what we would say if "pvt lang" is a language that by definition only one can speak one sense of, "*necessarily* no one else could understand the language"). It is here that Malcolm can add: "The reason for this is that the words of the language are supposed to refer to what can only be known to the person speaking; to his immediate private sensations."[17]

But now we can see that the notion of "necessary privacy" need not enter into our account of the private language argument at all. It may be that, if the referents of the language are "immediate private sensations," and if to understand the words of the language is to know "what can only be known to the person speaking," then it follows uninterestingly that the language will be understandable to one and only one person. But it is not clear that "sensations are private" implies that "only one person can 'know' sensations," nor is it clear—if "know" is taken again in this very strong sense—that one has to "know" the reference in order to understand what is said. But we need not attempt to resolve this problem—the classical locus of discussions about private language—since Husserl is not concerned with sensations in any event. Even if it is some sort of "grammatical truth" that "sensations are private" in some sense (i.e., that only one person can "have" them), it is not at all clear that "phenomena are private" is even true, much less necessarily true.

It has been argued by several authors (e.g., D. Locke and J. Cook) that the notion of "necessity" need play no role in the private language argument. John Cook argues, for example, that the peculiarity of sensation-talk that Wittgenstein wishes to point to is not the alleged *privacy* of peculiar objects, but rather the peculiarity of the very notion of "privacy." A sensation is not a peculiar object, but *having a sensation* is a property of a person. Cook compares "he has his pain" to "he has his build," commenting that the latter case does not tempt us to speak of the "his" as a "his" of private access or ownership or of a build as a peculiar object that each person has only for himself. Extending this analysis to sensations, the conclusion to be drawn, for Wittgenstein, is that it is talk of both "privacy" and "objects" that is inappropriate here. And the notion of a necessarily private language does not collapse either because it is not a language or because it is necessarily private, but because "private" is meaningless in this context.

But this way of dealing with sensations still leaves us free to raise the kinds of questions Wittgenstein wanted to raise about privacy with reference to phenomena or intentional objects. As Husserl introduces these, they are clearly not properties of persons, and consequently are describable as objects independent of any properties of the viewer (even though it is a necessary truth that they must be viewed by somebody). But, with regard to phenomena, there is not even a temptation to suggest that they are necessarily private in the questionable sense in which sensations are said to be private. We can still talk about privacy, but "necessary" privacy need have no place in our discussion whatever.

4. Wittgenstein and Malcolm often argue against a private language by pointing out the impossibility of someone's learning the language. For example, the idea that sensations are "immediate and private" is attacked on the grounds that a child could not learn to refer to such objects but could be taught to properly ascribe having-sensations to himself according to behavior and circumstances which are publicly accessible. But it is important to stress the *logical* force of the private language argument; what is at stake is not whether one could be taught a private language but whether one could *exercise* his knowledge of such a language. Thus, again, Robinson Crusoe examples are tediously off the point.

For purposes of the argument, it might be supposed that people simply find themselves capable of speaking a language. Or, for our purposes, it can simply be pointed out that Husserl's "private language" is not "natural" in any sense, and it requires a set of philosophical manipulations in order to force someone (already linguistically competent) into "a new way of looking at things."[18] Phenomenological language is clearly parasitic on 'natural' language. In *Ideas*, 88–89, for example, Husserl marks the passage from the natural standpoint to the phenomenological standpoint by merely inserting quotation marks around the naturalistic terms. This would seem to indicate that Husserl himself believes that phenomenological terms have a different sense than naturalist terms. One great difficulty in Husserl is his failure to ever make adequate comment on this. However, it may just be that only the reference of the terms is altered and not the sense, and Husserl has just mistaken the reference for the sense. For example, his introduction of the *epoche* and his long discussions of the concepts of *meaning* might be used to argue that the reference of phenomenological terms is irrelevant to the meaning of these terms, and, furthermore, that the meaning of these terms in phenomenological and naturalistic contexts is the same. (But in one case they are used to refer, in the other they are not.)

5. But there is a more interesting way to view Husserl's conception of sense and reference here, one that parallels a similar conception in Wittgenstein. Wittgenstein has recently been attacked on the grounds that he has confused the sense and the reference of sensation-expressions. D. Locke, for example, argues at length that Wittgenstein confuses the publicity of the meaning of sensation terms with the privacy of their reference. Similar arguments appear in P. F. Strawson's famous review of the *Investigations* and elsewhere. Wittgenstein does not neglect but rejects the Fregean distinction. His "use"-theory of meaning (if he has any theory at all) demands that words and expressions do not have either meaning or reference, but rather that people use words and expressions to mean and to refer. But these "uses" are hardly separable in practice, and Wittgenstein argues, I think, not just that people *do* many things with words, but also that they rarely if ever use words in such a way that what they mean and what they denote can be distinguished at all.

With particular regard to the use of sensation-expressions, it seems that Wittgenstein is arguing, not that these are used with public meaning without private reference, but rather that the very distinction makes no sense in this case, between public and private or between meaning and reference. When I assert, "I have a pain," the distinction between what I mean and what I refer to is senseless. This is not to deny that I may sometimes say "I have a pain" when I do not have a pain, but this is not a matter of *meaning* the same as before but now without referring. The Fregean picture is too simple, and Wittgenstein playfully rejects it (see *PI*, 270): "means something known . . . [or perhaps refers to something. . . .]" And again, Wittgenstein's "use"-theory undercuts traditional talk of "necessity" ("This game is played"), and so it is extremely doubtful whether the notion of a "necessarily private language" can play any role in a consistent interpretation of the *Investigations*.

This means that the traditional formulations of private-language questions are inappropriate starting points; for example, "Is it possible for a word or expression to refer to a private object?" or "Is it possible for a word or expression to have a meaning which only one person understands?" Similarly, Malcolm's defense of the argument in terms of establishing "an essential connection between words and sensations" is inappropriate as well. One might continue to guardedly talk about the sense and reference of sensation-expressions, but surely no argument using those forms will be Wittgenstein's, and, one might argue, it is such talk about the meaning as opposed to the reference of sensation-expressions that causes the private-language dilemma in the first place.

In Husserl, we face a parallel problem in interpretation; Husserl's *epoche,* interpreted as a "bracketing of existence," would lead us to think that all of phenomenological investigation is concerned with meaning and never with reference. And, indeed, Husserl does go on to draw an equivalence between meaning and the intentional object. Yet he does insist continuously that the objects of phenomenological-investigation are the "things-themselves."[19]

A great deal of confusion has been generated in the exposition of Husserl's phenomenology by making a remarkable distinction between the meaning and the reference of intentional acts (not words). Phenomenology treats of meaning and never of reference (existence). But I suggest that this is to ignore the fact that Husserl's notion of "constitution" is tied up not only with what we mean, but also with the objects that we "intend," and this makes sense only if we give up the Fregean distinction in Husserl and interpret him, like Wittgenstein, as holding an "act"-theory within which the Fregean distinction cannot be drawn. Intentional objects are as much the meaning as the reference of intentional acts.

All of this discussion has led us to a number of restrictions on our discussion of both Husserl and Wittgenstein which will allow us to compare them on one particular point, the question of whether it makes sense to describe the objects of experience independently of any description of natural objects. In this discussion, we need make no further mention of Husserl's *epoche,* or of sensations, or of "private language" in its many specialized post-Wittgensteinian senses, or of the difference between the sense and the reference of expressions, or of the notion of "(logical) necessity" as it usually functions in private language discussions.

The idea of phenomenology is to describe the objects of one's experience *as if* they could be viewed and described only by the phenomenologist. There is no point in confronting Husserl with those many private-language arguments that show the impossibility of objects "which no one else could (logically) experience." What is at sake is rather whether one can describe objects such that it *may* not be the case that they can be (not a logical 'can be') experienced and described by anyone else. Intentional objects, we might say, are provisionally private; *perhaps* no one else experiences them. But this is not sufficient to allow Husserl to escape from the private-language argument in at least one of its central formulations. There may be something very wrong with the query, "what is left when I subtract the object I see from my seeing of it?" This perfect parallel with one of Wittgenstein's favorable examples in action-theory should show us that we are still close to the central intentions of the *Investigations.*

The Same Intentional Object

The heart of the private-language argument, at least as interpreted by many commentators (notably Norman Malcolm), centers upon the notion of a "rule of language." A language must have rules and a rule is something that is followed. But it is possible to follow a rule only insofar as it is possible to be mistaken in applying that rule. If one cannot be mistaken, one cannot be said to be following a rule and so cannot be said to be employing a language. A private language, it is then argued, does not allow for mistakes, and so cannot have rules, and so cannot be a language.

As introduced, this argument focuses upon the concept of a language and begins by defining a set of rules as necessary to a language. We need not worry over a general characterization of "language," and Husserl would insist that the issues at stake go beyond the bounds of any conception of a language. But Husserl would agree with Wittgenstein-Malcolm that *meaning* requires rules (whether or not it is the meaning of the use of words or linguistic expressions that is in question), and so we may begin with a modified first premise, that phenomenological description has meaning (and can refer) only if it is formulated in accordance with certain rules. It is not clear from Husserl's writings whether he would accept the second step: that it is possible to follow a meaning rule only insofar as it is possible to be mistaken in applying that rule. But Husserl clearly does believe that it is possible to formulate mistaken phenomenological descriptions, and so he at least believes that mistakes are possible, whether or not he would argue that the possibility of mistakes is necessary. But we can ask whether phenomenology really can make mistakes, and so whether there really are rules for the formulation of phenomenological descriptions.

The argument in Wittgenstein-Malcolm to the conclusion that a private language cannot include mistakes, *ergo* cannot have rules, *ergo* cannot be meaningful, begins by distinguishing my correctly applying a rule and my having the impression that I have correctly applied the rule. It is taken to be evident that, in a "public" language, my making a mistake can be recognized by others even if it is not recognized by me. This contrast between my applying a rule and our following a rule (i.e., the distinction between a "public" and a "private" language) is key to Wittgenstein's argument. Only other people can allow me to know of my mistakes, and so only in a "public" context can one have a language. But the simple extension of this argument from "my mistakes" to "our mistakes," from "I can't distinguish between what seems right to me and what is right" to "*We* can't . . . to *us*. . . ." would yield the conclusion that there cannot be a public language either. On these grounds, one might reject the private language argument, even if valid, on the grounds that it demands of a private language satisfaction of conditions that no human language could ever satisfy (e.g., the formulation of a completely adequate refutation of philosophical skepticism).

But the Hegelian demand that intersubjective agreement is adequate to distinguish "correct" and "seeming correct" is clearly an unspoken presupposition of the Wittgensteinian argument. "Intersubjectivity" and "objectivity" become equivalents on this account (at the end of his career, Husserl also came to make this equation [in *Krisis*]). But in a private language where I cannot appeal to the experiences of others, all correction must be self-correction. "In my own case," according to the argument, I cannot ever tell whether I have applied a rule correctly or whether it seems to me that I have applied it correctly. Wittgenstein tells us, "Whatever is going to seem right to me is right, and that only means that here we can't talk about 'right'." (PI, 258) If I can't distinguish between being correct and seeming to be correct, then I lose hold of the concept of "correct" and consequently the concept of "rule" as well. If I can't distinguish being correct and seeming to be correct, I cannot know whether or not I am following a rule, and consequently, it is argued, I cannot be said to be following a rule at all. And, therefore, my identifications and descriptions are meaningless.

Finally, if my identifications and descriptions are meaningless, they cannot identify or describe anything. Therefore, there are no objects which cannot be identified and described by others as well as myself. Let E be an object (leaving open whether it is a physical object, a sensation, or an intentional object), and let *"E"* be either an identifying name or a description of E. Then the private-language argument as outlined above will run:

> (1) If I cannot appeal to the experiences of others regarding E, then I cannot tell the difference between *"E"* being correct and *"E"* seeming to be a correct identification or description of E. (We need not make mention of either the notion "private language" or "private object" here.)
>
> (2) If I can't distinguish between *"E"* being correct and *"E"* seeming to be correct, then it doesn't make sense to speak of "correct" with regard to *"E"*.
>
> (3) If it doesn't make sense to speak of *"E"* as "correct," then *"E"* is meaningless.
>
> (4) If *"E"* is meaningless, there can be no E.

One familiar strategy of attack is to tentatively grant (1) and then argue that steps (2), (3), (4) are invalid and rest upon easily recognizable fallacies. (1), particularly with regard to sensations, might be thought harmless enough. If I am in pain (and the question of "appeal to others" is inappropriate), the difference between being in pain, believing that I am in pain, and knowing I am in pain—a few exceptional cases aside—is negligible, and many philosophers who reject the argument will yet accept the first premise. But 2, 3, 4, they might argue, depend upon a basic confusion of the meaning and the reference of *"E,"* a confusion between the meaningfulness of confirmability of *"E"* and the truth of *"E,"* between the applicability of *"E"* and the truth of *"E."* In step 3 it is argued that if *"E"* can't be used to refer (since we cannot speak of its being used correctly or incorrectly to refer), then *"E"* cannot be meaningful. And in step 4 the converse move is made, from the alleged meaninglessness of *"E"* to the inability of *"E"* to refer. Traditionally, both moves can be argued to violate the distinction between the sense and reference of *"E"*: terms can fail to refer and yet be meaningful, while terms might refer but not have a meaning (as has been argued by many philosophers to be the case for proper names). Similarly, step 2 might be said to confuse the equally traditional distinctions between truth and confirmation, or truth and applicability (meaningfulness). *"E"* may be true yet nonconfirmable; or *"E"* might be confirmable but not true. One might deny this if he joins Wittgenstein, according to Strawson, in "retaining the verificationists' horror of a claim that cannot be checked" and in collapsing the notions of confirmability and meaningfulness.

But I am not happy with any of these counterarguments, even though I am at least as unhappy about steps 2, 3, and 4. If, as I suggested earlier, Wittgenstein is concerned with rejecting the traditional Fregean distinction between meaning and reference, and—only partially in agreement with Strawson's indictment of Wittgenstein as a still-latent positivist—the distinction between rules for applicability and rules for truth of a concept, then the critique of the private-language argument that depends upon these distinctions begs the question. I agree that steps 2, 3, and 4 are invalid as stated, but I am not at all confident that a thoroughgoing Wittgensteinian could not restate the argument in more sophisticated terms such that these criticisms could not apply.[20]

Rather than pursue this line of argument, therefore, I will focus my attention on premise (1), which, I shall argue, can be used as a basis for defense of Husserl without attempting to reject the later steps of the argument.

The premise of the argument turns on the impossibility of identifying and reidentifying and describing the *same* object. If I do not or cannot appeal to others' identifications and descriptions of E, then only I can determine whether or not *"E"* is a correct identification or description of E. But how can I determine whether *"E"* is current or not? According to Wittgenstein, if E is a "private object" (e.g., a sensation), I cannot ascertain the correctness of *"E"* by appealing to another "impression" for "that would be as if someone were to buy several copies of the morning paper to assure himself that what it said was true" (*PI,* 165). And so, at least with reference to sensations, the correct identification/description of the sensation must refer beyond the sensation itself; but if, as in the Cartesian position, such appeal is ruled out, there can be no alternative identification or description of E, and *"E"* cannot be ascertained as either correct or incorrect.

Again, I do not wish to pursue this argument as it applies to sensations. But if we replace "sensations" with "phenomena," and thereby make it more questionable in what sense we are speaking of "private objects" (as we have argued earlier), the argument is clearly inadequate. Granting that *qua* phenomenologist, I cannot appeal to the experiences of other people in evaluating my description of *"E,"* I can appeal to the details of E and to other E's where E here is not a sensation or an impression but an intentional object—an object of my experience. E is a tree in a garden (as I experience it): I want to know if it is the same E that I experienced yesterday. I walk around the trunk and see the initials "W.B." carved three feet up the trunk. I wonder if my description of the tree as a dogwood was correct: I open up my fieldguide and match the leaf pairs of the tree to the pictures in the book. I want to know if the tree is a real tree (as opposed to a picture of a tree, a plaster-cast tree, a hallucinated tree); I kick it, climb it, and try to remember having been here before. In short *within* "my own case," I can do a great deal to confirm or disconfirm my identification/description *"E."*

As A. J. Ayer has pointed out, Wittgenstein's newspaper quip is misleading. Identifying E in my own case is more like buying different editions of different newspapers, not like buying different copies of the same newspaper. Intentional objects are systematically connected with each other; identifications/descriptions of intentional objects are logically connected to each other. Even within my own case, I can ascertain the correctness of *"E"* by examining the coherence of E with other intentional objects, and by examining the consistency of *"E"* with other identifications and descriptions I have made. Husserl calls these coherence relations the "noematic nexus" or the "system of noemata"; what ties them together is the *meaning* of the intentional object (*not* the meaning of the description). Similarly, Aron Gurwitsch, one of Husserl's best pupils, takes the notion of "the noematic nexus" to provide a sufficient account of the identity of intentional objects and therefore, we may add, to provide a sufficient account of the possibility of self-correction to reject the Wittgensteinian premise.

Of course, one might then argue that this defense holds only so long as it is particular phenomenological descriptions that are in question and not phenomenological reflection and description as a whole. One can correct a particular description by appeal to other intentional objects and other descriptions, but one cannot, by the nature of the case, correct descriptions in general by appeal to anything else. To this we will have to agree. The possibility of "internal checking" does not yet suffice to defend the idea of phenomenology on a more grand scale. It may be that, although the phenomenologist can check and correct himself, he still cannot ever ascertain that his identifications and descriptions as a whole can be checked or corrected.

One reply to this objection is to simply return to our observation that it is an objection that applies to every "public" point of view as well as to the phenomenological standpoint. *We* can never know whether *our* world view is correct or not because we cannot (again, by the nature of the case) ever check it against anything else. Wittgenstein seemed satisfied with this; it is particular judgments and corrections of particular judgments that concern him. Yet I do not want to let the phenomenologist off so easily: he has escaped the major dangers of the private-language argument as we have presented it; he can correct his (particular) phenomenological identifications and descriptions, and so these are not meaningless, so it makes sense to talk about and describe (intentional) objects. But the private-language argument may yet have a last bite to it, one which the phenomenologist cannot escape. I should like to briefly argue this objection in closing.

Objectivity

The private-language argument as advanced by Wittgenstein and Malcolm is an argument to the effect that one can only have a language when it is possible to identify, reidentify, describe, and redescribe the *same object*. I have argued that Husserl's language is therefore a language, that it can identify, reidentify, describe, and redescribe intentional objects, and that Husserl's language is "private" only in that it refuses (tentatively at least) to make appeal to the identifications, reidentifications, descriptions, and redescriptions of others. Once we have properly restricted the notion of "private language" as it applies to Husserl, we have shown that a "private language" is possible in the above sense. The coherence among intentional objects and among descriptions of intentional objects is sufficient to correct phenomenological descriptions.

But we have thus shown only that self-correction is possible; we have not yet shown that it is sufficient to meet a stronger interpretation of the private-language argument that Wittgenstein does not seem to emphasize. Namely, coherence among experiences: intentional objects and descriptions may not be sufficient to identify the *same* object after all. Husserl seems to rely upon a coherence notion of identity and also of truth. Aron Gurwitsch explicitly argues that the phenomenological conceptions of "identity" and "truth" *cannot* be more than coherence conceptions.[21]

But now suppose we bolster Wittgenstein's argument once again and demand of the phenomenologist not only that he show that he can make some corrections (i.e., of those mistakes that are incoherent), but also that he show that he can prove that a coherent set of descriptions is also *correct*. This is, in effect, a return to the demand that the phenomenologist defend not only this or that description, but the notion of phenomenological description *in general*. We might object (as we did before) that no viewpoint can do that, but at least the Wittgensteinian can go one step past the phenomenologist. While the phenomenologist can only rely on coherence, the Wittgensteinian and naturalists in general can rely on *argeement*. Can the Husserlian phenomenologist get us this far toward "objectivity"?

I will not attempt a summary evaluation of Husserl's notion of "objectivity"—a notion which preoccupies him throughout his career. But I think I can briefly point out the problem he faces—which is derivative of Wittgenstein's argument—and, perhaps more surprisingly, I think I can point out that Husserl both recognized this problem and came to believe that it could *not* be solved. The problem is whether a coherence theory of such key philosophical notions as "truth," identity," "existence" can ever be adequate to establish, as Husserl wants to establish, the "objectivity" of intentional objects and their descriptions. But, one wants to point out, a coherence theory always leaves room for accidents and coincidences; a description may cohere circumstantially without being true. An object may share any number of properties with another object without being identical to it; there might be any amount of evidence for the existence of an object which in fact does not exist. Such obvious considerations have led philosophers to see that mere coherence cannot be sufficient as a criterion of truth, identity, or existence. This is not to insist that one must then accept traditional correspondence theories, nor is it yet to insist that one must accept semantical theories of truth, identity, and existence. Husserl would surely insist that correspondence theories are seriously confused (as Frege before him and Heidegger after him argues at some length); and, since he argues that meaning, truth, identity, and so on are properties of phenomena and not of language, Tarskian theories of truth or Quinean theories of existence are ruled out as well. I will not attempt here to trace the various attempts that have been made or might be made to establish a more-than-coherence phenomenological theory of truth, identity, and existence. But it would seem that Husserl has already ruled out all of the standardly available analyses. None of this is to question for a moment the intelligibility of the phenomenological standpoint; but it is to throw doubt on one of Husserl's key claims for that standpoint: that it (alone) can establish the objectivity of what we each experience.

Near the end of his career, Husserl confided in a letter that "the dream of philosophy as a science . . .—this dream will never be realized ."[22] But if philosophy cannot show that phenomena are "apodictically" true and "objective," at least one can take one step beyond the threat of solipisism and establish that phenomena are "intersubjective" or "public." Toward the end of his work, Husserl made a radical change of direction, one which is often and surprisingly interpreted as a smooth transition from his earlier phenomenology. In his last decade of work, the problem of "intersubjectivity" came to dominate many of his analyses. Husserl is often interpreted as obtaining a concern for the problem that Wittgensteinians refer to as "the problem of other minds." In fact, Husserl had very little to do with this problem, which is a problem of how to prove the existence of other minds on the basis of what we know about other things (e.g., bodies and behavior). But Husserl was concerned with *beginning* with the notion of intersubjectivity and argued that *therefore* we have knowledge (i.e., objectivity), not that we have knowledge (of something) and therefore we can prove the existence of others. What Husserl did, I want to suggest, was to make just that sort of move that lies at the very basis of Wittgenstein, to equate objectivity with intersubjectivity and then *begin* analysis from an intersubjective or "public" viewpoint. This analysis becomes prominent in such later phenomenologists as Schütz, Heidegger, and Merleau-Ponty. Curiously, it is Jean-Paul Sartre who resists this move most thoroughly: he begins, rather, by simply insisting on the nature of objectivity as something which can simply be described as *given.* While I do not want to criticize this move here, I think it is worth pointing out that, despite his belief that he is attacking Husserl at the most basic level of analysis, he is in fact remaining the most orthodox with respect to Husserl's original intentions.

But Husserl's turn to intersubjectivity may be a convert admission that phenomenology as he defines it is intelligible but yet a failure: one can be a phenomenologist, *contra* Wittgenstein, but one cannot give a phenomenologically adequate account of those notions which would allow a phenomenologist to claim that his descriptions are *objective,* and not at most, coherent and intersubjectively agreeable. So Husserl *can* have his private language, but he cannot do with it as he likes, and phenomenologists will move along with Wittgenstein from a relatively clear philosophical solipsism to an increasingly skeptical philosophy that begins with the notion of intersubjectivity.

NOTES

1. *Ideas* I, trans. by W. R. Boyce-Gibson (New York: Collier Books, 1962), ch. 4, sect. 33, p. 101.

2. Ibid, p. 173, 7:64.

3. *Cartesian Meditations,* trans. by D. Cairns (The Hague: Nijhoff, 1960), ch. 2, sect. 5, p. 13. Here-inafter referred to as *CM.*

4. Ibid, I:8, p. 18.

5. Ibid, p. 21.

6. *Ideas* I, ch. 2, esp. sect. 20, 21, 25.

7. *CM,* I:10, p. 24.

8. *Ideas* I, ch. 6, sect. 62.

9. *Beyond Good and Evil* (New York: Random House, 1966), I:15.

10. *Foundations of the Unity of Science,* ed. by O. Neurath et al., (Chicago: University of Chicago Press, 1938).

11. L. Wittgenstein, *Philosophical Investigations,* trans. by G. E. M. Anscombe, 2d ed. (London: Basil Blackwell, 1963). Numbers parenthesized in text refer to sections of this edition.

12. Cf. V. Chappell. "For it is (roughly) just the absence of logical terms, and of what, in Casteñeda's view, this entails that makes the postulated language not a language according to Wittgenstein." In C. D. Rollins, ed., *Knowledge and Experience,* Oberlin Colloquium in Philosophy, 1962, 3d ed. (Pittsburgh: University of Pittsburgh Press, 1968), p. 109.

13. N. Malcolm, "Wittgenstein's *Philosophical Investigations,*" in G. Pitcher, *Wittgenstein* (New York: Doubleday, 1966), p. 66.

14. Ibid., p. 75.

15. J. Cooke, "Wittgenstein on Privacy," in Pitcher, op. cit.

16. Don Locke, *Myself and Others* (Oxford: Oxford University Press, 1968).

17. Op. cit., p. 66.

18. *Ideas* I, 39 (cf. Wittgenstein, op. cit., p. 144.)

19. *Ideas* I, ch. 4, Sect. 43.

20. R. Dancy, "Agreement and Privacy," *Journal of Philosophy* (1970).

21. "On the Intentionality of Consciousness," *Studies in Phenomenology and Psychology* Evanston, Ill., Northwestern University Press, 1966).

22. *Husserliana* VI, 508.

12

Sense and Essence:
Frege and Husserl

Pure or transcendental phenomenology will be established not as a science of facts, but as a science of essential being, as 'Eidetic' science; a
science which aims exclusively at establishing "knowledge of essences"
and absolutely no "facts."

(*Ideen,* p. 40, Introduction)[1]

It is singularly unfortunate that Husserl, who conscientiously avoided use of terminology with long and varied philosophical histories, should choose the notion
"essence" as a central concept in his philosophy. In the Introduction to *Ideen,* he
comments that "its equivocations are harmless." But this is far from true regarding the disastrous effects of his own use of the notion. His talk of "essential Being"
and "essences as objects of knowledge" has generated such antagonism among
American philosophers that the formulation of an acceptable interpretation of
Husserl's philosophy has become an almost thankless task. While most of his
supporters remain content to give their endorsement to the insistence that philosophy must concern itself only with *essences* and the *Being of essences,* Husserl's detractors have not found it difficult to dismiss all talk of "essences" as an
unwelcome remnant of a paradigm of philosophy long outmoded.

We find Husserl's philosophy thus dismissed in the dress of any number of
doctrines not his own: the doctrine of essential Being is dismissed as a regression
to Platonic "realism"; the notion that essences "inhere in" facts is rejected as a
hangover from Scholasticism; the notion of "intuition of essences" is suspected
to be an attempt to block all criticism; or, what is worse, it is thought to be a new
variety of mysticism. This same notion of "intuition of essences," coupled with
Husserl's own characterization of his philosophy as a "radical empiricism," has
given critics cause to claim that Husserl attempted to give an empirical analysis
of essences and essential truths. Other critics, focusing rather on Husserl's sharp
separation of fact and essence, complain that Husserl is altogether opposed to
factual science and causal explanations. All of these criticisms are misguided, but,
to show this, we shall require an overall reevaluation of Husserl's doctrine of
essence in much clearer analysis than Husserl ever affords us.

205

In this essay, I shall attempt to dislodge Husserl's notion of "essence" from "Platonic Ideas" and "Scholastic essences" as well as from the speculative metaphysics, the mysticism, and the too-radical empiricism with which it has been confused, and display it in the philosophical context in which it rightfully belongs. This context, I shall suggest, is one best defined by Husserl's contemporary and critic, Gottlob Frege. It has always appeared curious to me that Husserl and Frege are so often considered so very far apart, when the two men were, in fact, so similar in background, in interests, in the specific problems they encountered, and, I shall argue, in some of the solutions they offered to these problems. Of course, the two very different movements these two thinkers set in motion explains our tendency to think of them as so markedly different. But if, as I shall argue, the differences between them is largely a matter of terminology and emphasis, there may be real hope for a sympathetic meeting between "analytic" and "phenomenological" philosophies as well.

Why should Husserl want to talk about "essences" at all, much less make such a problematic notion the central concern of his philosophy? Of course, Husserl might easily have coined a new term in place of "essence" *(Wesen),* but some such term is indispensable, we will argue, in just the same way that similar concepts are vital in the philosophy of Frege.

In the 1880s both Husserl and Frege were probing the foundations of mathematics, attempting to discover the source of validity of the basic principles of arithmetic. Frege's *Grundlagen der Arithmetik* (1884) *(GA)* did not receive the attention it deserved, largely because it deviated so markedly from the then fashionable "psychologistic" approach to this and other philosophical questions. Husserl's dissertation at Halle (1887) and his first book, *Philosophie der Arithmetik* (1891) *(PA)* which did accept this approach, were much better received. Husserl had studied with Franz Brentano, and worked with Carl Stumpf, the leading proponents of psychologism, a theory in which all necessary truths, including the basic principles of arithmetic, were reduced to empirical laws of psychology. Thus Husserl, in these early works, argued that the laws of arithmetic are nothing more than causal laws governing our experiences of *counting* and "collective association." Frege, at first ineffectively, argued against the psychologists that such treatment neglected the *necessity* of mathematical truths, and that psychologism was a confusion of two very different disciplines, a "building of dangerous inroads of psychology into logic," (*GA* xiv).

Frege published his more important *Grundgesetz der Arithmetik* in 1893, which began with a renewed attack on psychologism, and, in 1894, he attacked Husserl's *Philosophie der Arithmetik* specifically (in a review of the book in *Zeitschrift für Philosophie*). Again, Frege argued that there was a decisive difference between numbers and whatever ideas people might have about numbers. Arithmetic, he argued, gives us precise and necessary principles, while psychology can give us only imprecise and at best probable generalizations. Psychology is incapable of clarifying the most important notion of *necessity* which is so characteristic of mathematical truths, and so there can be no reduction of necessary principles of arithmetic to psychological principles governing our experiences of numbers.

Husserl's reaction to this onslaught was admirable. He cancelled the projected second volume of *Philosophie der Arithmetik,* and, seeing the validity of

Frege's claims, utterly rejected his psychologistic approach to the philosophy of mathematics. In doing so, however, Husserl saw a general deficiency in the empirical methods he had learned from Brentano; they could not provide an analysis of necessary truth, and philosophy in general is concerned only with necessary truths. In his next work, the *Logische Untersuchungen* (1901) *(LU)* Husserl joins with Frege in a relentless attack on psychologistic methods. He begins by quoting Goethe, "One is opposed to nothing more severely than to errors recently laid aside."

After the traumatic encounter with Frege, Husserl's interest in philosophy turned to this newly discovered (very Kantian) problem—how is necessary truth possible? The introduction of the notion of "essence" is designed to solve this problem: " . . . and here is the place for the phenomenological analysis of *essence,* which however strange and unsympathetic it may sound to the naturalistic psychologist, can in no way be an empirical analysis" (Husserl, PRS).

Husserl, like Frege, came to see that the account of necessary truth must reject any appeal to experience. In particular, such an account must reject any thesis which maintains that necessary truths are derivable by abstraction from particular experiences, using as its foundation some such notion as John Locke's "abstract ideas." In *PA* Husserl had employed just such a notion, and Frege had since convinced him that this consisted in a

> . . . blurring of the distinction between image and concept, between imagination and thought. . . . The constituents of the thought, and *a fortiori* things themselves, must be distinguished from the images that accompany in some mind the act of grasping the thought-images that each man forms of things (Frege, BG 79).

Frege accuses Husserl of ignoring the distinction, which Husserl was later to adopt (and be given credit for), between empirical and essential generality: "It is surely clear that when anyone uses the sentence 'all men are mortal,' he does not want to assert something about some Chief Akpanya, of whom perhaps he has never heard," (Frege, BG, 83).

In the *LU,* Husserl turns to the notion of "meaning" *(Sinn)* to account for necessary truth. In *LU,* we are introduced to "meaning-structures" and "meaning-designation" and "constitution of meanings." "Meanings," we are told, "come from consciousness" and are "conferred on facts by consciousness." In the same context, we are introduced to "essences," which are also "in consciousness" and are given in a "categorical intuition." It is quite evident, both in *LU* and *Ideen,* that "meaning" and "essence" are intimately related. (In *Ideen,* Husserl even employs the two jointly in a hyphenated expression, "meaning-essence.") Essences or meanings exist in a manner very different from the existence of *facts:* the "Being" and the knowledge of essences or meanings and the assertion of necessary truths are distinct from the "Being," or experiencing, of *facts* or "individuals":

> The positing of the essence . . . does not imply any positing of individual existence whatsoever: pure essential truths do not make the slightest assertion concerning facts (Husserl, *Ideas* 4).

Knowledge of essences: independent of all knowledge of Facts (Husserl, *Ideas* 4).

It is a matter of indifference [with regard to the essence] whether such things have ever been given in actual experience (Husserl *Ideas* 4).

This independence of essences from actual existence or from facts illuminates a most important point about "essences": the intuiting or the knowledge of essences is completely independent of any ontological commitment concerning the actual existence or actual experience of "individuals" who "have" that essence. Necessary truths are not "about" the world and are true independently of there being any individuals about which they are true. "All perfect circles are round," as a necessary truth, remains true although there might be no perfect circles. The fact that there are no perfect circles has nothing to do with the necessary truth.

The independence of "essence" and "fact" allows us to understand another thesis of central importance to Husserl's thought. In his earlier writings *(LU)*, we intuit essences by concentrating on particular experiences of individuals: by *Ideen,* it is the role of *imagination* or *fancy* which occupies a central role in "grasping" essences. "The element which makes up the life of phenomenology as of all eidetic science is 'fiction,' that fiction is the source whence the knowledge of 'eternal truths' draws its sustenance," (Husserl, *Ideas* 70).

A geometer, who gives us necessary truths, and a physicist, who gives us empirical truths, can thus be distinguished by the role of "fancy" in their studies. A geometer, Husserl tells us, can prove his theorems on any figure he should like to employ: any triangle he imagines will suffice for a proof as well as any other. The physicist, however, must take into account only the results of actual experiments, not the possible results of any imaginable experiences. With geometric figures Husserl tells us, we "through direct analysis determine their immanent meaning" *(Ideas* 25). For a physicist, "experiments conducted in imagination would be imagined experiments" *(Ideas* 25).

The consideration of the role of imagination in "intuiting essences" allows us to understand yet another important Husserlian doctrine and shows us the way to a simple parallel in current analytic philosophy. Husserl tells us that, " . . . no essential intuition is possible without the free possibility of directing one's glance to an individual counterpart and of shaping an illustration" (Husserl, *Ideas* 3).

In other words, one intuits an essence (or, I suggest, 'understands a meaning') by considering all possible *examples* and *counterexamples.* One does not intuit an essence if he cannot think of a single example of an instance of that essence: again, one does not intuit an essence if he cannot distinguish a case that is not an instance of that essence from one that is. (Certain qualifications have to be made here if we are talking about "formal" essences; to grasp the "essence" of the law of contradiction, we should not require that someone can imagine a case in which the law would not apply.) We can now begin to understand the significance of Husserl's characterization of "essence" in terms of "what a thing is": "At first 'essence' indicated that which in the intimate self-being of an individual discloses to us *'what'* it is" (Husserl, *Ideas* 3).

Husserl sometimes relates "essence" to the concept of a "concept" (e.g., *Ideen,* 1:10, 2:22) and tells us that an essence is a "body of essential predicables."

This should afford us an easy interpretation of some of Husserl's more obscure comments on "essence." He claims that "essences are repeatable," and that,

> ... whatever belongs to the essence of the individual can also belong to another individual, (47, 1:2).

> Essential intuition is the consciousness of something, of an "object" ... but which then can be "presented" in other acts ... (49, 1:3).

An essence or meaning applies to idefinitely many particular instances. The word "dog" *means* not just this dog or that dog, but *means,* or is the essence of all possible dogs. As we shall see in a moment, Husserl's notion of *meaning (Sinn)* or essence is at least in this respect identical to Frege's notion of *Sinn.* In Frege's language, the *Sinn* of "dog" is such that "dog" can *refer* to any or every actual or possible dog.

We are told that *essences* are "non-spatio-temporal" but yet not "Platonically independent." By the first, we understand that there is a difference between the sense in which an essence exists and the sense in which "real" individuals which instantiate that essence exist: only the latter have spatial location or can be said to occur in or endure through time. However, Husserl is forced (for obvious reasons) to continually defend himself against charges of "Platonism" a postulation of the existence of essences "somewhere" other than the "real" (spatio-temporal) world. It is thus necessary for him to persistently deny that essences are independent of all *possible* facts. Husserl insists that essences always demand the *possibility* of individual "counterparts," and that essences, like these individual counterparts, are given in intuition.

For a fuller understanding of this notion of "essence," I suggest we turn to the comparatively enviably clear writings of Gottlob Frege. Frege introduces a distinction between *"sense" (Sinn)* and *"reference" (Bedeutung)* of a *name* or a *sign.* A name or a sign is to be construed as a linguistic expression, a word, phrase, sentence, or set of sentences, whether written or spoken, or simply thought. We have already employed the distinction in our discussion of Husserl, and indicated the more-than-notational similarity between Husserl's notion of *"Sinn"* and Frege's notion of *"Sinn." "Bedeutung,"* however, is an expression used very differently by the two authors. For Husserl, *"Bedeutung"* will refer to a special kind of *meaning,* very close, in fact, to Frege's notion of *"Sinn." "Bedeutung"* for Frege means *reference,* and the reference of a sign is an *object.* A sign "stands for" or "designates" or "denotes" (or, of course, "refers to") its referent. This object, however, need not be a material object, an "individual," but may be, for example, a number. Numbers are referred to by numerals (i.e., "1," "2," "3," ...) and numbers are therefore objects in the appropriate sense. Similarly, *concepts* or meanings can be the referent objects of a sign, as when we speak of "the meaning of the word ..." or "the concept of man. ..."

The sense of meaning *(Sinn)* of a sign must be distinguished from the reference of the sign. Frege allows that signs are often used simply to *refer,* but there are cases in which they clearly do not. We can speak, for example, of unicorns, where "unicorn" has a sense but no reference. We can asert, "unicorns do not exist," and what we say can only be intelligible if we suppose that "unicorn" in this sentence has a sense independent of any referents. We usually *learn* the sense of signs through our familiarity with their referents, but our learning the sense through reference is irrelevant to this distinction. Because of their mutual opposition to psychologism, this separation of learning a sense and the sense itself is vital to both Frege and Husserl.

"A sign *expresses* its sense" (BG 61). Each and every (grammatically well-formed) sign in language has a sense, whether or not it has reference. However, each sense may have indefinitely many signs: "It is raining" and "it rains" are two different signs with the same sense, as are "it is raining" and *"es regnet."* There are as many signs for a single sense as there are intertranslatable expressions within any language and among all *possible* languages.

Because it is Frege's notion of *"Sinn"* which we intend to utilize in our analysis of Husserl's notion of "essence," we must further inquire into the nature of this. One might think that the *Sinn* of a sign can be distinguished from both the sign itself and from the reference of the sign by taking the *Sinn* to be an "image" that one associates with the sign (e.g., Locke's theory or Husserl in *PA*), or a "picture" (e.g., Wittgenstein, *Tractatus,* 2.1). (I shall certainly not attempt to examine the very close connection between such "pictures" and sentences [*Satz*] in Wittgenstein. I simply work on the supposition that the "image-theory" which Wittgenstein later sets out to refute is not wholly distinct from the "picture-sentence" theory in the *Tractatus.*) Frege categorizes all such "associated images" as "Ideas."

> If the reference of the sign is an object perceivable by the senses, my idea of it is an internal image, arising from memories of sense impressions which I have had and acts, both internal and external, which I have performed (BG 59).

Husserl's early analysis of "number" in terms of counting and ideas of "collective association" would neatly fit this notion of "Idea." However, Frege, as evidenced by his rejection of Husserl's *PA,* will have no part of this as an analysis of *Sinn;*

> The reference and sense of a sign are to be distinguished from the associated idea (BG 59).
>   The same sense is not always connected even in the same man, with the same idea. The idea is subjective, one man's idea is not that of another. There results, as a matter of course, a variety of differences in the ideas associated with the same sense. A painter, a horseman, and a zoologist will probably connect different ideas with the name "Bucephalus." This constitutes an essential distinction between the idea and the sign's sense, which may be the common property of many and therefore is not a part of a mode of the individual mind (BG 59).

For our comparison of Husserl and Frege, it is vitally important that we take special note of two very different employments of the English term "Idea." For Frege, the "idea" *(Vorstellung)* is the associated image: for Husserl, "Idea" *(Idee)* is closely allied with "essence." We shall therefore avoid use of this term as much as possible, and simply restrict ourselves to a discussion of "images" and "essences."

"Image" for Frege, is contrasted with "thought" *(Gedanke),* and it is thoughts, not images, which constitute sense. Thoughts, unlike images, are *public,* not *private*. Images are "had" by one and by only one consciousness ("your images are 'yours' and my images are 'mine'"). In this sense of "image," it is logically impossible that you and I should "think the same thing." An image is not a property of a sign, it is a 'property' of individual men. However,

> It is quite otherwise for thoughts; one and the same thought can be grasped by many men (Frege, BG 79).
> For one can hardly deny that mankind has a common store of thoughts which is transmitted from one generation to another (Frege, BG 59).

With "thought," therefore, we can say that many men "think" the same "thought," or that you mean by "P" just what I mean by "P." (E.g., we both learn *the* Pythagorean theorem; I do not learn *my* pythagorean theorem: Frege, "The Thought," trans. Quinton, *Mind* 65 [1956], p. 302.)

This is clearly necessary for the sense of a sign—that it remain one and the same sense which is "expressed" by whoever employs that sign. A thought, therefore, is neither the object referred to by a sign, nor any image associated with the sign or arising from my perceptions or memories of the object, nor is it the sign itself, which only *expresses* the thought. The thought is the sense of a sign, and is independent of the particular employer of that sign, independent of any objects referred to in the employment of that sign, and independent of the sign itself (any thought can be expressed by any number of signs).

The analysis of Frege's "sense" *(Sinn)* thus reduces to an analysis of the notion of "thought," or "The Thought." I hope that it is now becoming evident just how Frege's "sense (thought)" is remarkably similar to Husserl's "essence." Both clearly refer to "meaning" in some sense, and both philosophers are utilizing these notions of "meaning" as an approach to the analysis of necessary truth. We are now in a position to begin to bring these two authors together, and, in doing so, clarify some most puzzling passages in Husserl. "Essence" is to be distinguished from all objects that are instances of it, and from all signs which might "express" that essence (Husserl also utilizes this notion of "expression"); and, most importantly, an essence is to be distinguished from all 'psychological' ideas which we might have associated with it, that is, all (sensory) experience and individual (factual) intuitions.

We can now begin to see how essences can yield necessary truths. Insofar as essences are senses or meanings, a statement about essences will be a statement which is nonempirical. To utilize one of Husserl's few examples, a statement about the essence of *sound* and the essence of *color* to the effect that "the essence . . . Colour is other than the essence . . . Sound" (Husserl, *Ideas* 5), or, differently, "A colour in general is different from a sound in general" (Husserl, *Ideas* 5) will be essentially true, a statement of "essential generality." The latter is implicitly, as the former is explicitly, not a judgment about color and sound but a judgment about the *essences* of color and sound. In a different vernacular, these judgments are not "about the world" but "about the meanings of words," "the senses of signs." This would explain the necessity of truths which are about essences, and would explain the nonempirical nature and "independence of facts" of our "knowledge of essences."

Our suggested equation between Husserl's notion of "essence" and Frege's notions of *"Sinn"* and "thought" thus begins to show us some reward. However, there are important differences between the two sets of concepts. We must ask ourselves, quite critically, to what extent this equivalence can be maintained, and to what degree "essence" and "sense" are markedly different. It is equally important to ask ourselves to what extent the differences between the two authors are not so much differences in the concepts of "essence," "sense-thought," but differences in their theories *about* essences and sense-thoughts. I shall argue that these concepts are equivalent, but that Husserl makes important claims about essences that Frege does not make about thoughts. Notably, Husserl claims that essences are to be "grasped" through *intuition:* Frege claims that thoughts are to be "grasped" through an examination of language.

It would certainly seem that the most important difference between Frege and Husserl, a difference more than sufficient to destroy our equivalence between Husserl's "essence" and Frege's "sense," lies in their very different attitudes towards language in their treatment of these two concepts. Frege is clearly a philosopher of language, and his analysis of "sense" is an analysis of the *sense of a sign.* Husserl, quite to the contrary, is dealing with essences *simpliciter,* not essences *of* verbal expressions. It would appear, therefore, that our attempted reduction of both *"Sinn"* and *"Wesen"* to the same notion of "meaning" is most implausible.

The standard picture of Frege as a strictly "linguistic" philosopher and Husserl as an antilinguistic philosopher is, however, an oversimplification in both directions. Frege is concerned with language, and his interest in *Sinn* is an interest in analyzing language, but the notion of *"Sinn,"* as I shall attempt to argue, is not itself a purely "linguistic" notion. Moreover, Husserl is not so antagonistic to a philosophy of language as we are often led to suppose. Although Husserl has little to say about language, there is some reason to suppose that he would not have been willing to make any claim as harsh as the denial that essences were relevant to and even, in an important but puzzling way, dependent upon language. Thus, I shall argue that the alleged difference between the two philosophers *vis-à-vis* the importance of language for philosophy does not reflect a difference between their respective notions of *"Sinn"* and *"Wesen."*

We have already stressed Frege's insistence that the *sense* of a sign (the thought) must not be confused with the reference of that sign, any image associated with that sign, or most importantly, with the sign itself. The distinction between sense and sign can be demonstrated in many ways: a given sense can be "expressed" by many different signs—the sense of the word "cat" can be expressed by this inscription, or by my pronouncing a corresponding sequence of phonemes, or by appropriate inscriptions or pronouncements in any other language. Moreover, we can refer to a sense without expressing it with a sign at all; for example, "Whatever that word means must be obscene in that context," and we can refer to a sense that could never be expressed at all; for example, "There are inexpressible thoughts." Therefore, a sense of a sign is not the sign itself, nor is it equivalent to any combinations or sets of signs.

From Frege's characterization of the sense as the *thought,* it becomes clear that the sense-thought is something quite apart from language and language users. But here we encounter a fascinating problem: what is this entity which Frege clearly claims is necessary for any adequate analysis of language (a necessity reclaimed by Russell, and more recently by Church[2]). But does the interpretation of the thought as an abstract entity necessary to do justice to an account of language give us the only possible approach to thoughts? Or, can one recognize and identify thoughts independently of their expressions in language? Unfortunately, we can say little more about Frege's own analysis of sense or thought, for he nowhere attempts to give us such a prelinguistic analysis. His informal introduction in "On Sense and Reference," and his essay, "The Thought," are attempts to make clear several things a thought is *not* (e.g., "Thoughts are neither things of the outer world nor ideas" (Frege, "The Thought," p. 302), but Frege then leaves us, much as Husserl leaves us, with a statement to the effect that *thoughts* have their own "mode of Being."

It might be helpful at this point if we were to digress slightly and note that this tendency to introduce nonworldly, non-"mental," nonlinguistic entities was not in the least peculiar to Husserl and Frege. Although German philosophy-psychology was well served by philosophers who simply treated all entities as either "physical" or "psychical" (e.g., Brentano and Stumpf), at least two very prominent philosophers of the nineteenth century shared this concern for peculiar entities. In the early part of the century, Bolzano had introduced the notion of "proposition-in-itself" *(Salz-an-sich)* and like notions of "truth-in-itself" and "idea-in-itself" to refer to those entities which were asserted, questioned, believed to be true but which were themselves neither assertions (sentences or statements) questions, or beliefs. In the later part of the century, Alexius von Meinong, whose reputation in Anglo-American philosophy has largely been administered in the not-always-reliable historical criticism of Bertrand Russell, introduced a new "objective" "world" of entities to suit the same purpose. In his "Theory of Objects," Meinong presents us with a world of "objects" which have *Being,* but not *existence,* in order to explain how it is the case that we can talk about *nonexistent* objects; for example, in "Unicorns do not exist." Of special interest to us, however, is a special sort of nonworldly (i.e., nonexistent) entity which Meinong refers to as an "objective." An "objective," like Bolzano's "proposition-in-itself," is that which is expressed in assertions, is believed, is doubted, and so on. The peculiar ontological status of Frege's *sense* and Husserl's *essence* is a common problem in 1890; what is it that is *expressed* by assertions?

Of particular importance in our discussion of Husserl is our understanding that Bolzano and Meinong, as well as Husserl, were not exclusively concerned with language and its uses but with the nature of *mental acts.* Asserting is a verbal expression of a *Satz-an-sich* or an "objective," but it is also an *act* of asserting. This is not to say that it is an act which is clearly different from the act of assertively expressing the same *Satz-an-sich* or "objective" in language, nor is it even to say that it is possible to assert without asserting through language. Rather, asserting through language is but one very special instance of a huge number of mental acts, only some of which have any connection with linguistic expression. Husserl, we must emphasize, did not *deny* any role to language in mental acts; he simply did not concern himself *primarily* with linguistic acts.

Frege, however, also distinguished between mental acts and linguistic acts. We have insisted that the *thought* is not itself a linguistic entity, but rather, "itself immaterial, [it] clothes itself in the material garment of a sentence and thereby becomes comprehensible to us" (Frege, "The Thought," p. 292).

Frege distinguishes:

1. The apprehension of a thought—(thinking).

2. The recognition of the truth of a thought—(judgment).[3]
3. The manifestation of this thought—(assertion).

Thus, for Frege, assertion (while it is a necessarily linguistic act), is already two steps removed from the apprehension of a thought. The difference between Frege and Husserl would thus not seem to be Frege's employing a strictly linguistic notion of *Sinn* as opposed to Husserl's nonlinguistic notion of "essence." The difference is rather one of emphasis; Frege concentrates his philosophical genius on the analysis of *assertion,* an essentially linguistic activity, and on an analysis of *judgments,* in which the truth-value of sentences (more properly of senses which sentences express) is recognized. Frege has little interest in the analysis of thinking itself, the prelinguistic mental act in which one has not yet attempted to evaluate the truth of a thought or its possible expression in language. Yet this is just what interests Husserl, who is not interested particularly in either judgments or assertions. Husserl and Frege differ not in their analysis of *thought,* but in their interest in it. Husserl is interested in the nature of thought *before* it gets captured in language. He is also interested in thoughts before they are recognized as true or false; this latter form of judgments "reduced" to unevaluated thoughts is the significance of Husserl's famous *epoche,* or "bracketing of existence." In phenomenology, he is interested only in the thoughts, that is, the essences, themselves, barring any possible questions concerning the value of that thought or essence, as a model of the "real" world.

I do not wish to leave an impression that Husserl maintained, much less argued, that the grasping of essences can dispense with any consideration of language in which thoughts are expressed. Rather, his position on this matter seems to be ambivalent (not to say confused) concerning the role of language in the essences to be examined. In his early essay, "Philosophy as a Rigorous Science," he tells us: "The phenomenologist . . . derives no judgments at all from word concepts, but rather looks into the phenomena *that language occasions by means of the words in question*" (Husserl, PRS, p. 95, my italics).

In *Ideas,* Husserl tells us again that "essences are distinguished from their verbal expression," but that verbal expressions, "relate to the essence and the essential connections which they *once fixated* and now express" (Husserl, *Ideas,* p. 67, my italics).

This would seem to indicate that language has a role in "fixing" essences (i.e., "we can learn to think [employ concepts] only by learning a language"); but Husserl pays no heed to the *origins* of our knowledge of essences, and so this claim is never investigated.

Husserl's views on language become yet more complex when we attempt to investigate further our reduction of both Frege's "sense-thought" and Husserl's "essence" to a notion of "meaning," as we did in the beginning of this essay. Husserl gives us three distinct notions of "meaning." Husserl notes that these different notions are used as equivalents in ordinary speech, but must, for purposes of philosophy be distinguished. They are:

    a. *Sinn,* "Sense of Meaning *simpliciter,*" or Sense in its most general meaning.

b. *Bedeutung,* "meaning at the conceptual level," "logical," or "expressing meaning."

c. *Meinung,* "meaning as a functional act," or simply "intentionality."

It is only (b) in which we are interested. The sense of "sense" *(Sinn)* (a) encompasses Frege's "reference" as well as "sense." (c) *Meinung* is a very general term of intentionality and would go far beyond the "sense" of a sign to whatever a person might *mean* (intend) in any act of consciousness. In this sense, every act of perception, imagination, becoming angry, falling in love, being hungry, or trying to insult someone would have a *meaning.* Again, this sense of meaning is much broader than the concept of "essence."

What Husserl says about (b) is perplexing. He says, " ... originally these words *(Bedeutung, bedeuten)* relate only to the sphere of speech, that of 'expression'" (Husserl, *Ideas,* p. 319), but then he immediately suggests we extend their meanings to all acts, "whether these are interwoven with expression acts or not" *(Ibid.).* But later in the same section, he tells us that when we "grasp a meaning,"

> This process makes no call whatsoever on "expression," neither on expression in the sense of verbal sound nor on the like as verbal meaning, and here the latter can also be present independently of the verbal sound.

and then,

> Every meaning *(Meinung)* of any act can be expressed conceptually *(durch Bedeutungen)* . . . Logical meaning is an expression.

and then,

> The verbal sound can be referred to as expression only because the meaning which belongs to it expresses: it is in it that the expressing originally lies *(Ibid.,* p. 320).

These passages indicate that Husserl clearly takes "expressing," including "conceptual expression" to be prelinguistic ("preverbal") notions. The expression of "meaning" *(Bedeutung)* is an act of consciousness which is distinct from and precedes "verbal expression" (Frege's "assertion"). We can express the meaning *(Meinung)* of every act of consciousness as conceptual meaning *(Bedeutung)* and can, in turn, express every such conceptual meaning in some linguisitc expression. Husserl would thus make a claim for language that is more ambitious than many "linguistic" philosophers would assent to: there is nothing that can be thought that cannot be expressed in language.

What I have argued thus far in this essay is what I believe to be a most important correspondence between the philosophies of two supposedly very different philosophers. Granted that Husserl benefits far more from this statement of resemblance than Frege, I should not like to leave the merits of Husserl's doctrine of *essence* wholly dependent on his similarity to Frege. To a certain extent, Husserl does repeat, more obscurely and less systematically, some of Frege's central positions. However, the difference in emphasis we have discussed is of considerably more than historical interest, for it holds a key, not only to the major breach between analysis and phenomenology, but also to some important disputes in contemporary analytic philosophy of language.

Neither the notion of "essence" nor the notions of "sense" and "thought" play as large a role in contemporary philosophy as they once did. However, current philosophy is quite occupied with notions derivative of these: "concept" is such a notion, and the ontological status of *concepts* remains as large a question for contemporary philosophers of the analytic tradition as the status of *essence* continued to be for Husserl. Of equal importance in current discussions is the problematic notion of a "proposition." Frege occasionally used *"Satz"* to refer to that entity which was not a physical sentence (also *"Satz";* which meaning is determinable in context), but which was expressed by a sentence. Thus, in Frege, we can suggest a third concept like "sense" and "thought," and we can draw a further equivalence between Husserl's "essence" and "proposition." However, we must understand that this use of "proposition" is foreign to Husserl (for whom "proposition" and "judgment" are equivalent), and rare in Frege. This modern use is due to Russell and Wittgenstein, not Frege and Husserl. Of importance to us is the remarkable similarity between the functions of propositions, senses, thoughts, and essences in these various philosophies. Today, "proposition" is the most acceptable name for that peculiar entity which "has meaning," is "expressed" by a sentence, is true or false, but which is distinct from worldly objects, expressing sentences, and any "mental" occurrences (intentions, images) of persons who "hold" that proposition. In other words, "proposition" is the new name for Husserl's "essence," Frege's "sense" or "thought": "It is clear that by "thought" expressed by a declarative, he [Frege] means what other philosophers call a "proposition."[4]

The status of propositions is not an isolated problem in the philosophy of language, however; it has rather become the (often-unrecognized) fulcrum of a wide-spread debate between what F. P. Ramsey called several *paradigms of philosophy.* The acceptance or rejection of these special entities, under whatever name, determines an entire philosophical outlook. I take the attitude toward the ontological status of *propositions (thoughts, essences)* to be the key point of departure of Husserl's phenomenology from analytic philosophy, as I take it to be the key factor in what at present is probably the largest single split among analytic philosophers.

The rejection of Russell's theory of descriptions by Strawson has often been interpreted, notably by Strawson himself, as a rejection of a single theory concerning referring expressions within a mutually accepted philosophical framework. In fact, however, the problem of referring is only a focal point for a most general problem in philosophy, namely, the subject matter of philosophical investigation. According to Bertrand Russell (and the "early" Wittgenstein, and most practitioners of "philosophical analysis") the subject matter of philosophy was the structure of *propositions,* an examination of which would show us the structure of "the world." Russell's philosophical analysis is an analysis of "propositions and their constituents"; the problem of philosophy must be the clarification of these. What are these? In his famous article "On Denoting," Russell sometimes indicates that the constituents of propositions are *words,* but that cannot be right, since the proposition and its parts are clearly to be distinguished from the language that expressed them. Elsewhere he mentions "single propositions of which the thing itself (i.e., the referent) is a constituent,[5] but that cannot be right either, for the proposition is to be distinguished from the things referred to. But the status of propositions and their constituents remains a problem unilluminated by Russell. Wittgenstein gave the problem its due attention, and his attitude, most representative of that to which Husserl is a viable alternative, is that "I don't know *what* the constituents of a thought are, but I know that it must have such constituents which correspond to the words of language."[6]

In this view, confusedly indicated by Russell, and expressly argued by Church *(op. cit.),* propositions (thoughts, essences) are entities which are expressed in language, which we can get to know *through* an analysis of language, but whose nature ultimately must remain a mystery. Wittgenstein, for example, adopts the same ploy used by Frege, and takes "thought" to be a logical "primitive," inexplicable apart from its necessary functions in language.

The alternatives to this mystical concept of *proposition (essence, thought)* lie in two very different directions. First, there is the rejection of the notion of *propositions* and a simple appeal to the *use* of language. Thus, for Strawson, J. L. Austin, and the "later" Wittgenstein, philosophy studies not propositions but *sentences* and the *uses of sentences.* Through this examination, we discover the "structures of the world," presumably the same world explored earlier by Russell and the "early" Wittgenstein. Strawson's own attack seemed to be quite unaware of the nature of the disagreement between the two philosophers. Strawson attacks Russell's analysis on the basis of its failure as an analysis of our everyday uses of statements, while Russell's analysis was of a very different nature—an analysis of the propositions which are expressed by (but exist independently of) our ordinary uses of language. Strawson's conclusion to his article "On Referring" is symptomatic of the misdirection of the entire attack on Russell: "Ordinary language has no exact logic." But Russell's concern was with propositions, which are true or false, while Strawson's concern was with our use of statements in ordinary language "to make true or false assertions." Russell's criterion for the success of his analysis was to capture the structure of those entities which were expressed in language; Strawson's criterion for success was to satisfy the "purposes for which we ordinarily use language." In short, the dispute between Russell and Strawson was not over an analysis of certain referring expressions; it was "whether in our everyday discourse we speak in statements or in propositions?" (Linsky, *op. cit.,* p. 99.)

But this, according to Husserl, Frege, and Russell, is not the problem of philosophy, which is concerned with truth, meaning, reference, and so on, but a matter which may be described as *empirical.* (If we all learned language from Russell's philosophy, we should speak in propositions.) The problems of philosophy, as characterized by Frege and Husserl at least, are not the empirical problems of how people do *in fact* use their language, but matters of *essence (thought and logic).* The problems raised by Russell's theory about propositions are no more vulnerable to ordinary language criticism than our proofs of geometry are vulnerable to empirical refutation.

But despite the misplaced battle between Russell and Strawson, the underlying dispute is of momentous importance. The rejection of the role of propositions (thought, essences) in discussions of philosophy has been best expressed by the unique philosopher who was prominent as a defender of both views. In his later writings, Wittgenstein looked back at his almost mystical analysis of propositions, and complained that, "We don't get free of the idea that the sense of a sentence accompanies the sentence, is there along side it."[7]

The "innocent" claim that the *thought* is "primitive" and has no extra-linguistic characterization is, Wittgenstein now argues, "the decisive movement in the conjuring trick,"[8] a "myth of our symbolism." Philosophy must forget about this "occult sphere" of propositions and thoughts (and essences) and restrict itself to looking at "the given," which is, for Wittgenstein, our uses of language to *do* things.

But when one gives up the notion of propositions, all sorts of old taboos are broken, and with troublesome results. Once again, philosophy seems to become an *empirical* study of how persons (we) use language. But this leaves open an old Fregean-Husserlian wound, what justification can this seemingly *empirical* search provide us for the sorts of philosophical, that is, *necessary,* truths that we seek?

Why should we accept or not accept the existence of propositions? One reason for not accepting them, from what we have seen above, is the sort of serious problems we encounter in attempting to say what these entities are. Furthermore, as evidenced (but not made fully explicit) in the Russell-Strawson dispute, the introduction of propositions can generate problems of its own. But most important is the question of whether these entities are *necessary* for adequate explanation of the behavior of langauge, and, in particular an account of truth, meaning and necessary truth, in order to compensate for the disadvantages of adding mysterious entities to our ontology and generating new problems. Church has recently argued that such entities *are* necessary for the purpose of explanation of language (Linsky, *op. cit.*). All of those who reject propositions, or all of those who accept the procedures of ordinary language analysis (whether or not they have questioned the existence of propositions), do not accept this necessity.

However, the standard dispute covered in the preceding paragraph bases itself on a supposition about the nature of propositions (thoughts, essences) which has not been questioned sufficiently in analytic circles (just as the analytic suppositions here involved have not been sufficiently examined by phenomenologists). All of these considerations assume that the only way to approach these peculiar entities is through an analysis of language, and the dispute between the two analytic camps thus rests upon a common ground—the assumption that, if propositions are anything at all, they must be entities which can *only* be expressed in language but not independently characterized in any way.

> There is, I think, a discoverable relation between the structure of sentences and the structure of the occurrences to which the sentences refer. I do not think the structure of non-verbal facts wholly unknowable, and I believe that, with sufficient caution, the properties of language may help us to understand the structure of the world.[9]

Husserl and phenomenology make an important claim: they maintain that the peculiar entities we have been discussing do allow themselves to be expressed in language by sentences, but that they can be characterized without such appeal to their expression in language through a direct reflection upon "intuition." Because we can investigate essences (propositions, thoughts) without appeal to language, it is therefore possible to reestablish the role of propositions in the examination of language, but on a different basis than their necessity for an adequate accounting for language. If we could show that intuition itself provides us with the data which make necessary truths necessarily true, which give us the prelinguistic structures of languages and the structure of thought, then philosophy would have to accept a very different paradigm indeed.

One turns to "use"-theory in philosophy precisely because of the seeming impossibility of getting an adequate grasp on propositions (essences, thoughts). Husserl and Frege would both find this approach abhorrent to their vision of philosophy; the alternative would be to turn to the direct examination of the "things themselves" or the "given"—in other words, the propositions, thoughts, or essences rather than what expresses these propositions, thoughts, or essences. The business of philosophy is to provide and practice a technique for "reducing" our intuitions to those "eidetic" elements about which philosophers have been talking in so many ways. It is the function of Husserl's "eidetic reduction" to display for us these "pure essences" (or propositions). If Husserl is correct, then philosophers need not grapple with inaccessible "abstract" linguistic-related entities, nor need they look at how people *in fact* use language. Rather, philosophy would consist of a *theory of intuition* and a method for extracting *essential structures* from intuition.

The problem with all this, of course, is that it has not clearly been done. Husserl's own stylistic paraplegia makes his doctrine most unwelcome reading, and, for those who do master his exposition of his method in *Ideen,* there is the disappointment, I believe, of discovering that the endless distinctions there are based upon an obscure foundation, if not an insecure one. But phenomenology has had few articulate spokesmen in this country, and very few who have allowed themselves to become sympathetic to the goals of analytic philosophers. In this essay, I have attempted to make some sense out of one of Husserl's most obscure and most central concepts. As a result, I hope that I have indicated the direction which philosophers on both sides of the analysis-phenomenology breach must follow if there is to be a serious meeting of philosophical cultures. I suggest that the problems confronting analytic and phenomenological philosophers are identical: what has yet to be proved, even to those of us who are hopeful about the possible fruits of Husserl's method, is that the phenomenological approach is a fruitful one.

NOTES

1. All references to *Ideen* are to the Gibson translation. *Ideas* (New York: Collier-Macmillan, 1962). Page numbers are included in parentheses in the texts or immediately following quotations, and followed by chapter number, section number. All references to Frege's *Grundlagen der Arithmetik* (1884) will similarly be abbreviated *"GA"* and enclosed in parentheses, as will Husserl's *Philosophie der Arithmetik (PA)* (1891) and his *Logical Investigations* of 1901 *(LU),* "Philosophy as a Rigorous Science" (PRS). Other references

to Frege and from Black and Geach, *The Writings of Frege* (BG). All of the above are included in my *Phenomenology and Existentialism* (New York: Harper & Row, 1972; University Press of America, 1979).

2. "The Need for Abstract Entities in Semantics" in *Structure of Language,* Katz and Fodor (Englewood Cliffs, N.J.: Prentice-Hall, 1964).

3. This use of "judgment" is at odds with a usage in "On Concept and Object." "Language presents the thought as a judgment" (BG 49).

4. L. Linsky, *Referring* (London: Routledge, Kegan Paul, 1967), p. 25.

5. E.g., in Feigl and Sellars' reprint of "On Denoting," in *Readings in Philosophical Analysis* (New York: Appleton-Century-Crofts, 1949), p. 115.

6. Wittgenstein, *Notebooks,* 1914, 1916, trans. Anscombe (Oxford: Blackwell, 1961), p. 129.

7. Wittgenstein, *Zettel,* no. 139, trans., ed., Anscombe and Von Wright (Oxford: Blackwell, 1967), p. 56 (e).

8. *Philosophical Investigations,* no. 308, trans. Anscombe and Von Wright (Oxford: Blackwell, 1967), p. 56 (e).

9. Russell, *Inquiry into Meaning and Truth* (London: Allen and Unwin, 1940), p. 341.

13

Husserl's Concept of
the Noema

The eye of the intellect sees in all objects what it brought with it the
means of seeing.

—THOMAS CARLYLE

1. Two Interpretations

It is generally agreed that the concept of the *noema* is one of the themes, if not
the central theme, of Edmund Husserl's phenomenological philosophy. Yet like
many of Husserl's key concepts, "noema" changed its meaning many times
throughout his repeated attempts to reformulate and strengthen his philosophical
position. From its introduction in the first volume of *Ideen*[1] in 1913 until his later
writings, this concept receives no definitive and unequivocal characterization. It
is variously described and employed in such ways that several very different interpretations have become defensible on the basis of published as well as unpublished Husserlian texts.

On the one hand, following Husserl's examples and his characterization of
the noema as "the perceived as such" (*Ideas,* sect. 88), several of Husserl's leading
students, notably Aron Gurwitsch[2] and Dorion Cairns,[3] have characterized the
noema with special reference to certain problems of perception, for example, the
identification and reidentification of particulars. On the other hand, following an
equally documented Husserlian insistence that the noema is a "generalization of
the notion of *Sinn* to the field of all acts" (*Ideen* III, p. 89), a heretical group of

This essay is a much-revised version of my reply to Dagfin Føllesdal in an American Philosophical Association symposium on phenomenology December 27, 1969, in New York. Føllesdal's paper,
"Husserl's Notion of Noema," was first published in *The Journal of Philosophy,* vol. 66, no. 20 (Oct.
16, 1969): 680–87. I have since benefited from private correspondence with Professor Føllesdal, from
discussions with Hubert Dreyfus, and from extensive conversations with Izchak Miller, to whom I
am deeply grateful.

more "analytically" minded philosophers, notably Dagfin Føllesdal,[4] has paid
special attention to the close relationship between Husserl and his (more or less)
philosophical colleague, Gottlob Frege. In this interpretation the noema becomes
an abstract intensional entity which is not perceived at all.

At first glance, no two interpretations could seem more opposed, and considerable antipathy between the two has consequently emerged. One might wonder
whether the "perceived as such" and this Fregean abstract *Sinn* are in fact interpretations of one and the same conception. Our problem here is to understand
the source of these differences and to develop a conception of the noema that does
justice to both. Of the greatest importance, of course, is our need to understand
the role of the noema in Husserl's own thinking—or at least in that phase of his
thinking that produced the conception of the noema in *Ideas.*

This is not the place to trace the vicissitudes of Husserl's difficult conception;
this has been accomplished elsewhere[5] and will not help us here. We may grant
from the outset that the concept is to be found in several different contexts and
that different emphases may reinforce different interpretations. One pair of contexts, however, stands out from all the others—a basic ambivalence that underlies
all of Husserl's thought. Husserl entered philosophy from the foundations of
mathematics with an interest in the nature of certain "ideal" entities (e.g., numbers) and the nature of certain necessary truths (e.g., arithmetical propositions).
But, like Frege, with whom he had considerable correspondence,[6] Husserl was
drawn into the broader philosophical arena, particularly to the problems of epistemology. Though his interests were always tied to the former, his examples and
his concerns often emerged from the latter.[7] His work in logic and the foundations
of necessity is often brilliant, comparable to the work of Frege; his suggestions in
the field of perception are typically sketchy and incomplete and are never pursued
with the intensity of his more formal concerns.[8] The problems of logic and the
problems of perception have their mutual dependencies, of course, but the paradigms they provide for philosophical analysis are worlds apart. (The historical
"schools" of rationalism and empiricism, which Husserl, like Kant, attempted to
synthesize, provide an apt illustration of the divergence which this choice of paradigms entails.) Attempting to solve problems indigenous to one sphere by using
paradigms more appropriate to the other gives rise to spectacular confusions (as
the history of modern philosophy is again quick to prove). Husserl's concept of
the noema is an attempt to establish a common ground for both the problems of
perception and the foundations of necessary truths and judgments. Accordingly,
we must be prepared for problems of equivocation, for conceptions which might
be readily applicable in one paradigm which are not appropriate in the other. For
example, the notion of "perspective," which looms so large in the Gurwitsch
interpretations of the perceptual noema, is not even a plausible candidate for clarifying the role of the noema in the foundations of arithmetic.

The dispute between the "orthodox" view of Gurwitsch, Cairns, et al. (what
Hubert Dreyfus has called "the New School school") and the "heretical" view of
Føllesdal and his students[9] can be seen largely in terms of their acceptance of one
of these competing paradigms and their relative neglect of the other. Gurwitsch,
who has also been a major contributor to the philosophical aspects of Gestalt
psychology,[10] takes perception and its problems to be the proper setting for Husserl's noema. Føllesdal, a first-rate logician and student of W. V. O. Quine, sees

in Husserl's conception of the noema an answer to certain puzzles in the Fregean theory of "indirect" or "opaque" intensional contexts.[11] Although Gurwitsch is agreeable to Husserl's characterization of the noema as "ideal" and "irreal" (as an "atemporal meaning"), he insists on casting the noema in strictly perceptual terms, as a "percept" and even as "perceptual phenomenon."[12] The concept of the noema is introduced to account for the identification of objects through changes and over time in different acts and different kinds of acts. Gurwitsch's examples, as well as his analysis, leave no doubt that the "objects" he has in mind are in virtually every case *material* (perceptual) objects.[13] Føllesdal, on the other hand, takes Husserl's noema to be very much like Frege's notion of the *Sinn* of a linguistic expression, generalized appropriately to nonlinguistic acts. Frege had sharply distinguished between an expression and its *meaning (Sinn),* and also between the meaning *(Sinn)* and the *reference (Bedeutung)* of an expression. Using this pair of Fregean distinctions, Føllesdal interprets Husserl's noema as the meaning or *Sinn* of an intentional act (or *noesis*)—as distinct from its reference (or intended object) as well as distinct from the act itself. Like the Gurwitsch interpretation, this view has a solid foundation in Husserl's writings.[14]

More enticing than the interpretation itself, however, is its consequences: the noema as a *Sinn* or meaning now falls into alignment with the various concepts of linguistic meaning that have been formulated and debated in the seventy years since Frege's pioneering efforts. And with this conceptual bridge between two initially different conceptions of meaning comes a bridge between two philosophical disciplines that have seemed to be mutually incomprehensible and irreconcilable.[15]

2. Noema and Intentionality

Husserl introduces the concept of the noema in his attempt to clarify his conception of intentionality, adapted from a similar notion in Brentano.[16] Along with the notion itself, Husserl adopts Brentano's celebrated doctrine of intentionality, which we may summarize as (1) "all consciousness is consciousness of something" and (2) one cannot infer from the fact that an act is directed toward something that that "something" exists. If it ever makes sense to say that "*S* sees *y*" when *y* does not exist, then it must be true that *S* sees something even if it is also true that there is not something which *S* sees. To resolve this apparent paradox, Brentano resurrected the scholastic concept of "intentional inexistence": the idea that the "object" of a mental act need not be a "real" object. Husserl, according to Føllesdal's account, rejects this part of Brentano:

> Husserl resolved this dilemma by holding that although every act is directed, this does not mean that there is always some object towards which it is directed. According to Husserl, there is associated with each act a *noema,* in virtue of which the act is directed towards its object, if it has any. . . . To be directed is simply to have a noema.[17]

Husserl's modification can be summarized as a denial of the thesis that every act of consciousness has a (real) object; yet every act is directed by virtue of its noema, whether or not it in fact has an object. To be "directed" is simply, to have a noema. But what is this noema? And how does it "direct" the act toward its object? Husserl's claim that the noema is a meaning ("a generalization of linguistic meaning") is clearly an attempt to extend Frege's notion of the *Sinn,* by virtue of which linguistic expressions have reference, to mental acts in general. But Frege's notion, even in its more restricted context, raises notorious difficulties; how, then, does Husserl attempt to clarify that notion?

It is to clarify the conception of the noema as meaning that Gurwitsch and Føllesdal offer us their interpretations. According to Gurwitsch and the "orthodox" view, the noema is nothing other than the "perceived as such," the object of perception (appropriately "bracketed" by the phenomenological epoche) from this particular viewpoint:

> To each act there corresponds a noema—namely an object just, exactly and only just, as the subject is aware of it and has it in view, when he is experiencing the act in question.[18]

It is what Gurwitsch elsewhere calls a perceptual *Gestalt,*[19] a *percept,*[20] and a *theme.*[21]

The key to the orthodox view of the noema is the notion of "perspective," for it is through a perspective—or rather a variety of perspectives[22]—that one comes to know an object. There are dangers here, as Gurwitsch has been the first to point out: there is the danger of turning the noema into a sensory object with "real" status of its own, thus forcing the phenomenologist into the subjective idealist position that Husserl always opposed. (It is important to stress, even though it is not our topic, that the sensory matter or "hyletic data" of perception are not introduced on the noematic side of the act but rather in the noesis itself. The purpose of this move is precisely to avoid making the sensory into an object.)[23] The noema is not the object of an act of consciousness but, rather, its *meaning.* In Husserl as in Frege, meaning and reference must always be kept apart. But what, then, is this concept of meaning *(Sinn)* that plays such an important role here?

Gurwitsch, attempting to remain faithful to Husserl on this matter, insists that the noema is a *Sinn* ("belongs to the sphere of sense").[24] But it turns out that Gurwitsch's conception of *Sinn* is extremely emasculated; quoting from Husserl, he tells us that the noema is a *Sinn* because of its "atemporality":

> i.e. in a certain independence of the concrete act by which they are actualized, in the sense that every one of them may correspond, as identically the same, to another act, and even to an indefinite number of acts.[25]

Gurwitsch, in other words, employs a conception of *Sinn* which embodies the reference of an act as well as its meaning. (Both of these hide under the rubric of "the noematic correlate.") By extending the concept of *Sinn* to include both meaning and reference, Gurwitsch (and at times Husserl) makes it extremely difficult to provide an adequate analysis of the noema. If the noema is a *Sinn,* then of course it cannot be unique to any particular ("concrete") act; but neither can it be wholly "independent of any concrete act."[26] And however much Gurwitsch may insist upon following Husserl in his distinction between noema and object, that distinction, in Gurwitsch's interpretation, always seems to appear as a scholarly fine point when he describes the noema (of perception) as

> the object just (exactly and only just) as the perceiving subject is aware of it, . . .
> the 'perceived tree as such' varies according to the standpoint, the orientation,
> the attitude, etc.[27]

Gurwitsch's "orthodox" interpretation has established its orthodoxy by virtue of the fact that it is a manageable interpretation of Husserl. But its onesidedness and inadequacy for the richness of Husserl's thought become obvious as soon as we ask, even with particular reference to perception, why Husserl should have thought the noema to be such an important conception. In Gurwitsch's view, the doctrine of the noema reduces to little more than a restatement of the epistemological platitude that we never simply "see" material objects, but only material objects from a certain perspective, within a certain context, and so on. Moreover, this conception of the noema leaves no room for an adequate analysis of the noemata of abstract judgments, arithmetical propositions, and the like. In the orthodox view, why should Husserl have introduced the concept of noema at all—or, for that matter, the concept of *Sinn?* If his concerns were limited to the Brentanesque problem of "intentional inexistence," would not his revolutionary conception of the epoche and phenomenological reductions have been sufficient? The epoche would allow the phenomenologist, from an exclusively first-person viewpoint, to describe the various "objects" of his experience without asking any ontological questions and so without being forced to make any peculiar ontological claims about the "subsistence" *("Sosein," "Aussersein," "Nichtsein,"* or *"Quasi-sein")* of those objects which did not "exist". Why could Husserl not have rested with this early conception of intentionality with reference to intentional objects, without bothering himself with the intricacies of the very difficult theses concerning the noema and the *Sinn?* Gurwitsch's interpretation does not provide us with a satisfactory answer to these skeptical questions. In his view, the noema is simply the object viewed from a perspective and *Sinn* refers us only to the easily statable fact than an act has transnoetic reference. Nothing much would be lost if we deleted these concepts from Husserl's theory altogether. "Intentionality" alone would be sufficient.[28]

The importance of the concepts of noema and *Sinn* becomes evident only when we free ourselves from an exclusively perceptual paradigm and turn to "the higher level spheres of intentionality." It is worth noting that Husserl's protracted discussion of the noema in *Ideas,* although it begins with a brief consideration of the noema of perception, is devoted almost entirely to a discussion of the noema of judgment. *That* is where Husserl's primordial interests lie, and it is the noema of conceptual judgments, not the noema of perceptual judgments or perceptual acts, that occupies the center of his attention.

3. The Individuation Problem

According to Husserl, and according to both the Gurwitsch and the Føllesdal interpretations, it is by virtue of the noema that consciousness relates to objects, but the noema is not itself the object of consciousness.[29] This point is often obscured by Husserl's characterizations of the noema as the "noematic" or "objective content" and the ambiguous relationship between the noema, the noematic "correlate," and the intentional object. The noematic correlate is something more than the noema, yet less than the object. Furthermore, there is some confusion regarding the relationship between the noema, the object, and the noematic *Sinn.* At times it appears that the "full noema" *(das volle Noema)* is equivalent to the object; other times it is only equated with the *Sinn.* Sometimes the noema is said to *be* a *Sinn;* elsewhere it *has* a *Sinn.* Moreover, there is a general problem in Husserl's discussions, which I will call the Individuation Problem: Husserl continuously writes as if the various acts or noeses and the various noemata could be distinguished and counted like so many sneezes or marbles. Thus he insists that each act has its own noema (as well as its own intended object), that different acts may have the same noema, and that each "act phase" has its own "noematic phase."[30]

But it is not at all clear, for example, when I am observing an object before me—whether moving or stationary (and whether I am moving or stationary)— how many *acts* I am performing. There is a sense in which intentional acts (as Husserl tells us in *Logical Investigations*) are not to be construed as actions or events, and it is not clear that acts can be so easily distinguished as actions or events, whether in terms of their intentions or by appeal to temporality.[31] The same can be said of the noema; it is not at all clear that noemata can be individuated as simply as Husserl's discussion suggests. Of course, there are evident distinctions: betweeen an object seen from the front and an object seen from the back—to pick the usual example—or looking once on Tuesday and again on Wednesday. Short of a criterion for the identity of noemata and noeses respectively, however, there is no substance to the frequent "one-many" and "one-one" correlations that appear in the writings of Husserl and his interpreters.[32]

This Individuation Problem makes an adequate analysis of the noema far more problematic than it appears to be in most discussions. The common model, made popular in Gurwitsch's commentaries, is that a single "view" constitutes a single noema, just as a single "viewing" constitutes a single noesis.[33] But this assumption turns wholly upon a "snapshot" paradigm that utterly dissolves upon reflection.[34] Why should we suppose that our experience is dissectible into such views and viewings? (Husserl's arguments, for example, in *The Phenomenology of Internal Time-Consciousness* have taught us better.) Should we not more accurately describe our experience in terms of flux and continuity? (These are the dynamic terms which Husserl, like William James, often uses.) But if we do, then the facile individuation of acts and noemata of acts is unwarranted. And if it is not clear how to distinguish a single act or a single noema, then the usual formulae for their "correlation" are inappropriate. But they are also unnecessary. Husserl's notion of an "act phase" and a "noematic phase" introduces a promising vagueness which the more static talk of "act" and "noema" leaves out.[35] How this more dynamic vagueness can be used to answer the Individuation Problem would take us far beyond our scope in this essay. But no discussion of the noema can be complete unless it can account for some of the confusion of identities that penetrates Husserl's theory: the convoluted relationship between the noema and the object, the complex relationship between the noema and the act, and the confused relationship between the noema and its *Sinn.* The Individuation

Problem does not resolve these complexities and confusions for us, but it explains why they arise. Quantifiable relationships that hold between countables cannot be coherently described between uncountables. Until some criterion has been provided for the individuation of intentional acts and their noemata, all talk of "noetico-noematic correlations" ought to be suspended.

Although Husserl introduces the concept of the noema in the context of (and with an example from) perception, he soon makes it clear that *all* acts have noemata—acts of judgment and expression as well as acts of perceiving and imagining. A perceptual noema may well be described as "the perceived as such,"[36] but that formula is of little help when extended to the sphere of judgment. Husserl speaks of "the judgment as such," of course,[37] but it is not at all clear how that phrase is to be clarified in comparison with the perception case. What is clear is that the judgmental noema is a *Sinn,* a *meaning,* and here the connection between Husserl and Frege is most in evidence.

Husserl tells us repeatedly that it is through the noema that we intend an object but that the noema itself is not the object. What does this mean? In the Gurwitsch interpretation, taking perception as its paradigm, the noema is the object "viewed"[38] from a particular perspective (e.g., the house viewed from this side; the tree viewed from this angle). Thus we "see" an object "through" its various perspectives, yet no one of those perspectives *is* the object. (Neither, of course, is it *other than* the object; thus Husserl does not say that the noema is "unreal" in the sense of a mere "image" or a "phantom," but only "irreal" in the sense that it is not by itself the object. We might borrow Husserl's terms from *Cartesian Meditations*[39] in this context: "actual" and "quasi-actual" as opposed to "actual" and "non-actual."

In the Føllesdal interpretation it is not perception but judgment that provides the paradigm, even though Føllesdal begins his essay with a set of examples drawn from perception. This is not an inconsistency on his part, however, but rather an important philosophical presupposition; the noema of perception—an abstract and nonperceived *Sinn*—is the *same* noema that one finds as the noema of judgment. Thus Føllesdal claims, against Gurwitsch and the "orthodox" view, that "noemata are not perceived through the senses," that they are abstract, and that they are intensional entities: meanings, not objects viewed from a perspective. Føllesdal's conception of *Sinn* seems to correspond with what Husserl calls the *Bedeutung:* "meaning on the conceptual level."[40]

Thus the phenomenological concept of inten*t*ionality becomes the equivalent of the neo-Fregean logical concept of inten*s*ionality. The first was introduced as the characteristic of *acts* of consciousness; the second was introduced as a characteristic of certain *sentences.* In Føllesdal's interpretation, the equivalence of noema and *Sinn,* the meaning of mental acts and the meaning of sentences, results in the further equivalence of inten*t*ionality and inten*s*ionality.[41]

4. The Opacity of Perception:
The Role of the *Sinn*

One of Husserl's spectacular insights (contrary to the usual view of phenomenology as a primarily epistemological [perceptual] investigation) is the reinterpretation of perception along lines of analysis that are usually reserved for such "conceptual" acts as asserting, believing, judging, doubting, and denying. While Frege limited the notion of *Sinn* to verbal expressions (and it was the expression, rather than the act, that had the *Sinn*), Husserl attempted to extend the notion of *Sinn* (through the noema) to all acts. Thus Husserl says, in his introduction of the concept of the noematic *Sinn,* that it is "an extension of *Sinn* to the field of all acts."[42] (He makes the same claim later regarding *Bedeutung,* but more of this later.) Frege was concerned about the nature of "opaque" contexts in language-related acts ("indirect discourse"), but Husserl extended this concern to all acts, including perceptual acts. Thus perception, even prior to all judgments, gives rise to a type of "opaque" context. This general opacity of all conscious acts is clumsily captured in the Gurwitsch analysis, which is well suited to the concerns of the psychology of perception. But that is not *Husserl's* interest, and Gurwitsch's "perspective" analysis is far too narrow to do justice to Husserl's interest in judgments and expression.

According to Husserl, "*S* sees *y,*" like "*S* believes that *p*" and unlike "*S* kicks *y*", does not maintain its truth value or its meaning for all substitutions for "*y*" and "*p*". (This is not only to say that a judgment *by S* about his perceptions gives rise to opaque contexts; it is also, and more radically, to say that a judgment about *S*'s perceptions gives rise to such contexts.) By extending the notion of opacity beyond its usual narrowly linguistic context, we may say that perception itself is opaque. Underlying this extension, as in all of Husserl, is a claim that is old (Kantian) but still radical (e.g., in Quine and Sellars): that all acts (including the most rudimentary acts of perception) are judgment- and concept-laden.[43] It is here, we may anticipate, that the conception of *Sinn* (and *Bedeutung*) will become of paramount importance. Not only acts of verbal expression but all acts, according to Husserl, display the "logic" that Frege and he had investigated in the more esoteric realms of intentionality.

Consider the act of asserting that-*p*. It is clear that one can perform that act although "*p*" is false. What, then, is the status of "that-*p*"? It is not a "fact" (for there is no such fact). One might say that it is a possible yet not an actual state of affairs. But this Leibnizian conception introduces a nightmare of ontological complications which Husserl's epoche wisely avoids. One might say, in line with many prominent philosophers in the analytic tradition, that that-*p* is a sentence, namely, the sentence that was asserted, *p*. Unfortunately, no particular sentence uttered has any such exclusive claim: the sentence *p*, in a different language, might also be an apt expression of that-*p*, and one might assert that-*p* without uttering any sentence at all (e.g., by nodding approval). This myriad of complications is too well known to bear repetition here. But the conclusion drawn from these problems by Frege is worth repeating: that-*p* is neither a sentence nor a set of sentences (no matter how complex); nor is that-*p* a state of affairs nor a mental image of any kind; that-*p* is an abstract entity, a *Sinn,* which is expressed by any number of sentences in any number of languages. It might also be expressed, we can add (going beyond Frege's interests), in any number of semiverbal acts (e.g., grunting agreement) and nonverbal acts (a gesture or a signal).

This conception of *Sinn* need not be limited to these linguistic contexts (assertion, etc.); it was also applied by Frege to belief contexts ("doxic" contexts in Husserl), prior to verbal expression. Carrying the matter one step further, Husserl extends this notion of *Sinn* to all acts, including perception. It has long been obvious to linguistic philosophers that "*S* believes that *p*" cannot be successfully analyzed as a relationship between *S* and the fact that-*p*; it might not be the case that-*p*, even though "*S* believes that *p*" is true. *What* one believes is not a fact but that-*p*, whether or not *p*. In the same vein, "*S* sees *y*" cannot be construed as a relationship between *S* and *y*, for there might be no *y*.

Granted, it might be argued that "sees" is one of those verbs that has its veracity built into it, such that "*S* sees *y*" cannot be true unless there is a *y* that *S* sees. But of course this is not what Husserl has in mind, for the existence of *y* has already been "bracketed out" as a consideration in the phenomenological description of "seeing *y*." Although this problem has occupied an embarrassingly voluminous place in British philosophical journals, it is a strictly pedantic one. If "sees" is considered such a verb (a "success verb"), "seems to see" is surely not, and in each case the latter can be substituted above. Accordingly, what one sees—for example in cases of illusion and hallucination—is not *y,* but (*y*). It is this (*y*) that Husserl calls the noematic correlate. It is not the case that (*y*) has anything like the ontological status of *y*. In fact, (*y*) has *no* ontological status; rather, it is the *candidate* upon which ontological status is conferred. It is like the meaning of a sentence, which itself is neither asserted nor denied, true nor false, appropriate nor inappropriate, sincere nor prevaricating. Assertion and denial, or truth and falsity, arise only when a sentence with a meaning is put to some *use*— made the object of an act. Similarly, seeing (*y*), as described by the phenomenologist, precedes all judgments about the existence of *y*. But it must not therefore be supposed that seeing (*y*) precedes all judgments about (*y*), any more than the meaning of a sentence is without "meaning" until it is asserted or otherwise expressed in the language. (J. L. Austin's distinction between "locutionary" and "illocutionary act potential" comes to mind here.) Seeing (*y*) is already laden with conceptual judgments. It is not mere "experience" or "intuition" to which judgments are added subsequently. And so it is that *Sinn* (and *Bedeutung*) become essential to all acts.

5. The Noema as a Generalization of Meaning: Føllesdal's View

The main theme of Føllesdal's interpretation of the noema is that

> the noema is an intensional entity, a generalization of the notion of meaning (Sinn, Bedeutung).[44]

It is worth noting from the outset that *Sinn* and *Bedeutung* are treated *in tandem,* and the remainder of Føllesdal's essay similarly treats these two different senses of "meaning" cooperatively, one reinforcing the other. Føllesdal's noema is a close relative to Frege's *Sinn*.[45] He takes Husserl like Frege: to be supporting an intimacy between "experience and judgment" in which language plays a central if perhaps silent role.

Føllesdal rightly comments that there is an ambiguity in Husserl's use of the term *Sinn:* sometimes he means the full noema; at other times just a part of it. For this reason Føllesdal asserts (thesis two) that the noema has two "components": one "common to all acts that have the same object," another that is different in acts with a different "thetic" (or positional) character.[46] Like Gurwitsch, Føllesdal fully agrees that it is the noema—particularly the noematic *Sinn*—that allows consciousness to be "directed" toward an object (thesis three). He also insists—again in full agreement with Gurwitsch—that the noema is not itself the object (thesis four).[47] And, ignoring what we have called the Individuation Problem, Føllesdal also agrees that there is only one object per noema (thesis five) and one noema per act (thesis six), but any number of different noemata and noematic *Sinne* per object (thesis seven).[48] Of the utmost importance in distinguishing the Føllesdal interpretation from the "orthodox" view are the following two propositions:[49]

Noemata are abstract entities. (thesis 8)
Noemata are not perceived through the senses. (thesis 9)

In a famous passage Husserl claims that the noema of a tree, unlike the tree, cannot burn or suffer chemical decomposition.[50] In the unpublished manuscript "Noema and Sinn" Husserl adds that the "*Sinne* are unreal objects," and "a *Sinn* does not have Reality."[51] Husserl also tells us, however, that the noema of perception is the perceived as such,"[52] and an unquestionable absurdity seems to arise when one suggests that "the perceived as such" is not itself perceived.

This apparent paradox may be resolved in a variety of ways. We must note that, as Føllesdal insists, thesis 9 is "an immediate consequence" of thesis 8. This means, first of all, that the two stand or fall together (i.e., the falsity of 9 entails the falsity of 8). But this logical relationship gives us an important clue to the nature of Føllesdal's use of the term "abstract" in thesis 8. "Abstract" does not mean, as it often means, "conceptual"; neither does it mean, as it has often meant in German idealism, "separable in thought but not in Reality." "Abstract" means, at least, "not perceived." And here we can see the source of the significant differences between Føllesdal's interpretation and the "orthodox" view. If it is judgment we are discussing, then clearly this conception of the noema ties in perfectly with Frege's characterization of the *Sinn* or meaning of a linguistic expression. Of course the *Sinn* of a *Satz* is not perceived through the senses; and of course, consequently, it is "abstract." If it is perception that concerns us, however, it is clear that the noema *must,* if it is what directs us to the object, be itself perceived. And though it might be called "abstract" in some other sense, it cannot be abstract in *this* sense. In perception, the noema must be perceived; yet Føllesdal's theses are intended for perception as well as for judgment. Like Husserl, Føllesdal would want to hold that all noemata belong intrinsically to a single supreme genus. How, then, can these difficulties be resolved?

It is important to note that, having distinguished between two "components" of the noema (his second thesis), Føllesdal proceeds to ignore this distinction. The quotes above do not argue for the abstractness of the *Sinn.* And on the following page Føllesdal makes a casual remark that earmarks the confusion of his ultimate thesis: "Again, Husserl is here talking about the noematic *Sinn,* but, as noted above, the remark presumably applies to all components of the noema."[53] But Føllesdal had also sharply distinguished the *Sinn* as one "component" of the noema; it does not follow, then, that we can "presume" that Husserl's remarks about the noematic *Sinn* apply to the noema itself.

In his discussion of thesis 8 Føllesdal argues that the noema is abstract because it is "not a spacial object," and this because "spacial objects can be experienced only through perspectives *(Abschattungen)*." But here Gurwitsch's interpretation strikes full force against Føllesdal's "heretical" view; of course a noema cannot be viewed "through perspectives," because it is itself characterized *in terms of* the perspectives through which the object is viewed. To argue that the noema is not therefore a spatial object (with which all interpretations agree) does not permit the conclusion that it is therefore abstract. The equation that seems to be operating at the root of Føllesdal's theses 8 and 9 is that something can be perceived and is not abstract only if it is a spatial object. And in this sense we might disinterestedly agree that the noema is not perceived and abstract, in some contentious sense of "perceived" and "abstract"; but we can continue to adhere to the Gurwitsch interpretation according to which the noema is indeed "the perceived as such."

It would seem that Føllesdal's interpretation of the noema leaves out something vital in the case of perception; but we have seen that Gurwitsch's interpretation leaves out something equally essential in cases of abstract judgment. But, returning to Føllesdal's second thesis about the "two components" of the noema, we can see our way out of this impasse. Although Føllesdal introduced the conception of a "thetic" component of the noema, he proceeds, once he has done so, to concentrate wholly on the noematic *Sinn.* Although Gurwitsch admits without concern the importance of the noematic *Sinn,* he focuses wholly upon the thetic components of the noema: those which change with different "perspectives" and acts and those which can be said, without contradicting Husserl, to be "perceived" in various acts of perception. In other words, the noema consists of both a *Sinn* and various changing "characters."[54] *Every* noema, we must insist—including the noemata of abstract judgments and ideal entities—consists of *both* of these components. In acts of perception the thetic component of the noema is partially determined by sensory data or *hyle* through which various "views" are constituted: "the tree viewed from this side" and "that side"; and the content of those views consists of colors, textures, and the like. (It is important to stress that the *hyle* or sensory data are not themselves perceived but rather determine what we perceive, namely, the thetic component of the noema. Yet the thetic component itself—colors, textures, etc.—surely can be said to be perceived through the senses. This point is a matter of some obscurity in Husserl and Gurwitsch, but surely goes against Føllesdal's thesis 9). In imagination, the thetic component also consists of views—but in this case they are not perceived through but are still imagined on the basis of the senses. In judgment, the thetic component might be suggested to be the various sentences—in either the same language or in any number of languages—which express the same thought. Insofar as we concentrate on these latter examples, the Føllesdal interpretation is valid without qualification. But when perception is considered, Føllesdal must be augmented by Gurwitsch, who has given us an exemplary development and characterization of the thetic components of perception. But, accordingly, there is no serious disagreement between the interpretations. It is merely a difference in emphasis and interest, not a difference in the supposed nature of the noema.

6. Husserl's Radical Thesis

Brentano believed that all acts were directed toward objects; and in order to maintain this thesis he wavered between a Meinongian idealism and an unsatisfactory realism, populating his ontology with "unreal" entities on the one hand, denying the reality of unfulfilled acts on the other.[55] Husserl resolved this dilemma by denying the universality of intentionality in *this* sense. In place of the thesis that consciousness always takes an object, he substituted the thesis that consciousness is always directed. It need not have an object, but it always has a *noema.* But this noema, we have seen, is not only an apparent object or an "appearance." (At most this claim would be a misleading account of the "thetic" noematic phases of putative objects of perception.) The noema is also a *Sinn,* or rather it *has* a *Sinn,* and "separates off a certain *'noematic nucleus'* from the changing *'characters'* that belong to it."[56] Once again, there is a problem of precision here; just as Husserl was found to be ambiguous on the relationship between noema and *Sinn,* so he is imprecise on the relationship between *Sinn* and noematic nucleus. It is clear, however, that the nucleus is something less than the noema as a whole and that it is intimately related to that "component" of the noema which remains common through various "thetic" changes, namely the *Sinn.* (The analogy with biology—the cell with its changing protoplasm and its unchanging nucleus—is not inappropriate here.) Moreover, the notion of the noematic nucleus warns us against taking the two "components" of the noema as independent and separate; rather they form an organic and inseparable unity, with the nucleus and the *Sinn* forming the common thread and organizing the indefinitely many noetic "characters" or "phases" that fulfill it. It is the noema—these indefinitely many noematic phases linked together and given meaning by the noematic *Sinn*—that allows our conscious acts to be directed toward object. But the familiar phrase "all consciousness is consciousness *of* something" no longer means that all consciousness is consciousness of a real object. It means, rather, that every act of consciousness is directed by virtue of its noema *toward* objects, and it is possible (though absurd to suppose) that our acts are *never* directed in fact toward a "real" world beyond our experience.[57]

Husserl is not simply offering us a modification of Brentano's thesis, he is giving us a radical alternative to it. That radical thesis is essentially a Kantian thesis:[58] the claim that concepts are basic not only to conceptual thought but to the most primitive perception and experience as well. Perception, like belief, judgment, and assertion, has "meaning" *(Sinn),* not simply reference (with which the meaning is often confused). All perception involves judgments, not simply "seeing" but always seeing-as, not simply a "this" but always a "what" as well. In Kantian terms, we would say that all our experience is concept-laden and *meaning*-full, that *what* we experience is "constituted" through our judgments. The Husserlian thesis is strikingly similar to this, except that he would speak of an "essence" where Kant spoke of "concept." But if all acts of perception are also (or are accompanied by—the Individuation Problem again) acts of *con*ception and judgment, then perception is subject to much the same "logic" as abstract thought, including in particular the characteristics of "opacity" that have been so celebrated in the Fregean tradition.

Every act, as also every act correlate, harbors—explicitly or implicitly—a "logical" factor.[59] We said earlier that this argument carries with it a merger of inten*t*ionality and inten*s*ionality, *Sinn* and *Bedeutung.* Like *Sinn, Bedeutung* originates "in the sphere of speech" and "conceptual meaning," but is extended to "the whole noetico-noematic sphere."[60] Husserl restricts the concept of *Bedeutung* to the sphere of articulate judgment and expression—but this does not entail that *Bedeutungen* are involved only in *actual* expression.[61] *Sinn* is given wider scope, such that *all* acts involve *Sinn.* But it must not be thought that *Sinn* thereby dispenses with linguistic concepts and meanings. The relationship between *Sinn, Bedeutung,* and verbal expression *(Ausdruck)* is not at all clear in Husserl. He often writes as if the "phenomena" described by the phenomenologist are wholly independent of the language used to describe them.[62] Then he will claim that words "occasion" the phenomena.[63] At several points he indicates that it is language that "fixes" the essences they express.[64] The differences between these positions are enormously important: the difference between Husserl's phenomenology and the analytic tradition following Frege turns on them. Whether language conditions our experience through *its* meanings or whether language serves as a vehicle for the expression of already constituted meanings is the primary focus of the confrontation between phenomenology and "analytic" philosophy.[65] With particular concern for the noema, the question is this: Is the noematic *Sinn* a product of language (and therefore based on *Bedeutungen*) or is the *Sinn* constituted prior to our ability to express it (and therefore independently of *Bedeutungen*)?

In *Ideas* (sect. 124) Husserl tells us:

> Whatever is "meant as such", every meaning *(Meinung)* in the noematic sense
> . . . of any act whatsoever *can be expressed conceptually (durch 'Bedeutungen').*

In this sentence, and many others like it, Husserl makes it clear that there is an essential connection between intentionality, noema, and conceptual expression. Contemporary analytic philosophy, following Wittgenstein in particular, would argue that the meanings we find in our experience are derivative of the language we use to describe that experience. Most phenomenologists, on the other hand, would argue that it is the prelinguistic meanings which constitute the experiences which provide the meanings expressed in language. But "prelinguistic" here is not the same as "preconceptual" or "prejudgmental," and it is important to stress Husserl's insistence upon the role of concepts and judgments even apart from their expression in language. *Bedeutungen* may be expressed in language, but they do not exist only in their expression. Like *Sinne,* they exist preverbally in our experience and judgments.

In *Cartesian Meditations* (compare *Ideas,* p. 126) Husserl mentions the possible divergence of *Bedeutung* and *Sinn,* the meanings of expressions and the meanings of experience. It is important to stress, in the face of the preceding quotation, that there is no guarantee in Husserl that language does or can accurately capture the preverbal meanings of experience.[66] If this were not so, there would be no need for a phenomenological inquiry which attempted to "cut below" the meanings of expression to seek the meanings of experience; nor would there be any need for the invention of a difficult new vocabulary. If the *Sinne* of experience were always captured by the *Bedeutungen* of language, then "ordinary language" philosophy would indeed be a far less difficult yet adequate approach to the meanings of our experience. As it stands, the meanings and structures of language provide at most a clue to the meanings and structures of experience—and it is important to stress, as above, that there is no guarantee that language and experiential meanings will be in agreement. This is why (as even Austin was forced to admit) philosophical investigation will always require a phenomenological component as well as an investigation of language. Yet we must also guard against the conclusion that, because *Sinn* and *Bedeutung* may disagree, they must therefore be wholly independent of each other.

It has now become virtually axiomatic among phenomenologists that the *Sinne* of experience stand independent of the *Bedeutungen* of linguistic expressions. It has become all but axiomatic among analytic philosophers that there is no meaning apart from language.[67] It is the concept of the noema that provides the link between them. The noema embodies both the changing phases of experience and the organizing sense of our experience. But these two "components" are not separable, for all experience requires meaning, not as an after-the-fact luxury in reflective judgments but in order for it to be experience *of* anything. It is important to stress, along with Husserl, that meaning must be found in our experience, not only in the expressions we use to describe our experiences. But there is no ground for separating, on this account, the *Sinne* of experience from the *Bedeutungen* of expressions in the extreme way which is common to both phenomenologists and analysts. There is nothing in Husserl to support the all too frequent radical separation of nonlinguistic and Fregean conceptions of *Sinn,* and there is much to support their interrelationship. Husserl's radical thesis regarding the noema does not yield the severe segregation of phenomenology and the more formal Fregean enterprise; on the contrary, it provides the grounds for the integration of his "subjective" enterprise with the sophisticated logical investigations in which he, with Frege, played such a vital role.

NOTES

1. *Ideen zu einer reinen Phänomenologie und phänomenologischen Philosophie,* vol. 1, translated into English as *Ideas* by W. R. Boyce Gibson and published in 1931 by Macmillan. I have used the Collier edition of 1962, and unless otherwise noted it is to this edition that I refer in parentheses.

2. Aron Gurwitsch, *The Field of Consciousness* (Pittsburgh: Duquesne University Press, 1964) and *Studies in Phenomenology and Psychology* (Evanston: Northwestern University Press, 1966).

3. "An Approach to Phenomenology," in *Essays in Memory of Edmund Husserl,* ed. by M. Farber (Cambridge, Mass.: Harvard University Press, 1940), and by widespread reputation in his now famous lectures at the New School for Social Research.

4. Føllesdal, op. cit. Also Hubert Dreyfus, "Husserl's Phenomenology of Perception" (Ph.D. dissertation, Harvard University, 1965).

5. Recently by Frederick Kersten, "Husserl's Doctrine of Noesis-Noema," in *Phenomenology: Continuation and Criticism*, ed. by F. Kersten and R. Zaner (The Hague: Nijhoff, 1973), pp. 114–44.

6. See "Husserl-Frege Correspondence," trans. by J. N. Mohanty, *Southwestern Journal of Philosophy*, vol. 5 (1974):83–96.

7. Although *Ideas*, together with *Cartesian Meditations*, are Husserl's best-known introduction to his phenomenology, *Logical Investigations*, trans. by J. N. Findlay (New York: Humanities Press, 1970), *Experience and Judgement* (Prague: Academic, 1948), and *Formal and Transcendental Logic*, trans. by D. Cairns (The Hague: Nijhoff, 1970), are far more representative of Husserl's interests in philosophy. The problems of perception have been given a far larger role in phenomenology than they received in Husserl's investigations.

8. I have yet to meet or read a philosopher, versed in phenomenology but "outside" the movement, who has not thought Husserl's *Logical Investigations* is his best work. To mention but two very diverse examples: J. N. Findlay's "Phenomenology," *Encyclopaedia Britannica*, vol. 14 (1957), pp. 699–702, and Gustav Bergmann's *Logic and Reality* (Madison, Wis.: University of Wisconsin Press, 1964), pp. 193ff. Even those who would not share this opinion would agree that his philosophy of logic is of far more enduring interest and its products far better developed than anything that might be called his "philosophy of perception."

9. Several studies have been published following Føllesdal's essay (op. cit.). His position has been well developed and defended in dissertations by Dreyfus, op. cit., reprinted in part in Robert Solomon, ed., *Phenomenology and Existentialism* (New York: Harper & Row, 1972), pp. 196–210, and by David Smith and Ronald McIntyre of Stanford University and Izchak Miller of U.C.L.A.

10. Gurwitsch, *The Field of Consciousness*, esp. chs. 1 and 2; "The Phenomenology of Perception: Perceptual Implications," in *Studies*, esp. pp. 175–286; and idem, *Invitation to Phenomenology*, ed. by J. Edie (Chicago: Quadrangle, 1965), pp. 17–30.

11. Føllesdal's doctoral dissertation was written on this topic under Quine's direction. See also Willard V. Quine, ed., "Reference and Modality" in *From a Logical Point of View* (Cambridge, Mass.: Harvard University Press, 1964), esp. pp. 142–59.

12. *Studies*, p. 55.

13. Gurwitsch's short pieces on nonperceptual themes (e.g., "On Objects of Thought," *Studies*, pp. 141ff.; "Philosophical Presuppositions of Logic," *Studies*, pp. 350ff.; and "On the Conceptual Consciousness") are notably lacking in development and concrete illustrations compared to his more famous essays on perception. Gurwitsch clearly holds to the "primacy of perception"—to use an expression of one of Husserl's most famous students.

14. Føllesdal makes particular use of Husserl's essay "Noema und Sinn" and other unpublished manuscripts.

15. I have discussed this thesis in some detail in "Sense and Essence: Husserl and Frege," *International Philosophical Quarterly*, vol. 10, no. 3 (1970): 378–401 [chapter 12 in this collection].

16. *Psychologie vom empirischen Standpunkt* (Leipzig: Felix Meiner, 1924), vol. 1, bk. 2, ch. 1. Brentano's views on intentionality changed considerably throughout his career. Husserl, through whom Brentano's concept is best known, often treated his teacher's views unfairly, in an unsympathetic if not misrepresentative way. Brentano's thesis and Husserl's adaptation of it are ably discussed in J. C. Morrison, "Husserl and Brentano on Intentionality," *Philosophy and Phenomenological Research*, vol. 31, (1970): 27–46.

17. Føllesdal, op. cit., p. 680.

18. *Studies*, p. 132, Cf. Alfred Schutz, "Some Leading Concepts of Phenomenology," in M. Natanson, *Essays in Phenomenology* (The Hague: Nijhoff, 1966), p. 30.

19. "Phenomenology and Psychological Applications to Consciousness," in Natanson, op. cit., p. 41.

20. *Studies,* p. 55.

21. Ibid., p. 185.

22. It is characteristic of material objects that they involve any number of perspectives. The concept of "transcendence" in Husserl refers to the fact that an object is never "exhausted" in any number of acts. Husserl often seems to argue that ideal objects, by way of contrast, can be grasped "all at once." This is a dubious thesis, however, since Husserl recognized that "ideal" objects, e.g., the number 7, also involve any number of noemata: 2×3.5, $\sqrt{49}$, $14/2$, etc. "Perspective" is surely inappropriate here.

23. See Gurwitsch, "On the Intentionality of Consciousness," in *Studies;* A. Lingis, "Hyletic Data," in *Analecta Husserliana* (Dordrecht, Holland: D. Reidel, 1972), 2: 96–103. Cf. Frege, "On Sense and Reference" (trans. by Black and Geach, [Oxford: Blackwell, 1960]), in which he compares the *Sinn* to the image of the moon on the glass of a telescope, contrasting it both with the moon itself (the object) and the sensory image.

24. Gurwitsch, "On the Intentionality of Consciousness."

25. Ibid.

26. See, e.g., Tugendhat, *Der Wahrheitbegriff bei Husserl und Heidegger* (Berlin: Gruyter, 1970), pp. 38ff.

27. *Studies,* p. 132.

28. It is worth considering the relative positions of *Sinn* and intentionality in *Logical Investigations* (vol. 2). *Sinn* is clearly the dominant conception. Despite the usual emphasis on intentionality, it is *Sinn* which dominates the discussion in *Ideas,* as well as in the later logical works. Intentionality provides the framework in which *Sinn* is the leading *Analysandum.*

29. *Ideas.* pp. 128, 129. Føllesdal (op. cit., thesis 4) says that the noema of an act is not the object of the act (i.e. the object toward which the act is directed). Gurwitsch, *Studies,* pp. 116ff., 131ff. See also J. Mohanty, "Husserl's Concept of Intentionality," in *Analecta Husserliana* (New York: Humanities Press, 1971), 1: 108ff., and *Phenomenology and Ontology* (The Hague: Nijhoff, 1970), p. 141. Cf. also E. Levinas: "The object of perception of a tree is a tree, but the noema of this perception is its complete correlate, a tree with all the complexity of its predicates and especially of the modes in which it is given" (*The Theory of Intuition in Husserl's Phenomenology* [Evanston, Ill.: Northwestern University Press, 1973], p. 54).

30. *Ideas,* sect. 93, p. 250.

31. *Ibid.,* sect. 35, pp. 105ff.

32. Cf. Gurwitsch, *Studies,* pp. 131–34; Føllesdal, op. cit., prop. 5, 6, 7; Mohanty, "Husserl's Concept of Intentionality," in *Analecta Husserliana,* 1: 108, and his "Note" in *Analecta Husserliana,* 2: 318.

33. Gurwitsch, *Studies,* p. 134.

34. Cf. Wittgenstein's puzzle in *Philosophical Investigations,* trans. by G. E. M. Anscombe (Oxford: Blackwell, 1958) concerning the picture of the man on the hill: "Is he going up or coming down?" At least the *Tractatus* was written before the advent of motion pictures.

35. Cf. Mohanty's criticism on his "Note," *Analecta Husserliana,* 2: 320.

36. *Ideas,* sect. 88–89, pp. 237ff.

37. Ibid., sect. 94, p. 251. The individuation of judgments is even more problematic than that of perceptual acts and noemata.

38. *Studies,* p. 133. The frequency of visual verbs in Husserl and Gurwitsch is noteworthy. But where Husserl often places such verbs in "inverted commas"—e.g., *"Sehen"* (*Ideas,* sect. 19, p. 75 et passim)—Gurwitsch, restricting himself to perception, takes them literally.

39. Third Cartesian Meditation, sect. 25, pp. 58ff.

40. Esp. *Ideas,* sect. 124, pp. 318ff. It is *very* important to warn ourselves about the difference between Husserl's use of *Bedeutung* and Frege's use. For Husserl, *Bedeutung* is conceptual meaning; for Frege, it means reference. Cf. "Über Sinn und Bedeutung," *Zeitschrift für Philosophie und Philosophische Kritik* (1892).

41. Thus we find Roderick Chisholm, and many other recent philosophers, attempting to analyze Brentano's concept of inten*t*ionality in terms of inten*s*ional contexts. See, e.g., his *Perceiving* (Ithaca, N.Y.: Cornell University Press, 1957), the last chapter, and "On Some Psychological Concepts and the 'Logic' of Intentionality," in H. N. Casteneda, ed., *Intention, Minds and Perception* (Detroit, Mich.: Wayne State University Press, 1960), pp. 11–35.

42. *Ideen III,* p. 89 (quoted in Føllesdal, op. cit.); also *Ideas I,* ch. 9 et passim.

43. Husserl avoids the heavily psychologistic term 'concept' *(Begriff).* He prefers 'essence' *(Wesen),* but the point is the same. Cf. *Ideas,* ch. 1, sect. 2–5.

44. Føllesdal, op. cit., thesis 1.

45. Føllesdal makes only brief mention of Frege in this piece. The relationship is developed in Dreyfus, "*Sinn* and Intentional Object," in Solomon, *Phenomenology and Existentialism,* pp. 1–17.

46. Føllesdal, op. cit., thesis 2.

47. Ibid., theses 3, 4.

48. Ibid., theses 5, 6, 7.

49. Ibid., theses 8, 9.

50. *Ideas,* sect. 89, p. 240.

51. Quoted by Føllesdal, op. cit.

52. *Ideas,* sect. 89, 90.

53. Op. cit. (in defense of thesis 9).

54. *Ideas,* sect 129, p. 333.

55. See Chisholm's discussion of Brentano, op. cit., and in Lee and Mandlebaum, eds., *Phenomenology and Existentialism* (Baltimore, Md.: Johns Hopkins Press, 1967).

56. *Ideas,* sect. 129, p. 333.

57. Ibid., sect 48, p. 133.

58. It is worth remembering how much Brentano came to dislike Kant's philosophy in considering this affinity between his student and Kant.

59. *Ideas,* sect. 117, p. 306; cf. "the universality of the logical," ibid., p. 307.

60. Ibid., p. 307.

61. See the first of the *Logical Investigations,* vol. II.

62. *Ideas,* sect. 19, pp. 74f.

63. *Philosophy as a Rigorous Science,* trans. by Q. Lauer (New York: Harper Torchbooks, 1965), p. 95.

64. E.g. *Ideas,* sect. 66, p. 176.

65. For an admirable attempt at such a synthesis, see J. N. Mohanty's essays "Language and Reality" in his *Phenomenology and Ontology* (The Hague: Nijhoff, 1970), esp. pp. 62f., 30–59. See also the last section of my "Frege and Husserl."

66. On the pessimistic side, it may be argued that there is no way to know if language can ever capture these prelinguistic meanings. This thought haunted Merleau-Ponty throughout his career and drove Heidegger beyond the attempts at metaphysics begun in *Sein und Zeit,* as it chased Mallarmé beyond the transcendental limits of his onetime devotion to poetry.

67. The violent reaction in analytic quarters to the notion of prelinguistic meanings extends far beyond the limits of phenomenology. It has been evident in the reactions to structuralism and, closer to home, to Chomsky's recent theories of prelinguistic structures of language.

14

An Introduction to Existentialism

It is a commonly accepted half-truth that existentialism is a revolt against traditional Western rationalistic philosophy. It is also a demonstrable half-truth that existentialist philosophy is very much a continuation and logical expansion of themes and problems in Descartes, Kant, Hegel, Marx, and Husserl. But two half-truths provide us with less than the truth. Existentialism is not simply a philosophy or a philosophical revolt. Existentialist philosophy is the explicit conceptual manifestation of an existential attitude—a spirit of "the present age." It is a philosophical realization of a self-consciousness living in a "broken world" (Marcel), an "ambiguous world" (de Beauvoir), a "dislocated world" (Merleau-Ponty), a world into which we are "thrown" and "condemned" yet "abandoned" and "free" (Heidegger and Sartre), a world which appears to be indifferent or even "absurd" (Camus). It is an attitude that recognizes the unresolvable confusion of the human world, yet resists the all-too-human temptation to resolve the confusion by grasping toward whatever appears or can be made to appear firm or familiar—reason, God, nation, authority, history, work, tradition, or the "other-worldly," whether of Plato, Christianity, or utopian fantasy. The existential attitude begins with a disoriented individual facing a confused world that he cannot accept. This disorientation and confusion is one of the by-products of the Renaissance, the Reformation, the growth of science, the decline of Church authority, the French Revolution, and the growth of mass militarism and technocracy. In philosophical terms, the new stress on "the individual" provides the key themes of the Enlightenment, the "Age of Reason," the philosophical rationalism of Descartes, Kant, and Hegel. In these authors, however, the theme of individual autonomy is synthesized and absorbed into a transcendental move-

238

ment of reason. But in a culture that harps so persistently upon the themes of individual autonomy and freedom, there will always be individuals who carry these to their ultimate conclusion. Existentialism begins with the expression of a few such isolated individuals of genius, who find themselves cut adrift in the dangerous abyss between the harmony of Hegelian reason and the romantic celebration of the individual, between the warmth and comfort of the "collective idea" and the terror of finding oneself alone. Existentialism is this self-discovery. Its presupposition is always the Cartesian *sum* (not the *cogito*).

So long as we think of philosophy as a set of (hopefully) true propositions, we will continue to be tempted by notions that philosophy can be a "science," that there is a *correct* way of doing philosophy, that a philosophical judgment or body of judgments can be *true*. If instead we allow ourselves to think of philosophy as *expression,* these rigid demands seem pointless or vulgar. Yet we surely do not want to reduce philosophy to *mere* expression, to autobiography or poetry, to "subjective truth" or psychic discharge. Although it is an expression of personal attitude, a philosophical statement is better compared to a piece of statuary than to a feeling or an attitude. The philosopher is a conceptual sculptor. He uses his language to give a shape to his prejudices and values, to give his attitudes a life of their own, outside of him, for the grasp of others. A philosophical statement, once made, is "in the world," free of its author, open to the public, a piece to be interpreted; it becomes universal. But "universal" does not mean "universally true."[1] Philosophical genius lies not in the discovery of universal truth, but in the seductiveness with which one molds his personal attitudes as universals for others. The philosopher builds insight onto insight, illustration into argument, joins metaphysical slogan to concrete observation, perhaps using himself as an example, his entire age as a foil. Nevertheless, the philosophy is never merely a personal statement; if it is the individual that has made existentialist philosophy possible, it is also the case that existentialism has deepened our individualism. Nor is philosophy ever merely an epiphenomenon of cultural attitudes; it gives them shape and direction, creates them as well as expresses them.

Existential philosophy, perhaps like all philosophies, typically finds itself going in circles, trying to prove axioms with theorems, converting premises into methodological rules, using repetition and restatement for argument and illustration for proof. Here "the individual" appears as a conclusion, there as the presupposition, and there again as the rule. The existential attitude finds itself in syndromes, interpreting a feeling as a mark of identity, converting an insight about oneself into an interpretation of the world, resolving self-doubt by exaggerating the self in everything. The existential attitude is first of all an attitude of self-consciousness. One feels himself separated from the world, from other people. In isolation, one feels threatened, insignificant, meaningless, and in response demands significance through a bloated view of self. One constitutes himself as a hero, as an offense, as a prophet or Antichrist, as a revolutionary, as unique. As a result of this self-exaggeration, the world becomes—whether apparently or "really" is irrelevant—more threatening. So one attacks the world, discovering, with both despair and joy, that its threats are themselves without ultimate meaning, that there are no moral facts, no good and evil, that "the highest values devalue themselves," and that the human world is typically, even essentially, a hypocritical world. And so one self-righteously finds himself as the creator of meaning, which heightens one's role as absurd hero, prophet, revolutionary, "underground man," rebel, saint—or buffoon. Then there is at least slight paranoia, me or us against the others, the authorities, the public, the herd, the bourgeoisie, the pharisees, the oppressors. As the world becomes more threatening, one is thrown into his exaggerated concept of self all the more; and as he becomes more self-conscious, the world becomes increasingly "his." Then one begins to feel important in the face of the responsibility for "his" world; it becomes more apparent how indifferent the world is, how contingent its events, how utterly absurd. One feels isolated from others, and in desperate loneliness one seeks comraderie, through rebellion, through art, through writing existential philosophy. In the existential syndrome every tension increases self-consciousness, every increase in self-consciousness exaggerates the irresolvable tension with the world that is always there. As the existentialist becomes more sophisticated, as his feelings become formulated into ideas, as the existential attitude becomes philosophy, it becomes a mantra for similar attitudes in others. When those attitudes finally manifest themselves in the sardonic irony of Kierkegaard, the utter loneliness of Nietzsche's Zarathustra, the pathetic spitefulness of Dostoevsky's Underground Man, the struggle against nausea and "bad faith" in Sartre, the struggle for the heights in Camus' Sisyphus, these attitudes are no longer personal syndromes but universal meanings that we can accept as our own.

According to many existentialists, every act and every attitude must be considered a choice. Yet the existential attitude itself is apparently not chosen. One finds oneself in it. Dostoevsky tells us that self-consciousness is a "disease"; Nietzsche adds, in his discussion of "bad conscience," that it is "a disease—but as pregnancy is a disease." Although many existentialists speak of the universality of "the human condition," this universality is itself a view from within an attitude which is less than universal. Most existentialists, no less than Descartes, Kant, and Hegel, take self-consciousness to be the home of a universal first truth about all men. But self-consciousness itself is not universal, although once one becomes self-conscious, he cannot go back, no matter how he denies himself, drugs himself, *leaps* or *falls* away from himself (the terms, from Kierkegaard and Heidegger respectively, carry their evaluations with them). In *Utilitarianism,* John Stuart Mill argues for "quality" of pleasures by contrasting the dissatisfied Socrates with a satisfied pig. The first is preferable, Mill argues, because Socrates has experienced both Socratic pleasures and pig pleasures and he, like other men, has chosen to remain Socratic. Actually Socrates has no choice. He can *act like* a pig, but he cannot enjoy himself as one. Socrates can no more imagine the selfless indulgence of pig pleasure than the pig can appreciate the arguments of the *Apology.* Once expressed, the existential attitude appears as a universal condition, but only to those who can understand it. It is a peculiarly Western attitude, and talk of "the human condition" is as presumptuous as it is overdramatic. Perhaps that is why, for many of us, Hermann Hesse is convincing, even in the wild fantasies of the magic theater, but lyrically unpersuasive as he attempts to capture the selflessness of his Eastern Siddhartha. If we begin by understanding Siddhartha's quest, it is because we, like Hesse, understand quests. However, we may well have difficulty understanding the peace and satisfaction of Siddhartha's repetitive routine as a ferryman. Of course we, like Hesse, can moon for that selflessness as a dream, a nostalgia for something lost. But for us, even selflessness is something viewed self-consciously, something that would have to be striven for by each of us as an individual. The existential attitude is not universal, and existential philosophy is not a truth about the human condition. As Camus says, for many of us it is simply a necessity. Most of us have experienced this existential attitude at several points in our lives. A threat of imminent death—or even a passing thought of our own mortality—is sufficient to wrench us out of our current involvements, even if but for a moment, and force us to look at our lives. Like Sartre's characters in hell in *No Exit,* it is perhaps every man's private dream to see his own funeral, to see his life after its completion. In life, however, there can be no such viewpoint, as Kierkegaard complains against Hegel, since "at no particular moment can I find the necessary resting place from which to understand [my life] backwards." Inevitably the thought of death prompts existential questions, What have I done? Who have I been? What have I wanted to be? Is there still time? But anxiety of death is only one preface to existential anxiety. As Camus tells us, "at any streetcorner the absurd can strike a man in the face." Imagine yourself involved in any one of those petty mechanical tasks which fill so much of our waking hours—washing the car, boiling an egg, changing a typewriter ribbon—when a friend appears with a new movie camera. No warning: "Do something!" he commands, and the camera is already whirring. A frozen shock of self-consciousness, embarrassment, and confusion. "Do something!" Well of course one was doing something, but that is now seen as insignificant. And one is doing something just standing there, or perhaps indignantly protesting like a housewife caught in curlers. At such moments one appreciates the immobilization of John Barth's Jacob Horner, that paralyzing self-consciousness in which no action seems meaningful. In desperation one *falls* back into his everyday task, or he *leaps* into an absurd posture directed only toward the camera. In either case, one feels absurd. One remains as aware of the camera as of his actions, and then of his actions viewed by the camera. It is the Kantian transcendental deduction with a 16mm lens: there is the inseparable polarity between self and object; but in this instance the self is out there, in the camera, but it is also the object. A *sum* (not a *cogito*) accompanies my every presentation. "How do I look?" No one knows the existential attitude better than a ham actor.

Enlarge this moment, so that the pressure of self-consciousness is sustained. Norman Mailer, for example, attempted in *Maidstone* a continuous five-day film of himself and others which did not use a developed script, leaving itself open to the "contingencies of reality." His problem was, as ours now becomes, how to present oneself, how to live one's life, always playing to the camera, not just as one plays to an audience but as one plays to a mirror. One enjoys making love, but always with the consciousness of how one appears to be enjoying himself. One thinks or suffers, but always with the consciousness of the "outer" significance of those thoughts or sufferings. A film of one's life: Would it be a comedy? a tragedy? thrilling? boring? heartrending? Would it be, as Kierkegaard suggests, the film of "a life which put on the stage would have the audience weeping in ecstasy"? Would it be a film you would be willing to see yourself? twice? infinitely? Or would eternal reruns force you to throw yourself down and gnash your teeth and curse this Nietzschean projectionist? And who would edit this extravagant film of every detail—of yet undetermined significances—of your life? How would the credits be distributed? Each of us finds himself in his own leading role—the hero, the protagonist, the buffoon. John Barth tells us that Hamlet could have been told from Polonius' point of view: "He didn't think he was a minor character in anything."

What does one do? "Be yourself!" An empty script; *myself* sounds like a mere word that points at "me" along with the camera. One wants to "let things happen." But in self-conscious reflection nothing ever "just happens." One seizes a plan (one chooses a self), and all at once one demands controls unimaginable in everyday life. Every demand becomes a need, yet every need is also seen as gratuitous. During the filming of *Maidstone,* Mailer was attacked by one of his "costars" (Rip Torn), and his candid reaction exploded the film's pretense of reality. No one can be an existential hero and also accept fate, yet no one is more aware of contingencies. Camus tells us that Sisyphus is happy, but perhaps he is because his routine is settled. He can afford to have scorn because his mythical reality is entirely structured within its predictable contingencies. Could Sisyphus remain the absurd hero if he were alive? How much does Camus' absurd hero and the existential attitude require the routine and leisure of the bourgeoisie? Perhaps there are no existentialists in foxholes.

The hero? The buffoon? Does any of us really think of himself that way? As Odysseus, Beowulf, James Bond, Woody Allen, perhaps not. But as the center, the one who endows all else with meaning, that is an attitude we recognize easily. Yet at the same instant we recognize ourselves as pelted by meanings, "sown on our path as thousands of little demands, like the signs which order us to keep off the grass" (Sartre). The existential attitude is the constant confusion of given meanings and our own. As this confusion becomes better formulated, one begins to suspect both. Today, I am Dr. Pangloss, and the world is spectacular; yesterday I was a Schopenhauerian fecal monist, grumbling over a fine wine in a rotten world. Each day values are given to me, but each day I find changes to explain how yesterday's differing values depended on differences in the world. (Yesterday I was there, now I'm here; yesterday she was friendly, today she insulted me.) My friends assure me, typically, that what has changed is only me, and that yesterday's depression was a symptom of a very real problem. It is today that is the illusion; my happiness is merely another symptom of my problem. But the values remain a problem, outside of me. Then, the exaggerated insight: It is all me (mine). No one can begin in the existential attitude without feeling sometime the hero, the megalomaniac (Nietzsche: "I am dynamite"). But again, one need not, should not, take this attitude for the truth. The realization that "I am the world" is a necessary step in the awakening of self-consciousness. In the existentialists' self-conscious sense, perhaps one has never existed if he has never once seen himself as everything.

What is self-consciousness? According to some recent existentialists, there is no *self* as such. And what is consciousness? "It is nothing," Sartre tells us, and for Heidegger it is scarcely worth mentioning. One looks at paradigm cases. One is self-conscious because of the camera: "He is self-conscious about his baldness." To be self-conscious is to be embarrassed, to be ill at ease. Or is that a peculiarly American paradigm? Descartes sees self-consciousness as a propositional attitude; consciousness of one's own existence seems in the light of reason to be not much different from a mathematical postulate. Hegel is centrally concerned with self-consciousness in his master-slave parable, but self-consciousness in Hegel carries with it a sense of dignity, pride, autonomy. We might well suspect that semantics is here becoming an ethology as well. What we begin to see, in our moviemaking example as well as in Descartes and Hegel, is that self-consciousness is neither a subject aware nor an awareness of an object (the self) so much as it is a motivation, an attitude that illuminates the world as well as the individual in the world. Self-consciousness is not, strictly speaking, awareness of self, for there is no self. Rather, self-consciousness in the existential sense is this very recognition that there is no self. The self is an ideal, a chosen course of action and values. Self-consciousness does not add anything to the world or to consciousness; it is neither a Lockean "turning back on itself" nor a Cartesian reflective substance. Self-consciousness robs the world of its authority, its given values, and it robs consciousness of its innocence. Self-consciousness is not a premise or an object for study. It is rather the perspective within which existentialism attempts to focus itself.

Existentialism is forced to be centrally concerned with problems of justification. In self-consciousness one holds all given values suspect. How much of reason might be no more than *our* reason, the anonymous consensus of "the public"? How many of our values might be no more than relics of dead authority or products of our weaknesses, our fears of isolation, failure, or meaninglessness? How many of our values are prejudices, how much reason mere rationalization? Nevertheless, to simply pronounce the nihilist thesis that the highest values are without justification is not sufficient. The problem, we hear from every author, is to live. And so we continue to seek courses of action. We look to Kant and try to act in a way that would universalize our principles of action for everyone. But that supposes that we can identify those features of our own action which would be so universalizable. And then, already caught in the existential attitude, each of us realizes that he is always an exception. I can accept moral principles by the tabletful, but I am always without the rule which teaches me to apply such principles to my own case. One is tempted to turn away from principles to the concrete—to his feelings and attitudes. Yet to do so, as Kant had already argued, is to give up morality. And which feelings can I trust? How does one build a way of life on a foundation of tenuous, passing feelings? How much does one value happiness? Pleasure? Self-interest? Feelings for others? Simple perversity and spite? Must my values change every time my feelings change? And how can decisions for the future always depend upon the undependability of passing whims, a bad night's sleep, too much coffee, or a hassle on the subway? To be consistent, in such a scheme, one must be impotent. Still, all of this supposes that there are feelings, that they are given—with directions and instructions—like concrete and intuited moral principles of the moment. But a feeling does not have an identity or a direction before it is already made self-conscious. For one who is not yet self-conscious, a feeling can be a cause of behavior. In one who is self-conscious, a feeling is but an obscure text which requires an interpretation, and that presupposes a set of values. In one and the same situation I might be ashamed or embarrassed, depending on my own sense of responsibility, angry or afraid, depending on my sense of value, indignant or amused, depending on my sense of morality. One can always find values given, in his everyday tasks, by "the public," but the existential self-consciousness has already closed this escape behind itself. One can no longer turn to religion, for Kant has destroyed its authority and reduced it to a mere "postulate" of morality. So, one *creates* a criterion, "leaps" to a set of values, to a life of one's own. Camus calls this "philosophical suicide," for every such attempt to adopt a value is at the same time a pretense that the value is justified. However, no one can simply rest in the existential attitude of the absurd, any more than he can relax in Hegel's dialectic. Kierkegaard's "leap," like the lie in Kafka's *Trial*, becomes for existentialism a universal principle.

The existential attitude, as we have been describing it, is not merely a piece of psychology, much less psychopathology. Existential statements are at once both personal and general. Personal, however, is not autobiographical. The same Kierkegaard who complains of the lack of passion in his age is thus described by a friend: "There is nothing spontaneous about him: I am surprised he can eat and sleep." The Nietzsche one might have met in Sils Maria in 1886 was surely not the Dionysian epic hero one pictures from his writings. This is not hypocrisy. It is the mark of these great philosophers that their personal discomfort could be so brilliantly transformed into matters of universal concern and inspiration. Kierkegaard describes himself as a "stormy petrel" (a bird that appears "when, in a generation, storms begin to gather") and as "an epigram to make people aware." Nietzsche often feared that he would be considered either a saint or a buffoon. (Hesse remarked that "a nature such as Nietzsche's had to suffer the ills of our society a generation in advance"; his personal suffering was at the same time "the sickness of the times themselves.") And Camus gives us, not just *his* feelings of alienation, but "an absurd sensitivity that is widespread in our age." If these feelings are not universal, neither are they exceptional. What is exceptional is their expression in these authors and their ability to provoke others who hold these still unformed and unexpressed existential attitudes as personal failures and not yet as philosophical insights. Kierkegaard and Nietzsche wrote only for "the few": Camus and Sartre write to generations. Nevertheless, in each case the philosopher is not simply striving after merely the truth, but after converts as well. The philosopher becomes the seducer, the *provocateur*. The Socratic gadfly kept people annoyedly aware of reason. The existentialist Don Juan draws his power from desires, from loneliness, from feelings of inadequacy that we already share.

One might object that this sketch of the existential attitude and its philosophical expression has failed to give a definition of existentialism. But existentialism is not a dead doctrine to be bottled and labeled. It is a living attitude that is yet defining and creating itself. As Nietzsche warns us in his *Genealogy of Morals,* "Only that which has no history can be defined." And Sartre, rejecting an invitation to define existentialism, says, "It is in the nature of an intellectual quest to be undefined. To name it and define it is to wrap it up and tie the knot. What is left? A finished, already outdated mode of culture, something like a brand of soap, in other words, an idea" (*Search for a Method*). Although one might develop a working definition of one aspect of one twentieth-century existentialist "movement," namely that series of attempts to develop an existential phenomenology in extension of and reaction to Edmund Husserl's "transcendental phenomenology," existentialism is but a growing series of expressions of a set of attitudes which can be recognized only in a series of portraits.[2] Existentialism is not a movement or a set of ideas or an established list of authors. It is an attitude which has found and is still finding philosophical expression in the most gifted writers of our times. But little more needs to be said *about* existentialism, for nothing could be further from the existential attitude than attempts to define existentialism, except perhaps a discussion *about* the attempts to define existentialism.

NOTES

1. I follow Hegel here in distinguishing between "universally available" and "universally applicable."

2. See my *From Rationalism to Existentialism* (New York: Harper & Row, 1972).

15

Camus's *L'Étranger* and the Truth

Lying is not only saying what is not true. It is also and especially saying more than is true and, as far as the human heart is concerned, saying more than one feels.

—ALBERT CAMUS[1]

What would it be—not to lie? Perhaps it is impossible. It is not difficult to avoid uttering falsehoods, of course. One can always keep silent. But what if lying is also not *seeing* the truth? For instance, not seeing the truth about oneself even in the name of "not lying"? What then would it be not to lie?—to see oneself and one's feelings as brute facts, as matters already fixed and settled? The very idea of not lying would then be a lie.

The lie—the very heart of French existentialism. It is the infamy of the human condition for Sartre, the gravest sin for Camus. But where Sartre suspects that the lie—or what he calls *mauvaise foi*— is inescapable, Camus glorifies his characters—and apparently himself—as men without a lie. Meursault of *L'Étranger,* Camus tells us in a retrospective interpretation, "refuses to lie ... accepts death for the sake of truth."[2] Dr. Rieux of *The Plague* refuses to release information to Tarrou the reporter unless Tarrou reports "without qualification." Clamence of *The Fall* has been living a lie. He is now in purgatory (the seedy inner circles of Amsterdam), a judge-penitent: a judge, we come to see, of other people's hidden falsehoods, a penitent for his own past lie of a life. In *The Myth of Sisyphus,* it is "the absurd" that becomes the ascertainable truth, and it is the absurd hero who "keeps the absurd alive" with his defiant recognition of that truth. In the turmoil of French leftist politics through the Algerian crises and the Stalin show trials, Camus portrays himself in his *Journals* and in *The Rebel* as the "independent intellectual," the spokesman for the truth who refuses to accept the necessary political fabrications of the left during a time of crisis and change.

This research was supported by the Centre Universitaire International of the University of Paris.

Accordingly, Camus has himself been interpreted and praised as the hero and martyr for the truth, as "Saint Just," the absurd hero and existential champion.[3]

L'Étranger is the best known of Camus's works, and it is on the basis of this early short novel that the interpretations of Camus's philosophy reasonably begin. But virtually every interpretation of this work has resulted in what I shall argue to be a false claim—that Meursault is a totally honest man, the "stranger" who does not lie. In his own interpretation of *The Stranger,* Camus writes,

> . . . the hero of the book is condemned because he doesn't play the game. In this sense he is a stranger to the society in which he lives; he drifts in the margin, in the suburb of private, solitary, sensual life. This is why some readers are tempted to consider him as a waif. You will have a more precise idea of this character, or one at all events in closer conformity with the intentions of the author, if you ask yourself in what way Meursault doesn't play the game. The answer is simple: He refuses to lie. Lying is not only saying what is not true. It is also and especially saying more than is true and, as far as the human heart is concerned, saying more than one feels. This is what we all do every day to simplify life. Meursault, despite appearances, does not wish to simplify life. He says what is true. He refuses to disguise his feelings and immediately society feels threatened. He is asked, for example, to say that he regrets his crime according to the ritual formula. He replies that he feels about it more annoyance than real regret and this shade of meaning condemns him.
>
> Meursault for me is then not a waif, but a man who is poor and naked, in love with the sun which leaves no shadows. Far from it being true that he lacks all sensibility, a deep tenacious passion animates him, a passion for the absolute and for truth. It is a still negative truth, the truth of being and of feeling, but one without which no victory over oneself and over the world will ever be possible.
>
> You would not be far wrong then in reading *The Stranger* as a story of a man who, without any heroics, accepts death for the sake of truth. I have sometimes said, and always paradoxically, that I have tried to portray in this character the only Christ we deserved. You will understand after these explanations that I said this without any intention of blasphemy and only with the slightly ironic affection which an artist has the right to feel towards the characters whom he has created.[4]

And throughout the standard interpretations, the same theme is unquestioningly repeated, for example, " . . . this indifferent man is intractable in his absolute respect for truth,"[5] and "his principal characteristic appears to be a kind of total sincerity which disconcerts us because it is virtually unknown in our world."[6]

This view has been challenged, but only in its scope, not in its essence. Notably, C. C. O'Brien, in a recent book and article on Camus, has argued that "Meursault of the actual novel is not quite the same person as the Meursault of the commentaries. Meursault in the novel lies. He concocts for Raymond the letter which is designed to deceive the Arab girl and expose her to humiliation, and later he lies to the police to get Raymond discharged, . . . It is simply not true that Meursault is 'intractable in his absolute respect for the truth.' These episodes show him as indifferent to truth as he is to cruelty."[7] O'Brien continues to point out that Meursault, as the mirror of his author, is also indifferent to the realities of the hostility of the Arabs, the political tensions and sufferings of the Arab population and the pretensions and arrogance of colonialism in which he plays an undisputed part. Perhaps O'Brien does not make enough of the distinction between lying and being simply *indifferent* to the truth, saying less than is true. In the passages in question, it is more indifference at stake than outright lying; for example, Meursault passes no judgment on Raymond's action apart from a straight appraisal of his means to an end: "I agreed it wasn't a bad plan—it would punish her all right" (p. 40). And there is nothing in the description of the letter or his testimony before the police to make us certain that he has lied. But Camus, again in his commentary, explicitly points out that lying is not just saying what is not true; it is "also saying more than is true" and, we may safely extrapolate, saying less than is true as well. On this basis, we ought to agree with O'Brien that Meursault is, even if he does not lie outright, less than the ideal honest man. But ultimately, even O'Brien joins in the standard interpretation, qualifying it beyond the usual blanket judgment:

> There is just one category of phenomena about which Meursault will not lie, and that is his own feelings. Neither to give pleasure to others nor to save them pain nor to save his own skin will he pretend that he feels something that he does not feel. Logically there is no reason why this should be so. There is no reason why he should not use lies to get himself out of the trouble which he got himself into by lies. Indeed, in the second case the motivation is (one could imagine) infinitely stronger than the first. Yet it is only the second he resists. The reason can only be that his own feelings, and his feeling about his feelings, are sacrosanct.[8]

But I want to argue that this standard interpretation in all its forms is unconvincing, not just in detail, but in essence, and in spite of the fact that the author has endorsed it himself. I want to argue that the whole question of Meursault's "honesty" and "the lie" should be replaced by an examination of the presuppositions of honesty and a new kind of thinking about "feelings." For I want to argue that the character of Meursault is not to be found in the reflective realm of truth and falsity but exclusively in the prereflective realm of simple "seeing" and "lived experience." On the basis of certain phenomenological theories which were circulating around Paris in the 1940s and with which Camus was surely familiar, I want to argue that Meursault neither lies nor tells the truth, because he never reaches that (meta-)level of consciousness where truth and falsity can be articulated. Moreover, he does not even have the feelings, much less feelings about his feelings, to which he is supposed to be so true.

1

If *L'Étranger* has so often been defended as a celebration of pure and honest feelings, it has also been said that Meursault is "strange" because he has no feelings. This is certainly not true.[9] He enjoys the warmth of the sun and Marie's company. He can be annoyed—by the sun or the fact that it's Sunday. But he does not feel regret for his crime nor sorrow for his mother's death. He is confused when Marie asks him if he loves her, not because he is undecided, but because he does not understand the question. What Meursault does not do is make judgments. As the narrator of the novel he describes, but he does not judge, the significance of his actions or the meaning of events, other people's feelings or his own. Accordingly, he does not reflect; he has few thoughts and is only minimally self-conscious. He cannot be true to his feelings, not only because he does not know what they are, but because, without judgments, he cannot even have them. His "true feelings," the feelings he actually has, are an emotionally emasculated and crippled portrait of human experience.

For those who construe Meursault as hero for the truth, his simple world of feelings must be treated as wholly autonomous, independent of reflection; his honesty is precisely the fact that he does not claim to be feeling anything more than what he actually feels. It is, in other words, as if the feelings were simply given and reflection merely commentary, a set of judgments *about* our feelings, with which we, according to Camus, "simplify" and thereby lie about life. In French phenomenology, which Camus knew well enough when he wrote *L'Étranger,* this reflection-and-feeling duality was well summarized in Sartre's distinction between reflection and prereflective "lived experience" (*le vécu*), adapted from Heidegger's distinction between the "ontological" and the "ontic" and repeated again by Merleau-Ponty. These distinctions provide the two-part structure of Camus's novel.

To state my interpretation baldly, Meursault is a philosophically fantastic character who, for the first part of the novel, is an ideal Sartrian prereflective consciousness, pure experience without reflection, always other than, but also *nothing* other than what he is conscious of at the moment. He is a demonstration, even despite the author's intentions,[10] of the poverty of consciousness, for it is only with judgments and reflection that the feelings we consider most human are possible. But then, in the second part of the novel, prison deprives him of his rich fund of totally involving Mediterranean experiences; his trial robs him of his indifference to others' opinions of him, thereby forcing him to reflect on himself and providing him with such emotions as regret, guilt, and anger; the threat of immanent death finally forces him into a Heideggerian celebration of the "privilege of death" and the "happy death" which is a constant theme in Camus' novels (the last line of *The Plague,* the title of *La Mort heureuse*) but a clumsy paradox in his philosophical essays. In part II, Meursault begins to become a person, because he is condemned.

In his later writings, Camus employs the same duality. *The Myth of Sisyphus* explores the tenuous relation between experience (life) and the value of experience through reflection. Ultimately, Camus confusedly argues, it is *only* life that has value, but we can see the value of this value (in Nietzschean phrase) only by "keeping the absurd alive," that is, by reflectively accepting it. It is apparent that the "metavalue" becomes relevant only after reflection—one might add, *inadequate* reflection—has cheated the first of its value. Later, in *The Fall,* the delicate balance between experience and reflection is again destroyed by the absurd, and we there meet Clamence, a character who is pure reflection and apparently without experience; he barely tastes the gin he is always drinking, and he does not look at the painting he is hiding. He is only reflectively aware of its significance. Like Meursault at the end of *L'Étranger,* Clamence refers to "the life which is no longer mine." This is the nightmare image of pure reflection. (Compare Kierkegaard, who often speaks of himself, because of his hyperreflectivity, as "one who has already died.") At the end of experience, there is only reflection on experience. "Experience," in this formulation, can only mean spontaneous and unreflective experience. This is Meursault's final realization and consequently his only possible conception of an afterlife (p. 150).

In the first part of the book, Meursault does not reflect; he rarely speaks at all. He does not think. Those sporadic occurrences where a thought does appear to him, like a weed that has surprisingly pushed its way through the concrete, only illustrate how unthinking he is; for example, "For some reason, I don't know what, I began thinking of mother" (p. 50) and " . . . just in time, I remembered I killed a man" (p. 78). This is not thinking, certainly not reflecting. It is at most simply "having thoughts."

A problem: Who is the narrator of part I? It cannot consistently be the same Meursault who is unreflectively experiencing. It must be another Meursault, a reflective Meursault, other than the experiences to which he has special access. Philosophy, of course, abounds in such detached observational egos, from the *cogito* of Descartes to the "transcendental ego" of Kant and Husserl. It is this second Meursault who is the narrator, a necessarily reflective but not at all imaginative or philosophical reporter. But notice that the report is not contemporaneous with the experience: even though the novel begins in the brutal present ("Aujourd'hui, Maman est morte"), it very soon (second paragraph) changes to the French present perfect tense and remains there. While the experiences are in ordinary temporal sequence, the reporting is not. On page 13, the narrator says, "But now I suspect that I was mistaken about this," and on page 70, "but probably I was mistaken about this." When is this *now?* It can only be in the time interval of part II of the novel, in prison but (obviously) before the execution. On page 95 (in prison) the narrator reports, "it was *then* that the things I've never liked to talk about began."

If *L'Étranger* were written from a third-person standpoint, Meursault would certainly not seem "strange," but he would have no character at all. It is from the first-person standpoint that Camus allows the Kantian or Husserlian ego to report on the utter blandness of Meursault's prereflective consciousness as it matter-of-factly describes his world. Now, going back to Camus' warning, "lying is not only saying what is not true. It is also saying and especially saying more than is true"; neither applies to the prereflective Meursault, who does not say enough to lie. But what of the reflective narrator? What is "true" for him would appear to be the flat, uninterpreted reporting of prereflective Meursault's experience, without addition or comment. But here we suspect that the entire first part of the book—however brilliant and sensitive—is a lie, for there can be no description of experience without some conceptualization, interpretation, and unavoidable, if minimal, commentary. Meursault of part I is an impossible character because he is both the reflective transcendental narrator and the unreflective bearer of experience. And if one finds just that same coupling in such luminary philosophers as Kant and Husserl, it was in the late 1930s and 1940s that it was starting to be rejected by philosophers in general. (Sartre's "Transcendence of the Ego," Wittgenstein's seminars in Cambridge, the circulation of Heidegger's work in France and Germany.)

Meursault is neither a hero nor an "antihero." He is more like the space from which the reader watches a world discover itself. It is a simple world, without interpretation and without personality. Meursault is Sartre's nothingness of consciousness, John Barth's Jacob Horner, but unlike Sartre or Horner, Meursault does not see himself as nothing, he simply is nothing; he does not see himself as anything at all. (It is impossible to be unhumorously grammatical in these matters.) Meursault might be described by others as "the man who . . .," but he himself has no self-image until his trial, when he is for the first time forced to see himself as the "criminal": "I too came under that description. Somehow it was an idea to which I could never get reconciled" (p. 87). (Compare Sartre describing the young Genet in "The Dizzying Word": "Someone has entered and is watching him. Beneath this gaze the child comes to himself. He who was not yet anyone suddenly becomes Jean Genet. . . . A voice declares publicly: 'You're a thief'. . . . It is revealed to him that he *is* a thief."[11]) He is learning what it is to apply ascriptions to himself, to "see himself in a social context." Early in the novel, in his flat, he says "I glanced at the mirror and saw reflected in it the corner of my table . . . " (p. 30); like a vampire, *he* has no reflection, for reflections do not precede but are consequent upon concern with self-image. In prison, self-image becomes almost an obsession: he polishes his food tin to make a mirror, studies his face and his expression (p. 101), does the same again later and critically reflects upon his "seriousness." Once, he hears his own voice, talking to himself.

It is not as if Meursault has been deprived by his author of a single superfluous dimension of human existence. He has been deprived of *human* existence altogether. On this point, the pompous prosecutor is right, even if his overloaded references to Meursault's "shameful orgies" (i.e., sleeping with Marie and watching a Fernandel film) and Meursault's virtual guilt for the parricide (his lack of visible mourning for his mother) easily lead us to dismiss everything he says. The prosecutor looked into Meursault's "soul," and "found a blank, literally nothing . . . ," "nothing human," "not one of those moral qualities" and "devoid of the least spark of human feeling" (pp. 127 and 129).

Meursault the character is a piece of flat, colorless glass, allowing us to sense the warmth of the sun and smell the brine on the pillow, to crave a cigarette or a cup of coffee or conjure up a vision of thin-haired, hunched-up, skin-blotched Salamano dragging his mule-like mangy dog. We feel the flash of light reflected from the blade of a knife "sear our eyelashes and gouge our eyeballs," spot a "black speck on the sea that might be a ship," but we get no feeling for the *significance* of anything, not even enjoyment or disgust or fear. And it is judgments of significance that make most feelings possible.[12] Meursault has no expectations, no desires other than immediate needs and urges, no sense of responsibility so no sense of guilt or regret, no ability to make moral judgments—and so feels neither disgust nor alarm at the sight of cruelty or danger. He has no conception of either commitment or fidelity, so such notions as love, marriage, and honesty have no meaning to him. He has no ambition, no dissatisfactions. (Even in prison he says, "I have everything I want.") He can feel vexation, an immediate feeling of malcontent and resentment, but not regret, which requires a view of oneself and the past for which one is responsible. He can feel desire but not love; he feels fondness for his mother but not grief; he has thoughts but does not think; he exists but does not think of himself as existing as anything.

Meursault lacks that human dimension that the Greeks had identified as "rationality" and which modern philosophy, since Descartes, has pinpointed in self-consciousness and reflection. For Meursault, there is no "I think," and there is no "I am"; he simply is. But without self-consciousness, Meursault also lacks feelings and, in an important sense, does not acknowledge other people. Edmund Husserl, who best defined the phenomenological ideal of "pure description," was far more concerned with the analysis of knowledge than the analysis of feeling. But when his techniques are turned on the "appetitive" and "volitional" parts of the soul, the consequences may be bizarre. Unlike the objects of knowledge, these vanish like phantoms and explode like bubbles of froth. In Sartre's brilliant early analysis of the emotions, and in his later phenomenological works, "Transcendence of the Ego" and *Being and Nothingness,* he scrutinizes the "givenness" of feelings and watches them disappear as so many everyday illusions. Emotions, he tells us, are "magical transformations of the world." They are not primitive phenomenological givens, but involve meanings, reflections and interpretations. There are no emotions "in themselves," atoms adrift in the stream of consciousness to be simply felt and observed. Emotions—"feelings" in the grander sense— are reflections of a self-conscious subject on his position in the world. Accordingly, Meursault, who is not self-conscious, can have no feelings.

It has always seemed curious to me that the standard interpretation of Meursault as a man faithful to his feelings should persist in the face of the embarrassing fact that, throughout part I of the novel, Meursault never has any significant feelings, even where it seems obvious *to us* that he *ought* to feel something. There are blanks and gaps in the narration where feelings ought to be in exactly the same way that there is an abyss where Meursault's "soul" ought to be. He is not disgusted by Salamano's treatment of his dog nor by Raymond's cruelty to the Arab woman; he is not frightened by the knife-wielding Arab nor moved by his mother's death nor by Marie, for whom his only "passion" appears to be the immediacy of sexual desire. Although there is at least one instance of shared enjoyment, Meursault typically treats Marie as a source of sensations. Any hint of personality on her part appears to Meursault merely as a stimulus. ("When she laughs I always want to kiss her" [p. 44].) He shows no sign of jealousy when he sees Raymond flirting with her, and he is at most "curious" when Marie "has other plans for the evening." He never thinks of Marie when she is not with him, until he is in prison, that is, when his thoughts are rather aimed at "some woman or other," but even those primitive sexual desires are apparently satisfied by his "doing like the others."

In a rightfully famous and startling passage, Marie asks Meursault if he loves her. "I said that sort of question had no meaning, really: but I supposed I didn't" (p. 44). Exactly the same question and answer appear a few pages later (p. 52). (It is not clear whether the second phrase occurs in the conversation, whether it is a reflective commentary or a thought occurring to Meursault at the time.) When Raymond asks Meursault if he would like to be "pals," he responds with similar indifference. With love and friendship, as with his mother's death, "nothing in my life has changed." One would not expect Meursault to be an interesting lover, but we can see that he could not be a lover at all. It is not a matter of his not loving Marie in particular nor a question of his not "saying more than is true." Meursault has no *concept* of love (or friendship or family). If "love" would mean anything to him, it would have to be a sensation, something like the pleasure he feels from the warmth of Marie's body or the smell she leaves behind her. But love, as Camus must have been aware—if not from Sartre at least from his early idol André Gide—is not simply a feeling, but a system of judgments, meanings, expectations, intentions, regrets, reflections, fears, obsessions, needs and desires, abstract demands and metaphysical longings. Of course there may also be pleasurable sensuous contact and feelings of animal warmth and comfort, but these are—however desirable—less essential than the more judgmental components of love, involving a conception of oneself and another which Meursault does not have.

In *The Myth of Sisyphus,* Camus comments, "But of love I know only that mixture of desire, affection, and intelligence that binds me to this or that creature. That compound is not the same for another person. I do not have the right to cover all these experiences with the same name."[13] But Camus the philosopher here makes the same error that he builds into his unreflective creation; love is not simply an experience nor a set of experiences, however complex. It has a necessary dimension which one might call "commitment," not in any legal or moral sense, but in that series of demands, memories, intentions, expectations, and abstractions which add up to a relationship which cannot be simply "for the moment." ("Will you love me forever, [even if just for this weekend?]") Meursault, who understands only his sensuous feelings, can have no concept of love, which is not a sensuous feeling; nor can he understand friendship or the abstract love of a son for his distant mother.

Since Meursault has no sense of commitment, we would expect that he must have an equally uncomprehending view of love's institutional variant (or fossilization), marriage:

> Marie came that evening and asked me if I'd marry her. I said I didn't mind; if she was keen on it, we'd get married. . . . I explained that it had no importance really, but if it would give her pleasure, we could get married right away. I pointed out that, anyhow, the suggestion came from her; as for me, I'd merely said, "Yes." Then she remarked that marriage was a serious matter. To which I answered, "No." She kept silent after that, staring at me in a curious way. Then she wondered whether she loved me or not. I, of course, couldn't enlighten her on that. (p. 53)

For Meursault (and, one sometimes suspects, for Camus), only spontaneous experience ("life") is meaningful. Ironically, Meursault, who has only such experiences, can find no meaning in his experience. He cannot know love or friendship, nor grief for his mother or regret for his crime. He is, as he tells us later, "too absorbed in the present or immediate future." He has no expectations, and consequently no fears or disappointments. In short, he has no feelings of consequence.

It is entertaining to find commentators struggling to identify the "feelings" to which this "honest" man can be faithful. It is at least peculiar to call a man "honest" because he allows himself to enjoy the sun and the sea, the warmth of a woman's body and *café au lait,* because he doesn't go to a brothel on account of "not feeling like it" and refuses to call the cops because he "doesn't like the police." And when Camus praises his character for "refusing to simplify life," he seems to be thinking that the systematic interpretation of the innumerable feelings and judgments that compose our notions of "love" or "grief" or "anger" is "simplification." The underlying Faulknerian metaphor appears to be that feelings are concrete flotsam in a Mississippi flood of consciousness. Consciousness is complex, names are simple. But it is rather pure consciousness, not our systematization of it, that is simple. Or rather, empty. And Meursault is as effective an illustration of that point as Hegel's labyrinthine arguments to the same end. Meursault's consciousness betrays an inability to go beyond the vacuous, while Camus seems to see it as fidelity to the complex. Human feeling and human experience begin, not end, with reflection. Of course, feeling and experience can be suffocated by overintellectualization, as in Dostoyevsky's pathetic, hyperconscious Underground Man. But Camus' antireflective reaction is, as Kant said in the days before air pollution, like trying to avoid breathing impure air by not breathing at all.

O'Brien, agreeing with this part of Camus' interpretation, suggests that Meursault will not lie about his own feelings: "neither to give pleasure to others or to gain pleasure himself . . . will he pretend that he feels something that he does not feel."[14] But the notion of "pretending" here, like its complementary notion of sincerity, is curiously out of place. When Meursault, who has already agreed to marry Marie, will not say that he loves her, that is not a matter of refusing to pretend but a matter of refusal to understand, not a word, but a human relationship. To pretend, one must have a conception of what one does feel as opposed to what one apparently feels. In the flourish of Anglo-American concern with "pretending" (J. L. Austin et al.) and French concern with "sincerity" (the difference of interests may be of some cultural interest besides), a point jointly driven home by, among others, the curious troika of Austin, Gide, and Sartre, is that pretending to feel and feeling (where the feeling at stake is not a mere sensation) are not distinct and in many cases are identical. But this is because feelings are interpretations born in action, not the brute sensations which Camus uses as his paradigm. It is true that Meursault does not pretend to feel what he does not feel. But this no more makes him sincere than his awkward silence makes him honest. (Compare John Barth, *End of the Road:* "She had looked deeply into herself and found nothing. For such a person, the notion of sincerity makes little sense.")

One might hypothesize, in good philosophical tradition, that Meursault could not possibly sense feelings in others if he cannot comprehend them in himself. Quite right, but the logic of the argument—at least since Wittgenstein and Sartre—might better be reversed: It is only with an understanding of feelings in others that one can have an apprehension of one's own feelings. And if understanding feelings is a necessary condition for having feelings, one can argue that, unless one apprehends feelings in others, one cannot *have* them oneself. And so for Meursault. His "indifference" to other people and his indifference in general are two aspects of the same impossible opacity: his inability to interpret, his unwillingness to judge, to "say more than he feels."

Accordingly, people do not exist for Meursault. He only "observes" other people, as he once claims some Arabs viewed him, "like blocks of stone or dead trees," not without interest, but without compassion. At the vigil for his mother, Meursault watches the old people soundlessly usher themselves around the coffin: "Never in my life had I seen anyone so clearly as I saw these people; not a detail of their clothes or features escaped me. And yet I couldn't hear them, and it was hard to believe they really existed" (p. 10). "For a moment I had the absurd impression that they had come to sit in judgment of me" (p. 11). They are all "details of clothes and features." So of course it is "absurd" to think that they can judge him. He sees that the old people cry, but he does not see them grieve. He sees Marie pout at his responses to her, but he does not see that she is hurt. He hears Raymond's girlfriend scream, but he does not see her pain. He sees Raymond bleed, but he does not see his pain or his anger. The Arab Meursault shoots evidently feels or expresses nothing whatever. They are all "little robots," like the woman seated opposite him in Celeste's restaurant.

What I have said in detail about feelings applies as well to the concept of "action." One can try—and occasionally succeed—in describing an action as a set of physical movements. But something is irretrievably lost in such a description: the concept of agency, and consequently the concept of action itself. But the breach between movement and action is again not "given" to experience, but a matter of interpretation. Meursault has no feelings because he will only "feel," but not interpret. He is not aware of other people *as people* because he sees them as "details of clothes and features." Similarly, he is not aware of actions—especially his own actions—because he will not interpret them as actions. There is surprisingly little action in *L'Étranger.* Most importantly, Meursault's crime is only barely an action, and as described it is not an action at all. In the brilliant description of that scene, Meursault is aware of the heat, the sun, the sea, a black speck that might be a ship, the wind, and the "keen blade of light flashing up from the knife scarring my eyelashes and gouging into my eyeballs" (p. 75). He is aware of his sensations; "everything reeled before me," and "every nerve in my body was like a steel spring." Mechanical tension, not fear or anticipation. Then there is what we and the court later interpret as "the killing." But all we are told is, "The trigger gave, and the smooth underbelly of the butt jogged my palm" (p. 76). That is all. Not the slightest indication of his *doing* anything. He appears as much a Newtonian victim of the reaction of the revolver as the unnamed, undescribed victim is of the action of the bullet. The whole event is impersonal, like an accident that happened to him, a mere "it." "And so, with that crisp, whipcrack sound, *it* all began" (p. 76). It is only then that Meursault performs any action, as an afterthought, a reaction to what has already happened; "I shook off my sweat. . . . I fired four shots more into the inert body . . . " (p. 76). He is unable to explain, either to the magistrate or to himself, why he fired those four extra shots. But the mystery which is not broached in the trial—or in Meursault's reflections—is not only why but even whether he fired the first shot.

2

The movement from part I to part II of *L'Étranger* is a movement from innocence to awareness, but not only in the "Christian" sense which has so often been pointed out. It is a movement from pure unreflective experience to reflection and philosophy. It is the second part of the book that carries us into *The Myth of Sisyphus.* It is not in prereflective "indifference" or "honesty," but in his reflection before death that Meursault becomes a model of the absurd hero, like Sisyphus, whose tragedy and whose salvation lies in the fact that he is "conscious" (*Myth,* p. 89).

In the early stages of the indictment and interrogation, Meursault regards his case as "quite simple" (p. 77). He is just beginning to characterize himself, to give himself an "essence" on the basis of his past, as Sartre would say. It is not his case but his reflections that are still "simple." As he learns to reflect on himself, his actions and his past, he loses his former spontaneity, for example at the prosecutor's office: "When leaving, I very nearly held out my hand and said 'Goodby': just in time I remembered that I'd killed a man" (p. 78).

In part I, Meursault invisibly observes the little "robot woman" in the restaurant; in part II, at the trial, he notices only that she is *looking at him.* To reflect is to "see yourself," and to "see yourself" is to make yourself vulnerable to the look of others. In court, Meursault learns of the existence of other people, not as "details of features and clothing" but as his *judges*: "It was then that I noticed a row of faces opposite me. These people were staring hard at me, and I guessed they were the jury. But somehow I didn't see them as individuals. I felt as you do just after boarding a streetcar; and you're conscious of all the people on the opposite seat staring at you in the hope of finding something in your appearance to amuse them" (p. 103). Meursault develops an ego, a bit of French vanity. At first he is delighted at the attention he is receiving. Later he feels left out of the camaraderie of the courtroom, "de trop," "a gate crasher" (p. 105), "excluded" (p. 130). But finally, the looks take their effect: the prosecutor's "tone and the look of triumph on his face, as he glanced at me, were so marked that I felt as I hadn't felt in ages. I had a foolish desire to burst into tears. For the first time, I'd realized how all these people loathed me" (p. 112); and then, " . . . For the first time I understood that I was guilty" (p. 112).

"Guilt" here is not a premonition of the verdict, any more than the desire to burst into tears is a reaction of fear. Nor is the sense of guilt here a *feeling* of guilt. This is rather a far more metaphysical claim, the loss of innocence, not for a particular crime and not before a particular human tribunal, but that loss of innocence that comes from being judged, and recognizing oneself as being judged, by anyone or anything. It is Sartre's "look" (*le regard*), through which we become brutally aware of others. It is this "look," bursting upon Meursault's life as a trauma, that is so terribly regarded by Clamence in *The Fall.* For him, the reality of other people's judgments, even the judgment of a sourceless laugh in the street or the possible judgment yet made by no one of an act unperformed (his failing to try to save the life of a drowning woman), is sufficient to collapse the delicate structure of unreflective innocence. His response is vindictive: "judge that ye not be judged." Meursault's guilt is Clamence's guilt, "Christian" guilt in the sense that mere awareness of oneself is in itself sufficient cause for damnation.

The function of the Kafkaesque trial, on this interpretation, is to force Meursault to reflect on his life, not to try him for murder. This is why the focus of the trial is not a plea of self-defense, which would have been reasonable and convincing (against an Arab with a knife who had already stabbed a friend, in a country already exploding with anticolonial resentment). O'Brien (in *Camus*) has made this political point most forcefully:

> In practice, French justice in Algeria would almost certainly not have condemned a European to death for shooting an Arab who had drawn a knife on him and who had shortly before stabbed another European. And most cer-

tainly Meursault's defense counsel would have made his central plea that of self-defense, turning on the frightening picture of the Arab with a knife. There is no reference to the use of any such defence or even to the bare possibility of an appeal to European solidarity in a case of this kind. This is as unreal as to suppose that in an American court, where a white man was charged with killing a black man who had pulled a knife, defense counsel would not evoke, or the court be moved by, white fear of blacks. (pp. 22–23)

Accordingly, it is artistically and philosophically (even if not legally) appropriate that Meursault is tried for not weeping for his mother, for his friendship with a pimp, for his "liaison" with a woman. In each case, he is forced to see for the first time what his unthinking habits and relations appear to be "from the outside." (E.g., " . . . he kept referring to 'the prisoner's mistress,' whereas for me she was just 'Marie'" [p. 125].) It is true that the trial is a political mockery, but its purpose is not to demonstrate some perverse injustice or to make a victim out of "innocent" Meursault. It is a trial of Meursault's uneventful life, not for justice, but in and for himself.

With reflection, Meursault begins to talk about his feelings, and his lack of feelings. Ironically, it is only at this point that he finally *has* feelings. At first simple feelings, boredom, vexation, hope (p. 89), then annoyance and frustration (p. 95), and finally, full-blown anger (p. 151ff.). He begins to understand desire. In part I, all that he would want he has. It is only with deprivation that he learns what it is to desire. When Marie visits him in prison, he still says he has everything that he wants (p. 91). This is not a lie on his part, but a symptom of his still primitive ability to reflect, and consequently to want. A bit later, he realizes that he cannot smoke in prison. (We were hardly aware that he did smoke in part I.) At first he suffers faintness and nausea. Then he comes to understand that "this is part of my punishment . . . but by the time I understood, I'd lost the craving, so it had ceased to be a punishment" (p. 97).

It is with desire and frustration that Meursault begins to be a philosopher. At first he is "hardly conscious of being in prison" (p. 89), but he soon finds himself facing the awful breach between the concrete but vacuous reality of his former existence and the abstract but rich possibilities of thought. At first it is simple daydreaming, "my habit of thinking like a free man" (p. 95), but soon imagination begins to take the place of lived experience, and imagination, as we know from Descartes, Kant, and of course from Sartre, is the beginning of all philosophical reflection. At first, Meursault's philosophy is imitative and adolescent, at best: "One of mother's pet ideas . . . in the long run one gets used to anything" (p. 96). It is with his increasing frustration that his philosophy matures. In the half-humorous dialogue with his jailer, Meursault learns of *freedom,* now lost. It is with the sudden deprivation of his everyday routines (Heidegger's "hurly-burly of everyday life," or the "wake, meal, streetcar, work, meal, work, streetcar, meal, Monday, Tuesday, . . ." of Camus's "Absurd Reasoning" [*Myth,* p. 10]) that reflection sets in. It is with the loss of the freedom which Meursault never knew he possessed that the "Why" of philosophy begins. It is only with the frustration of his desires that he begins to ask what is worth desiring. It is only with the lack of life's routine that life becomes a problem ("how to kill time" [p. 98]). To avoid frustration and boredom, Meursault invents a routine, a purely reflective routine.

He practices remembering the contents of his room at home. And it is at this point that the most dramatic philosophical turn of the book occurs: "So I learned that even after a single day's experience of the outside world a man could easily live a hundred years in prison" (p. 98). Here is the final twist: Reflection no longer serves experience, but experience serves reflection. One lives in order to be able to reflect, and now "life" is over. ("A life which was mine no longer" [p. 132].) Accordingly, Meursault's only conception of an afterlife is "a life in which I can remember this life on earth" (p. 150).

With the loss of freedom and the loss of "life" in this peculiar sense, Meursault can, like Sartre's damned trio in *No Exit,* view his life in its entirety. Like Clamence in his own "hell" in an Amsterdam bar, he can pass judgment upon it. The fact that he is also condemned to death by the court becomes almost incidental, a vehicle to insure that his reflections are not contaminated by *hope,* that his judgment is not moved by the possibility of "living" once again.

Meursault's gain of self-consciousness is at the same time a transcending of self. Once he begins to reflect on life, it is not simply *his* life itself. It is not his execution, but the idea of execution that puzzles him (compare Camus's later "Reflections on the Guillotine"). It is not his death that torments him but death itself. In reflection, Meursault becomes, as Sartre once said of Camus, a "Cartesian of the absurd."

In part I, Meursault had commented to his employer that "one life is as good as another" (p. 52). Now, more philosophically, he argues, "I'd been right. I was still right, I was always right. I'd passed my life in a certain way, and I might have passed it in a different way, if I'd felt like it. I'd acted thus, and I hadn't acted otherwise. I hadn't done *x,* whereas I'd done *y* or *z.* And what did that mean? That, all the time, I'd been waiting for this present moment, for that dawn, tomorrow's or another day's, which was to justify me. Nothing, nothing had the least importance" (p. 152). This curious notion of death as "justification" is as close to Heidegger's early philosophy as it is to Camus' own *Myth.* "What difference could they make to me, the deaths of others, or a mother's love, or his God, or the way a man chooses to live, the fate he thinks he chooses, since one and the same fate was bound to 'choose' not only me but thousands and millions of privileged people who, like him, called themselves my brother. . . . Every man alive was privileged; there was only one class of man, the privileged class. All alike would be condemned to die one day" (p. 152). Here is Heidegger's Being-Unto-Death with a vengeance, overwhelming all questions of value and worth. It is "that dark wind blowing from the future" that fogs over all ethics and chills all vanities. That one "brutal certitude" undermines Kierkegaardian "leaps" and Sartrian "projects." Here is a peculiar inversion of the central theme of the *Myth,* "whether life is or is not worth living." Death is the end (not just the termination, but the goal) of life: "whether I died now or forty years hence, this business of dying had to be got through, inevitably" (p. 143).

In the shadow of death, Meursault's reflections tend towards but inevitably fall short of the suicidal conclusion that Camus attacks in *The Myth of Sisyphus*: "It is common knowledge that life isn't worth living anyhow" (p. 142). For Meursault, the meaning of life resides only in the spontaneous and momentary lived experiences of part I. In part II, Meursault learns that his lost immediacies, the sun and sand, the smell of brine and Marie's hair, the taste of *café au lait,* were valuable in themselves. ("I'd been right. . . . ") To the chaplain, Meursault replies that "all his certainties were not worth even a single strand of a woman's hair" (p. 151). The value of reflection, in its turn, is just this understanding, reflected in Meursault's unique conception of an afterlife. In other words, Meursault perversely sees that, on reflection, it can be seen that reflection is worthless. It is here that Meursault is more persuasive than his philosophical creator, for he has no pretensions of creating a second value—over and above "life"—in the very reflection within which life can be seen to be without value. Life is not of value *for* anything, yet it is worth living for itself. (Compare *Myth,* p. 7.) But Camus, not Meursault, adds another value, "keeping the absurd alive" "a matter of living in the state of the absurd" (*Myth,* p. 30). Because Meursault is condemned to death, he will not be in a position to live in defiance and revolt (*Myth,* pp. 41, 47). For Camus, the loss of prereflective innocence appears more terrible than a sentence of death. For Sisyphus and Clamence and, one might argue, for Camus himself, reflective defiance soon turns to scorn and resentment.

For Meursault, reflection is not cold and deliberate. It climaxes in "a great rush of anger, which washed me clean, emptied me of hope" (p. 154). Emotion and reflection, it seems, not emotion and innocence, go together. It is in the impassioned hopelessness of reflection, just before his execution, that Meursault faces "the absurd" as a final revelation: "Gazing up at the dark sky spangled with its signs and stars, for the first time, I laid my heart open to the benign indifference of the universe. To feel it so like myself, indeed, so brotherly, made me realize that I'd been happy, and that I was happy still" (p. 154).

How different is Meursault's "benign indifference of the universe" from Camus's "revolt of the flesh" (*Myth,* p. 11). And how different is Meursault's acceptance of it from Sisyphus' scorn and struggle and Clamence's vicious bitterness. For Meursault, there is no "mind and world straining against each other" (*Myth,* p. 30), but a recognition of identity and brotherliness." The universe itself, like Meursault, is unreflectively "indifferent." One might take note, however, that this proposition, as soon as it is stated by Meursault, becomes self-refuting. Meursault is perhaps the only character of Camus' creation, including the author himself, who knows the "happy death" that is his constant theme. "With death so near, Mother must have felt like someone on the brink of freedom, ready to start life all over again. . . . And I, too, felt ready to start life all over again" (p. 154).

Now what are we to make of this? Is it inconsistent with all that has gone before it? What could it mean in this context "to be free" or to "start life all over again"? Meursault's euphoric indifference is a falsification of his emotion, like Camus' calling Sisyphus' scorn of the gods his "happiness," like Jean-Jacques Rousseau, the philosophical champion of innocent "indifference," portraying his bitter resentment as righteousness and even joy. Something has gone very wrong, for the "feelings" to which Meursault is supposed to be faithful are not as they seem. If readers identified with Meursault in part I (as I once did) for his honesty, this does not show that he does not lie but only that we too, like Rousseau, are pleased to fancy our innocence beneath a veil of social conventions and reflected sentiments. And that is a lie. And if readers are moved (as I once was) by Meursault's acceptance of an unjust death, this does not show that "he is willing to die . . . for the sake of the truth," but only that we too would like to be "innocent" even after committing a murder, satisfied with our lives even in the face of absurdity. But that too is a lie. Meursault, who was created with a paucity of feelings, dies with a feeling that is fraudulent. But given his hope to be hated ("all that remained to hope was that on the day of my execution there should be a huge crowd of spectators and that they should greet me with howls of execration" [p. 154]), he failed to be true even to that.

NOTES

1. Albert Camus, preface to *L'Étranger,* ed. by Germaine Brée (New York: Appleton-Century-Crofts, 1955).

2. Albert Camus, *The Stranger,* trans. by Stuart Gilbert (New York: Knopf, 1946). All page references are to this English-edition, in consultation with the Livre de Poche edition (Paris: Gallimard, 1957). Camus's preface appears only in the French edition.

3. E.g., Germaine Brée, *Camus and Sartre* (New York: Delacorte, 1972), esp. p. 122ff.

4. Camus, preface to *L'Étranger,* ed. by Brée, op. cit.

5. Rachel Bespaloff, in Germaine Brée, ed., *Camus: A Collection of Critical Essays* (Englewood Cliffs, N. J.: Prentice-Hall, 1962), p. 93. See also John Cruickshank, *Albert Camus and the Literature of Revolt* (Oxford: Oxford University Press, 1959).

6. Brée, in *Camus,* ed. by Brée, op. cit., p. 7; also p. 12, "the young man's total sincerity."

7. Conor Cruise O'Brien, *Camus* (London: Fontana-Collins, 1970), p. 21. (The article originally appeared in *The New York Review of Bookds.)*

8. Ibid. pp. 21–22.

9. Some of these ideas were originally suggested by Frithjof Bergmann in 1963. He is in no way responsible for what I have done with them since.

10. See, e.g., Jack W. Meiland, "Interpretation as a Cognitive Discipline," *Philosophy and Literature,* vol. 2 (1978): 23–45.

11. Jean-Paul Sartre, *St. Genet: Actor and Martyr* (New York: Braziller, 1963), p. 17.

12. Robert C. Solomon, *The Passions* (New York: Doubleday-Anchor, 1976). Also, cf. "What we call feeling is merely the abstract unity and the meaning of discontinuous impressions."—Jean-Paul Sartre, in his review of *L'Étranger* in Sartre, *Literary and Philosophical Essays,* trans. by Annette Michelson (New York: Collier, 1962), p. 33.

13. Camus, *The Myth of Sisyphus* (New York: Vintage, 1955), p. 55. Hereafter cited as *"Myth."*

14. O'Brien, op. cit., p. 21.

16

Sartre on Emotions

What are the emotions? Ancient poets described them in terms of madness and brute forces. ("Anger is like riding a wild horse," wrote Horace.) Medieval and modern poets alike have talked of the emotions in terms of physiological disruptions—the breaking of hearts, the outpouring of bile, spleen, and gall. Our present-day language of the emotions is riddled with metaphors of passivity: "falling" in love, "struck by" jealousy, "overwhelmed by" grief, "paralyzed by" fear, "haunted by" guilt, "plagued by" remorse. Not surprisingly, the first full-blown psychological theory of the emotions, the so-called James–Lange theory (simultaneously formed by William James in America and C. G. Lange in Denmark), was nothing other than a scientific canonization of these metaphors; the emotions are physiological disturbances with certain epiphenomenal "affects" in consciousness. Similarly, Sigmund Freud describes the "affects" as we might speak of hydraulics, in terms of various pressures and their outlets: filling up ("cathexis") and discharge ("catharsis"), channeling ("sublimation") and bottling up ("repression"). Like James and Lange, Freud links this "hydraulic model" to scientifically acknowledged operations of the central nervous system.[1] In each case, the emotions are viewed as untoward and disruptive forces or pressures, erupting in "outbursts" or manifesting themselves in behavior that is aimless and "irrational,"degrading and often embarrassing, inimical to our best interests and beyond our control. They are not our responsibility (except, that is, in their *expression,* which we are told we *ought* to control).

Jean-Paul Sartre was among the first writers on the subject to break with this tradition. He did so incompletely, but I shall argue that he must nonetheless be credited with the initiation of a persuasive alternative to the ancient model of invasion by alien physiological and animal forces assailing our normal patterns of behavior and thought. In his "Esquisse d'une théorie des émotions,"* Sartre defends a view of the emotions as conscious *acts,* as purposive and "meaningful" ways of "constituting" our world, for which we must accept responsibility. The essay is the only published portion of a projected four hundred-page manuscript that was to be called "The Psyche."[2] It is worth noting that it was written in 1939, about the same time as *Nausea,* Sartre's first "existentialist" novel, and only a short time after "La Transcendance de l'ego,"[3] his best-known phenomenological essay. The "Sketch" on the emotions not only anticipates but actually argues many of the familiar themes of *Being and Nothingness,*** mapping out its phenomenological presuppositions with a simplicity that is lacking in the larger work. (In fact, I have suggested to my students that they read the "Sketch" as an introduction to *Being and Nothingness* in place of the opaque so-called introduction to that work, in which the paradoxes of phenomenological ontology often obscure the existential themes that occupy Sartre for the next several hundred pages.[4])

Since the "Sketch," Sartre has not attempted to develop his "theory" of the emotions as such. Its basic structures, however, are prominent throughout *Being and Nothingness* and his later "psychoanalytic" studies. In his brilliant analysis of the career of Jean Genet,[5] for example, the conception of an emotional "transformation of the world," the key to the theory of his early "Sketch," is also the key to Genet's "word magic" and his "poetic use of language." And the evidence of the first volumes of his gargantuan study of Flaubert[6] demonstrates that no matter how his interests over the years have shifted (in scope if not in direction), Sartre has continued to hold and to use the theory he sketched for us four decades ago.

Sartre's Method: Phenomenology (Introduction)

The introduction to Sartre's "Sketch" tells us that the key to his approach to the emotions lies in an appreciation of the fact that "the consciousness which must be interrogated and what gives value to its responses is precisely that *it is mine*" (8;11, my italics). He contrasts this precept with what he characterizes as "the methods of the psychologist," in which "our knowledge of the emotion will be added *from without* to other knowledge about the physical being" (6,;7). What difference will appreciation of this fact make? It will allow us, according to Sartre, to investigate "the very structure of human reality," the possible conditions of emotion (ibid.), arrived at by the same Kantian style of inquiry that will be central to *Being and Nothingness.*[7] The psychologist reports the "objective" and "empir-

*"Esquisse d'une théorie des émotions" ("Sketch of a Theory of the Emotions") in *Actualities scientifiques et industrielles,* ser. no 838 (Paris: Hermann, 1939, copyright February 23, 1940). This work, translated by B. Frechtman, first appeared in English in 1948 as *The Emotions: Outline of a Theory* (New York: Philosophical Library). All references here are to the 1949 (second) Hermann edition with translations based on the Frechtman 1971 Citadel Press edition. The page numbers that appear in parentheses in the text refer first to the French, then to the English.

**All quotes from *Being and Nothingness* are from the 1972 printing of the Washington Square paperback edition, translated by Hazel Barnes (New York: Philosophical Library, 1956). This work is hereinafter cited in parentheses as *B&N.*

ical" physiological facts of human behavior and, if he allows himself, examines certain "states of consciousness" through introspection (which Sartre insists is equally "objective" and "empirical"). What is missing in the psychologist's method, Sartre complains, is a consideration of consciouness as a *meaningful activity* in and for itself, a consideration that "cannot come to human reality *from the outside*" (11;17).

From the outset Sartre rejects the notion of the emotions as sporadic and inessential disruptions of behavior with conscious "affects"; rather, he says, the emotions are "essential" and "indispensable structures of consciousness" (10;15). Moreover, emotion must not be considered as a set of empirical facts gained through introspection or as a "corporeal phenomenon" (12;19), but rather as "an organized form of human existence" (11;18). This approach Sartre appropriately couches in the now familiar but then novel and exciting language of *phenomenology*. The idea of a form of investigation that goes "beyond the psychic, beyond man's situation in the world, to the very source of man, the world, and the psychic," is essential to Husserl's "transcendental phenomenology," which Sartre endorsed enthusiastically during this period. (See as well his essay "Intentionality" and his *La Transcendance de l'ego,* both written a few years earlier, and his essay "L'Imaginaire" a year later.) The phenomenologist, according to Sartre, attempts "to describe and fix by concepts precisely the essences which preside as the transcendental field unrolls" (8;11). Again anticipating the central theme of *Being and Nothingness,* Sartre argues that it is "just as impossible to get to essence by accumulating accidents as to reach 1 by adding figures to the right of 0.99" (5;5). Sartre's "phenomenology of emotion" would, following Husserl, "put the world in parentheses" in order to study "emotion as a pure transcendental phenomenon," "to attain and elucidate the transcendental essence of emotion as an organized type of consciousness" (8;12).

It is worth noting to what extent Sartre then accepted what he was soon to reject in Husserl—not only the idea of the *epoche,* or "putting in parentheses," but also the very idea of a "transcendental phenomenology" as Husserl conceived it. What is more, it is interesting to note that in these same passages of the introduction Sartre expounds and endorses views of Heidegger, "another phenomenologist" (8;12), who adds to Husserl's transcendental method the need to "assume" human reality, "to be responsible for it instead of receiving it from the outside like a stone," "to 'choose' itself in its being" (8–9;12, quoting Heidegger from *Sein und Zeit*). Sartre does not seem to see the radical disagreements between these two, as if he felt that Husserl's transcendental phenomenology and Heidegger's existential phenomenology could embrace each other without conflict. (For example, he mentions Heidegger's *Dasein,* or "being-in-the-world," along with Husserl's *epoche* apparently without noticing that the one is a radical rejection of the other.)

Sartre analysis is peppered with phenomenological jargon, not always accurately employed but virtually always superfluously, more by way of fetish than conceptual need. Throughout, we find mentions of "neomatic correlate" (33,37;58,65), "noesis" (43;79), "hyle" (34,40;60,73) "thetic consciousness" and "non-thetic consciousness" (29,32,42–43;51,57,77), but it is clear that then, as later, Sartre adopted the language of other theorists only insofar as it suited his own creative intentions. It does not surprise us that all that would remain of this

Husserlian enthusiasm in *Being and Nothingness* was its basic Cartesianism, its emphasis on the "first-person standpoint" and its stress on "subjectivity." The substantial doctrines, on the other hand, would be drawn more from Heidegger than from Husserl, the idea that "man makes himself" (27,28;46,49), that he has no "essence" (2ff;2ff.), that one "lives his body" (*le vécu*) (41;75), that one "assumes" or "chooses" himself and takes responsibility for even his feelings: "it is senseless to think of complaining since nothing foreign has decided what we feel, what we live, or what we are" (*B&N,* 708).

The emotions in particular are to be viewed as "essentially" acts of consciousness, and therefore as intentional and as purposive. An emotion is a mode of consciousness that "by its synthetic activity, can break and reconstitute forms," "transforming an aspect of the world" (24;40), "One can understand emotion only if he looks for *signification*" (24;41). And this means, within the phenomenological framework Sartre is presupposing, that we must ask what its "intentions" are, in a double sense: what it has to do with the world (its "*intentionality*"), and what *purposes* it serves (its "finality" [*finalité*]). As opposed to merely reporting "the facts" of our emotions—their manifestations in behavior, physiology, and "states of consciousness"—Sartre intends to tell us what we are *doing*.

Sartre's Critique of Traditional Theories
(Chapters 1 and 2)

Given his phenomenological approach, the thrust of Sartre's criticism of traditional psychological theories of emotion should be evident. Such theories pay attention only to "the facts," not to the essence of emotion; they regard an emotion as passive, that which afflicts us or, in Freud, "invades us" (29;49); they regard an emotion as disruptive, purposeless, and meaningless. And most importantly, they do not see an emotion as a structure *of* consciousness, as a conscious *act,* but rather as a state or occurrence with manifestations *in* consciousness (as "affect"), as well as in behavior and physiology. Such "peripheric theories" of emotion have in common the thesis that consciousness "is a secondary phenomenon," that what is primary is the bodily response, what William James calls the "expression" of emotion (thus his famous observation, "A mother is sad because she weeps"[8].)

Sartre singles out for attack two theories: that of James, which holds that the conscious "affects" of emotion are mere "epiphenomena" of certain physiological (particularly visceral) disturbances, and that of Janet, whose theory places far greater stress on behavior and "organization" than on physiology. Yet the true target of Sartre's attack is far larger, including all the variations on physiological theory (e.g., those of Cannon and Sherrington: 16;24–25:25;41–42); all versions of "behaviorism" that attempt to do away with "consciousness" and conscious purposiveness; and all the numerous varieties of "philosophical behaviorism" that have sprung up in the wake of the later Wittgenstein and of Gilbert Ryle's *Concept of Mind,*[9] in which emotion is reduced to "agitation," a breakdown in normal, "rational" behavior patterns. These theories may, as in Janet (and subsequently in Freud), involve a "hydraulic" model of accumulated tension and nervous energy, or they may confine themselves to the operational definitions and pure behavioral descriptions of latter-day behaviorism. What they all have in common is a radically de-emphasized conception of consciousness as an "epiphenomenon" (James) or "secondary phenomenon" (Janet), or as no phenomenon at all (as in behaviorism). Against them all, Sartre argues, as anticipated in his introduction, that there can be no accounting for emotions in a model that is not purposive and that does not explain their *significance*. He draws from the German Gestalt psychologists Köhler, Lewin, and Dembo, but he quotes only the Frenchman P. Guillaume at considerable length (20–23;33–36) in order to show, by way of a single example, that our emotions *must* be interpreted "functionally," as purposeful and meaningful yet neither explicit nor deliberate. Anger, for example, "is neither an instinct nor a habit nor a reasoned calculation. It is an abrupt solution of a conflict, a way of cutting the Gordian knot" (22;36–37). It is "an escape" (ibid.). Thus, against Janet in particular (but against all such theories in general), Sartre insists that reference to "finality" is unavoidable and that we "return to consciousness, with which we should have begun" (24;40).

Of particular interest is Sartre's interpretation and critique of Freud's psychoanalytic theory of the emotions (ch. 2:24–29;41–49). He credits this theory with being "the first to put the emphasis on the signification of psychic facts, that is, the fact that every state of consciousness is the equivalent of something other than itself" (25;43). (Freud, who had studied with Brentano, also referred to this equivalence as the "meaning" of a psychic act.) According to psychoanalysis, an emotion is "a symbolic realization of a desire repressed by censorship" (26;44). As in *Being and Nothingness* (pt. I, ch. 2; pt. IV, chs. 1, 2) Sartre's interpretation of Freud's complex and evolving theories in the "Sketch" is oversimplified and highly critical, aiming doubly at (1) the problem of self-deception (anticipating his analysis of "bad faith" in *Being and Nothingness* as not dishonesty as such, yet as needing both "to know and not to know"), and (2) causal determinism. On the one hand, Sartre acknowledges that the psychoanalytic theory recognizes the emotion as meaningful and purposive, but as *symbolically* so. On the other hand, "one *undergoes* it; it takes one by surprise; it develops in accordance with its own laws and without our conscious spontaneity's being able to modify its course appreciably" (25;42). Thus it "invades us in spite of ourselves" (24;49). But this is "a flagrant contradiction" (27;46), Sartre complains, and in support of this assertion he cites reasons similar to those he will marshal to attack the Freudian notion of "the unconscious" in *Being and Nothingness*: "It cuts off consciousness from itself"; in Saussurian language, "The thing signified is entirely cut off from the thing signifying" (Le *signifie* es entièrement coupe du *signifiant*) (26;45). One must be conscious of his own symbolism, but at the same time he cannot be (the same paradox that constitues the "lie to oneself" of "bad faith" in *Being and Nothingness*). The argument, again as in *Being and Nothingness,* turns on the Cartesian conception of the *cogito* and its Kantian conditions of possibility: "If the cogito is to be possible, consciousness is itself the *fact,* the *signification* and the *thing signified*" (27;46).*

Sartre distinguishes sharply, as he will in *Being and Nothingness,* between the intentional model of emotions as meaningful and the mechanical model of

---

*Sartre's italics.

emotions as caused. These are, he assumes, mutually exclusive antitheses. "The profound contradiction of all psychoanalysis is to introduce *both* a bond of causality and a bond of comprehension between the phenomena it studies" (28;48). (Similarly, he accuses Janet [from whom Freud borrowed heavily in his early years] of wavering between "a spontaneous finalism and a fundamental mechanism" [20;32–33].)

Thus the Sartrean position emerges from the rubble of tradition: the fundamental emphasis must be on consciousness, its purposiveness and its signification, only secondarily on the "expression" of emotion in behavior and its physiological correlations. There can be no "unconscious purposes" and therefore no "unconscious emotions," although we may well find ourselves in a position of *refusing* to recognize our own emotions and their purposes. But the very idea of refusal leads us to suspect that it is itself motivated, as a way of "saving face." Accordingly, the phenomenological sketch that follows is of paramount importance in unmasking the various deceptions about ourselves that Sartre will lay bare four years later in *Being and Nothingness*.

Sartre's "Sketch" of a Theory of the Emotions (Chapter 3)

We have already anticipated that Sartre's theory will be based on the idea that an emotion has meaning ("signification") and purpose ("finality"). It is not merely a "state of consciousness" but an *intentional act*, something we *do*, a mode of behavior (*conduite*[10]) that has distinctive purposes and characteristics. The act is inseparable from its object ("the affective subject [*le sujet ému*] and the affective object [*l'objet émouvant*] are bound in an indissoluble synthesis" [30;52]). The emotion is "not absorbed in itself" but "returns to the object at every moment" (30;51). Nor is an emotion an isolated disturbance of consciousness; an emotion is "a certain way of apprehending the world" (30;52), a "transformation of the world" (33;58), a "mode of existence of consciousness" (49;91), an "existential [*existentielle*] structure of the world" (45;83). "There is," Sartre tell us, "a world of emotion" (44;80) (as there is a world of dreams and there are worlds of madness).

Although this is only a "sketch" (*esquisse*) or a theory that has yet to be filled in, the phenomenological structures of Sartre's theory are here spelled out with a clarity that is sometimes missing from *Being and Nothingness*. For example, a defining characteristic of the emotions in this theory is that they are "unreflective" (*irréflechive*), and Sartre here gives us (30ff;52ff.) the explication of that conception which is so painfully opaque in the introduction (sec. III) of *Being and Nothingness* (although he had also provided such an explication in his "Transcendence of the Ego" two years earlier). He defines "unreflective behavior" (*conduite irréflechie*) as behavior without consciousness of self, and insists that "in order to act it is not necessary to be conscious of the self as acting" (32;56–57). (In the next section, we shall raise objections against both this shift from "reflective consciousness" to "unreflective behavior," and this characterization of "unreflective.") The point is that emotion involves purposive and meaningful acts which are not themselves objects of consciousness. This is not to say that they are "unconscious," Sartre insists, but only that they are "nonthetic" (32;57) or "non-positional" (29;51), thus anticipating a long familiar phenomenological paradox that emerges in the opening pages of *Being and Nothingness* (esp. pp. 9–17).

An emotion is "significant"? But wherein lies its significance? Certainly not in pure "intentionality" (which Sartre, like Husserl, takes to be primarily a *cognitive* conception). Sartre follows Merleau-Ponty in avoiding the term (just as Merleau-Ponty replaces Husserl's term with his own conception of "motility"[11]). He rather borrows from the German Gestaltists the concept of the *Umwelt*—the world of our desires, our needs, and our acts (32;57). The objects of our emotions are not merely "things to be known," but objects of personal concern. Thus the meaning of an emotion must be referred to its *purpose*. And what is this purpose? It is not one we would readily acknowledge. The purpose of our emotions is to allow us to cope with a world that we find *difficult,* frustrating and, in Camus' quasi-paranoid terms, "indifferent" if not "hostile":

> When the paths traced out become too difficult, or when we see no path, we can no longer live in so urgent and difficult a world. All the ways are barred. However, we must act. So we try to change the world, that is, to live as if the connection between things and their potentialities were not ruled by deterministic processes, but by magic. (33;58–59)

We cannot change the world itself, but we can change "the direction of consciousness" (33;59), our "intentions and behavior" (34;60). It is thus that our emotions "transform the world." An act is impossible and so we seek "magical" compensation. Choosing a familiar example from Aesop, Sartre analyzes the emotional structure of the "sour grapes" attitude. He sees a bunch of grapes as "having to be picked," but he cannot reach them. By way of compensation, he then sees them as "too green." This is not a change in the chemistry of the grapes, but a change of attitude. So it is with all emotions. In order to cope with frustration, they change our view of a world we cannot change.

Such behavior is not "effective" (34;60), if what we mean by that term is "effective in changing the world." It surely is effective in another way, however, in allowing us to cope with our own impotence. But neither is it merely "symbolic"; we cannot believe our behavior to be a wholly satisfactory substitute. Every emotion has the purpose of allowing us to live with our own "unbearable" conflicts and tensions without explicitly recognizing them. Sartre calls such behavior "magical" because of this ineffective yet effective change, not in *the* world, but in *our* world. Every emotion "sets up a magical world by using the body as a means of incantation" (39;70). In a sense, we fail to *do* anything, that is, anything effective; but in another sense, we are very decidedly "doing something," namely, transforming the world to suit ourselves, through our "magical comedy of impotence" (*comédie magique d'impuissance*) (37;67).

Thus we can understand how it is that an emotion is not to be taken as a mere "disruption," as "a trivial episode of everyday life" (*un banal épisode de notre vie quotidienne*) (48;89). It is a "total alteration of the world" (47;87), even "an intuition of the absolute" (*l'absolu*) (44;81). It is not a disorder, but a response to an emergency. We must not allow ourselves to be stunned by this Hegelian terminology; what Sartre means is something quite ordinary: an emotion is not a distraction in our lives, like an itch on the calf or an arthritic shoulder. It is not an isolated interruption of consciousness but a "mode" of consciousness, an "existential structure of the world" (45;83), even a world unto itself (44;80). (This ambiguity seems not to have bothered Sartre.) It is a structure in which we *live,* often an obsessive structure, which extends forward into the indefinite future (44;81) and may well establish a durable if not permanent view of the world. In some emotions, notably spite and resentment, envy and hatred (the "poisonous emotions," perhaps the "deadly sins" as well), this premonition is evidently self-fulfilling. (On a happier note, however, we could argue that the same may be true of love.)

Borrowing from Heidegger, Sartre analyzes the difference between the "magical," ineffective behavior of our emotions and our effectively doing something in terms of "instrumentality" (compare *Sein und Zeit,* pt. I, div. 1, sec. 3: "die Weltlichkeit der Welt"). In action, the world appears as a "complex of instruments," in which "each instrument refers to other instruments and to the totality of instruments; there is no absolute action or radical change that one can immediately introduce into this world" (48;89). In other words, we do something *in order to* do something else (for example, we pull a trigger to shoot a rifle to propel a bullet to kill a dictator to open up the way for democracy so that we can . . .). In the "magical" world of emotion, however, this "world of instruments abruptly vanishes" (49;90) and we act as if to "transform" the world (in fact, however, transforming only our view of the world) in one "magical act." It is as if one wanted to produce a house not brick by brick and board by board, but by a simple magical incantation, a wish pronounced to a thankful genie or one of those wish-giving witches we find in fairy tales. The "magic" is this extraordinary and ineffectively effortless attempt to transform the world without effectively doing anything. But, Sartre reminds us, this is "not a game" (33;59) or a joke (34;61); quite to the contrary, our emotions are typified by their "seriousness" (41;74), by the fact that they require *belief* (40ff.;73), even to the point where we "cannot abandon it at will" (ibid.).

It is worth noting that Sartre distinguishes two forms of emotion, one in which "we constitute the magic of the world," the other in which "it is the world which abruptly reveals itself as being magical" (for example, a face appears at the window) (45;85). Thus he introduces a distinction *within* the emotions between active and passive. This distinction betrays a weakness in Sartre's theory which we shall presently examine.

What is an emotion, according to Sartre? It is a "magical transformation" of an "unbearable" world, a compensating and necessarily unreflective (and thus easily—but not necessarily—self-deceptive) way of changing our intentions and behavior toward the world when the world itself will not satisfy us.

A Critique of Sartre's Theory

Traditionalists will respond, of course, that Sartre has too glibly neglected the physiological correlates of emotion and attributed too much to consciousness and too little to simple behavior; that he has made sound too voluntary what is demonstrably involuntary;[12] and that he has obscured a fairly simple set of "primitive" reactions by his use of phenomenological, Hegelian and occultist terminology. Our complaint, however, is the very opposite. Although Sartre's "sketch" of a theory needs to be supplemented with more detailed arguments against traditional physiological, behaviorist, and "emotions-are-simply-feelings" theorists, the theory itself is a major step in the right direction—that is, away from the view of emotions as passive disruptions, invasions from a Freudian "id," or disorders in our physiology which are registered as "states of consciousness" that are no more our doing than are headaches, itches, and pains in the shoulder. From our point of view, the problem is that Sartre has not gone *far enough* in this early work, that he has retained *too much* of the traditional view of emotions as patterns of behavior and reaction, as irrational, disruptive, passive, and degrading. Using the radically voluntarist philosophy in *Being and Nothingness* as our basis (though our arguments can be duplicated in a broader framework), I want to argue that Sartre's early theory of emotion must be further radicalized, according to the very principles he himself has been so instrumental in formulating.

Our first objection is a familiar one, and it points up an error that is often repeated or uncritically accepted by a great many phenomenologists. It concerns the confusion of *reflection* with *self-consciousness*. These must be distinguished, although the reason they often are not is that the usual contrasts between prereflective chores or mechanical skills and the clearly reflective self-consciousness of philosophy gives us no reason to suspect *two* sets of distinctions. But we can be reflective without being self-conscious (for example, in thinking about a problem, even a problem concerning ourselves); and we can be self-conscious without being reflective (as in experiencing embarrassment or pride). Sartre long struggled with these two distinctions, between reflective and prereflective and self-conscious and unself-conscious, and developed a convoluted but demonstrably unsatisfactory conception of the *prereflective cogito* in response. In any theory of the emotions this is a serious error, for it does not follow that because the emotions are prereflective they are therefore without self-consciousness. In fact, I would argue that every emotion, as part of its essential structure, involves consciousness of oneself.[13] This is not to disagree with Sartre's contention that emotions are prereflective (although I would disagree that they are essentially so); it is rather to say that his oft-cited example of "my writing but not being aware of *my* writing" (see, for instance, 31;54; "Transcendence of the Ego," ch. 2) has confused many readers because he claims too much. It would be sufficient for him to say, simply, that such acts are unreflective. It does not follow that they are not self-conscious.

Our second objection also turns on a problematic distinction, though one that has long been central to most theories concerning the emotions. The distinction between an emotion and its *expression* has often been considered absolute, with the emotion as some mental occurrence or state, and its expression the behavioral manifestation of that occurrence. This concept of "expression" has been expanded by some theorists (by James, for example) to include various physiological manifestations as well. Thus the emotion becomes "the emotion felt," while expression includes "vigorous action" as well as ineffective gestures, physiological flushing and grimaces, and "faces" and facial "expressions."[14] Sartre, anxious to reject these Cartesian distinctions between "mind" and "body," "inner" and "outer" (even as he firmly retains a related dualism at the very core of his phenomenological ontology), denies these distinctions and characterizes the emotions in terms of behavior, in terms of "our body *lived*." Sartre's characterization also obscures our understanding of the emotions, however. He has criticized Janet for asserting that emotions are *just* behavior; "Behavior pure and simple," says Sartre, "*is not emotion*" (39;71). In pretense, for example, we feign emotional behavior without having the emotion; such behavior "is not sustained by anything," he tells us (40;72). The definitive element here is our belief and the "seriousness" of the emotion (40,41;73,74). Yet the emotion, according to Sartre, is a mode of behavior, an employment of the body as a way of changing one's relations with the world (34;61), as "a means of incantation" in "setting up a magical world" (39;70). Thus he moves immediately from his discussion of unreflective consciousness to a discussion of "unreflective behavior" (30;52). In his examples it is always behavior that attracts his emphasis although it is "change of intention" that is his thesis. (For example, he singles out "acting disgusted" in his description of the "sour grapes" phenomenon, when it is the "magical conferring of a quality" ["too green"] that is the point of the example.) He concludes, "an emotion is not a matter of pure demeanor [*comportement*]. It is the demeanor of a body which is in a certain state" (41;74).

It is noteworthy that Sartre sees that the need for a second "form of emotion," in which "the world reveals itself as magical," arises because in certain instances (a face appearing at the window) "there is no behavior [*conduite*] to take hold of" (45;82–83), and so "the emotion has no finality at all" (45;83). This second "form of emotion" threatens to betray Sartre's entire thesis, for it presupposes that emotion is a way of behaving, rather than a mode of *consciousness*. And, even without bringing into question the important Sartrean (and later Merleau-Pontean) doctrine of the "lived body," we must protest that this conception of emotions is too nearly a return to Janet and the behaviorists (a return evidently welcomed by Merleau-Ponty). Sartre, of course, insists that such behavior is purposive and "meaningful," that it requires consciousness in order to be so, but nevertheless, it is in terms of behavior that our emotions must be understood.

Sartre has not taken seriously enough the phenomenological viewpoint which he introduced with such fanfare but evidently with too little devotion. In particular, he has not taken seriously enough the Husserlian conception of "constitution" with its Kantian overtones, the concept of an "act of consciousness" that need not be viewed in terms of any resultant behavior. Our "setting up of a world that is magical" need have no such manifestations. Sartre is surely right that, through our emotions, we "constitute" and "transform the world." But the notion of "ineffective" which he adds to this idea of transformation only betrays his thinking that an emotion *ought* to be effective, that its behavior is ineffective and therefore "inferior." But not all emotions involve behavior, effective or otherwise. It is the very essence of certain emotions—for example, guilt, resentment, or envy—that they refrain from any expression no matter how "ineffective," even from facial expression, for they find it much more to their interest either to hide from view entirely or to show the world a bland and superficial smile, a pretense of hearty handclasps, and an "expression" of self-confidence. One can feel even love or fear and yet express nothing in word or stance, in gesture or grimace. We want to say that expression and emotion *must* be distinguished, even if it is true, as it probably is, that the phenomenological view must deny any such absolute distinction *when there is expression*. We want to say that it is not essential to an emotion that it be expressed. We do not need to act disgusted in our "sour grapes" attitude, nor do we need to break down in tears in our sadness or shout insults in our anger. In resentment, we may well mutter silent curses, but we need not thereby *behave* in any distinctive way. This point is crucial to our understanding of the emotions: they are transformations of our world through "acts" of consciousness, but they need not involve our behavior and they need not entail expression of any kind whatever.

Our most serious objection follows from the idea that emotions represent ineffective behavior or, to use the term Sartre borrowed directly from Janet, "inferior behavior." Despite his persuasive rejection of the traditional theories in which the emotions are viewed as disruptions, as irrational and degrading, Sartre has retained many of these attitudes in his own theory. He says, for example, that "in order to believe in magical behavior, it is necessary to be highly disturbed" (42;75). An emotion is "an irrational synthesis of spontaneity and passivity" (46;84), a "collapse of the superstructures laboriously built by reason" (ibid.). Emotions "obscure" consciousness (43;76)[15] and fail to see "the event in its proper proportions" (47;87). In language more reminiscent of Freud than of his own theories, Sartre tells us that "*captivity*" (43;79) is typical of the emotions, that they are "undergone" (ibid.), and that they are a "trap" in which we are "caught" (43;78). We "cannot abandon [an emotion] at will," and "we cannot stop it" (40f;73). When he tells us that there is "a world of emotion" (44;80), he adds "as of dreams of madness" (ibid.) as he had earlier compared emotions to "dreaming and hysteria" (43;78). And he tells us that "when, with all paths blocked, consciousness precipitates itself into the magical world of emotion, it does so by *degrading* itself (43;75–76, my italics), and again, "the origin of emotion is a spontaneous and lived degradation of consciousness in the face of the world" (42;77); and again, "consciousness is degraded" (45;83).

In short, Sartre has fallen prey to the very attitudes he seeks to refute. Despite his contributions to our thinking, he evidently believes that our emotions are "inferior," "irrational," and "degrading." They are meaningful, but their meanings are *de*-meaning; they have purposes, but their purposes serve to compensate for impotence. They may be our own conscious "acts," but they are nevertheless beyond our control, "traps" in which we are "caught," "a consciousness rendered passive" (46;84). What he had yet to realize is the revolutionary vigor of our emotions,[16] the fact that they are as important in sustaining our *effective* behavior as in rationalizing our failures and our impotence.

The Emotions: Ideology and Magic

If emotions are "transformations of the world," those transformations are not always "magical." For Sartre, the concept of magic serves to underscore the *ineffectiveness* of emotional behavior, the fact that our emotions merely change the direction of consciousness without really changing *the* world at all. Like Janet, and like the Gestaltist from whom he borrows his most extensive example, Sartre treats the emotions in general as isolated modes of frustration behavior, as ways of *coping* or "escaping" from a world that is "too difficult." But our emotions are much more than this. Using the doctrines of *Being and Nothingness* and the examples of his more recent works, we can offer a far more vital and existentially inspiring account of the emotions.

Sartre insists that our emotions are "meaningful." In his "Sketch," however, this meaningfulness is minimal, capturing the rudiments of Husserl's thesis of "intentionality" but surely giving us much less than the "meaningfulness" which Sartre (and so many other philosophers) have sought and demanded in other contexts (for example, in the sense of "the meaning of life" or the concept of "meaningful action"). The problem is that Sartre continues, in the fashion of those psychologists whom he castigates, to treat the emotions as "isolated" and the "world of emotions" as a world that is distinct from the "real" world of effective action and commitment. But it is our emotions which motivate our actions and sustain our commitments. The "fundamental project" that dominates so much of Sartre's writings is by its very nature an emotional project, one in which we heavily invest ourselves, even to the extent of reorganizing ("transforming") our entire world around its demands. Thus Nietzsche, following both Kant and Hegel, proclaimed that "nothing ever succeeds which exuberant spirits have not helped to produce."[17] It is through our emotions that we constitute not only the magical world of frustration and escape, but the living and often radical ideologies of action and commitment. In *Being and Nothingness,* Sartre himself tells us: "A Jew is not a Jew *first* in order to be subsequently ashamed or proud. It is his pride of being a Jew, his shame, or his indifference which will reveal to him his being-a-Jew; and this being-a-Jew is nothing ouside the free manner of adopting it" (p. 677). On the same page, Sartre speaks of "my own choice of inferiority or pride," which appear "only with the meaning that my freedom confers upon them." In other words, an emotion, such as pride, is not an isolated conscious transformation, restricted to those cases of reaction and frustration to which Sartre limits himself in his early "Sketch." The emotions are the constitutive structures of our world. It is through them that we give our lives meaning. Thus the emotions are, in Sartre's own philosophy, elevated from their traditional status as "degradations" and "disruptions" to those very "existential structures" of our existence with which Sartre has been concerned throughout his career.

In view of Sartre's more recent emphasis on "the power of circumstances"[18] and the demands of politics, it is necessary to go beyond the view of emotions as frustration reactions and to stress the idea that every emotion has as part of its essential structure an *ideology,* a set of demands regarding how the world *ought* to be changed. Some of these—for example, moral indignation and anger, love of mankind and Rousseauian "Sympathy"—may have straightforward political ramifications. Others—notably guilt, envy, and resentment—may betray precisely that apolitical and self-indulgent "sour-grapes" attitude that Sartre discusses in his "Sketch." But the point is to recognize *both* kinds of ideology, radical as well as ineffective and reactionary frustration, and to appreciate the power of the former as well as to reject the latter as "degradations of consciousness."

Regarding the *expression* of emotion, it is similarly an error to restrict our attenton to "emotional outbursts" and frustration and emergency reactions. Our emotions may also be solid and durable structures of our lives—dedicated love to a spouse, a friend, or a child; "wholehearted commitment" to a cause or a project; or passionate involvement in a movement, a faith, or a relationship. Such emotions are not even plausible candidates for "irrationality" and, though *some* emotions surely are irrational, it is obvious that *not all* are. Nor can such emotions—which may not only last for, but give meaning to, a lifetime—be plausibly classified as "disruptions" or as "degradations of consciousness." Quite to the contrary, they are precisely those constitutive structures with which we prove ourselves to be most human, of which we are rightly most proud, and in which we justifiably feel ourselves to be the most "uplifted" rather than the "degraded."

This conception of emotional ideologies merits a brief examination, though this is not the place to work it out in detail.[19] In anger and indignation, we demand rectification, vindication, the righting of a wrong, whether it be a minor personal affront or a social injustice embedded in the political structures of the contemporary world. In sadness and grief we desire the redress or return of a loss; in shame and remorse we seek to redeem ourselves; in love and hate we work toward the welfare or the ill-fare of our lover or our enemy. This conception of ideology allows us to clarify that most abused notion of emotional "expression." The expression of an emotion (the "natural expression," if you like) is precisely that action or set of actions which will most effectively and directly satisfy its ideological demands. This is, of course, not what is usually implied by that term. The "expression" of an emotion is often taken to be the least effective, the least voluntary, and the least "meaningful" of gestures and movements, the grimace of the face and the gnashing of teeth. Many psychologists (James, for example) have even included one's physiological responses as part of the "expression" of emotion. But focusing on these expressions (which are indeed typically frustration reactions and "outbursts") only underscores the fallacious view of the emotions as "disruptions" and as "ineffective," a view which is all too evident even in Sartre's "Sketch." Turning rather to the concept of the "fundamental project" of *Being and Nothingness* and the ideological language of his later writings, we can revise Sartre's thesis and take direct and effective expression as our paradigm: Mathieu's grabbing the machine gun or Hugo's finally resolute (if ambiguous) assassination of Hoerderer, Inez's double suicide or Sartre's own lifetime of "engaged" literature. The expression of an emotion is, first of all, *the realization of an ideological demand.* What is so often called the "expression" of emotion is only that by way of derivation, a suppressed or inhibited action that might otherwise be effective, a gesture instead of an act, a grimace instead of a battle, the gnashing of teeth in place of an articulated threat, the knotted fists held rigid at one's side rather than a well-thrown and much-deserved punch to the jaw.

But if expression is the realization of an ideological demand, we must now turn back to Sartre's conception of the "magic" of emotions in order to understand the nature of ineffective expression. Sartre is correct, of course, when he suggests that often such ineffective expressions are a means of coping or escaping. They are not so much the expression of the emotion as expressions of frustration, namely, the frustration of the emotion, as, for example, when I beat my cane against a tree in anger whose true target is a person (not the tree). Even if this answer is correct, however, it is not illuminating. Why this mode of frustration behavior rather than another? And why any behavior at all, given its evident ineffectiveness? The traditional idea that we thereby "vent"[20] our emotion is not only metaphorical—a return to the "hydraulic model" of the psyche as an ethereal pressure cooker. It is also false. Such ineffective modes of expression have precisely the opposite result; they do not satisfy the emotion but rather *intensify* it.

Consider yourself reviewing a minor offense—perhaps a slighting comment by a friend—and grimacing, gesturing, cursing, perhaps even stamping and kicking and literally "working yourself into a rage." It is often suggested that such behavior is "symbolic," that you are acting *as if* the curses you mutter would be "magically" effective (like the "incantations" Sartre mentions), as if your stamping and kicking register some mysterious pain to the shins of your malefactor (as if by voodoo). The "symbolic" analysis only underscores the question, "Why should we indulge in such useless practices, knowing all the while that they will be without effect and consequently will only increase our demands for satisfaction?"

The very idea that such so-called expressions intensify rather than satisfy our emotions provides us with our answer. It is an answer that has so long been overlooked precisely because of a general uncritical acceptance of the "hydraulic model" of the emotions, which posits a need to "get them out" and "discharge" them, a need that seems evident even in the etymology of the word "ex-press": to "force out." But though we demand satisfaction of our emotions, we demand something more as well. The emotions, we have already argued, sustain the "fundamental projects" of our lives, "give our lives meaning" and provide the constitutive structures within which we live. If this is so, we can see that we have good reason for *not* satisfying them—in order to keep them alive and, in a great many cases, to intentionally intensify them and their demands. Thus some lovers take delight in histrionic responses to small infidelities, "expressions" of love in a sense but, more literally, *im*pressions which intensify (and surely do not "relieve") that same emotion. Dostoevsky's man of spite acts—or does not act— merely in order to intensify the bitterness and resentment through which he constitutes his dubious conception of "freedom."[21] And Sartre himself, to take our most important example, has engaged his life in the pursuit of an ever-intensified sense of injustice and indignation, sometimes even at the cost of excruciating self-imposed guilt and despair, simply, in his own words, "to move history forward by recommending it, as well as by prefiguring within himself new beginnings yet to come."[22] If there is "magic" in the emotions, surely that magic is here, in these *chosen* ideologies through which we dramatize our lives in struggle against an unsatisfactory if not indifferent world, *against* the "power of circumstances," making that world, if not better, at least less "indifferent" through these very choices. And these choices are—our emotions.

Thus we must insist, taking our cues from Sartre's "Sketch" but our substance from his later works, that our emotions are nothing other than our own *choices,* views of our world for which we alone are responsible. The development of this Sartrean thesis might be a fitting tribute to the philosopher whom I would not hesitate to call the Socrates of our century.

NOTES

1. See, for example, his early "Project for a Scientific Psychology" in James Strachey, ed., *The Standard Edition of the Complete Psychological Works of Sigmund Freud,* vol. 3 (London: Hogarth, 1953—).

2. According to Simone de Beauvoir, *Coming of Age* (New York: Putnam, 1973), p. 253, and M. Contat and M. Rybalka, *The Writings of Jean-Paul Sartre,* an extensive bibliography translated from the French by Richard C. McCleary (Evanston, Ill.: Northwestern University Press, 1974), p. 65.

3. *Recherches Philosophiques,* vol. 6 (1936–37): 85–123. Translated by Forrest Williams and Robert Kirkpatrick as *The Transcendence of the Ego* (New York: Noonday, 1957).

4. See also Contat and Rybalka, op. cit., p. 83.

5. *St. Genet, comédien et martyr* (Paris: Gallimard, 1952); trans. by B. Frechtman as *St. Genet, Actor and Martyr* (New York: Braziller, 1963).

6. *L'Idiot de la famille* (Paris: Gallimard, 1972).

7. See, e.g., his formulation of the question of "Bad Faith" (*B&N,* 85, 87, 96).

8. W. James, "What Is an Emotion?" *Mind* (London), 1884.

9. (New York: Barnes & Noble, 1949), esp. ch. 6.

10. Sartre uses this term except where I have otherwise noted.

11. In *Phénoménologie de la perception* (Paris: Gallimard, 1945).

12. Thus Paul Ricoeur, to take but one prominent example, retains the traditional view of the emotions, placing them on the "involuntary" side in his most important work, *Le Volontaire et l'involontaire* (Paris: Aubier, 1950); see *Freedom and Nature,* vol. I, trans. by e. Kohak, (Evanston, Ill.: Northwestern University Press, 1966).

13. See my *The Myth of the Passions* (New York: Doubleday, 1976), esp. pt. II.

14. In this light, it is worth rereading Sartre's early essay "Faces," in Maurice Natanson, ed., *Essays in Phenomenology* (The Hague: Nijhoff, 1966). See also D. Rapaport's *Emotions and Memory* (New York: International University Press, 1971).

15. Leibniz once argued that emotions were "confused intelligence."

16. Gilles Deleuze and Felix Guattari have argued this position in their *Capitalisme et schizophrene: l'anti-oedipe* (Paris: Editions de Minnit, 1972).

17. *Twilight of the Idols,* in Walter Kaufmann, *The Portable Nietzsche* (New York: Viking, 1954).

18. See *Between Existentialism and Marxism,* trans. by John Mathews (New York: Pantheon, 1975).

19. I have done so in op. cit. above.

20. See, e.g., Wittgenstein's discussion of Fraser's *The Golden Bough* in Synthese (1975).

21. *Notes from Underground,* trans. by R. Matlaw (New York: Dutton, 1960).

22. *Between Existentialism and Marxism.*

17

Jean-Paul Sartre, 1905–1980

April 15, 1980. Jean-Paul Sartre died today. Or was it yesterday? It is hard to tell from the initial press release. But it doesn't really matter; the greatest philosopher of our time is dead.

"I do not believe it," he wrote twenty years ago in *France Observateur,* upon hearing of the sudden death of his onetime friend, Albert Camus. Now it is our turn not to believe, despite the fact that Sartre's death followed a decade of blindness and ill health. I never met him and yet, it is as if I knew him, as if he were always there reminding us of our responsibilities, jabbing us with his teasing humor, impressing us with our own importance, puncturing our easy pretentions—the true Socratic gadfly.

"Death haunts me at the heart of my projects," he wrote in the early 1940s; and yet, he added, "it is always beyond me." An indeed, it was. Sartre criticized his former mentor, Martin Heidegger, for his gloomy emphasis on the importance of death for life; for Sartre, the emphasis was wholly on life, on "existence," and his writings have been badly characterized, by those who have not enjoyed them, as themselves "gloomy" and ridden with anxiety and loneliness. But Sartre was nothing if not playful—even about death. *No Exit (Huis-clos)* is a play set in hell, a black comedy with the dead as its characters; along with the seriousness, Sartre was always the comic. He considered himself the great optimist, declaring one day in the mid-1960s that he had never been unhappy in his life.

Sartre captured the term "existentialism" so thoroughly that others who might have applied it to themselves, indeed, who had influenced him in his use of it—such as Camus and Heidegger—felt forced to reject it in order to avoid being lost in his shadow. And if existentialism is one of the few philosophies to survive its fashionable phase in Paris, that too has been due to the genius and the persistence of Sartre, who, by speaking only to a select group of initiates and addressing topics that escaped the masses, never allowed himself to become a cult figure. He was always accessible; he saw himself as the spokesman for the workers of the world, who no doubt rarely read him. Like Socrates, who used his wit and his convictions to keep difficult issues alive and put an end to easy complacency, Sartre was a philosopher of the streets. His political opinions were often mistaken, sometimes downright foolish. But he always exemplified his own philosophy: that one must be "engaged" and committed, and avoid scrupulously a posture of "waiting to see what will happen." Perhaps, despite his brilliance with words, he never fully understood the media and the dynamics of public opinion; for example, when he did not condemn some young German terrorists outright but admitted that he at least understood their frustration, it was widely assumed that he supported them. He always insisted on calling himself a Marxist—a label which in America at least, is too easily interpreted in exactly the wrong manner—as if its bearer rejected individual freedom, had nothing but praise for Soviet society, and accepted the totalitarian features of Russian Communism.

But the watchwords of Sartre's philosophy, from the 1930s to the present, have always been *freedom* and *responsibility*. The key to Sartre's thought is that every individual must choose and act for himself or herself. He insisted that we are always responsible for what we do, no matter what the ready excuses or the circumstances. He always rejected what he called "vulgar" Marxism, which denied individual choice and responsibility and hence a place at the very center of history, and which sought to replace individual responsibility with abstract forces over which society has no control. And if this philosophy seems like a "burden" or a "predicament," as so many authors have concluded, or as "gloomy" and "full of despair," as the popular press likes to declare, it is only so to those who prefer to excuse themselves—deceive themselves, Sartre would say—into thinking that they as individuals do not count, that they are mere pawns of the universe. But there is nothing necessarily "gloomy" about self-acceptance and the sense of taking one's life in one's own hands.

Sartre wanted nothing less than to change humanity through his writings. From his German mentors—Hegel, Marx and Heidegger—he learned his global perspective with all of its complexities and traumas. But at his philosophical heart he was totally French, and his ultimate model was René Descartes, that paradigm of clarity and reason, that champion of freedom—in particular, freedom of mind. It is mind that distinguishes being human from everything else; and we can imagine, we can dream, we can scheme—virtually anything. And it is in this confrontation between our imaginative consciousness and the obstinate resistance of the world that Sartre's existentialism was born. To change the world, to try to, to reject those who say "we can't," to encourage those who think that we can—that was Jean-Paul Sartre's philosophy.

He wrote of Camus: "He represented in this century, and against history, the present heir of that long line of moralists whose works perhaps constitute what is most original in French letters." We can now say that of Sartre too.

"A man is nothing else but the sum of his actions," he wrote in 1947, "he is nothing but what his life is." But he was wrong about that; Sartre was always more than the sum of his actions, even more than his life. For us, he remains what it means to be a philsopher, and, perhaps, what it means to be human.

The call came suddenly, as if in a dream. "Monsieur Sartre will see you now." Although I could not determine the direction of the voice, the enormity of my excitement overshadowed my confusion. Shortly, a very distinguished if hungry-looking gentleman in formal dress appeared and led me down a seemingly endless corridor to an anonymous white door. Without a smile or a gesture, he opened that door as if to show me, rather than introduce me to, a small and fragile man smoking a heavy pipe and wearing thick glasses, whom I immediately recognized to be Sartre. His age was indeterminable, and, in any case, the person before me seemed more a parody of Sartre than a flesh-and-blood human being—rather a projection of what I thought of him and what he thought of himself. His eyesight, in death, had evidently been partially restored, for while he was seated at a small café table, a half-finished carafe of wine before him, he had apparently been reading various newspapers from around the world, in which his death had just been reported. A large mirror behind him dominated the room. A clock ticked loudly on the mantle, and the unexpected but distinct sound of crickets was discernible—although there were no windows in the room. "Here he *is*," announced the valet, with a note of dry humor. Sartre obviously caught the irony, and looked at the man askance with his good eye. "Yes, I *am*" he responded cooly, "at least until you and the others have decided what to do with me." I wasn't sure whether the latter part of this remark had been addressed to the valet or some more authoritative voice, or—the thought occurred to me—to me. But, in any case, the valet bowed slightly and, with a bit of a smirk—barely detectable—backed out the door.

SARTRE: You are surprised they allowed you to see me, I suspect.

RCS: I certainly am, especially now that you're . . . gone.

SARTRE: Dead, you mean. But death is nothing, and so it makes no difference.

RCS: But according to your own philosophy, sir, it would seem to make *all* the difference.

SARTRE: Yes, that's why it makes no difference at all. I am—or was—my life, and nothing else. Jean-Paul Sartre is now, as I once wrote about Proust, nothing more than his works.

RCS: But surely there is something more than that: your plans and ambitions, the people you influenced, the enormous impact you have had on all thinking people in the twentieth century—even those who have never really read you. . . .

SARTRE: My plans and ambitions are no more; only the works themselves live. And they are for the most part unread—or misunderstood. Most of the people whom I influenced would have been so influenced without me, and my "impact," as you call it, is a creation of the press. I was merely an excuse, except to myself and a circle of friends. I do not believe in being admired; I do not want to be an institution.

RCS: Is that why you turned down the Nobel Prize for literature in 1964?

SARTRE: Yes.

RCS: But you are an institution, you know that, don't you?

SARTRE: I do not care.

RCS: But how do you react to these obituaries? For example, this one, which calls you "existentialist giant," or this one, "a modern Don Quixote"?

SARTRE: But that is not *I*; that is a fabrication which for the rest of history will bear the name "Jean-Paul Sartre, 1905–1980." The stories will change, and "Jean-Paul Sartre, 1905–1980" will change along with them. I have never believed in obituaries, although I've written some. No one can confer meaning on another, at least not without reducing him or her to a mere thing, an object with such and such characteristics, which in the case of myself is utterly irrelevant, at least to me.

RCS: Perhaps I can go back and set the record straight.

SARTRE: No, I am nothing, and there is nothing to tell.

RCS: But you want them to get it right, don't you, sir?

SARTRE: It makes no difference.

RCS: I can go back with my notes of our conversation.

SARTRE: You will see that no one will believe you.

RCS: I can describe you to them.

SARTRE: Go ahead, describe me to me.

RCS: Well, you're . . . I guess I can't. You seem to change as I look at you.

SARTRE: Indeed, you should see what happens when I look at myself, in the mirror over there, for example.

RCS: I thought . . . well, in your play, *No Exit* . . . you make a great point of insisting that there are no mirrors in hell, no way of seeing ourselves, and therefore we are at the mercy of others and their opinions. "Hell is other people," you wrote in *No Exit,* and seemed to prove it.

SARTRE: Ha, ha, yes. That was one of the many things I believed back then. Incredible, isn't it, that I actually believed that?

RCS: That there were no mirrors in hell, you mean?

SARTRE: No, no. Besides, we're not exactly in hell here, you know. I mean the idea that self-reflection is the touchstone of self-recognition, and other people are obstacles—distorting mirrors, as it were.

RCS: In *No Exit,* I remember that the young coquette Estelle, who is wholly absorbed in her looks, is desperate for a mirror, and even wonders whether she exists without one.

SARTRE: Yes, and in desperation she pleads with the others to look at her. I have changed my mind about that; "they" gave me the mirror in this place out of spite, no doubt. They've read everything, you know, and carefully—as if to impress on me daily that my reflection, whether in the mirror or in my mind, is of no significance at all. And that which is of significance, perhaps all that is of any importance, is the reality of other people.

RCS: So hell is not other people?

SARTRE: No, hell is not other people.

RCS: Well then, why did they let me see you here in hell?

SARTRE: I told you, we are not in hell . . . because you don't matter at all. My friends, of course, they count for everything. And a handful of readers in Paris, many of whom I've lost in one way or another. If only I could be with them now. But you . . . you're just a phantom yourself, one of those hundreds of people who write books and articles about me and my work and have the senseless idea that you are somehow connected to me. But you're not, and so you make no difference at all. Thus, they have let you see me in order to tease me. For you, this is an interview with a celebrity, a unique opportunity; for me, it is absurd. Tedious too, if there weren't all the time in the world to kill.

RCS: You mean, *out* of the world. But whom would you like to see?

SARTRE: Simone,[1] of course. François Jeanson. And, if it were possible, my one-time friends, Maurice Merleau-Ponty, Paul Nizan,[2] and Albert Camus. [*looks upward, dreamily*] We had such good times together, in the old days. [*getting angry with himself*] and inevitably split apart because of our differences. What a waste! The friendships were always what counted.

RCS: Camus?

SARTRE: He was, perhaps, my last good friend.

RCS: Why did you break?

SARTRE: I? No, it was he. He was always mad at me for something, something I said, something I wrote, something I didn't write . . . a good fellow, however.

RCS: And Simone de Beauvoir?

SARTRE: Simone? She has been the other half of my life, of course, much more than a friend; my essence, perhaps.

RCS: You seem to have changed your mind quite considerably from the forties, from the "Hell is other people" philosophy of *No Exit* and the "Relations with others is essentially CONFLICT" of *Being and Nothingness.*

SARTRE: Yes, I change, or rather *changed,* my mind quite often. Each time I was quite certain I was correct; but later, I would see that I was only one-half or one-quarter right. Incredible, isn't it? But mainly, amusing. [*muses to himself, chuckling*]

RCS: I'm surprised to find you so jolly. That is certainly not the person I expected to find here.

SARTRE: You mean, because I'm here? Oh, you mean because my philosophy is so full of desperation and hopelessness? [*laughs*] Look at this. [*picks up a newspaper and reads, in passable English:*] " . . . his view of the human condition as angst-ridden and despairing." Or this one, " . . . man as a responsible but lonely being, burdened with the terrifying freedom of choice." Ha, ha, ha.

RCS: Not so?

SARTRE: I have never been in despair, and I have never imagined despair as an emotion that could ever belong to me. Even here, [*looks around the room, fixes his glare at his reflection in the mirror, sticks out his tongue and giggles.*]

RCS: But your philosophy—?

SARTRE: I know. In the 1940s, and for obvious reasons, despair was all the fashion in Paris. We all paid homage to it in our writings: Camus, obviously, with his concept of the absurd; Malraux; [*pauses*] all of us.

RCS: So what do you think "the human condition" really is, now that you've been through it?

SARTRE: "Been through it?" Oh, goodness, my boy, no one ever "goes through it." We each have our taste of it, and that's enough. But this "human condition"—where did you hear about that?

RCS: From you, I thought.

SARTRE: [*chuckling, lighting his pipe*] Yes, yes, I suppose I did believe in something like that. Funny how it changes every time my philosophy changes. And every time the world changes. No, the human condition—the "essence of man," you might call it—is another fabrication, like your idea of me as "Jean-Paul Sartre, 1905–1980." We create it as we go, all of us. But there's no such thing. And if there is a *"condition humaine"* it certainly would not be anxiety.

RCS: What might it be?

SARTRE: History, time, the fact that we are thrown into situations not of our choosing, that we must make our own condition, making history on the way.

RCS: One of your followers who is popular in America, Rollo May, has called our time "the Age of Anxiety." How do you feel about that? Could your philosophy have been true for its time?

SARTRE: "True for its time"? What does that mean? In 1940, I wrote that "Whatever the circumstances, and whatever the site, a man is always free to choose . . ." When I read this, I say to myself, "That's incredible! I actually believed that!" But it wasn't any more true then than it is now. And that's the case with "the Age of Anxiety" as well.

RCS: So you've changed your view of freedom too?

SARTRE: Changed it? Well [*momentarily serious*], I don't know that I have. I've come to grips with it. Times have changed. The "either-or" choices we faced during the war have been replaced by much more real and complex choices about how to create a society worth living in for everyone. But I would say freedom is still the central concern of my entire philosophy, the freedom one has. The responsibility for what one is, even if there has been little that one could have done about it. The responsibility for what one makes of what is made of one, perhaps. But, no, I haven't changed my mind about freedom and responsibility.

RCS: "Man makes himself."

SARTRE: I still believe that simpleminded little slogan.

RCS: "Man makes himself"; but you just said that sometimes one can't help what is made of oneself.

SARTRE: No, I said one is still responsible for what one makes of what is made of oneself. There is always that glimmer of freedom, the possibility that one will refuse to give back that which his conditioning has made of him and expects him to return, the possibility of saying "no!" even when all else is lost.

RCS: Freedom is just another word for nothing to lose?

SARTRE: Freedom is everything to lose. And now I've lost it.

RCS: But you seem free enough here. They leave you alone. They give you newspapers . . .

SARTRE: But nothing, you notice, with which to write.

RCS: I'd be delighted to leave you my pen and some paper.

SARTRE: It wouldn't do any good. Look. [*snatches RCS's pad and pen, which RCS is already extending to him. He writes, but the lines disappear.*]

RCS: But you're free to think, at least.

SARTRE: Free to think? What is that worth? By itself, I mean. I have always considered thinking to be an adjunct of writing; in fact, I can't really think unless I am writing. The purpose of writing is to get your cause across to other people, to cajole them, to convince them, at least to arouse them. What would Socrates have done if he could only have written notes to himself, instead of arguing in the public square?

RCS: I don't know.

SARTRE: Of course you don't! He couldn't have done anything. He wouldn't have been Socrates. Writing is my way of reaching people, of engaging the world. Thinking is merely the prelude to action. And here there's no action. No people. No conflicts. No causes.

RCS: You could fight with me. Convince me of something.

SARTRE: [*laughs*] No, you don't count. They thought of that.

RCS: Thanks a lot.

SARTRE: Don't be offended. You think you know me, but I'm just the bug you study in your library to find something to write about. And why? What are you trying to change? What is the *point* of your writing?

RCS: Uh well, I don't know. Well, to try to get people to understand your writings.

SARTRE: As I said, you don't count.

RCS: [*speechless*]

SARTRE: But I don't want to discourage you. This is an original project you have here, and the first interview I've had since I died. So go ahead, ask me anything you want.

RCS: Anything?

SARTRE: It doesn't matter.

RCS: Why are you here?

SARTRE: What do you mean? Oh, for example, what was my crime? You don't seem to understand the situation here. It's not heaven if you're good and hell if you're bad, with someplace in between until "they" decide. No. This is nothing more than the echo of life, turned into a joke, that is, if you have a sense of humor. If you don't, it's torture. But it's not a question of good or bad, reward and punishment. I've committed no crime. I've no regrets . . .

RCS: *No* regrets?

SARTRE: No regrets. I'm content with everything—the way in which I lived my life, that is. What would be the point in feeling any other way?

RCS: What is that clock doing over there? I thought there could be no time here.

SARTRE: Perhaps you would be pleased with a clock with no hands?

RCS: Er, yes, it did occur to me.

SARTRE: My life hasn't been that much of a cliché, has it?

RCS: No, but . . . that clock seems to be keeping perfect time.

SARTRE: Indeed it is, or maybe it is. Anyway, I wouldn't know how to check. But that isn't the point. The clock is there for me to make of it what I will. I can watch the time passing, think of the infinity of moments yet to come, or contemplate what must be happening among the living, or ignore it as one of the pointless peculiarities of this most unpeculiar room. Time doesn't mean anything, in itself.

RCS: It's what we make of it.

SARTRE: And as there's nothing for me to do, there's nothing to make of it.

RCS: I guess that makes sense.

SARTRE: Certainly it does.

RCS: O.K. What are the crickets in the background? I came here through some labyrinthine hallway, and yet, the feeling I have in here is that we're out in the countryside somewhere.

SARTRE: Yes, yes. [*laughs a little*] I have always despised the country. The banality of nature. It is the intercourse of men and women that I love, the life in the city. So, of course, they gave me crickets.

RCS: Pretty diabolical!

SARTRE: Not at all. I wouldn't have done it differently myself.

RCS: Can I ask you about your philosophy?

SARTRE: You mean, the philosophy of "Jean-Paul Sartre, 1905–1980"?

RCS: Yes, that's the fellow.

SARTRE: Well, I'm not sure I know much more about it than many other people who would have been much easier to interview, but go ahead.

RCS: Do you still consider *Being and Nothingness* to be your most important book?

SARTRE: What *I* consider is irrelevant. Those who like to make me an "existentialist" will certainly think so.

RCS: Aren't you an existentialist?

SARTRE: I? I'm nothing.

RCS: [*a little exasperated*] I mean Jean-Paul Sartre (1905–1980).

SARTRE: I'm sure he has no objection to that.

RCS: [*frustrated silence*]

SARTRE: During the later years of my life, I saw mainly the flaws in that book, and so I moved on, sometimes as if the book did not exist. If you had asked me that question in 1960, I would have said my *Critique of Dialectical Reason,* which cost me my health, among other things. But if you had asked me at almost any other time, I would have said that my most important work was the one I was working on, or had just completed. I can give you an answer, however: my novel *Nausea,* which I wrote in 1938. I still think it is the best thing I ever wrote. A couple of plays, *No Exit* and perhaps *The Devil and the Good Lord.* My two large philosophical works, but especially the *Critique of Dialectical Reason.* I would be happy to be remembered for those. That would be enough.

RCS: Why did you never follow up *Being and Nothingness?*

SARTRE: Ah, but I did. See, that is why these retrospective "interpretations" of my work will never give you even Jean-Paul Sartre (1905–1980); I wrote a long treatise that I never published, which means that even the experts don't know all my work. I'm certain you will see it soon. No doubt someone has unearthed my manuscript—since I never threw things away—and will publish it as a new wealth of insights into "what JPS *really* meant."

RCS: There's a second volume of the *Critique* too, isn't there?

SARTRE: Yes, that was about to see the light.

RCS: Will these two new works change what we think of your philosophy?

SARTRE: That depends on what you think my philosophy is.

RCS: Well, I know you won't like this, but . . .

SARTRE: Oh, I like just about everything these days.

RCS: Let me go through your writings and your career with you. O.K.?

SARTRE: "O.K."

RCS: Your childhood. You have said that you were without friends, but you thought yourself a genius. Your great uncle was Albert Schweitzer, who won the Nobel Peace Prize in 1952. You were raised without a father and consequently, or so you said, "without a superego." You were raised by women, and so have always preferred their company.

SARTRE: Yes, but you left out the most important element in the childhood of Jean-Paul Sartre (1905–1980): *words.*

RCS: Oh yes, *The Words.*[3]

SARTRE: I never liked my body; in fact, I have always been ugly as a toad. I distrusted authority, but I generally obeyed. I was cynical about religion, even with a great Christian in my family, and I was extremely naïve about, and later shocked at my own unwitting complicity in, politics. So I came to trust one thing, the quintessence of things—words. Words have always been my *métier,* my way of meeting people, relating to them, my way of defining myself, my way of taking hold of things, my hold on the world.

RCS: But as a student, as a philosopher, you became a phenomenologist, that is, one of those philosophers who sought to have direct contact with "the things themselves" as Husserl put it.[4]

SARTRE: Yes, I was initially a "phenomenologist," if you like. *Being and Nothingness* is certainly a very phenomenological book.

RCS: It is subtitled "An Essay in Phenomenological Ontology."

SARTRE: But that already shows you that it was not just a piece of phenomenology, for Husserl always tried to insist that phenomenology is not ontology.

RCS: Just a moment, Monsieur Sartre. What is phenomenology? What is ontology?

SARTRE: It is quite simple, really: Husserl defined phenomenology as the study of the essential structures of consciousness. Ontology is the study of beings, a theory about the basic things in the world that make up "reality." Now what I did—and I was guided by one of Husserl's own pupils, Martin Heidegger— was to say that one could not do phenomenology without doing ontology, too. It is impossible to treat consciousnsess as if it were some free-floating realm detachable from the world. To understand the one meant to understand the other. I have always been a realist, but without sacrificing consciousness to the reality of mere things.

RCS: You mean, without denying that consciousness is real?

SARTRE: Yes—consciousness confronting the brute existence of the world—that was my philosophy then.

RCS: I have always admired one passage of your work, perhaps more than any other. It is where you apply this so-called phenomenological method in your novel *Nausea.* I see you have all your books here; could I ask you to read it to me?

SARTRE: "They" put the books here. But certainly, I have no objection to entertaining you. I take it that you mean the encounter with the chestnut tree. [*pulls the book off the shelf, separates a couple of pages and reads*]

I was in the park just now. The roots of the chestnut tree were sunk in the ground just under my bench. I couldn't remember it was a root any more. The words had vanished and with them the significance of things, their methods of use, and the feeble points of reference which men have traced on alone in front of this black, knotty mass entirely beastly, which frightened me. Then I had this vision.

It left me breathless. Never, until these last few days, had I understood the meaning of "existence." . . . It is there, around us, in us, it *is* us, you can't say two words without mentioning it, but you can never touch it. . . . Even when I looked at things, I was miles from dreaming that they existed: they looked like scenery to me. I picked them up in my hands, they served me as tools, I foresaw their resistance. But that all happened on the surface. If anyone had asked me what existence was, I would have answered in good faith, that it was nothing, simply an empty form which was added to external things without changing anything in their nature. And then, all of a sudden, there it was, clear as day: existence had suddenly unveiled itself. It had lost the harmless look of an abstract category: it was the very paste of things, this root was kneaded into existence . . . this hard and compact skin of a sea lion, . . . this oily, callous, headstrong look. This root, with its colour, shape, its congealed movement, was . . . below all explanation. . . . To exist is simply to be there. . . .

RCS: Terrifying. Now what does that mean?

SARTRE: What do you think it means?

RCS: That consciousness confronts existence and is repulsed by it; that the abstract categories of the mind are not—as many philosophers seem to think—the basis of reality.

SARTRE: Not bad. Yes, the central theme of that whole part of my career—which I think you might call quite rightly the phenomenological phase rather than the existentialist phase—was characterized by a basic duality: consciousness on the one side, brute existence on the other. Both are real, and neither is reducible to the other.

RCS: Sounds very Cartesian.

SARTRE: But of course. Every French boy learns Descartes' basic philosophy, with its fundamental split between mind and body and the centrality of the "I," while still in grade school. I was no different, and it always remained my ontological model.

RCS: Despite your reading of Heidegger and Kant and other German philosophers?

SARTRE: Yes.

RCS: And this then provides the theme for *Being and Nothingness*?

SARTRE: Yes, but you're jumping ahead of the story. In 1936, before I wrote *Nausea* and almost five years before *Being and Nothingness,* I published an essay called "The Transcendence of the Ego." It was a basic exercise in phenomenological description, and my main point was to show that an adequate description of consciousness did not disclose, as both Descartes and Husserl thought it would, an "ego," a "self," an "I."

RCS: I think you said, "My 'I' is out there in the world, like the 'I's of other people."

SARTRE: Yes, the point being that the self is not something experienced as such, but only, as I argued later, something that we create through our actions. But this changes the nature of that dualism between consciousness and brute physical existence. Consciousness is not "I," it is not *self*-consciousness, or much less, as Descartes thought, something that can be translated "I think, therefore I am." Consciousness is much more than thinking, but much less than an "I." In fact, consciousness is empty; it has no contents; it is only that activity, that tendency—like a wind blowing from nowhere—toward everything in the world.

RCS: I'm not sure I see the distinction. Can you give me an example of consciousness without an "I" in it?

SARTRE: Certainly. When you are running after a streetcar, you are not conscious of the thought, "Here I am, running after this streetcar." Or at least, it would be very odd if you were. What you are conscious of is the phenomenon of "the-streetcar-to-be-overtaken." The "I" does not appear until later; for example, if you become embarrassed.

RCS: So "the transcendence of the ego" means that the self is not *in* consciousness but rather a potential object of experience, reflected back at us in the world?

SARTRE: Yes. Consciousness never catches itself in the act, so to speak; it is always ahead of itself and always escapes our scrutiny. I try to catch myself thinking *now*—but the "now" is already gone, and I'm only trying to remember. The passage you asked me to read in *Nausea* is the other side of that duality; whereas consciousness is essentially ephemeral, empty; physical existence, on the other hand, is full, a *"plenum,"* a brute presence which confronts us whether we like it or not.

RCS: And the self?

SARTRE: It stands uncomfortably in the middle, not quite existing, but not nothing, either.

RCS: Thus your title, *Being and Nothingness—L'Etre et le néant.*

SARTRE: Yes, the *"le néant"* (nothingness) is consciousness, and I take that quite literally. Consciousness is not a possible object of consciousness and so it is nothing. But also, it is through consciousness that negation comes into the world; it is only according to our demands and in line with our expectations that something is absent, or changed, or destroyed. Otherwise, the world just exists, one way or another. Thus, Descartes could doubt everything, even the existence of the world; and a terrorist can plan the destruction of everything. Being simply *is*: it is *what* it is; it is *as* it is; it just *is*. But the ideas of destruction and reconstruction, seeing the world as it is not, as it could be otherwise—those are the products of consciousness. And the being through whom nothingness comes into the world must itself be nothing.

RCS: But the fact that it is nothing also means that it has no "essence," right? Because it is not "something," it can't be something in particular.

SARTRE: Right! Consciousness itself cannot be fat or stupid or shy or friendly or cowardly or old. But you're jumping ahead of the game. Let's establish the basic ontology first.

RCS: All right.

SARTRE: Now I distinguish two kinds of being—although this may sound paradoxical at first: being-*in-itself* (en-soi), the brute existence of things, and being-*for-itself* (pour-soi), the existence of consciousness. This is, as you have commented, quite thoroughly Cartesian. I define being-in-itself simply as being *as* it is, *what* it is, simply *being*—like the chestnut root in the park. But being-for-itself I define in terms of negation, as nothing—or to use one of my favorite paradoxes, it is what it is not, and it is not whatever it is. Being-for-itself, unlike beings-in-themselves, is not yet anything at all. Being-for-itself has the power of *transcendence*.

RCS: You used the same word a moment ago to describe the fact that the self was outside of consciousness. Now I'm confused.

SARTRE: What I mean by transcendence is the ability to imagine alternative possibilities, to plan ahead, to formulate projects and ambitions, to create oneself. Thus, the "transcendence" of the self. It is a project, a possibility, rather than a thing to be found already in consciousness. And we create our selves not by looking inward but by acting, by changing the world.

RCS: But mere things can change the world, too. A tornado, for example. Does the tornado thereby create a self?

SARTRE: No. A tornado moves things around, breaks them apart, of course, but it is only through human consciousness that one arrangement rather than another *means* anything.

RCS: So transcendence is essentially a property of consciousness, because things have meaning only to a being that is conscious?

SARTRE: Yes—this is why I say, again following Heidegger, that things, beings-in-themselves, don't have transcendence, don't have what Heidegger calls "possibilities." They can't project themselves into the future. They can't have conscious *projects.*

RCS: So consciousness is quite essential to your view of human existence?

SARTRE: Of course.

RCS: And this is the same as saying that consciousness is simply freedom?

SARTRE: Yes and no. That is the formulation that is provided by Kant, for instance, and in a simpler version by Descartes. I too want to say that consciousness is essentially freedom; this is why I am so adamant in insisting that it is nothing, because that means that it cannot be anything determinate, or anything determined by anything else. But I do not want to say, as Descartes and Kant seem to have believed, that there is a realm of human consciousness that is distinct from nature, immune from the causal laws of nature, and a kingdom unto itself.

RCS: You say, "consciousness *is* freedom"; why don't you just say "consciousness is free" or "man is free"?

SARTRE: It is a device that I borrowed from Kant; it is a way of *protecting* freedom. If you say simply "consciousness has freedom, as one of its properties," then it is possible to suggest other properties that are more important, or to find excuses why, in some particular case, one wasn't really free—because of an emotion, or an illness, or some particularly pressing set of circumstances. But by insisting that consciousness itself *is* freedom—an awkward way of putting it, I admit—these excuses are blocked. There are no conditions for freedom, and no ways of cancelling it—except, of course, obliterating consciousness itself.

RCS: But how can you have both—the view that consciousness is essentially freedom, and the view that consciousness is not apart from the determinacy of nature in general? Do you believe in the general causal determinism of nature, that every event has its sufficient natural causes?

SARTRE: Of course I do. I have never said and have never believed that consciousness is an ontological exception to the laws of nature. That again is why I insist on saying it is nothing. But insofar as it is something—that is, insofar as we find ourselves filled with desires, inculcated values, motives and emotions, insofar as I have this body and exist in this place and at this time—we are, I am, indeed determined. My thesis is rather this: as we said earlier of the clock here ticking away on the wall, the important consideration is what we are to *make* of these things. For nothing is wholly determined in our experience. Everything, even the direst emergency, is presented for our consideration as an opportunity, never as a causally complete determinate factor, such as a coiled spring in a watch, or the instinctual mechanism in a bird building its nest or flying south for the winter.

RCS: You say you are a determinist?

SARTRE: I do.

RCS: And you believe that every event has its natural causes?

SARTRE: Yes.

RCS: And yet you insist that all human actions are free, that we are always responsible for what we do, even when we seem to have no alternatives?

SARTRE: That bothers you? Well, in fact, it is in part an old argument of Kant's: that the question of freedom is not a question of the lack of causal determination. I agree with him that the very suggestion is nonsense. The question of freedom is a question of subjectivity, a question of how the subject must see his own situation.

RCS: Give me an example, please.

SARTRE: Certainly. Suppose that we are reliving the Resistance, and that one of our friends is a known coward, a man who has panicked in every action of any intensity in his entire life. He knows it. His friends know it. It is agreed by all that he is a coward, and he says so himself. But now the chips are down, and for various reasons a vital and dangerous action must be entrusted only to him. There is no other workable option. Now, let us say that he thinks about this, reflects on his history and on what he and everyone else consider to be his "character"—that is, one of a coward—and he says to himself, "I am going to panic. I am going to fail. I have always done so. My character causes this to be so. And I will always do so." What will happen? Well, of course, he is going to panic. It is as if he has already set himself to it. But now suppose he steels himself in the following manner: he looks at his past; he reflects on his cowardice, and he vows this time to succeed. His friends are doubtful; we expect the worst. But he does not listen to us. He insists and, perhaps, he succeeds. But the point is not whether he does succeed. The point is that, even if we were to suppose that there is something "in him," some determinate quality which makes him act as a coward, this is not for him to acknowledge. For his acknowledgement is thereby also an act of resignation: in effect, a decision that there is no use trying to act otherwise. His freedom to choose, in other words, has nothing to do with what he in fact will do. One can choose the most hopeless of causes, and in doing so, one proves oneself free.

RCS: But can you generalize that example? Is that true of ordinary human activities as well?

SARTRE: Of course. Giving up smoking, for example. Whether in fact one *can* do it is not the question of freedom. It is rather a question of *will.*

RCS: But now it sounds as if freedom is nothing but having a certain intention.

SARTRE: But one cannot have an intention without trying to act on it, and thereby acting. The assassin whose rifle jams at the crucial moment, in one sense does no more than move his finger; but he has acted no less than if he had succeeded. Success does not depend on one's freedom alone, and freedom does not depend on success.

RCS: Then what does it mean to be free?

SARTRE: I think that the best account of my view of freedom was in my book about Jean Genet, a petty criminal but a master writer. Genet was *made* a thief by the people around him, while he was still a child. These "good citizens" did not directly make him steal, of course, but when they found the young urchin taking some things, they called him a "thief." He accepted the description and became a thief. It is a tiny change, from the imposition to the acceptance, but this tiny change, was the beginning of a long process in which Jean Genet became both thief and poet, both an exile from and in the limelight of society. His is not a happy freedom, to be sure, but it *is* freedom; he marked out in increments a road in life which was not, at any stage, given to him. But in retrospect, of course, one can always look back and say, "Ah, we knew he would end up this way all along; it could not have been different." And one can always find evidence to show why this is so. But retrospect is not the domain of freedom, and on the road to freedom, things might always be different. At least, we cannot help but believe that they might be.

RCS: But do you not defend a doctrine that you call "absolute freedom," at least in *Being and Nothingness?*

SARTRE: Ah, yes. I've since given that up as too extreme, but I still believe in the basic idea of it: that consciousness always has that small if infinitesimal gap between itself and pure being; that one is *never* in a position of utter helplessness; that we are never mere pawns of forces beyond our control. Perhaps it is merely a question of perspective, always insisting on the question "What can I do?" or, after the fact, "What could I have done?"

RCS: Don't you believe that we do things beyond our control, compelled, for example, by unknown desires or repressed fantasies?

SARTRE: That is, of course, an important question, the question of "the unconscious." But you have to remember that I was raised in the land of Descartes, believing in the crystalline transparency of consciousness and the immediate, even infallible, knowledge we have of our own states of mind. Freud was virtually an undiscussed figure in France until only a few years ago, when suddenly a number of Frenchmen began to behave as if they had invented him. But the unconscious in the land of Descartes, that was blasphemy. So, no, I did not give any credence to the idea that there were hidden forces in the mind itself which, unbeknownst to us, determined our every move and desire. I rejected and I still reject the *mythology* of the unconsciousness that psychoanalysts use to explain human behavior. I reject their attempt to reduce all relationships to a single primal relationship, and I especially reject what I call the mechanistic cramp in Freud's own description of his theory, the biological and physiological language he uses, and words such as "repression" and "instinct." But having said this, I hope you will also recognize that although I am in complete agreement with the *facts* of repression and disguise, I do not describe them in that manner. In fact, the whole of *Being and Nothingness* is, in one sense, a diagnosis of the various ways in which we hide our own intentions and decisions from ourselves. But it is something *we* do, not a mechanism inside of us. But I totally agree with Freud that what we hide from ourselves can trap us and limit our freedom.

RCS: In emotions, for example?

SARTRE: Yes, emotions, in particular, are often (but not always) traps which we set for ourselves with our own freedom of mind. You may not know this, but I wrote a book in 1937-or-so on the mind, one part of which has been published as *The Emotions: Sketch of a Theory,* in which I argue that our emotions are "magical transformations of the world": in effect, actions of just such a kind. They are a subtle form of escape behavior, ways of coping with the obstinacy of the world by avoiding it. But we pretend that they "happen to us" and force us to do this or that, when indeed they are rather our strategies for preventing action, avoiding situations.

RCS: For example?

SARTRE: Do you know Aesop's fable about the fox and the grapes? I'm certain that you do. The fox lusted after the grapes but could not, however he tried, get them in reach. And so he concluded that they must be sour. Now the grapes didn't change their chemistry. He changed them by his view of them. That is what I mean by "a magical transformation of the world." And it is a method of avoiding responsibility.

RCS: So you do believe in the unconscious?

SARTRE: NO. I do not and cannot make any sense of what you call "the unconscious." What I do know is that people often conveniently ignore their own decisions and their own activities, sometimes under the guise of "forgetting" but usually by simply ignoring them. All those behaviors that are attributed by Freudians to the mysterious forces of the unexplorable "unconscious" can be explained thereby.

RCS: It sounds as if we have reached one of your major themes. You have said repeatedly that freedom and responsibility were your most enduring commitments, but what about the *avoidance* of responsibility? The *denial* of freedom?

SARTRE: Of course; that is what I call "bad faith" or *mauvaise foi,* to deny what one is—or is not. We do it all the time. In fact, I have sometimes suggested that we cannot help but be in bad faith, that it is as much a part of human nature as the demand for freedom itself.

RCS: "Human nature"?

SARTRE: Well, yes, in a manner of speaking. You might say that the essence of being human is to be free, which means not to have an essence. But let's not dwell on this kind of paradox now. The point is rather that human existence revolves around one enormous complexity, which perhaps I can best present in traditional philosophical form. I have already cited my allegiance to Descartes and his division of everything (apart from God) into being-in-itself (of things) and being-for-itself (of consciousness). Well, I also said that being-for-itself has one all-important aspect, which I call transcendence—the ability to envision oneself as something other than one is, to see things as other than they are.

RCS: And that is what you call freedom.

SARTRE: Yes, but the obvious fact about all human existence is that it is not *only* this, for the ability to make oneself other than what one already is presumes that one already *is* something. And this starting point, which for every one of us seems so astonishing, so outrageous, so . . . coincidental, is just as much a part of us as our transcendence.

RCS: For example?

SARTRE: Well, the fact that I was born with my particular face and body; the fact that I was born in Paris of white, European parents. The fact that I was born in this century, as opposed to any other. And this totality of facts about me I call (I borrowed the term from Heidegger) my *facticity.*

RCS: Facticity is then opposed to transcendence?

SARTRE: No. It complements transcendence. There are no facts about us that are beyond our overcoming, albeit often at considerable cost. And there is no imaginable change that is not grounded in the way in which we already are— our race, our class, our age, our education.

RCS: But if we can change anything, what is left as a brute "fact" about us? The year of one's birth? One's height?

SARTRE: Not even such things as those. One can take great pains to lie about one's birth, hide the facts and create the appearance of new ones.

RCS: But one doesn't change the fact of one's birth date.

SARTRE: No matter; it is what one makes of it that counts, a matter of pride, a matter of embarrassment, an utter irrelevancy, a point of controversy.

RCS: And your height?

SARTRE: Haven't you noticed how some very tall men slouch a lot, as if to hide their height? And do you know about the artist Toulouse-Lautrec who compensated for his dwarfish appearance by acting every inch the dominating giant around Paris?

RCS: Then how do you know what the difference is, between those aspects of you that are given as facts—your facticity—and those aspects which are open to change—your transcendence?

SARTRE: You cannot know.

RCS: Oh!

SARTRE: And that is how bad faith becomes so essential. Bad faith, to be more precise, is a denial of either one's facticity or one's transcendence.

RCS: How is that?

SARTRE: Well, some cases of bad faith are easy to spot. For example, in *Being and Nothingness* I gave the example of a waiter in a café. His movement is a little too precise. He is a bit too eager, his voice and expression a bit too solicitous. When he takes an order, and when he turns to the bar, there is that inflexible stiffness, like some kind of automaton, as he carries his tray with the control of a tightrope walker, forever avoiding loss of balance by the masterful movements of his arm and hand. It is as if his movements were mechanisms, as if he were playing a game. But what game? We need not watch long before we can see that he is playing at *being* a waiter in a café.

RCS: I can see that you long for those cafés.

SARTRE: Yes, but let me stick to the example. The condition is one of ceremony. It is an obligation of all tradesmen. The grocer is expected to act like a grocer, a tailor like a tailor. Each is expected to deny his transcendence for the convenience and comfort of his customers. But if these examples seem innocent enough, consider the soldier who acts as he is expected to act—as a military machine—a soldier-*thing,* who obeys his orders without a murmur, who does what he does as part of his *function.* Then you can see the horror of bad faith; men who deny their ability to choose—even if the only alternative is death— by pretending that they are things, by acting as if they were pure facticity. That is bad faith. That is the negative role of my existentialism.

RCS: It is a concept, like your example of the soldier, that was evidently given a powerful impetus by your heroic experiences in the war and in occupied Paris.

SARTRE: Oh, my own experiences were nothing heroic, but, yes, you are right. Like most of my ideas, this one was formulated and received its importance from that particular situation.

RCS: And after the war?

SARTRE: I was still sensitive to bad faith, but in more subtle areas—anti-Semitism and racism, for example. The anti-Semite, for instance, turns the Jew into a thing in order to deny his own faults, and to blame someone else for his failures. The anti-Semite is a man who is afraid—not of the Jew, of course, but of himself—of his conscience, of his instincts, of his responsibilities, of solitude, of change, of society, and of the world, of everything *except* the Jews. Thus he chooses himself as a person, with the permanence and the impenetrability of a rock, the total irresponsibility of the warrior who obeys his leaders—and he has no leader. The Jew is only the pretext for his bad faith; if he were elsewhere he would be equally prejudiced against blacks or Orientals. Anti-Semitism, in a word, is fear of one's fate.

RCS: In some of your more recent writings, you seem to indicate that bad faith isn't so much a universal human condition as a condition of the bourgeoisie.

SARTRE: Let me be careful here. In my early works, *Nausea,* for instance, the bourgeoisie I despise is the fat and complacent majority of most middle-class societies, for example, those in provincial France or suburban America. Now, I use the term more as Marx did, to signify an economic class—the rich, basically. But in both cases, there is a philosophical pretention to be attacked—namely, that the interests of the bourgeoisie are the interests of humanity in general. And I should say that *Being and Nothingness,* in my opinion now, is bourgeois in this sense also: I claimed to express the essence of being human, but in fact express primarily the concerns of a middle-class Parisian intellectual in 1940.

RCS: I want to go back to something you said a while ago, about the essential human dilemma. You said that bad faith is the denial of transcendence and the retreat into facticity, or vice versa. Then you gave the examples of the waiter and the soldier. But some time ago you suggested to me that there was no way in which to know one's facticity from one's transcendence. Isn't this an essential incoherence in your theory?

SARTRE: No. It is rather an essential ambiguity in human existence. Consider, for example, any of those features of a personality that psychologists so matter-of-factly label "traits": shyness, or cowardness, or friendliness. They look like facts, and to so accept them is to indeed make them into facts, to make them true. But their actual function is as excuses: [*falsetto voice*] "Oh I can't do that, I'm too shy." But the explanation is precisely the opposite of what the situation involves: one does not refuse to do something because of shyness; one excuses one's decision not to do something by becoming shy. And so too with cowardice, or friendliness, or any other human trait.

RCS: So you are saying that many of the so-called "psychological facts" about us are actually excuses, decisions, and thus part of our transcendence.

SARTRE: Yes, but it works the other way around too. In one of my first novels, *The Age of Reason,* I invented a character called Mathieu, who obviously resembled me in many ways. He was a thirty-seven-year-old philosophy professor (I wrote the novel in the mid-1940s) who had a professional commitment to be free. That is, he *talked* about freedom all of the time. He refused to marry the girl with whom he had more or less been living for years, and whom he had just made pregnant, all "in order to preserve his freedom." He did not join his friends in the civil war in Spain, "in order to keep his options open." But he was, as his older and very bourgeois brother pointed out to him, in total conformity with all of the institutions he claimed to despise and reject. He too was in bad faith, but in an opposite manner from our waiter-machine and soldier-thing; he pretended to be all freedom, all transcendence, refusing to acknowledge how he was restricted by the facts of his life.

RCS: Is there a middle way, a kind of balance, in which one can avoid bad faith?

SARTRE: I do not know whether one can be both wholly engaged in an activity and sufficiently aware at the same time. I do know that every time I was sufficiently removed from one of my own opinions or activities to look it squarely in the face, I could see that I had been guilty of bad faith too.

RCS: Is that what you are going through now?

SARTRE: Essentially, but with a sense of humor that only death makes possible. And that makes all the difference.

RCS: One thing you haven't mentioned at all, and that surprises me, is God. You don't believe in God?

SARTRE: You know very well that I do not. But not out of any bitterness. I just do not believe "by instinct" as Nietzsche once said.

RCS: But don't you argue in *Being and Nothingness* that man wants to be God, and that this is his tragedy?

SARTRE: Did I say that? Incredible! Well, yes, everyone wants to be God, but what I mean by that is an argument that you will find in the hardly radical writings of the scholastics of the thirteenth century. Each of us consists of both facticity and transcendence, as I've said, and bad faith emerges from both the tendency to think of oneself as all facticity—as if one could identify with the list of credentials on a job application form—and the tendency to wish oneself totally free—as if by some magical stroke we could become somebody else, perhaps by joining some exotic religious cult, or throwing oneself into a new love affair. But if you take both of these tendencies at once, what do you get? A wish to be totally in-itself and for-itself at once, all possibility without restriction, and yet something secure, given, permanent, eternal. And this, of course, was just how some of the medieval philosophers defined God. And they even said—as did Saint Thomas Aquinas, for instance—that man wanted to be like this, too, and therein lies his longing for the divine. Well, I guess that I believe that too, except that I don't see it as a tragedy. It's just the way things are.

RCS: But it doesn't mean that you believe in God?

SARTRE: No. It means that I believe that God is an impossibility.

RCS: And that is why man is without a purpose? Without an essence?

SARTRE: What!

RCS: You know, the argument you presented in 1947 in your lecture "Existentialism Is a Humanism," that a paper knife or cookie cutter has a function because it is designed to serve a certain purpose, but, because there is no God, we do not have any such purpose, or any predetermined "human nature."

SARTRE: Did I say that? Incredible! Well, the argument is obviously fallacious; whether or not there is a human nature depends on something more than God's intentions. But more important, you shouldn't take that lecture too seriously. It was a mistake, an attempt at popularization that didn't come off.

RCS: It was the most widely read of your works.

SARTRE: Oh my God! . . . Sorry. Oh well, too bad. No, my arguments about the nature of human existence have virtually nothing to do with the question of whether there is or is not a God. If there were a God, the arguments would be precisely the same. And if there is not . . . no matter.

RCS: Do you still believe that now?

SARTRE: Of course. I haven't changed my mind about everything.

RCS: You know, it has often been commented how Christian your philosophy is, despite your atheism. The concept of inescapable bad faith, for instance, has often been linked to the concept of original sin; your emphasis on action and will with the Lutheran doctrines of good works and conscience; and your equation of virtue with the continual overcoming of temptation.

SARTRE: And why should that worry me? I have also been called a dogmatic Marxist by the conservatives, a traitor and a revisionist by the Marxists, a puritan by the libertines and a libertine by the moralists. I don't really care what people say about me.

RCS: Ah, but didn't you say that you had retracted your old philosophy of the autonomous, isolated individual, in favor of a new emphasis on the importance of other people?

SARTRE: Yes, but not other people in general, such as readers I've never met and people who know me only from the newspapers. I do think that virtually everything in my consciousness was affected by and mostly created with other people, but that doesn't mean that I have to explain myself to every clown and critic who thinks that existentialism is a fine tune to dance to.

RCS: Let me ask you about your views of other people, and how they have been changed. In *Being and Nothingness* you argued that the essence of our relations with other people is *conflict*. Is that not right?

SARTRE: Right that I said it, wrong as a thesis.

RCS: And there you argued that "being-for-others" was a third ontological category, along with being-in-itself and being-for-itself, right?

SARTRE: Yes, but I also insisted that it was ontologically on a par with the other two, and not derivative from them.

RCS: Nevertheless, it is introduced several hundred pages along in the book.

SARTRE: That's true, I clearly saw relationships as secondary—or as a threat—to individual consciousness.

RCS: And you must admit that the very title "being-*for*-others," as opposed to "being-*with*-others," for example, is already a little paranoid. It sounds as if you see yourself at the mercy of other people, rather than seeing them as friends, companions, playmates, and so on.

SARTRE: Yes, but that was what we were thinking in those days. Think of Camus' *Stranger,* for instance, in which an innocent, solitary man is destroyed by those around him. In the days of the Resistance, we naturally suspected everyone—felt at their mercy. In my own examples, I discuss that draining experience in which one's solitude is interrupted by the intrusion of another person, as if the landscape is sucked into the sinkhole of the other person's consciousness. And, my favorite example, the awkward instance in which I am peering through a keyhole—I do not say exactly at what—and someone else arrives on the landing; *the look (le regard)* of the other throws me into a paroxysm of self-consciousness, and I am no longer aware of what I was looking at before, but now only of myself, being *looked at*. We *are* at the mercy of other people. They have the power to make us into what we are.

RCS: And that is where the self arises?

SARTRE: I do not see it quite that way now, but yes, that is where one finds the origin of self-consciousness, not in the solitude of Cartesian self-reflection, but in the reflection of others.

RCS: An embarrassing source of self-consciousness.

SARTRE: In English, of course, "self-conscious" means precisely that—"embarrassed."

RCS: That's true, but that, surely, is not all there is to selfhood.

SARTRE: I never said so. It is just one of those existential traumas that continuously reminds us of ourselves.

RCS: The distinction between an occasional existential trauma and the nature of human existence dosen't always come through clearly in your writings.

SARTRE: It doesn't usually come through clearly in life either.

RCS: There is one question we keep avoiding, the one you called "paradox" a few moments ago. Is there such a thing as "human nature" or "human essence"? With your famous slogan of 1947, "existence precedes essence," you argue that we create our essences. I know you have dismissed that lecture as a "mistake," but I am not clear about what you do believe.

SARTRE: I have always believed that there is something essential to man, because man is conscious, and that is *freedom*. If you like, to be free is human nature, not, mind you, simply the desire to be free, but *being* free. But to say that

man is free is to say that many of the motives and drives by which philosophers and other theorists have tried to define human nature—for example,
the idea that people are basically selfish, or that everyone needs to be loved,
or that we are "naturally" social animals, or rational animals, or anything
else—must be viewed as options and choices, not as necessities.

RCS: So you do not believe that any specific characteristics, apart from freedom,
can characterize humanity in general?

SARTRE: Well, yes and no. There are no given characteristics, in the form of determinate drives, instincts or motives, which make it necessary for people to act
this way or become that. We are not, in a sense, a part of nature, as Descartes
argued too; we have given up the guarantees that other creatures, from cock-
roaches to cattle, obtain from nature regarding what they are to do. But there
is one argument in that lecture which I still find enormously convincing: the
idea that, just as one creates his own character through the acts he performs,
so he also contributes to the creation of the character of humanity as a whole
by being an example, by making it true, at least in this one case, that humanity is capable of selfless heroism, or utter selfishness.

RCS: Is that like Kant's imperative, "act so that the principle of your action can
be universalized as a law for all men"?

SARTRE: It is related to Kant, except that he thinks the principles precede the act
and are already rational; that is, if they are worth doing. I do not believe in
such rational principles but rather insist that one creates one's principles in
acting; in the beginning is the act, not the word, not the principle. And that
means that one has no assurances that what one does is "right"; one does it,
that's all. One sets an example and hopes that the world will follow.

RCS: Your own political commitments, which have been much in the news for
many years now, have hardly been followed by the world. Indeed, you've
repudiated many of them yourself, in retrospect.

SARTRE: "In retrospect" again; it is so easy. But at the time all I know is what
seems to be the right course of action. And so I act, even if my action is
nothing more heroic than handing out handbills on a street in central Paris,
surrounded by the press and television and providing coverage for a workers'
movement which would otherwise be ignored.

RCS: How do you know it is the "right" course?

SARTRE: I don't, in one sense; but I obviously follow a rule of thumb in such
matters: that it is always the most radical alternative, the farthest to the left—
that will be the "right" one. Even if, later on, it turns out that it was not as
it seemed.

RCS: Isn't that fairly dogmatic? What of all the arguments of the intellectuals on
the right? Don't you even listen to them?

SARTRE: There *are* no intellectuals on the right. Functionaries of the bourgeoisie,
perhaps. Practical theoreticians. But an intellectual stands for the universal,
for humanity, even though his roots and even his personal interests are
wholly on the side of a particular class or social group.

RCS: Can one stand for what you call "the universal"?

SARTRE: Obviously, I have believed so for the last decades of my life. As a student, and even when I was writing *Being and Nothingness,* I was oblivious

to my own class interests, and I thought—or pretended—that I was writing for all humanity. I found out that I was wrong, but I did not change my ambition, only the class on behalf of which I was writing. And I agree with Marx, of course, that the only universal class is the working class, the "proletariat," for their interests will not be served until there are no classes at all.

RCS: This is obviously not the place to argue politics with you, Monsieur Sartre, but let me at least ask you to comment on what you have said you consider your most important book, *The Critique of Dialectical Reason,* which came out in 1960.

SARTRE: Yes, I nearly killed myself writing that book—too many amphetamines, too little sleep—but I felt an urgency, not so much for myself but for the book itself. It was my corrective to *Being and Nothingness*; and it was my ultimate attack on the Communists.

RCS: Weren't you yourself a Communist?

SARTRE: Every French intellectual flirts with the Party, but I have always kept my distance from them, and they have always despised me. In fact, my existentialism was at one time branded "ideological public enemy number 1." I have often shared their opinions about international politics, that is, when they were not merely toadying to the USSR, but my philosophy has always been incompatible with their vulgar materialism and their reduction of men to mere cogs in the dialectic. My Marxism, and Marx's too, begins with a theory of individual freedom. "Man makes history," Marx wrote, and Communism has ignored him ever since.

RCS: But the *Critique* itself is about Marxism.

SARTRE: No, it is not *about* Marxism; it *is* Marxism. And in it I try to prove that Marxism and existentialism are not incompatible, but rather, properly understood, they presuppose one another.

RCS: How does the *Critique* differ from *Being and Nothingness*? How does it correct it?

SARTRE: Well, to begin with, *Being and Nothingness* was about individuals, about consciousness and contact between individuals. The *Critique* is about society, about groups, In fact, it is more a work in sociology than what you would probably consider philosophy.

RCS: Some critics have contended that the book loses sight of the individual altogether.

SARTRE: But it is not a book about individuals. I did not mean for the *Critique* to replace *Being and Nothingness,* but to correct its one-sidedness and to complement it.

RCS: How does it do that?

SARTRE: In *Being and Nothingness,* I said much too little about how individuals are molded and affected by the large and largely static institutions that make up society, or what I call the "practico-inert." And that is what the *Critique* is about. And in *Being and Nothingness* I considered man as mainly a consciousness with a body, but I worried almost exclusively about the demands of consciousness. In the *Critique,* I worry more about the needs of the body, and the basic questions of economics.

RCS: What about freedom?

SARTRE: Freedom is still there, at the very core of the theory, of course. I should add that, with my usual propensity for exaggeration, I sometimes insist that, insofar as man is victim of his own institutions and inequities, he is a slave and not free at all. But don't take that too seriously. It is still freedom that is the course of everything, and one of my main arguments in the *Critique* is against the common tendency to treat groups and societies as organic units, with individuals merely as "members."

RCS: And you disagree with that?

SARTRE: Fundamentally. Groups are not organisms but tenuous collectives of individuals, sometimes but not always held together by a common past and shared interests (the "practico-inert" again), but always liable to disintegration. Most sociologists worry about the structures of groups; I am more concerned with their formation and disintegration, and that comes back, once again, to a matter of individual freedom.

RCS: What do you mean by "dialectical reason"?

SARTRE: Very simple. "Analytical reason" is trying to understand something by watching it, or dissecting it; "dialectical reason" is understanding through participation, by being part of what you are trying to understand.

RCS: You prefer dialectical reason?

SARTRE: In all matters concerning human conduct, yes.

RCS: "Dialectic" is what you used to call "engagement."

SARTRE: In a sense, but "dialectic" is also a bit more aware than I was of history and the limitations of the individual.

RCS: You have a reputation for having encouraged violence in politics; was that true?

SARTRE: You sound shocked. But violence is not always the worst alternative, and to eschew violence on principle is to let others have their way by violence, and thus be their accomplice. Do you remember the speech in my play *Dirty Hands*: "How frightened you are of dirtying your hands. Oh well, stay pure! What good will it do anyone and why did you join us? Purity is a monk's ideal. You intellectual and bourgeois anarchists, you make it an excuse for doing nothing. Do nothing, then. Wear gloves, but as for me, I've got dirty hands, dirty up to the elbows."

RCS: How would you describe your politics?

SARTRE: My politics? I've always been an anarchist.

[*The valet steps quickly through the door. He says nothing, but waits for* RCS *to join him.*]

RCS: Monsieur Sartre, this has been the dream of my life.

SARTRE: Indeed, that is all it has been.

RCS: I was always so certain that you would be dogmatic and authoritative and impossible to talk to.

SARTRE: [*chuckles*] I was, but it no longer matters what I say. My conversation with you was like looking into a mirror.

RCS: You mean . . .

SARTRE: No. I mean only that, ultimately, perhaps, it does not matter with whom one speaks, that what one always finds is another human being, like oneself.

RCS: I cannot accept that; talking to you has been a rare and special experience.
SARTRE: Perhaps, then, you still have something to learn. But not from me.

NOTES

1. Simone de Beauvoir, one of France's leading novelists and essayists, was Sartre's companion for fifty years. Her works include *The Second Sex, Force of Circumstances, The Mandarins,* and *Memoirs of a Dutiful Daughter.*

2. Maurice Merleau-Ponty was a friend of Sartre's from college and, second only to Sartre, the leading philosopher in France until his death in 1961. He coedited *Les Temps Modernes* with Sartre and wrote some of the most important works in the phenemenological movement in France, particularly *Phenomenology of Perception,* which was written at the same time as Sartre's *Being and Nothingness,* with which it has many affinities.

Paul Nizan, another college classmate of Sartre's, was the most politically active of the group and a committed member of the Communist party. Nizan was killed in World War II, but Sartre considered him a victim of the tension between his own idealistic marxist principles and the vulgar marxists of the establishment left. He was the model for the character Brunet in Sartre's trilogy, *Roads to Freedom.*

Francois Jeanson remains Sartre's most loyal disciple in Paris. It was his review of Camus' *The Rebel* in Sartre's journal that triggered the ultimate break between Camus and Sartre. Jeanson often provided the bridge between Sartre's philosophy and his radical politics. His work *Le problème moral et al pensée de Sartre* was published in 1947.

3. Sartre's autobiography, trans. by Bernard Frechtman (New York: Braziller, 1964).

4. Edmund Husserl (1859–1938), Czech-German philosopher and founder of the phenomenological movement.